Crimes
and
Criminals

Nick Vandome

Chambers

EDINBURGH   NEW YORK   TORONTO

Published 1992 by W & R Chambers Ltd
43–45 Annandale Street, Edinburgh EH7 4AZ

British Library Cataloguing in Publication Data

A catalogue record for this book is available from the British Library.

ISBN 0 550 17012 X

Cover design   Blue Peach Design Consultants Ltd
Typeset by Alphaset Graphics Limited, Edinburgh
Printed in England by Clays Ltd, St Ives, plc

Acknowledgements

Chambers Compact Reference Series Editor   Min Lee

Illustration credits

Page		Page	
5	© Hulton-Deutsch/Keystone Press Agency	136	© Hulton-Deutsch
		140	© Hulton-Deutsch
33	© Hulton-Deutsch/Bettmann	143	© Hulton-Deutsch/Bettmann
34	© Hulton-Deutsch/Bettmann	145	© Hulton-Deutsch/Bettmann
50	© Hulton-Deutsch	147	© Hulton-Deutsch
55	© Hulton-Deutsch/Bettmann	167	© Hulton-Deutsch
63	© Hulton-Deutsch	174	© Hulton-Deutsch
70	© Hulton-Deutsch	184	© Hulton-Deutsch
81	© Hulton-Deutsch/Bettmann	186	© Hulton-Deutsch
89	© Hulton-Deutsch	195	© Hulton-Deutsch
99	© Hulton-Deutsch	199	© Hulton-Deutsch/Bettmann
106	© Hulton-Deutsch	202	© Hulton-Deutsch
114	© Hulton-Deutsch	209	© Hulton-Deutsch
117	© Hulton-Deutsch	218	© Hulton-Deutsch/Keystone Collection
127	© Hulton-Deutsch/Bettmann		
131	© Hulton-Deutsch	234	© Hulton-Deutsch
133	© Hulton-Deutsch	237	© Hulton-Deutsch

Front cover John Dillinger © Hulton/Deutsch/Bettmann
Spine Handcuffs by John Marshall

Contents

Crimes
and
Criminals

Other titles in
Chambers Compact Reference

To be published in 1993

Introduction

Crime is a topic which both fascinates and horrifies us all: we shudder at the exploits of the murderer, but are drawn to the newspaper headline telling his story; we are shocked when a major robbery takes place, but secretly admire the audacity of the thieves; the actions of criminals have aroused interest throughout history.

Murder is one of the most obvious and emotive subjects in the criminal world. Some of the murderers in this book are included because their names have passed into popular as well as criminal folklore. Dr Crippen, Lizzie Borden, Burke and Hare, Ruth Ellis and Charles Manson are all names with which we are well acquainted, but how much do we really know about their crimes?

Other murderers are included because their cases mark an important breakthrough in criminal investigation: in 1905 the Stratton brothers became the first people to be convicted using the technique of fingerprinting, while in 1927 Frederick Browne and William Kennedy became the first people in Britain to be convicted of murder using ballistics evidence.

A number of the murderers — Ted Bundy, the Boston Strangler, and the Son of Sam — are examples of serial killers (people who kill again and again, usually following a similar pattern). This is considered to be a modern phenomenon and particularly an American one. However, the United Kingdom has had its own mass murderers. Mary Ann Cotton is thought to have killed at least 15 people in the 1860s and 1870s and by the time Burke and Hare were caught in 1829 they had acounted for at least 16 victims. Serial killers may be a modern concept but the mass murderer is certainly not a product solely of the 20th century.

Although methods of murder vary greatly, poison has always been one of the most popular ways of disposing of the victims. Doctors, logically enough, have been particularly prone to use poison and several,

including William Palmer and Neill Cream, have been foiled in their attempts at committing the elusive 'perfect murder'.

Poison has also featured prominently with female murderers. In the Victorian era there were four cases which generated enormous public interest; Madame Lafarge in France, Madeleine Smith in Scotland, and Adelaide Bartlett and Florence Maybrick in England. All four were accused of poisoning their partners, an act which stunned the staid Victorian societies in which they lived. The fact that Smith and Bartlett were not convicted only served to heighten interest in the cases.

The concept of pure evil is often discussed in connection with murder but a more common motive is greed, lust or sheer frustration. The name of Dr Crippen is often cited as an example of evil but in reality he was a mild-mannered man who killed his overbearing wife because he was in love with another woman. It was an unremarkable act but his name has become notorious because of the way he was apprehended while trying to escape to Canada with his mistress. However, apparently motiveless, evil actions are documented in the book, most notably in the Moors murders and the case of the Scottish murderer Peter Manuel, who was described at his trial as, 'Bad but not mad'.

An unsolved murder creates even greater interest than a convicted murderer. The lack of a culprit allows everyone to construct their own theories and imaginatons are free to indulge in the wildest fantasies. Jack the Ripper remains the most celebrated unsolved case in history but he has since been followed by other notable cases including the assassination of President Kennedy and the disappearance of Lord Lucan.

Theft does not usually hold the same appeal as murder and modern-day robberies tend to be violent, clumsy affairs. However, two that have been included captured the public's imagination not only for the amount of money stolen but also because of the meticulous planning that went into the crimes. In 1950 the Brinks robbery occurred in Boston, USA which netted the perpetrators a total of $2.5 million. This was followed in 1963 by the Great Train Robbery in England. Both crimes were carried out with military-style precision and the public had much greater sympathy with the criminals than the authorities.

The fallibility of the legal system is illustrated in a number of cases in the book. The executions of Timothy Evans and Derek Bentley for crimes they did not commit did much to hasten the abolition of capital punishment in the United Kingdom. Similar cases in the USA, the executions of the spies Julius and Ethel Rosenberg and convicted kidnapper Caryle Chessman, created outrage around the world but they had little effect on the policy of capital punishment. But not all miscarriages of justice centre around the death penalty. In 1895 a captain in the French Army, Alfred Dreyfuss, was convicted of espionage on the flimsiest of evidence. The ensuing arguments brought France to the brink of civil war before Dreyfuss was eventually fully exonerated in 1906.

The pages of history are littered with notorious criminals and several of them are included here. However, one effect history can have on crime is to glamorize it and turn it into something romantic and noble: every year we 'celebrate' the attempt by Guy Fawkes to blow up several hundred people. The idea of doing this for a modern mass murderer is unthinkable. Similarly, Dick Turpin and Bonnie and Clyde have been depicted in numerous books, films and plays as popular heroes, fighting a just cause. In reality Turpin was a pitiless thug and Bonnie and Clyde were outlaws in the truest

sense of the word. It seems that the excesses of some criminals are overlooked with the passing of time.

A number of conspirators appear in the book and two points need to be made about them. Firstly, one man's conspirator is another man's patriot and it depends on your viewpoint as to whether you judge them as criminals or not. Secondly, the most remarkable fact about the conspirators dealt with is their almost total failure in achieving their objectives. In some cases this was due to the greater quantities of idealism than good judgement and in others it was because of the extremely efficient intelligence networks of the governments of the day.

Forgers, fraudsters and fakers are some of the most popular criminals — as long as you are not the dupe. The sheer audacity of the likes of financial fraudsters Horatio Bottomley and Jabez Balfour has to be admired, while the art forger, Tom Keating, took great delight in revealing his chicanery, in order to show up the pretensions of the art world. He subsequently went on to become a minor celebrity. In the 18th century another forger, William Dodd, was not so fortunate. He was executed in 1777 for forging a financial bond, illustrating, if nothing else, how our attitudes towards capital punishment have changed over the years.

This book is not an attempt to analyse the actions of criminals but rather a collection of notable malefactors and their deeds. However, through the exploits of serial killers and conmen, bank robbers and traitors, forgers and highwaymen, imposters and gangsters it is possible to see some of the motives and characteristics of the criminal mind. Crime may not pay but it certainly fascinates.

A6 Layby murder

(1961)

James Hanratty

A cold-blooded killing that resulted in a possible miscarriage of justice.

On the evening of 22 August 1961 two lovers, Michael Gregsten and Valerie Storie, were in a Morris Minor parked by a field near Slough, Buckinghamshire. Unexpectedly, they heard a tap on the window; when Gregsten wound it down there was a man pointing a gun at his head. The man got into the back seat and although he seemed uncertain, he ordered Gregsten to start driving.

There then followed a bizarre 30-mile drive which ended at a layby on the A6, between St Albans and Luton. The gunman asked Gregsten to hand over a bag but when he tried to do so he was shot twice in the head. The killer then raped Valerie Storie, shot her and left her for dead on the roadside.

Paralysed but alive

Although Valerie was paralysed she survived and gave a description of the killer. The police appealed for witnesses and two people came forward who had seen a man driving Gregsten's car in Ilford, Essex. Their descriptions differed from the one given by Valerie Storie so two identikit pictures were issued.

The first person that the police suspected was a man named Peter Louis Alphon. He had stayed in the Vienna Hotel, Maida Vale, the night after the murder and bullets matching those that killed Gregsten were found in his room. However, Valerie Storie failed to recognize him in an identity parade.

Gregsten's widow came forward and claimed she had seen her husband's killer in the street. The man was James Hanratty, a petty criminal, and the police soon discovered that he had used the same room as Alphon in the Vienna Hotel. When they found the murder weapon under a seat on a London bus, Hanratty was arrested. Valerie again failed to pick him out of an identity parade, but when she heard him speak she claimed he had the same accent as the killer and that she now recognized him.

Change of alibi

James Hanratty's trial began on 22 January 1962. The defence was based on Valerie Storie's failed identifications and the fact that Hanratty did not resemble either of the identikit pictures. He also claimed to have an alibi in Liverpool at the time of the killing but he would not name the people involved. There seemed to be sufficient doubt to avoid a conviction but then Hanratty inexplicably changed his alibi and said that he had been in Rhyl, North Wales. The jury deliberated for nine and a half hours before reaching a verdict of guilty. James Hanratty was hanged at Bedford Prison on 4 April 1962.

Many people still believe there was insufficient evidence to convict Hanratty. After his execution several witnesses claimed they had seen him in Rhyl at the time of the murder.

Discrepancies

There were a number of flaws in the prosecution case: Valerie Storie said the killer was pale when in fact Hanratty had a ruddy complexion; she said he was a nervous passenger but Hanratty was a confident driver; and there was not even any evidence to suggest that Hanratty possessed a gun.

Abershaw, Louis Jeremiah (Jerry)

(1773–95)

Highwayman

An audacious robber who revelled in flaunting authority and the law.

Jerry Abershaw was born at Kingston-on-Thames and became a postillion during his teenage years. However, this was rather too subdued for his flamboyant character, so at the age of 17 he turned to highway robbery. His daring nature and his riding ability soon made him one of the most feared characters in the south of England.

Abershaw operated on the roads between London, Kingston and Wimbledon and made his headquarters at a pub called the Bald-faced Stag, near Kingston. Most passengers who passed this way were subjected to Abershaw's violent form of robbery. On one occasion he held up a carriage which was being driven by a young man named Richard Ferguson. Ferguson recognized him as a fellow customer of a local prostitute and in return for his silence Abershaw took him on as his apprentice.

Safe house

Despite his youth, Abershaw was soon one of the most wanted criminals in the country and he frequently had to go into hiding in a house near Saffron Hill. It was ideal for his purposes as it had dark closets, trap-doors and sliding panels. As well as sheltering Abershaw it was also a safe haven for other criminals of the time, most notably Jonathan Wild and Jack Sheppard.

In January 1795 an informer went to the police to tell them that Jerry Abershaw was hiding at the Three Brewers public house in Southwark. Two officers, David Price and Bernard Turner, were sent to arrest him but when they arrived Abershaw shot Price dead and wounded Turner. His efforts were in vain though and he was arrested.

Contempt for judge

Abershaw was tried at the Croydon assizes on 30 July 1795. Turner was the chief witness and it took the jury just three minutes to find the accused guilty. However, there was a flaw in the indictment which invalidated the charge of murder and so Abershaw avoided the death sentence. Unfortunately his relief was short-lived; he was found guilty of the felonious shooting of Turner — a crime that also carried the death penalty. As the judge donned the black cap Abershaw showed his contempt for the law by putting on his own cap and staring menacingly at the judge, on one occasion calling him a murderer.

Before his execution Abershaw obtained a bowl of cherries and used them to paint his cell walls with scenes from his crimes. He was hanged at Kennington Common on 3 August 1795. A huge crowd gathered to witness the death of such a famous criminal and he gave them a performance that delighted them. He went to the gallows with his shirt open and a flower in his mouth and laughed and joked with the crowd. His last act was to remove his boots — to disprove his mother's prophecy that because of his criminal ways he would die with them on.

Far-reaching reputation

A doctor who was treating Abershaw on one occasion was offered an escort back home by the highwayman. The doctor, unaware who he had treated, replied that he feared no one, not even the notorious Jerry Abershaw.

Adams case

(1957)

Dr John Bodkin Adams

An Eastbourne doctor who benefited financially from the suspicious deaths of several of his patients.

John Bodkin Adams was born in 1899 and brought up in Northern Ireland. He trained as a doctor and when he qualified he moved to the English seaside town of Eastbourne. Although he was an unattractive man he had a calming bedside manner and he soon built up a highly respectable practice. He was particularly popular with elderly patients, who enjoyed the compassion he showed them. It soon became noticed that several patients altered their wills in favour of Adams shortly before they died.

Rumours began to circulate about Adams and some people claimed that he drugged his patients and then persuaded them to change their wills in his favour. It was even suggested that he went on his rounds with a bottle of morphine and a blank form. It was not usual for patients to survive very long once they had made their wills over to Adams.

Financial gain

In 1936 Mrs Alice Whitton died after receiving treatment from Adams. In her will she left him £3000, a small fortune at the time. Mrs Whitton's daughter contested the will in the High Court but Adams won and was allowed to keep the money.

Adams was impressed with the ease at which he could persuade people to change their wills and several suspicious deaths in Eastbourne followed. These included a lady who broke with the family tradition of only naming relatives in a will, and gave £8000 to Adams; a retired bank manager who died after treatment for a broken ankle, and gave Adams £1000 in a will signed in the doctor's presence with a shaky X; a widow who bequeathed Adams £5000 and then died of pneumonia after being left in a freezing room with no bedclothes over her; and an heiress to a cotton fortune who went into a coma and then died after being treated by Adams for influenza.

Suspicious circumstances

Although there was no proof to suggest that Adams was murdering his patients there was strong circumstantial evidence. He frequently telephoned solicitors and asked them to come immediately to witness the signing of a new will in his favour. As to the

Dr John Bodkin Adams

5

cause of death Adams invariably claimed that cerebral haemorrhage or cerebral thrombosis had accounted for his patients. In later years when some of his patients were exhumed this was shown to be untrue.

In 1949 an elderly widow named Edith Morrell moved to Eastbourne. She suffered from severe arthritis and turned to Dr Adams for relief. He prescribed heroin and morphine, while at the same time making various attempts to persuade her to change her will. She died on 12 November 1950 and Adams profited with a Rolls-Royce, an antique cupboard and a chest of silver.

Police activity

By 1955 the police were beginning to take an interest in Adams and the mysterious deaths that seemed to be connected with him. Towards the end of the year Adams treated Jack Hullett, a retired Lloyds underwriter, for a heart condition. Hullett died in 1956 and left Adams £500 in his will. Following her husband's death Gertrude Hullett turned to Adams for drugs to help her sleep. The doctor supplied them willingly and very shortly she was addicted. She died four months later, on 23 July 1956, and Adams certified death as the usual cerebral haemorrhage. But the Home Office pathologist, Dr Francis Camps, disagreed and claimed that she had died from barbiturate poisoning. The inquest found that she had committed suicide and Adams was reprimanded for 'an extraordinary degree of careless treatment'. No doubt he was consoled by the Rolls-Royce that Mrs Hullett had left him in her will.

Unsatisfied customer

The wife of one of Adams' patients took forceful measures after he tried to persuade her husband to change his will: 'I grabbed my gold-headed walking stick and struck out at the doctor and chased him around the bed. He ran out of the room and as he dashed down the stairs I threw my stick at him. Unfortunately it missed, and broke a flower vase. It was the last I wanted to see of him. I certainly would not tolerate the idea of Adams trying to get into my husband's will'.

This latest death was the final straw for the authorities and the Director of Public Prosecutions decided to prosecute Dr Adams for murder. After an intense police investigation he was charged with the murder of Edith Morrell, which was a strange choice in many ways, particularly as the body had been cremated. Following this there were to be two more cases against him and the Crown believed they had enough evidence for a further three murder charges.

Inspired defence

The trial of John Adams began at the Old Bailey in March 1957. The prosecution, led by Sir Reginald Manningham-Buller QC, were confident of a quick conviction, but the defence, led brilliantly by Geoffrey Lawrence QC, had other ideas. Lawrence discredited some of the evidence given by the nurses who had attended Mrs Morrell and then he pulled off a master-stroke by not calling Adams to the witness stand. This meant that information connected with several other deaths could not be allowed as admissible evidence. Without this the prosecution's case fell apart and the jury took just 45 minutes to find Dr Adams not guilty.

Charges dropped

The trial was such a disaster for the Crown that the Director of Public Prosecutions decided not to proceed with the other cases against Adams. The police were infuriated, particularly as they knew that Adams had been the beneficiary of 132 wills, amounting to £45 000 in cash. However, there was nothing further that they could do. One of the officers on the case believed that Adams had murdered a minimum of nine patients. The more charitable suggested that he merely practised a form of euthanasia.

Following his trial Adams resigned from the National Health Service. In July 1957 he was fined £2400 after pleading guilty to 14 charges including the forgery of National Health Service prescriptions. Four months later he was struck off the Medical Register. He was reinstated in 1961 and maintained a modest practice in Eastbourne, but understandably he was never completely trusted again. Dr Adams died in 1983, leaving an estate of over £400 000.

Aram, Eugene

(1704–59)

Convicted murderer

An English schoolmaster who was convicted of murder 14 years after the event.

Eugene Aram was a scholarly man who was born at Ramsgill in Yorkshire. He was largely self-educated and by the time he was 30 he had an excellent command of Greek, Latin and Hebrew. In 1734 Aram moved to Knaresborough where he took up a position as a private schoolmaster.

A scholarly murder

One of the acquaintances that Aram made in Knaresborough was a shoemaker named Daniel Clarke, who had recently married and who liked to boast of his wife's wealth. Aram encouraged him in this and persuaded him to show him some of this reported fortune. On 8 February 1745 Clarke met Aram and a weaver named Robert Houseman, bringing with him a considerable quantity of silver and jewellery. Clarke was then lured out of town and murdered by Aram. Although Aram and his accomplice were later arrested for possession of Clarke's belongings they were released because no one knew what had become of the shoemaker.

With his share of the jewels Aram fled to London and finally settled in King's Lynn. Apparently having committed the perfect murder he continued his scholarly life and added Arabic and other eastern languages to his linguistic repertoire.

Justice after 14 years

On 1 August 1758 a labourer was digging for limestone near St Robert's Cave on the outskirts of Knaresborough when he dis-

covered some human bones. Although it was 13 years since Clarke had disappeared it was immediately presumed that these were the remains of the shoemaker. Houseman was the first to be arrested and he wasted no time in implicating Aram in the murder.

Eugene Aram was tried for murder on 28 July 1759 and he conducted his own defence. He argued with considerable eloquence that he was not the type of character to commit murder for financial gain and that at the time he had been so ill with distemper that he had barely been able to walk. He also claimed, with some justification, that there was no proof that the remains were those of Daniel Clarke and he cited several cases where the remains of hermits had been discovered in isolated caves. He concluded that he was, 'without interest, without power, without motive and without means' to commit murder.

Commendable defence

The trial judge, Mr Justice Noel, was greatly impressed by the way Aram conducted his defence and the defendant may have been acquitted if it had not been for the damning statement of Robert Houseman, who turned King's evidence. After he had been found guilty Aram tried unsuccessfully to commit suicide on the morning of his execution, but he was completely conscious when he was taken to the gallows near York on 6 August 1759.

Medical exhibit

Following his execution Aram's body was hung in chains for several years near Knaresborough. It was tradition for his widow to pick up the bones as they fell. One night a doctor removed the skull and it is now on exhibit in the Museum of the Royal College of Surgeons in London.

Arm in the shark case

(1935)

Anonymous shark-feeder

The discovery of a human arm in Australia that led to an unsolved murder inquiry.

On 25 April 1935 a crowd of onlookers at the Coogee Beach aquarium, near Sydney, were shocked when a tiger shark began to regurgitate the contents of its stomach. They became even more horrified when they saw a human arm appear. It had a piece of rope attached and on the arm was a tattoo of two boxers.

The police were called immediately and after a forensic examination and fingerprinting it was identified as belonging to a known criminal named James Smith. A police surgeon also declared that the arm had been severed with a knife, thus ruling out the possibility of a shark attack.

Criminal associate

On 17 May 1935 the police interviewed Patrick Brady, a petty criminal and a known associate of James Smith. Under interrogation, Brady admitted having stayed with Smith on the same stretch of coastline where the shark had been caught but he denied any involvement in a crime of any sort. Using divers and chartered aircraft the police searched the coastline but they could find no further sign of Smith.

While he was being interviewed Brady gave the police the name of Reg Holmes. At first Holmes denied knowing Brady but three days later the police discovered him with a superficial bullet-wound to the head. He now talked freely and claimed that Brady had killed Smith and then disposed of the body.

Death of star witness

After Holmes's confession Brady was arrested and charged with murder, but Holmes was found murdered on the eve of the Coroner's Inquiry into the arm in the shark case. The coroner then ruled that an inquest could not be held without a complete body. Brady was sent for trial, but there was no conclusive evidence and after refusing to admit as evidence a statement from Holmes signed before he died, the judge directed the jury to acquit Brady. Two men were tried for Holmes's murder but they too were acquitted.

Patrick Brady died in August 1965, after spending over 20 years of his life in prison for various offences, including theft and fraud. He never gave any clues as to the solution to the arm in the shark case and he continued to protest his innocence. The case remains unsolved.

Pyjama girl case

An equally bizarre Australian murder case occurred a year before the Arm in the Shark Case. On 1 September 1934 the partially burned and pyjama-clad body of a woman was found near Albury, New South Wales. Identification proved difficult so the body was preserved in a bath of formalin at Sydney University. It remained there for 10 years, when a newly appointed Commissioner of Police decided to have the body dressed up to see if it would aid identification. Immediately seven people said that it was the body of Linda Agostini. Her husband, Antonio Agostini, was interviewed by the police and claimed that his wife had died as a result of gunshots following a struggle. The jury were not convinced and in June 1944 Agostini was found guilty of manslaughter. He served six years' hard labour and was then deported to Italy.

Armstrong, Herbert Rowse

(1869–1922)

Convicted murderer

A respected solicitor who poisoned his domineering wife and then tried to do the same to one of his professional rivals.

To the residents of Hay-on-Wye, on the the Wales–England border, Herbert Armstrong and his wife Katharine appeared to live a prosperous and highly respectable existence. He was a graduate from Cambridge, a member of the Territorial Army and one of only two solicitors in the town. One thing that was frequently commented on however, was Mrs Armstrong's nagging of her mild-mannered husband, to the point of forbidding him to smoke or drink alcohol.

In July 1920 Mrs Armstrong made a new will that left everything to her husband. Shortly afterwards her health began to decline and she was committed to an asylum. In January 1921 she was allowed to return home but she soon had a relapse and died on 22 February 1921. The cause of death was put down to gastritis and she was duly buried.

Lack of grief

Armstrong seemed unperturbed by his wife's death and after her funeral he went on a long holiday, most of it spent in the company of a young lady friend.

With his wife out of the way the only cloud on Armstrong's horizon was Oswald Martin, the rival solicitor in Hay. The two men were on amicable terms but on one occasion they had a dispute over a litigation case. Shortly afterwards Martin and his wife received a box of chocolates from an anonymous source. They gave them to guests at a dinner party, who all became violently ill.

The chocolates were found to be laced with arsenic.

In an effort to solve the problem of the litigation, Armstrong invited Martin to his house for tea on 26 October 1921. Armstrong offered him a scone, apologizing for using his fingers as he passed it to him. When Martin got home that evening he was violently ill. Th doctor who examined him was suspicious about his symptoms and asked for an analysis of his urine. It was discovered to contain arsenic.

Long wait

The next two months were agonizing for Martin. Scotland Yard had been notified and they were making exhaustive, and secret, inquiries. All through this period Martin was trying to avoid taking tea with Armstrong again. He managed to hold out and on 31 December 1921 Armstrong was arrested and charged with attempted murder.

Once Armstrong was in custody it was decided to exhume his wife's body. It was found to contain three and a half grains of arsenic, one of the largest quantities that the analyst had ever seen in a murder case. Armstrong was tried for the murder of his wife and the defence that he had bought arsenic to kill dandelions was rejected and he was found guilty. Herbert Armstrong was hanged at Gloucester prison on 31 May 1922 — the first solicitor to suffer this fate.

Arsenic

Invented by an Arab alchemist, arsenic has been a favourite with poisoners for hundreds of years. It can pass for sugar or flour and has very little taste, making it easy to mix with food. The symptoms it produces can be ascribed to other illnesses and, most importantly, its effects are cumulative.

Armstrong, Johnnie

(?–1530)

Freebooter

A cattle-rustler from the borders of Scotland whose life-story appears in a number of different forms.

Johnnie Armstrong of Gilnockie was born in the Borders at the turn of the 16th century and he soon developed a strong dislike of what he saw as English persecution. To compensate he became a freebooter and survived by plundering the English countryside, from his home at the Hollows, near Langholm, to Newcastle. He led a gang of 24 expert horsemen and the name of Johnnie Armstrong soon became feared wherever he went. He never attacked a Scotsman and his chief target was cattle.

Troublesome reivers

On 28 March 1528 James V held a parliament at Edinburgh. It was clear that he was becoming tired of the activities of the reivers (cattle-rustlers) and he consulted his lords and barons as to what could be done about the problem. It was eventually decided that all the lords barons, and gentlemen in the kingdom should bring a month's supplies to Edinburgh and prepare for an expedition against the freebooters of Teviotdale, Annandale and Liddisdale.

When Armstrong saw what was happening he tried to pre-empt the King's actions. He offered James the service of himself and 40 of his men, undertaking to round up any English dukes, earls or barons that he wished. James wisely rejected the offer and in disgust Armstrong exclaimed, 'It is folly to seek grace at a graceless face'. In reply James arrested Armstrong and his men and hanged them at Carlanrigg Chapel, on the road to Langholm, in 1530.

Alternative versions

Following his death Armstrong immediately became a national hero and the ballad writers were quick to adopt him as a figurehead. Several other accounts of his life have also been put forward. One of them claims that he was equally severe on the Scottish and the English and that after being tricked into going to see the King he was ambushed and taken to James as a prisoner. This version of the story claims that he was saved when his brother turned informer.

Apocryphal tales

The English also have ballads that feature Johnnie Armstrong, one of which has him appearing after the battle of Bannockburn. After fighting bravely he was called to Edinburgh but then denounced as a traitor. A violent battle ensued with Armstrong and his followers eventually being slain in the streets of Edinburgh.

Several of these versions of Armstrong's life are undoubtedly apocryphal, and although he was almost certainly a daring freebooter his image may have become romanticized due to the ballads that have been written about him.

Famous in song

One of the most famous ballads about Johnnie Armstrong tells of his fate once he had been captured:

John murdred was at Calinrigg.
And all his galant companie;
But Scotland's heart was never sae wae
To see so many brave men die
Because they saved their country dier
Frae Englishmen; nane were sae bauld,
When Johnnie lived on the border-syde
Nane of them durst cum neir his hald.

Axeman of New Orleans murders

(1911–19)

Unsolved murders

A series of murders that caused panic in the Italian community of New Orleans.

In 1911 there were six identical murders in New Orleans. All six of the victims were Italian grocers and their wives and they were killed by an axeman who gained entry to their houses by chiselling out the door panel. The police were baffled by the crimes and assigned them to the unsolved file.

On 23 May 1918 the Axeman struck again. This time the victims were Joseph Maggio and his wife, again both Italian grocers. They had been struck with an axe and then had their throats cut. Joseph Maggio's brothers were arrested but later released since they had alibis. As with the 1911 killings, the police had no leads.

Killings continue

After an initial burst of media attention the case of the Axeman faded from prominence. Then, on 28 June 1918, Louis Besumer and his common-law wife, Harriet Lowe, were attacked by the Axeman. Harriet died but Besumer survived and was charged with her murder. The police were relieved to have a suspect at last but while Besumer was in custody there was another Axeman murder. This time the victims survived and the police were able to compile a rough description of the assailant — a tall, well-built white man.

On 10 March 1919 the Axeman chiselled out the door panel at the house of Charles and Rosie Cortimiglia. He hacked their two-year-old daughter to death and then fled, leaving behind his bloodstained axe. Following the murder Rosie Cortimiglia accused an Italian family, the Jordanos who

owned a rival grocery store, of killing her baby. Again the police were eager to make an arrest, so Frank Jordano and his father were charged with murder. Their trial was a farce, with Charles Cortimiglia vehemently denying his wife's claim that the Jordanos were responsible. Despite this they were found guilty and Frank Jordano was sentenced to death.

Unexplained halt

The arrest of the Jordanos did not halt the Axeman attacks either. There were three incidents when people were attacked but lived to tell the tale and then, on 27 October 1919, the Axeman committed his last reported killing. The victim was a grocer named Mike Pepitone.

Shortly after the Pepitone murder Rosie Cortimiglia went to the offices of the *Times–Picayune* and admitted that she had lied about the Jordanos having killed her baby. Frank Jordano and his father were released immediately.

By this time the citizens of New Orleans were in a state of hysteria, but unaccountably the Axeman murders suddenly stopped. There was no explanation for this, but there was one curious incident in December 1920. Mike Pepitone's widow shot a man named Joseph Mumfre, claiming he was the Axeman. This was possible but he was never arrested. The Axeman case remained unsolved and theories ranged from Mafia involvement, to a vendetta against Italian grocers.

Axeman fever

At the height of the Axeman craze there was not a single person in New Orleans who did not have a theory. People held 'Axeman' parties and a songwriter wrote a tune entitled 'The Mysterious Axeman's Jazz'.

Babington, Anthony

(1561–86)

Conspirator

*The leader of a Catholic
conspiracy, whose aim was to
assassinate Elizabeth I and free
Mary, Queen of Scots.*

Anthony Babington's family can be traced back to the Norman era and he was born in the Derbyshire town of Dethick. His father died in 1571 and he was brought up by his mother and two guardians. Although officially Protestants, all three had strong Catholic sympathies, which were duly passed on to the young Babington.

Before Babington married, in 1579, he served briefly as a page to Mary, Queen of Scots while she was imprisoned at Sheffield. It was during this time that he became devoted to her and her cause. When he left her service in 1580 he went to London and wasted no time in forming a secret society for the protection and maintenance of Jesuit missionaries.

The plot is hatched

After returning to Dethick and assuming control of his property, Babington went to the continent. In France he met Mary's emissaries at Paris and then went to Rome where he met several members of the Roman Catholic secret society. By the time he returned to England in 1585 he had already been marked out by Mary's friends as being a suitable leader of a Catholic insurrection against Queen Elizabeth.

At the end of 1585 Babington was persuaded by John Ballard, a Catholic priest from Rheims, to take command of a plot to kill Queen Elizabeth and free Queen Mary. With the promise of a foreign invasion to follow, Babington readily agreed, with the help of a number of men from his secret society formed in 1580. The conspirators met frequently throughout June 1586. Babington corresponded with Mary on a number of occasions, detailing how the preparations were proceeding.

Foiled by spies

Unfortunately for Babington and his fellow conspirators they were surrounded by spies planted by Elizabeth's principal secretary Sir Francis Walsingham. Their letters were intercepted and deciphered and their activities in June and July were reported to the government. On 4 August Ballard was arrested and, realizing that they had been discovered, Babington fled to St John's Wood. Although he disguised himself by cutting off his hair and staining himself with walnut juice he was captured by the end of August and taken to the Tower.

Between 13 and 16 September 1586 Babington and 13 of his fellow conspirators were sentenced to hanging and quartering. When Elizabeth heard of the brutal circumstances of his death on 20 September, she ordered that the rest of the conspirators were to be hanged to death.

The Babington Plot was the excuse Elizabeth had been looking for to put Mary, Queen of Scots on trial. The letters that Mary had received from Babington and her coded replies were damning evidence of her approval of the plot to kill the Queen.

Disposal of lands
Although Babington was worried about how his property might be divided after his death he need not have been too concerned. The majority of his lands went to his brothers, although some of his personal property was granted to Sir Walter Raleigh, and Elizabeth herself even took a valuable clock.

Balfour, Jabez Spencer
(1843–1912)

Fraudster

An eminently believable swindler who used one fraudulent company to finance the next.

Jabez Balfour's upbringing ensured that he had the one thing that was invaluable to a con man — an air of respectability. His father worked in the House of Commons and his mother was a writer who enjoyed considerable success with books entitled *Women of Scripture* and *Moral Heroism*. This enabled Jabez to be educated in France and Germany.

Business mind

Balfour's vocational ambitions inclined towards land and property and he joined the Lands Allotment Ltd and The Liberator Building Society. His manner was one of reassuring authority and in 1870 he was made a managing director of Lands Allotment. In his new role he championed the cause of the small investor and this helped him become a Justice of the Peace and a Liberal Member of Parliament.

But Balfour's main interest remained business and by 1885 he had increased the capital of Lands Allotment from £15 000 to £750 000. Never one to stand still he consolidated by forming a succession of new companies, which he ran under the umbrella of the Balfour Group.

The Balfour snowball

On paper, Balfour's companies seemed to be a great success and the business community and the investing public had the utmost faith in him. Unfortunately, what they did not know was that Balfour had founded his empire on the 'snowball' technique, where shares are floated and then the money is used to finance another company. The investors were unaware of this because they always received their dividends, even though it was money from another company.

In 1882 Balfour formed the London and General Bank, a dubious institution whose main task was to juggle the figures of the Balfour Group, while ensuring that its founder was always receiving handsome payments. For the next 10 years Balfour's snowball kept growing and embracing more new companies.

The snowball melts

In 1892 the business world were stunned when one of the Balfour Group companies collapsed with debts of £8 million. Slowly, Balfour's financial intrigues were unravelled, and the revelations were all the more shocking because no one had suspected him of being a fraudster. Over 25 000 small investors were ruined at the collapse of the Balfour Group and the only person who was not surprised at the outcome was the perpetrator himself. He was well prepared and before the authorities could move to arrest him he fled to Argentina, leaving financial chaos in his wake.

In 1895 Balfour was recognized in a small village and after a lengthy legal battle he was extradited to Britain. He was tried at the Old Bailey in November 1895. The evidence against him was overwhelming; he was sentenced to 14 years' penal servitude, after which a fatal heart attack in 1912 curtailed his proposed financial comeback.

Prison diary
While in prison Balfour emulated his mother and took up writing. His book *My Prison Life* is considered to be one of the best works of prison reminiscences.

Bank of England swindle

(1873)

MacDonnell, Noyes and the Bidwells

An attempt by four Americans to steal £100 000 from the Bank of England.

At the beginning of 1873 four Americans arrived in London and took a suite at the Savoy Hotel. The foursome consisted of George Bidwell, a shrewd, businesslike con man, his younger brother Austin, a forger named George MacDonnell, and Edwin Noyes. They had come to London to take advantage of the British banking system whereby bills of exchange could be cashed at a bank, but were not presented to the relevant finance house until the end of the financial quarter.

George Bidwell knew that the most important part of the operation was to gain the bank's confidence; for this he used his charming younger brother. Austin was sent to a Saville Row tailor and, after ordering a new suit, he asked the tailor to look after some money for him. The tailor went one better and said he would introduce him to his banker, Mr Francis of the Bank of England.

Gullible banker

Austin, using the alias of Frederick Warren, impressed the banker and when he presented a genuine Rothschild bill for £4500 Mr Francis congratulated himself on landing a wealthy American client. He was so confident about Austin's credentials that he did bother to check his identity or his references.

After Austin's initial success George MacDonnell went to work producing forged bills of exchange. He was a skilful craftsman and when Austin presented the bills to the clerk at the Bank of England they were honoured immediately. George Bidwell had calculated that the gang could continue to operate for four weeks. By that time they would have over £100 000 and they would be well within the time limit by which the bills would be presented to the finance house.

Faulty forgery

The plan progressed smoothly and the biggest problem for George Bidwell was keeping Austin away from the young ladies in London. Shortly before the gang's time limit was up MacDonnell made an elementary mistake with two of his forgeries and forgot to put the date on them. When Mr Francis received them he sent them to the finance house, in this case Rothschild, to have the dates inserted. Rothschild sent them back saying that they were not genuine bills of exchange. By then the gang had swindled the 'Old Lady of Threadneedle Street' out of over £102 000.

Once they knew the game was up the gang went to ground: Noyes stayed in London and was the first to be caught; Austin Bidwell was traced to Cuba and arrested; George was apprehended in Edinburgh after a dramatic chase; and George MacDonnell was held by the authorities in New York and extradited. They were sent for trial at the Old Bailey in August 1873 and they were all sentenced to penal servitude for life.

Ailing con man

Although his accomplices spent 18 years in prison George Bidwell had no intention of being detained for so long. After serving six years he convinced the prison doctor that he was dying and was released on compassionate grounds. He proceeded to make a remarkable recovery from his fatal illness.

Barker family

(c.1930s)

Gangsters

A family of bank robbers and murderers who were led by the formidable Ma Barker.

Arizona Donnie Clark was born in 1872 in Springfield, Missouri. She was a spirited woman and after marrying George Barker and having four sons she encouraged them in their youthful criminal activities. She also changed her name to Kate but was more commonly known as Ma.

Herman Barker, born in 1894, was the eldest brother, followed by Lloyd (1896), Arthur, known as 'Doc', (1899), and Fred (1902). Under their mother's guidance they quickly graduated from petty robbery to more menacing crimes. They roamed through the midwest of America, from Minnesota to Texas, leaving a trail of carnage behind them. The gang were joined by a gangster named Alvin Karpis but this did not prevent them being dubbed the 'Bloody Barkers'.

Criminal record

The Barker gang were not fussy about how they obtained money or who they killed in the process. They robbed banks, payrolls and post offices, and also engaged in kidnapping. One of their most successful escapades was when they kidnapped a wealthy brewer and a bank president. They received $100 000 and $200 000 for the men respectively, and released their captives. Others were not so lucky and at least 10 people lost their lives to Ma Barker and her sons. In all the Barker gang accumulated more than $3 million from their raids.

In keeping with their way of life, all of the Barkers met with violent deaths. In 1927

Herman was tracked down by the Kansas police and surrounded. Rather than let himself be taken alive he committed suicide. In 1939 Doc was killed while trying to escape from Alcatraz, where he was serving a life sentence. Lloyd, the loner in the family, was imprisoned from 1922–47 and he received an unpleasant homecoming — he was killed by his wife two years after his release.

FBI assault

The FBI eventually tracked down Ma and Fred Barker in 1935. Following Doc's arrest in January they discovered a map with a circle drawn around Lake Weir in Florida. When they arrived at the location they found Ma and Fred barricaded into their house, with a considerable arsenal of weapons. During a 45-minute gun battle the FBI bombarded the house using tear-gas bombs, machine guns and rifles. When the assault was over the bodies of Ma and Fred were found inside. Ma was still clutching a machine gun.

George Barker, who had been deserted by his wife in 1927, collected the bodies of his wife and son and buried them at Welch, Oklahoma.

No 1 Rat

Alvin Karpis, whom J Edgar Hoover, the director of the FBI, called 'Public Rat No 1' was arrested in 1935. He was convicted of kidnapping and was sentenced to life imprisonment in Alcatraz.

Hard-hitting reward

During the 1930s American banks became thoroughly fed up with the activities of the likes of the Barkers. To deter them, various rewards were offered, one of which read: '$5000 Reward for DEAD bank robbers. The Association will not give one cent for live bank robbers'.

Barrington, Sir Jonah

(1760–1834)

Corrupt judge

A high-profile Irish judge who stole money from his court in an attempt to finance his lavish lifestyle.

Jonah Barrington was born near Abbeyleix, Queen's County, Ireland. He was one of 16 children in a staunch Protestant family and his upbringing was a happy one, and he made a number of useful contacts.

Barrington studied law at Trinity College, Dublin, and soon showed himself to be a talented scholar. Initially it was thought that he might pursue a career in the army. With this intention he was offered an ensign's commission by General Hunt Walsh. But Barrington, who was always a strong supporter of self-preservation, heard that the regiment was going to be sent for immediate service in America, so he declined the commission. He graciously told General Hunt to give the commission to 'some hardier soldier'.

Political aspirations

In 1788 Barrington joined the legal profession when he was called to the Irish bar. Due to a circle of influential friends and his social position his rise was swift. He also took an interest in politics and in 1792 he was elected to the Irish House of Commons as MP for Tuam, and a year later he took silk. In the same year he became a judge at the Admiralty Court. He had numerous political and legal connections, many of whom he liked to entertain on a lavish scale.

Barrington lost his seat of Tuam in 1798 but was returned as the member for Bannagher the following year. He was politically active when the idea for a union between the British and Irish parliaments was suggested. He was a fierce opponent of this proposal and his stance cost him the lucrative post of the solicitor-general. He left parliament in 1800 following the Act of Union and concentrated on his legal career. However, this had stagnated due to his political activities and he now found he was unable to entertain on the same scale as before. This did not worry him though and his expenditure began to greatly exceed his income.

Court theft

In an effort to bolster his dwindling finances Barrington undertook a number of questionable activities and in 1805 he turned to his own court in an attempt to pay off some of his debts. He stole money from the court but this only eased the situation temporarily. In 1806 and 1810 he stole again from the court.

Barrington's activities remained undetected for 20 years but in 1830 a commission of inquiry was set up to examine the workings of the Irish Courts of Justice. Among their findings was the evidence of Barrington's illegal activities. He was thrown out of office in disgrace and, rather than face the shame of staying at home, he moved to France where he pursued a literary career. He died at Versailles on 8 April 1834.

Talented author

Following his downfall Barrington wrote a number of critically acclaimed literary works. These included the provocative *The Rise and Fall of the Irish Nation* (1833) and *Personal Sketches of his own Time* (1827–32). The latter included a number of pictures that displayed Barrington's fine eye for detail and his cutting sense of humour.

Murder of Eliza Mary Barrow

(1911)

Frederick Henry Seddon

A mean and spiteful murder that was motivated by sheer greed.

Frederick Seddon was born in 1871 and he grew up with one preoccupation: hoarding money. By 1910 he was married with five children and worked as a district superintendent for a London insurance company. The family lived in a large house at 63 Tollington Park, Holloway, and Seddon charged his two teenage sons six shillings for the pleasure of sharing the family home.

In July 1910 Seddon decided to let out the top floor of the house to Eliza Mary Barrow, a 49-year-old spinster who was slovenly, argumentative and as mean as Seddon himself. She brought two friends with her, Robert Hook and his wife, and her 10-year-old nephew, Ernest Grant. True to character she soon fell out with the Hooks, and Seddon helped her in removing them from the premises.

Rich tenant

This action won Seddon the confidence of Miss Barrow and she was soon asking him advice about financial matters. She owned several properties, including a pub and a barber's shop, in addition to £1600 in India stock, and at least £420 in gold coins. Seddon quickly realized that his lodger was a very rich lady.

On 14 October 1910 Miss Barrow transferred the £1600 of India stock to Seddon in return for an annual annuity of £103. Three months later, in January 1911, Seddon persuaded her to transfer the leaseholds of the pub and the barber's shop into his name. For this he gave her a further annuity of £52 a year and, uncharacteristically, allowed her to live rent-free.

At the beginning of September 1911 Miss Barrow fell ill with vomiting and diarrhoea. She took to her bed and her slovenly habits ensured that the room was soon full of flies. To counteract this Mrs Seddon bought four flypapers, containing arsenic, and placed them around the room. But Miss Barrow's condition worsened and she died on 14 September. The cause of death was given as epidemic diarrhoea.

Suspicious relatives

In her will Mary Barrow gave everything to Seddon. When her relatives heard of this they were furious; suspecting foul play, they went to the police with their suspicions and persuaded them to exhume the body of Miss Barrow, which was discovered to contain arsenic, the real cause of death. Both Seddon and his wife were arrested and charged with murder.

The Seddons' trial began on 4 March 1912 at the Old Bailey and lasted for 10 days. Mrs Seddon was a quiet and submissive witness but her husband was overbearing, conceited and arrogant. This could have been a governing factor in the jury's decision; they found him guilty but his wife not guilty.

The odious and miserly Frederick Seddon was hanged in Pentonville Prison on 18 April 1912.

Fellow masons
Before being sentenced to death Seddon gave a ritual masonic sign and said to the judge, 'I declare before the Great Architect of the Universe, I am not guilty'. The judge, a fellow mason, was unimpressed: 'Our brotherhood does not encourage crime — on the contrary, it condemns it'.

Bartlett case

(1886)

Adelaide Bartlett

A celebrated Victorian case in which an adulterous wife was accused of poisoning her husband with chloroform.

Little is known about Adelaide Bartlett's early life but she was born in Orleans, France, in 1856, and educated in a convent school. When she was 17 she moved to England to complete her education and stayed with a guardian in Kingston, just outside London.

In February 1875 she met Edwin Bartlett, a partner in a grocery business, and it was quickly decided by the Bartlett family and Adelaide's guardian that it would be advantageous if the couple married. Adelaide soon became bored with her industrious husband as she had to endure long periods alone. To compensate for this she had a brief affair with her husband's brother, Frederick, but when her father-in-law found out about this there was a fierce row and the liaison was broken off.

Clerical affair

By 1885 Edwin Bartlett was becoming concerned that his wife was not involved enough in society. He introduced her to one of his friends, the Reverend George Dyson, and an intimate relationship soon developed. Bartlett was aware but unconcerned about the affair and he even changed his will, leaving everything to his wife and naming Dyson as the executor.

In December 1885 Edwin Bartlett, who had always considered himself in the best of health, fell seriously ill. He died on 1 January and at the post-mortem it was discovered that he had a large quantity of liquid chloroform in his body. When it was revealed that Dyson had bought chloroform only days before Bartlett's death both he and Adelaide were arrested.

Lack of evidence

The case against Dyson was dropped due to lack of evidence, but Adelaide Bartlett was charged with murder and sent for trial at the Old Bailey. At the trial it was soon established that the Bartletts had formed a 'platonic compact'. Adelaide's defence council, Edward Clarke, suggested that Bartlett had taken the poison willingly, hoping to soothe a raging toothache.

When Adelaide took the stand she gave a superb performance. She hinted that her husband had some strange sexual preferences and admitted giving him chloroform on a handkerchief, but only to curb his sexual advances towards her. This may not have been completely true but it weighed heavily with the Victorian jury who saw Adelaide as something of a heroine, warding off the unwanted attentions of a perverted husband.

But the most important piece of evidence was that there was no trace of burning in Bartlett's mouth and throat — as there would have been if Adelaide had administered the poison orally. The jury agreed that there was insufficient evidence to convict Adelaide Bartlett; she was acquitted and emigrated to America. After the trial a famous surgeon commented, 'Now that it is all over, she should tell us in the interests of science how she did it'.

My Birdie

Who is it that hath burst the door
Unclosed the heart that shut before
And set her queen-like on the throne
And made her homage all her own?
My Birdie!
Poem from Dyson to Adelaide Bartlett.

Bath Racecourse betting conspiracy

(1953)

Francasal

A major betting fraud in which two identical horses were switched, and heavy bets placed on the substitute.

On 16 July 1953 a French bred and trained horse named Francasal won the Spa Selling Plate race at Bath Racecourse. The starting price was 10–1 and a few individuals who had bet on the horse stood to win £60 000.

However, immediately after the race the authorities became suspicious of Francasal's victory and withheld all bets. Their chief cause for concern was the fact that immediately before the race 'the blower' system had been out of order. This is a telephone network between bookmakers and their agents whereby they monitor the bets on races all over the country. If someone is betting heavily on a particular horse then the odds can be adjusted accordingly to ensure that the bookmakers do not lose too much money. However, when 'the blower' went down at 1.30pm on 16 July 1953 the bookmakers had no idea that large bets were being placed on Francasal.

Conspiracy uncovered

After an investigation by the Post Office and Scotland Yard it was shown that the overhead telephone wires just outside Bath had been tampered with and a man was later charged with causing malicious damage to the wires. This confirmed the authorities' suspicions that there was something amiss with the Francasal race, particularly as the horse had disappeared immediately afterwards.

On 20 July the police in Berkshire discovered Francasal and an almost identical horse in a stable in Reading. After forensic examinations the other horse was identified as Santa Amaro, which had been bought in France on 12 May 1953 by Victor Robert Colquhoun Dill and Henry George Kateley. It was raced at Worcester six days later and to the men's satisfaction it won easily. They then returned to France and bought the near identical, and untested, Francasal.

Switched horses

On 16 July Francasal was entered to race at Bath and Santa Amaro was due to race at Newmarket. However, the two horses were switched and Santa Amaro ran at Bath, benefiting from the generous odds that had been assigned to the unknown 'Francasal'. While this was going on the real Francasal was being shipped out of the country, in case anyone at Newmarket inspected him too closely.

Once the betting conspiracy had been uncovered Dill, Kateley and three of their associates were arrested and sent for trial at the Old Bailey. It began on 12 January 1954 and the men's defence claimed that no conspiracy had taken place and that the horses had been switched as the result of a genuine mistake. They cited five previous cases where this had happened in British racing history. On 2 February the trial ended with the jury unable to reach a verdict; a re-trial was ordered and on 17 March 1954 four of the defendants were found guilty. Kateley's sentence was for three years and Dill's was nine months.

Kidnapping

On 9 February 1983 Shergar, the 1981 English Derby winner, was kidnapped in Ireland. A £2 million ransom was demanded but the kidnappers never showed themselves and Shergar has never been seen again.

Beane family

(c.1600)

Murderers and cannibals

A family of cave-dwelling savages who murdered up to 1000 people.

Sawney Beane was born in East Lothian, eight miles east of Edinburgh, during the reign of James I of Scotland and England. His father was a hedger and ditcher but Sawney was a lazy, unruly child who avoided all manual labour. He soon tired of his home life and moved to the Galloway coast, taking with him a vicious-minded woman of ill repute.

For the next 25 years Beane, and his frequently expanding family, lived in a cave and launched a reign of terror on travellers who came within his territory. Over the years dozens of people disappeared without trace in the Galloway area and it was thought that there could be a large pack of wolves operating in the area. To be seen to be doing something the authorities executed a number of tramps and innkeepers but it did little to halt the disappearances.

First survivor

While James I was on the throne, 1567–1625, a man and his wife were attacked by a large group of savages in Galloway. The woman was stabbed to death and her attackers began drinking her blood and eating her flesh. The man fought wildly and was eventually saved by the arrival of 30 people who were on their way home from a local fair. Immediately the savages vanished, leaving behind the only person to have survived one of their attacks.

When James heard of this clan of savages he decided to take direct action, and went to Galloway with 400 men. As they were investigating along the shoreline, one of the dogs in the party began barking at the entrance to a small cave. When the soldiers entered they discovered that it opened into a huge cavern and inside were Sawney Beane and his family. They put up a brief fight but were soon overpowered by the soldiers.

Cannibals' lair

Inside the cave there were the remains of dozens of human bodies and it was obvious that the captured clan were not only murderers but also cannibals. They attacked unsuspecting travellers, robbed them, and killed them to make sure that no one reported them. They then took the bodies back to their cave to eat.

The Beane family numbered 48 in all — Sawney and his mate, eight sons, six daughters, 18 grandsons and 14 granddaughters. They all looked and behaved like wild beasts and although it is impossible to know how many people they killed it could have been as many as 1000.

The Beane clan were taken to Edinburgh and briefly imprisoned in the Tolbooth. They were then taken to Leith and executed. Since they behaved like animals they were treated as such and did not receive a trial. They went to their deaths without the slightest remorse and died cursing and shouting at their executioners.

Brutal executions

The members of the Beane family were put to death in a particularly brutal fashion. The men had their arms and legs cut off and were left to bleed to death. The women were made to watch this and were then burnt on three separate fires.

Beck, Martha and Fernandez, Raymond

(1920–51) and (1914–51)

Convicted murderers

Known as America's 'Lonely Hearts Killers', Beck and Fernandez swindled and murdered lonely spinsters.

Raymond Fernandez was born in Hawaii and moved to Spain during the 1930s, where he served with Franco's forces during the Civil War. He later worked for British intelligence in Gibraltar and in 1945 he returned to America, working his passage on an oil tanker. During the voyage he was hit on the head by a hatch cover and this changed his personality dramatically. Once he reached America he settled in New York and began swindling hundreds of women, whom he contacted through lonely-hearts magazines.

Unlikely lovers

In December 1947 Fernandez met Martha Beck, an overweight nurse with a voracious sexual appetite. The couple began a strange relationship which was based on sexual perversions and jealousy. When Martha discovered her lover's occupation she joined him with enthusiasm, aiding in the swindles by posing as his sister.

Beck and Fernandez moved to Illinois in August 1948 and Fernandez married Myrtle Young. However, Martha was intensely jealous and refused to allow Fernandez to consummate the marriage. Instead, Young was given a fatal overdose of barbiturates. Beck and Fernandez made $4000 from her death.

Following their first murder the couple moved to Albany, New York, where Fernandez charmed a widow, Janet Fay, out of a $6000 insurance policy and then beat her to death. The couple buried the body in their cellar in New York City.

Bodies in the cellar

Beck and Fernandez reached Grand Rapids, Michigan, early in 1949. Using lonely-hearts columns they contacted a 28-year-old widow named Delphine Dowling. Again, Martha's jealousy got the better of her and Delphine, and her daughter Rainelle, were murdered. Afterwards Beck and Fernandez went to the cinema for the evening. When they returned they found the police waiting for them. When the house was searched the bodies of Delphine and Rainelle were found cemented into the cellar floor.

After their arrest Beck and Fernandez confessed to their two earlier killings. Since there was no death penalty in Michigan the police began a long legal battle to have their trial moved to New York, where they would be tried for the murder of Janet Fay. Eventually the police got their way and the trial of the 'Lonely Hearts Killers' began in New York in July 1949.

The trial lasted 44 days, with the press and the general public revelling in the details of the couple's sordid sex-life and murderous activities. There was little sympathy when they were found guilty. Martha Beck and Raymond Fernandez were electrocuted at Sing-Sing Prison on 8 March 1951. It is thought that they killed up to 21 other women.

Prolonged death

Martha Beck wrote, 'Now that I know Raymond loves me I can go to my death bursting with joy'. Hers was an agonizing death, her severely overweight body shuddering for several seconds as the current made its impact.

Becker, Charles

(1872–1915)

Corrupt policeman and convicted murderer

A New York police detective who turned to murder to help maintain his protection racket.

In the years before World War I New York was rife with illegal gambling dens and corrupt policemen. The gambling joints faced a double risk in the form of raids by the police and also attacks from rival organizations. One of the biggest operations was run by a man named Herman Rosenthal. However, he was continually frustrated by police raids. He opened a saloon at West 116th Street, but this was quickly closed down. When he tried again, at West 45th Street, he fared little better and suffered frequent raids and two bombings by rival gangs.

On the make

Frustrated by these attacks Rosenthal knew he needed to act quickly if he was to remain in business. He approached a detective on the New York Police force, Charlie Becker, who had a reputation for corruption. He was the head of the city's Gambling Squad and in this capacity he was able to organize an efficient protection racket involving various gambling joints. Some paid him handsomely while those who refused had numerous charges falsified against them. Rosenthal offered Becker a 'business' partnership on the condition that he received adequate protection. Initially this was satisfactory to both parties.

Threat of exposure

In 1912 Becker asked Rosenthal for $500 to help defend his press agent who had been charged with murder. Rosenthal refused and in a rage Becker ordered a raid on his club. In retaliation Rosenthal threatened to expose Becker to a reform-conscious District Attorney named Charles Whitman, who was sworn to clamp down on police corruption.

When Becker heard of this threat he decided to act. He offered $2000 and freedom to an imprisoned gangster named Jack Zelig, if he would kill Rosenthal. Zelig agreed and once he was released he enlisted the help of four fellow gangsters for the task. Their first attempt was unsuccessful but on 15 June 1912 Herman Rosenthal was gunned down outside the Hotel Metropole.

Witness assassinated

After the killing the gunmen were quickly traced and Zelig wasted no time in implicating Becker in the murder. He would have been a vital witness at the trial but he was shot dead before he had a chance to testify.

The trial of Charlie Becker and six of his associates took place in October 1912. Several gangsters were offered immunity by Charles Whitman if they testified against Becker and they did so. The former detective was found guilty of first degree murder but the judge's summing-up was so prejudiced that a re-trial was ordered. This did Becker little good and he was found guilty again. He was electrocuted on 30 July 1915, after Charles Whitman, who was now State Governor, had refused a plea of clemency.

> **Libellous plaque**
> Becker's wife placed a silver plate on her husband's coffin that read, 'Charles Becker, murdered 30 July 1915 by Governor Whitman'. However, she was advised to remove it as she could have been accused of criminal libel.

Bender family case

(1873)

Suspected murderers

A traveller's inn run by a family who robbed and murdered their guests.

In 1871 the Bender family moved into a house on a desolate prairie road in Labette County, Kansas, 14 miles from the frontier town of Independence. The family were of German extraction and consisted of John Bender, a surly 60-year-old, his wife, and their children, 27-year-old John jnr and 24-year-old Kate. Kate claimed to be a spiritualist; she called herself Professor and gave lectures in neighbouring towns. She also asserted that she could communicate with the dead.

Deadly inn

The Benders set up their house as a store and an inn. They had a steady trade of customers in the form of travellers who were pioneering the west at this time. By the autumn of 1872 it was noticed that several of the guests who stayed at the Bender's inn were never seen again. However, since few of the travellers were known in the area this caused no more than passing comment.

Persistent brother

On 10 March 1873 Dr William H York was returning to his home in Independence. He met some friends on the road and told them that he was going to stop at the Bender's inn for something to eat. This was the last that was seen of him. After a few weeks his brother, Colonel A M York became suspicious and began to investigate the doctor's whereabouts. He visited the Benders on 24 April but found nothing suspicious: they suggested that he might have been attacked by bandits after leaving their inn.

Colonel York was unhappy about the Bender's casual manner and on 5 May he returned to their home with a group of armed men. They found the house deserted. After examining the contents of the house Colonel York looked outside and exclaimed, 'Boys, I see graves yonder in the orchard'.

Grisly garden

When York and his men started digging in the orchard they soon found the body of Dr York. On further investigation they unearthed 11 more bodies — nine men, a woman and a little girl. The men and the woman had all been killed by severe blows to the head with an implement like a sledgehammer, while the girl had been buried alive. It was deduced that the Benders had murdered their victims by striking them from behind while they were having dinner. Some of the more imaginative theorists suggested that Kate Bender hypnotized the victims before they were killed.

Despite an intensive search the Benders were never seen again. It has been suggested that they were caught and hanged in Oklahoma, shot by a gang of vigilantes in Independence, or that they joined a gang of desperadoes in the Indian Territory. Whatever the truth, they were never brought to justice and escaped scot-free with the proceeds of their crimes — over $7000.

Hysteria

Following the discovery of the bodies at the Benders' inn their neighbour, Rudolph Brockmann, was set upon by a mob because he had a German accent. They twice half-hanged him but when he refused to confess they decided he must be innocent and released him.

Berkowitz, David Richard

(1953–)

Convicted murderer

New York's Son of Sam killer who claimed he was driven to kill by demon voices in his head.

David Berkowitz was an illegitimate child and his natural mother gave him up for adoption when he was three years old. He grew up with a feeling of rejection and he joined the Army in the hope of finding an identity. He served briefly in Korea but left the Army after refusing to carry a gun while on duty. He returned to New York where he worked in several menial, dead-end jobs. He was shy in female company and this slowly grew into a strong dislike of women.

In November 1975 Berkowitz took a month off work and virtually became a recluse in his apartment in the Yonkers. He nailed blankets over the window, slept on a bare mattress on the floor and only went outside to satisfy his cravings for junk food. While he was incarcerated in his apartment he wrote messages on the wall: 'In this hole lives the wicked King', 'Kill for my Master', and 'I turn children into Killers'.

Demons in his mind

On Christmas Eve 1975 Berkowitz felt the need to kill. He later claimed that he heard demonic voices that told him that people had to be sacrificed. He drove to Co-op City, where he used to live, and tried to stab a woman with a hunting knife. It was a clumsy, ineffectual attempt and the victim escaped virtually unharmed. As Berkowitz was running from the scene of his first attack he saw a 15-year-old girl standing in a doorway. In a frenzy he struck out at her and stabbed her six times. The girl survived and Berkowitz 'celebrated' his attack by gorging himself on junk food.

On 28 July 1976 Berkowitz's demons were demanding 'blood'. He put his gun, a Charter Arms .44 Special Bulldog, into a paper bag and went to the Bronx. He came across a parked car with two girls sitting talking inside and went up to the window, firing indiscriminately. One of the girls, Jody Valenti, was severely injured, and the other, Donna Lauria, was killed.

Three months later Berkowitz went to Queens and shot a young couple who were embracing in a parked car. They both survived, as did two teenage girls who were shot on 26 November 1976. The bullets from these attacks were found to match the ones that had killed Donna Lauria.

Vendetta continues

By the beginning of 1977 Berkowitz had overcome his initial nervousness about killing and he continued his campaign in a more ruthless manner. On 30 January he went to Queens, again looking for victims to satisfy the demanding voices in his head. He saw two lovers in a car and as they embraced he shot the woman, Christine Freund, who died in hospital a few hours later.

On 8 March 1977 Berkowitz was in the Forest Hills area of New York. As usual he had his gun with him and, as he approached an Armenian student named Virginia Voskerichian, he pulled it out and shot her through the mouth. She died instantly.

Despite the biggest operation ever mounted by the New York Police Department (100 police patrolled Queens every night), the killings continued. On 17 April 1977 Berkowitz was again prowling around Queens. In the early hours of the morning he came across a couple in a parked car and shot them both. Valentina Suriani was killed instantly, while her lover, Alexander Esau, died later in hospital.

Son of Sam

After the latest killings the police found a note that had been left by the killer. It was addressed to Captain Borrelli of the New York Police and read: 'I am deeply hurt by your calling me a wemen-hater(sic). I am not. But I am a monster. I am the Son of Sam'. A further missive from the Son of Sam was also sent to a columnist on a New York newspaper. Once the killer had acquired his new sobriquet he achieved a macabre celebrity status.

On 26 June 1977 Son of Sam struck again. This time his targets were Salvatore Lupo and Judy Placido who were in a car in Bayside, Queens. They both survived the attack but a month later Stacy Moskowitz was not so lucky when she and her boyfriend, Robert Violante, were shot on 31 July. She died in hospital and Violante was blinded.

Parking ticket clue

This was the last killing by the Son of Sam. While he had been attacking Moskowitz and Violante a woman had seen a policeman put a parking ticket on a car, and then minutes later a man rush into it and drive away. When the records were checked the car was found to belong to David Berkowitz. When the police went to investigate they saw a gun in the back of his car and a note in the same handwriting as the Son of Sam letters. Berkowitz was apprehended as he left his apartment and he announced calmly, 'I'm Sam'.

When Berkowitz was captured he was found to be a small, overweight man with a childlike grin. He was diagnosed by psychiatrists as being neurotic, schizophrenic and paranoid but nevertheless he was judged fit to stand trial. He made this unnecessary by pleading guilty to all the charges against him. He was sentenced to a total of 365 years' imprisonment. He was sent to prison in August 1977 and he has since made considerable sums of money from writing, and selling the film rights to his life story.

Son of Sam

Berkowitz took the name Son of Sam from his neighbour, Sam Carr. Carr had a black labrador that kept Berkowitz awake at night with its barking. He claimed that the 'real' Sam, who tormented his mind, was a 6000-year-old man who was inhabiting the body of the labrador.

Sensation-seekers

Following Berkowitz's arrest his apartment at Pine Street in the Yonkers was besieged by macabre sensation-seekers. They stole door-knobs, chipped pieces of paint from the front door and even shouted, 'David, come out', in the middle of the night. The owner was forced to change the numbers in the building in an effort to divert attention.

Biggs, Ronald

(1929–   )

Train robber and fugitive

One of the Great Train Robbers, who became a national figure after events following the robbery.

Although Ronnie Biggs took part in the Great Train Robbery in 1963 (see p29) he was not an original member of the gang. He was brought in at the last minute, after much heated debate, to provide the gang with a substitute train driver. As it transpired Biggs's companion lost his nerve on the night and was not used.

Before the Great Train Robbery Biggs had been a small-time thief in London, who tended to get caught with monotonous regularity. In keeping with this he was one of the first to be arrested after the robbery, having left his fingerprints at Leatherslade Farm, the gang's hideout. On 15 April 1964 he was sentenced to 30 years' imprisonment for his part in the largest robbery in British history.

Jailbreak

Not relishing the prospect of a long prison sentence Biggs decided to escape, and on 8 July 1965 he used a rope-ladder to scale the wall at Wandsworth Prison. After staying in hiding for several weeks he fled to the continent and while in Paris he underwent extensive, and painful, plastic surgery. Using the services of an underground outfit called 'The Organization', Biggs obtained a new passport in the name of Terence Furminger and on 31 December 1965 he flew to Australia.

Biggs quickly took to the relaxed Australian way of life and settled in Adelaide, intent on living a quiet life using his proceeds from the robbery. In June 1966 his wife, Charmian, and their sons, Nicky and Chris, joined him. However, this domestic bliss was shattered when Biggs was recognized from a picture in a newspaper. Once again he returned to a life on the run, narrowly missing capture in Melbourne.

Fugitive

With the police hot on his trail Biggs left Australia and, with considerable help from a friend, he entered Brazil in March 1970. At first he missed his family terribly but Charmian insisted that he stayed where he was and kept his freedom. Biggs soon found solace with his Brazilian girlfriend, Raimunda, and the couple had a child. In 1974 the British police tracked down Biggs and tried to extradite him. However, they were thwarted by a Brazilian law stating that fathers of Brazilian children cannot be extradited. The policemen returned home in disgrace, while Biggs revelled in another moment of triumph.

In his new home Biggs became a celebrity and occupied his time with, among other things, making a record with the Sex Pistols and taking drinks aboard a Royal Navy ship. He is currently living in Rio de Janeiro, giving press interviews and indulging his passion for jazz music.

Final straw

When Ronnie Biggs was sent to prison in 1964 his wife Charmian said, 'I married you for the rainy days as well as the fine ones'. She stuck to her words for 10 years, joining her husband in a life on the run. In 1974 she visited him in Brazil, only to find him with his Brazilian girlfriend. This proved to be the final straw. Charmian returned to Australia, completed her arts degree at Melbourne University and divorced Ronnie Biggs.

Black Dahlia murder

(1947)

Hollywood killer

The murder of a Hollywood bit-part actress which produced a spate of confessions, but no killer.

On 15 January 1947 the Los Angeles police discovered the mutilated body of a young woman on a piece of waste ground. The body had been crudely cut in half and the initials BD had been carved deep into one thigh. Identification proved difficult but the police eventually discovered it was the body of 22-year-old Elizabeth Short, known as the Black Dahlia.

Elizabeth Short had been born and brought up in Medford in Massachusetts and from an early age her life followed an unfortunate pattern. When she was six her father left, and her mother had difficulty keeping the rest of the family together. By the time she was 16, in 1942, Elizabeth had decided to start a new life in Miami.

Elizabeth Short was a very attractive young woman and in Miami she had no shortage of American servicemen for company. She became engaged to one of these men but unfortunately he was killed during World War II. At this news Elizabeth became increasingly promiscuous and began drinking heavily. On one occasion she was found drinking by the police and arrested as a juvenile delinquent.

Tragedy again

In 1944 Elizabeth became engaged to another serviceman and returned to her mother to await her fiancé's return from the war. He never came back and in 1946 Elizabeth received a telegram saying that he had been killed in action. This shattered Elizabeth and she decided to go to California and make a fresh start.

When she reached the West Coast she achieved moderate success as a film extra. She enjoyed her Hollywood lifestyle and earned the nickname the Black Dahlia because of her preference for dressing entirely in black. But her success was short-lived and she soon turned to waitressing and sank into a vicious circle of alcohol and promiscuity. It is likely that one of the men she picked up was responsible for her brutal murder.

Flood of confessions

When the murder of the Black Dahlia was discovered there was a flood of 'confessions'. It seemed as if every crank in Los Angeles wanted to claim responsibility for killing this beautiful, troubled woman. The police were able to quickly discount most of these 'killers' because some of the injuries that Elizabeth suffered were so horrific that they had not been reported to the public.

The one genuine piece of evidence that the police received was a letter sent to a Los Angeles newspaper. It had been made from newspaper clippings and read, 'Here are Dahlia's belongings. Letter to follow'. Enclosed were Elizabeth Short's birth certificate, address book and social security card. Crucially, one page of the address book was missing and the author of the letter never did get in contact again.

Despite the fact that over 50 people came forward to confess to the murder of the Black Dahlia the case remains unsolved.

> **Red herring**
> A waitress in LA thought she had found the killers when she overheard two men talking about the killing. When they were arrested they turned out to be two off-duty detectives.

Blunt, Anthony Frederick

(1907–83)

Spy

A respected art historian who was an espionage contemporary of Guy Burgess, Kim Philby and Donald Maclean.

Anthony Blunt was born into an upper-class family in Hampshire. He was exceptionally intelligent and while his father was working in Paris he developed a passion for French art and architecture. He attended Marlborough College and then won a scholarship to Trinity College, Cambridge, in 1926. He excelled in his studies and in 1932 he became a fellow after writing a superb history of art dissertation.

While still at Cambridge Blunt was invited to join the Apostles, an exclusive and elitist club, the members of which believed they were above the normal moral rules of society. Several of them were homosexuals and it was here that Blunt developed his own homosexual tendencies.

Being a passionate anti-Fascist, Blunt soon met Burgess, Philby and Maclean. He was particularly fascinated by the flamboyantly homosexual Burgess and this led to his acquiescence when Burgess asked him to become a Russian spy. His initial task was as a 'talent-spotter' — picking suitable candidates for recruitment to the Russian intelligence service.

Russian provider

In 1939 Blunt joined the army and then served briefly in France with the Field Security Police. In 1940 he joined MI5 and served with them in the counter-espionage department during World War II. Throughout this period he provided the Russians with valuable information on British operators at home and abroad. Although his work was not as damaging as that of Philby, Burgess or Maclean, it is likely that he was indirectly responsible for the death of a number of British agents.

Blunt's espionage activities virtually ceased in 1945 when he left MI5 to resume his academic career. However, in 1951 he aided Burgess and Maclean when they defected to the Soviet Union.

Pillar of society

After the war Blunt's career flourished. From 1947 to 1974 he was director of the Courtauld Institute of Art, and from 1945 to 1972 surveyor of the Queen's Pictures. In 1947 he received the Commander of the Royal Victorian Order (CVO) and he was knighted in 1956.

After several years of investigation by the security forces, MI5 discovered an American who had been recruited by Blunt during his time at Cambridge. When confronted with this information, in return for immunity from prosecution, Blunt told them everything. To prevent a public scandal the information was kept secret and he remained in his official posts.

In 1979 Andrew Boyle published *The Climate of Treason*, revealing damaging information about espionage activities in Britain. To avoid further speculation it was announced that Anthony Blunt was also in the Philby, Burgess and Maclean spy ring. His knighthood was annulled and he was roundly condemned by the community. He died in London on 26 March 1983.

No remorse
Following his exposure Anthony Blunt did himself few favours. He appeared on television and declared arrogantly, 'I did not betray my conscience'. He then refused to speak of his espionage activities, hypocritically citing the Official Secrets Act as the reason for his silence.

Bogle – Chandler case

(1963)

Dr Gilbert Stanley Bogle and Margaret Chandler

An unsolved Australian double murder in which the cause of death was never satisfactorily proved.

On the night of New Year's Eve 1962 Dr Stanley Bogle, a high-ranking government scientist employed at the Commonwealth Scientific and Industrial Research Office near Sydney, attended a party given by friends at Sydney's North Shore. At 3.45am he offered to drive home Mrs Margaret Chandler, a family friend. It was the last time that they were seen alive.

The bodies of Dr Bogle and Mrs Chandler were discovered on the morning of 1 January 1963, by two teenagers. At first the police thought it was a suicide pact between two lovers, but there was no evidence to support this. Both of the victims were happily married and there was no sign of sexual intercourse having taken place. However, both bodies were partially naked and had been covered with clothes and cardboard. Even more mysteriously the bodies were 50 feet apart.

Untraceable poison

The police were quick to discount the suicide theory and treated the case as a double murder. When it was discovered that both of the victims had been violently sick shortly before their deaths it was assumed that they had been poisoned. However, the police scientists could find no trace of poison and an eminent professor of pharmacology came to the conclusion that the poisoner was 'virtually a biological genius'.

The official inquest concluded that Dr Bogle and Mrs Chandler had died of acute circulatory failure of an unknown cause. There then followed a fierce debate about why the couple had been killed. The tabloid newspapers had a field day speculating about secret work on a death-ray. There was considerable discussion about whether Dr Bogle was killed by enemy agents. Far fetched as it may seem this theory was given some credence when it was revealed that Dr Bogle was due to start work on a research programme of military importance to the United States government.

LSD user?

In 1977 Margaret Fowler, a former lover of Dr Bogle's, died. It was then discovered that she had attended the inquest in 1963 but had been refused permission to give evidence. Some people now voiced the belief that she would have told the inquest that Dr Bogle was a LSD user and that he could have died of an overdose of the drug. In light of the forensic evidence this seems unlikely but if the tests had been carried out with today's advanced technology the results could have been quite different.

The case of Dr Bogle and Mrs Chandler is still officially unsolved, although the conspiracy theory is kept alive by the knowledge that the FBI hold a file on Dr Bogle.

Unsolved

Another celebrated unsolved murder involving poison occurred in 1978 when Georgi Markov, a Bulgarian defector living in London, was assassinated by an umbrella-gun. A pellet of poison was injected into his leg from the point of an umbrella. He developed a fever and died three days later. An inquest revealed that he had been poisoned — by a rare and barely detectable poison called ricin. The assailant was never caught.

Bonney, William H (Billy the Kid)

(1859–81)

Outlaw

A legendary gunslinger who was charming, quiet — and a deadly killer.

William H Bonney was born in New York City but moved with his parents to Coffeyville, Kansas in 1862. Billy's father, William Bonney, died shortly afterwards and his mother, Kathleen, decided to move to Colorado. She then lived briefly in Santa Fe before settling in Silver City, New Mexico. Throughout these wanderings Billy received a rough education and it soon became evident that most of his schooling was going to be done in saloons and on gambling tables.

Youthful killing

It is alleged that Billy committed his first murder at the age of 12. During a bar-room argument a man insulted his mother, to whom he was devoted, and even though he was not yet a teenager he had no second thoughts about stabbing him to death. When Billy was 16, he and a friend mercilessly slaughtered three Indians in Arizona, as they were taking furs to town for sale. The pattern for Billy's life was already set.

Billy's mother died when he was 15, thus removing the only constraining influence in his life. He engaged upon a series of wild and reckless adventures which resulted in more deaths and short periods in prison for minor offences. Once he escaped from captivity by climbing a chimney and jumping to his freedom from the roof.

Cattle war

In 1877, after two years of raiding both sides of the border and killing another 12 men,

Billy joined the ranch owner J H Tunstall as a cowhand in the Pecos Valley in New Mexico. His arrival in the area coincided with the outbreak of a violent cattle war that was centred on Lincoln County. The instigators of this were the Murphy gang and when they murdered J H Tunstall Billy resolved to take revenge. He took over the leadership of the McSween gang and indulged in violent attacks on the Murphys and their associates. One of these was a notoriously corrupt sheriff named James A Brady. On 1 April 1878 Billy incurred the wrath of the authorities when he killed Brady and a deputy sheriff. By this time his activities were gaining widespread publicity and he soon acquired the nickname of Billy the Kid.

Amnesty rejected

Following the shooting of Sheriff Brady, General Lew Wallace was sent to Lincoln County to try and put a stop to the cattle war. He reasoned that the easiest way to do this would be to remove Billy the Kid from the scene. In August 1878 he urged the Kid to surrender, offering him amnesty and a promise that he would not be prosecuted. Understandably, Billy was sceptical of the offer, claiming that he would be shot the minute he laid down his gun. Instead he surrounded himself with a band of bloodthirsty outlaws and embarked on a spree of cattle-rustling, robbery, and killing.

Although Billy soon became known as a violent and ruthless outlaw he was remarkably innocuous to look at. He was slender, five foot eight in height, with a pale, thoughtful face. He tended to be quiet and unassuming and walked with a languid grace. When he was in town he dressed well, liked to frequent balls and fandangoes and he was never short of female companionship.

Despite his social graces the authorities were becoming increasingly anxious to bring Billy the Kid to justice. In 1880 a group of worried cattlemen persuaded an erstwhile friend of Billy's, Patrick F Garrett, to become sheriff of Lincoln County and track down the notorious outlaw.

Capture and escape

Garrett entered into his task with enthusiasm and made it his declared intention to destroy Billy and his gang. He nearly achieved this in November 1880 when he and his posse surrounded the Kid at Greathouse Ranch, but they eventually had to retreat because of the perishing cold. A month later, on Christmas Eve, the Kid had again been tracked down but he escaped after one of his gang members had been mortally wounded. His reprieve was short-lived though and he was captured a few days later, with three of his accomplices.

In March 1881 Billy the Kid was tried for the murder of Sheriff Brady. He was found guilty and sentenced to death, only to escape from Lincoln jail, on 28 April 1881, by killing both his guards. By now Pat Garrett's patience was beginning to wear thin and he decided to take matters into his own hands. Drawing on personal knowledge he reasoned that sooner or later Billy would visit a friend of his named Pete Maxwell, who lived at Fort Sumner.

Final act

On 14 June 1881 Garrett travelled to Fort Sumner. When he encountered Billy he wasted no time on pleasantries and fired two shots from his Colt. Billy the Kid died of his wounds and although he had 19 notches on his guns it has been calculated that he was responsible for a minimum of 21 murders. Although it was acknowledged that he was in many ways a heartless killer he was mourned by a number of women at Fort Sumner. A monument now stands near the spot where he was killed.

Courteous robber

Not all criminals of the West were bloodthirsty and devoid of feelings. Black Bart was a robber whose behaviour bordered on the chivalrous. He held up stagecoaches and robbed them, but he never hurt anyone and only stole from treasure boxes and mailbags, never personal belongings. In 1875 he stopped a stagecoach in California. One of the terrified passengers threw him her purse but he picked it up, bowed and returned it to her.

Jim Hulme, the chief detective of Wells Fargo, was appointed to track down Black Bart. He eventually did so and discovered that this folk hero was in fact an elderly, grey-haired man, named Charles Bolton. He was convicted but the judge took pity on him and gave him a lenient sentence of six years.

Crooked judge

Even the law makers in the West at this time tended to have a trace of the outlaw in them. The worst was probably Judge Roy Bean. He had been a guerilla in the Civil War, a gambler, a saloon-keeper and a smuggler before he was appointed as judge in Vinegaroon, Texas, on the grounds of learning a little law while running a construction camp saloon. His court was a complete farce. He made up new laws to suit himself and most of the fines that he imposed went straight into his own pocket. He was also renowned for passing whisky around the courtroom and interrupting proceedings to play a couple of hands of poker.

Definitive account

The first, and undoubtedly the most comprehensive, history of Billy the Kid, *The Authentic Life of Billy the Kid*, was written by Pat Garrett in 1882. A new edition of this definitive work was published in 1954.

Bonnie and Clyde

Bonnie Parker (1910–34) and Clyde Barrow (1909–34)

Gangsters and murderers

Two of America's most notorious gangsters who left a trail of murder and mayhem across the southern states during the early 1930s.

Bonnie Parker was born in the small agricultural community of Rowena on the Texas plains. Her family were comfortably off and Bonnie grew up as a high-spirited, fun-loving girl. When she was 16 she married one of her classmates, Roy Thornton, but the marriage floundered for two reasons: Thornton was a crook who spent much of his time in prison, and Bonnie had an overwhelming dependency on her mother. This never left her and even when she was on the run she made frequent visits to the family home.

New partnership

In January 1930 Bonnie moved to Dallas, where she worked as a waitress. One day a young man named Clyde Barrow walked into her cafe and she fell in love with him immediately. He was a slim young man who had been brought up in a small township 30 miles south-east of Dallas.

By the time Bonnie and Clyde met he had already been in trouble with the police for car theft and petty crime and in 1930 he was sentenced to 14 years in the state penitentiary for robbery. This experience had a profound effect on both of them: Bonnie was desperately lonely, while Clyde despised the strict prison regime and developed a lasting hatred of authority. On 2 February 1932 Clyde was unexpectedly given parole and released.

Life on the run

Despite Bonnie's attempts to find Clyde a steady job so that they could live a 'good, honest life', the couple were soon involved in their first joint illegal venture. Clyde had planned a robbery with a jail companion and, rather than spend more time on her own, Bonnie went to join him. The robbery was a complete farce — the car they escaped in broke down, so Bonnie and Clyde tried to escape on a couple of mules. Clyde succeeded but Bonnie was captured.

While Bonnie was awaiting trial Clyde committed several robberies and two needless killings. When she was released without going to trial, on 17 June 1932, she returned briefly to her mother but soon willingly joined Clyde in a life on the run.

The couple spent much of their time driving around the southern states of America, living out of the cars they stole. Clyde was the driving force of the couple but Bonnie was a very able companion, never afraid to carry, and use, a gun. For six months the couple, and a young man named Jones, drove from state to state committing robberies and occasionally murder. Surprisingly, their largest haul was little more than $1500, but their escapes were always memorable and newsworthy.

The Barrow Gang

In March 1933 Clyde's elder brother, Buck, was released from prison and he and his wife Blanche went to Joplin, Missouri, to see Clyde and Bonnie. After two weeks the police became aware of their presence and surrounded the house. A brief gun battle followed, during which the fugitives escaped and two policemen were murdered.

After the Joplin killings the police found a film that the gangsters had left in their apartment. The Barrow Gang were soon known across the country and their pictures were splashed in newspapers and on wanted posters. They achieved instant notoriety and even the *New York Times* wrote about them.

Bonnie injured

The robberies and killings continued, interspersed with trips to the Barrow and Parker families in Texas. After one of these visits Clyde crashed their car at a bridge near the Oklahoma border and Bonnie was badly burned in the resulting explosion. She was taken to a nearby farmhouse but one of the farmers informed the police and the gang fled. Clyde drove non-stop to avoid capture and they ended up in a tourist camp at Fort Smith just over the Arkansas border.

The familiar pattern of robbery followed, which only increased the pressure for their capture. In July 1933 they were ambushed at the Red Crown Tavern in Platte City, Missouri. Again, Bonnie and Clyde escaped but Buck died from the wounds he received and Blanche was captured.

In September 1933 the couple returned to the Dallas area to see their families. Shortly afterwards Jones left the Gang. He chose an opportune time because on 22 November 1933 the police, led by Sheriff Smoot Schmid, carried out an ambush. It was a hopeless failure and only served to add to the Bonnie and Clyde legend.

During the early months of 1934 Clyde instigated the breakout of some convicts he had met in the state penitentiary. They proved to be argumentative and troublesome and Bonnie and Clyde soon parted company with them. However, one of the convicts went to the police and informed on the gangster duo.

Ambushed

The police, headed by Sheriff Smoot, staged another ambush, this time near a town named Gibsland, Louisiana. They waited for two days and eventually a car driven by Clyde Barrow appeared, with Bonnie Parker by his side. Bonnie and Clyde were killed when the police literally riddled the car with bullets. Such was their notoriety that a crowd gathered and tried to loot the gangsters' possessions.

Clyde Barrow

Contrary to their wishes Clyde Barrow and Bonnie Parker were buried separately: he in the West Dallas Cemetery, she in Fish Trap Cemetery. Their daring escapades soon passed into legend, despite the fact that they had murdered at least 12 people.

Ford V–8

Clyde Barrow's favourite car to steal was the Ford V–8. He was so impressed with it that he even wrote to Henry Ford: 'While I have still got breath in my lungs I will tell you what a dandy car you make. I have drove Fords exclusively when I could get away with one. For sustained speed and freedom from trouble the Ford has got every other car skinned'.

The story of Bonnie and Clyde

Shortly before her death Bonnie Parker wrote a poem that foretold her own demise:
Some day they will go down together
And they will bury them side by side
To a few it means grief
To the law it's relief
But it's death to Bonnie and Clyde.

Borden case

(1893)

Lizzie Andrew Borden

One of America's most notorious murder cases, in which Lizzie Borden was accused of hacking her father and stepmother to death with an axe.

Lizzie Borden was born in 1860, the second surviving child of Andrew and Sarah Borden, in the small Massachusetts town of Fall River. She was a moody child who used to spend hours gazing out of her bedroom window. In 1863 her mother died and two years later her father married Abby Durfee Gray, an overweight, dull woman to whom Lizzie immediately took a dislike.

A troubled family

Although the Borden family were one of the wealthiest in Fall River they lived in 92 Second Street in a shabby three-bedroomed house that had hardly changed since the Civil War. Borden's only indulgence was on Lizzie and her elder sister Emma. In 1892 Borden agreed to purchase his sister-in-law's house, to save her from possible eviction, and put it in his wife's name. This infuriated Lizzie who saw it as a ploy by Abby to usurp her father's fortune. From then on relations between the two women were almost non-existent — Lizzie already called her Mrs Borden and refused to eat at the same table as her.

Events came to a head in the Borden household in the sweltering summer of 1892. For a few weeks Lizzie had been buying small quantities of prussic acid, a deadly poison, and on 3 August she was refused any more without a prescription. That evening everyone in the family, except Lizzie, were violently ill.

Summer murder

On the morning of 4 August 1892 Andrew Borden left home after breakfast to check on his businesses. Lizzie's uncle, John Morse, who was staying for a few days, left to visit

LIZZIE BORDEN.   EMMA BORDEN.   REV. MR. BUCK.   MRS. C. J. HOLMES.   MR. C. J. HOLMES.
THE PRISONER AND HER FRIENDS IN COURT.

Lizzie Borden Trial 1893

relatives in town. Mrs Borden was dusting the bedrooms while Bridget, the maid, was washing the windows. Lizzie was alone in her room and Emma had left Fall River to stay with friends.

At approximately 9.30am on 4 August Abby Borden was brutally murdered as she dusted in the spare bedroom. She was struck 20 times with an axe. Andrew Borden arrived home at 11am and entered the house, unaware of what had happened. He never found out because as he lay on the sofa in the living room he was murdered in the same fashion as his wife, receiving 10 blows of the axe.

The initial suspicion for the double murder fell on John Morse, more for his calm reaction than any real evidence. He returned to the Borden home at about midday, by which time a large and inquisitive crowd had gathered around the house. Rather than going to see what had happened Morse went into the garden and started eating fruit from the trees. He then gave the police such a precise alibi that he became a prime suspect. His alibi, however, proved to be legitimate.

Lizzie is prime suspect

Suspicion then fell on Lizzie, as it was reasoned that the murders must have been committed by someone who was already in the house. It would have been impossible for someone to enter the house and commit two murders without Lizzie or Bridget hearing anything. In addition, Lizzie's dislike of her stepmother was common knowledge.

At the inquest on 9–11 August Lizzie claimed she had been in the loft of the barn at the time of the murders. When this was investigated the dust in the loft was undisturbed. There were other pieces of contradictory evidence and as a result Lizzie was arrested and charged with both murders.

At the time of her arrest public opinion was strongly against Lizzie and the news-

paper were adding their own opinions to the known facts. However, by the time the trial opened at New Bedford on 5 June 1893, there had been a dramatic U-turn in public opinion. The nation was horrified that such a God-fearing, respectable woman could be accused of such a horrific crime. Flowers and good luck messages poured into Fall River from all over America.

Shaky evidence

Although the state had a certain amount of circumstantial evidence Lizzie had a number of factors in her favour: although the axe-head had been found, finger-printing was not allowed in Massachusetts at this time so it could not be linked to her; one of the witnesses, Miss Russell, claimed that although Lizzie had burnt a dress three days after the murder it had not had any blood on it; and the judge ruled that the fact that the defendant had tried to buy prussic acid the day before the murders was irrelevant.

Lizzie Borden's trial lasted 10 days and at its conclusion there was loud applause when a verdict of not guilty was announced. That evening she attended a lavish party held in her honour, but afterwards she dropped out of Fall River society. With her father's money she bought a bigger house but she gave up all of her social activities and lost all local popularity. She even quarrelled with her sister Emma, who left her and went to live in New Hampshire. Lizzie Borden died alone and uncared for in 1927, aged 67.

Forty whacks

'Lizzie Borden took an axe
And gave her mother forty whacks
When she saw what she had done
She gave her father forty-one.'
This famous rhyme is not entirely fair to Lizzie Borden but it shows the interest that the case generated. There have also been over 16 books, five stage plays and a ballet written about the case.

Bottomley, Horatio William

(1860–1933)

Politician and swindler

An extraordinary gift for persuading thousands of people to invest money in fraudulent business ventures.

Horatio Bottomley's parents died when he was a young child and he grew up in an orphanage. He ran away to become successively an errand-boy, a clerk in a solicitor's office and a shorthand reporter in the Law Courts. It was in the latter that he learned about the workings of the legal system, an education that was to be invaluable in years to come.

A career in fraud

Bottomley had a great love of the high life and he soon decided that he wanted to make large quantities of money — preferably at the expense of other people. His first attempt at this was in 1889 when he promoted the Hansard Publishing Union, a dubious venture that was supposed to merge printing and publishing works in Britain and Austria. Most of the money that was subscribed went straight in to Bottomley's pocket, and in 1893 he was prosecuted for conspiracy to defraud. Thanks to his legal experience he defended himself brilliantly and achieved a full acquittal. But his appetite for fraud had been whetted and he proceeded to pursue this cause with considerable enthusiasm.

By 1905 Bottomley had made an estimated £3 million, and had been served with 67 bankruptcy petitions and writs. Many subscribers who saw no return on their capital came to see him to demand their money back, but they invariably left his office having promised to subscribe more.

In 1905 Bottomley became Liberal MP for South Hackney and a year later he founded the weekly periodical *John Bull.* This suited his style because he could now air his outspoken views and also use it to advertise his fraudulent companies. In 1908 he was again prosecuted for conspiracy to defraud but the case against him collapsed.

Victory Loan Scheme

During World War I Bottomley heightened his public profile by touring the country giving patriotic speeches and lectures, for which he made sure he was well paid. He also used *John Bull* to promote his greatest, and last, swindle. He created the Victory Bond Club, an organization designed to buy shares in the Government's Victory Loan Scheme. This appealed to the general public and by the end of 1919 the amount subscribed was half a million pounds. Of this, at least £150 000 was used by Bottomley for his own personal diversions — to run his racing stable, to maintain his numerous mistresses and to indulge his fondness for champagne.

In 1922, when these activities were discovered, Bottomley was charged with fraudulent conversion of Victory Club funds. As usual he defended himself and in his summing-up he declared, 'The jury has not yet been born that would convict me on this evidence'. However, the jury disagreed and he was found guilty and sentenced to seven years' penal servitude.

Released in 1927, he failed to regain his former glory and died in poverty in 1933.

Medicine
During the course of his trial Bottomley asked if he could have an adjournment at 11 o'clock each morning to take his 'medicine'. This consisted of a bottle of champagne, which he drank to sustain himself.

Bougrat, Pierre

(1887–1962)

Convicted murderer

A French doctor who was convicted of murder but escaped captivity to become a successful practitioner in Venezuela.

Pierre Bougrat began his medical studies in Lyons before the outbreak of World War I. He then served with exceptional merit in the army, receiving both the Croix de Guerre and the Legion of Honour. He completed his studies with distinction in 1920 and set up practice in Marseilles. By this time he had also married the daughter of an established doctor.

Red-light districts

Despite his apparent high standing in society Bougrat soon tired of his conventional lifestyle. Instead of spending time with his loving wife and daughter he preferred the company of the local prostitutes and spent much of his time in the Marseilles red-light districts. In 1924 his wife became tired of her husband's behaviour and divorced him. Apparently unconcerned, Bougrat took one of the local prostitutes as a mistress.

Bougrat spent a great deal of time and money on his mistress, as a result of which his practice suffered and he became heavily in debt. On 14 March 1925 he thought he had found the answer to his problems. An old friend, Jacques Rumebe, whom he had been treating for several years, arrived at the surgery with a bag containing his firm's wages, totalling 20 000 francs. The temptation was too great for Bougrat; he administered an overdose and then hid Rumebe's body on top of a medicine cupboard.

It took three months for the police to find Rumebe's body but when they did

Bougrat was charged with his murder. (At the time of his arrest he was in prison for passing dud cheques.) The legal system then moved incredibly slowly: it took a year for a magistrate to hear Bougrat's side of the story and during that time he was imprisoned with a one-eyed swindler who was also an informer.

Controversial trial

When Bougrat was eventually tried, in March 1927, it was obvious that the court was prejudiced against him. They listened diligently to the informer but virtually ignored evidence given by medical experts who said that Rumebe could have died from an unexpected side-effect from a prescribed drug. The jury were unimpressed by the experts and found Bougrat guilty. Perhaps because of his war record the death sentence was commuted to hard labour for life in the Guiana settlements.

Bougrat began his sentence on the island of Cayenne where he was employed in the prison hospital. After five months he had not only acquired various tropical medicines but also a ship's compass. He managed to escape with seven other prisoners and in October 1927 they landed in Caracas, Venezuela. Due to his medical experience Bougrat was allowed to stay and he later married a Venezuelan. He became the only doctor on the island of Margarita and when he died, in 1965, he was a much-loved figure.

Reformed character

The citizens of Margarita held Bougrat in high regard and placed a plaque on his tombstone: 'Doctor and exemplary citizen, he rendered himself worthy of the affection, the admiration and the respect of all'. There is also a Bougrat museum on the island.

Boyle, Jimmy

(1944–   )

Convicted murderer

A Glasgow gangland killer who has become Scotland's most respected reformed criminal.

Jimmy Boyle was born in the notorious Gorbals of Glasgow and he grew up surrounded by crime. He soon became involved himself and when he was 13 he was sent to Larchgrove Remand Home for theft. A spell in borstal followed this, as did a two-year prison sentence for serious assault.

In between periods in prison Boyle became involved with violent gangs and he gained a reputation as 'Scotland's Most Violent Man'. Through his gang activities he was twice tried for murder but acquitted on both occasions. He was again imprisoned for serious assault and on his release it was clear that he had not forsaken his criminal ways. He continued to be heavily involved in several violent and illegal underworld activities and in 1967 he was charged with the murder of Babs Ronney. This time there was no acquittal and Jimmy Boyle was sent to prison for life.

Harsh treatment

Due to his reputation Boyle was treated with great severity when he first went to prison and he spent long periods in solitary confinement. Not surprisingly, he took an active part in various prison riots.

In 1973 Boyle's life changed dramatically when he was transferred to the newly-opened Barlinnie Prison Special Unit's rehabilitation programme. He flourished in this new atmosphere of encouragement and support and he proved himself to be a man of intelligence and artistic ability. He developed into a talented sculptor and wrote his biography *A Sense of Freedom.*

Jimmy Boyle was released in November 1982 and since then he and his wife Sarah have been actively involved in social work, particularly helping drug addicts and homeless teenagers.

Predecessor

Born in Glasgow in 1906 Patrick Carraher had a similar upbringing to Jimmy Boyle's 40 years later. From the age of 17 onwards he spent his life in and out of borstal and prison, for crimes ranging from housebreaking to assault.

In August 1938 Carraher was sentenced to three years' penal servitude for culpable homicide. On his release he teamed up with his brother-in-law Daniel Bonnar. They had a city-wide reputation for violence and in 1945 three brothers named Gordon crossed them. On 23 November Carraher solved the problem by stabbing John Gordon to death. He was arrested, convicted of murder and hanged at Barlinnie Prison on 6 April 1946.

Bravo case

(1876)

Charles and Florence Bravo

An unsolved Victorian poisoning which resulted in an inquest returning a verdict of murder, but not naming a culprit.

At the end of 1875 Charles Delauny Turner Bravo seemed to have it all: a promising career as a barrister, a luxurious home at The Priory, Balham, and a new bride — a wealthy, attractive, 25-year-old widow named Florence Ricardo. The new Mrs Bravo had inherited £40 000 when her first husband died and she was a strong-minded and vivacious women. Before she married Bravo she was having an affair with a 64-year-old doctor named James Gully. Bravo was aware of the liaison but took his wife's word when she told him that she had ended the affair before her second wedding.

After their wedding the Bravos settled down to life at The Priory. Despite the fact that Florence drank more than was normal for a lady in her position there was only one small cloud on the horizon; this was her constant companion, Mrs Jane Cannon Cox, a 43-year-old widow with three sons. Despite Florence's best efforts Mrs Cox and Bravo did not get on and they openly distrusted each other.

Convulsive death

At Easter 1876 the Bravos decided to spend a day in London (Florence was convalescing after her third miscarriage). They returned on 18 April and Charles ate a substantial evening meal consisting of whiting, roast lamb and anchovy eggs. He then retired to his bedroom. At 10 o'clock that night he was heard calling for water and when Florence and Mrs Cox went to investigate they found Charles in considerable distress and vomiting frequently.

Florence Bravo insisted on the best medical attention for her husband. One doctor asked Bravo what drugs he had taken but all he said was that he had rubbed some laudanum on his sore gums. The doctor was unable to help and Charles Bravo died on 21 April 1876. At the subsequent post-mortem it was revealed that he had between 20 and 30 grains of antimony in his body.

Second inquests

At the inquest it was argued that the poison had been administered by mistake by an unknown person. An open verdict was returned even though there were suspicions against both Florence Bravo and Mrs Cox.

The Lord Chief Justice was unhappy about the case and he quashed the findings of the first inquest and ordered a new one. It began on 11 July. The public interest in the case was increased still further when it was disclosed that Florence was still having an affair with the ageing Doctor Gully. He strongly denied that he had been a party to a plot to kill Bravo and, although the coroner had suitable doubts to return a verdict of wilful murder, he added, 'There is insufficient evidence to fix the guilt upon any person or persons'.

If Florence Bravo knew the truth about her husband's death she took her secret to the grave, dying in Southsea on 13 September 1878 from alcoholism.

> **Famous patrons**
> Florence Bravo's lover, Doctor Gully, was renowned for his advocacy of the water-cure. Dozens of ladies sought his advice and his patients included Dickens, Tennyson and Bulwer-Lytton.

Brinks robbery

(1950)

Joe McGinnis and others

One of the most audacious and successful robberies in American history, and one that remained unsolved for six years.

Like the Great Train Robbery in Britain the Brinks robbery was the result of months of careful planning and research. The gang of men who undertook the operation numbered 11, with their leaders being Joe McGinnis, an ex-convict and a nightclub owner, and Anthony Pino. Their target was The Brinks, Inc, an armoured-car express company in Boston, who were responsible for transferring money to and from the banks in the city. The Brinks depot at North Terminal Garage was chosen as the site for the robbery.

Meticulous plans

Eighteen months of planning were undertaken before the robbery was attempted. This included the vetting of the gang members, a study of the premises and a careful watch on the employees' habits.

The initial research by the gang concerned the vault where the money was kept. Two of them went to Washington DC to check the vault specifications held in the US Patent Office. They then set about the locks within the building itself. In all they made 27 secret visits to the depot and in this time they managed to remove the locks from all the relevant doors and make copies of the keys for them. The night-watchman was followed for several nights and his movements noted to the second. The gang even broke into a burglar alarm company so they could study the same type of alarm system that was used by Brinks.

Trial runs

Two weeks before the robbery itself the gang made four practice runs. Then, on 17 January 1950, the raid was made for real. It was a bitterly cold night when the gang entered the North Terminal Garage and seven of them made their way quickly to the vault using their own keys. The remainder of the gang kept watch and organized the getaway car.

When the robbers arrived in the vault, shortly after 7pm, they were all wearing Hallowe'en masks, chauffeur's caps, navy jackets, grey trousers and gloves. With military-style precision they gagged and tied the five employees and then began loading the money into large canvas bags. They worked tirelessly for a few minutes and then loaded the sacks into a van and drove away from the scene of the crime. They were in the North Terminal Garage for less than 17 minutes.

Massive haul

When the robbery was first discovered it was thought that only $100 000 had been taken. However, when the accountants went to work it was calculated that the gang had got away with $1 218 211 in cash and $1 557 183 in securities and cheques. It was a staggering sum and it attracted the undivided attention of both the American public and the FBI. Despite the fact that the gang had removed such a large sum of money they left behind very few clues — a chauffeur's cap, a few pieces of rope, and some adhesive tape. When the getaway car was later discovered it was found to be totally devoid of fingerprints. One of the largest manhunts in American history followed, but the police came up with no positive leads.

Unfortunate gang member

All 11 members of the gang quickly established alibis and although they were all known criminals and therefore questioned by the police they did not put a foot wrong. One member of the gang, Joseph 'Specs' O'Keefe, gave his share of the money to another gang member for safe-keeping. In 1954, after serving a brief sentence for possessing stolen guns, O'Keefe tried to get his money back but he was only given $5000 out of $100 000. Then, on 16 June 1954, he survived an assassination attack by a hired killer. To make matters worse he was then arrested for violation of his parole and sent back to prison for a year.

Nick of time

When O'Keefe was released from prison, in 1955, he told the rest of the gang that if he did not receive his full share of the money then he would go to the police. The gang did not believe him but O'Keefe stuck to his word and on 12 January 1956 he went to the FBI and told them the whole story about the Brinks robbery. He did this just in time because if he had waited another few days the statute of limitation on robbery in Massachusetts would have expired and no one could have been tried for the crime.

The eight surviving members of the gang (two had died of natural causes since the robbery) were arrested and charged on 108 counts, ranging from armed robbery to putting persons in fear with intent to rob. All eight men were found guilty and sentenced to life imprisonment. O'Keefe pleaded guilty at his own trial and was released from prison on 22 June 1960.

Understandably he immediately went into hiding. On his release the district attorney said, 'He's made himself a sitting duck for murder'.

Despite intense police and FBI activity only $60 000 was recovered from the Brinks haul. The whereabouts of the rest of the money has never been traced.

Early Bird

In 1961 the Brinks theft was surpassed as the largest robbery in North American history when a flamboyant playboy named Georges LeMay took the contents of 377 safety deposit boxes from the Bank of Nova Scotia in Montreal. The haul totalled over $4 million. Two years later, using the newly-launched Early Bird telecommunications satellite, Scotland Yard, the FBI and the RCMP combined to flash pictures of wanted men around the world. A man in Fort Lauderdale recognized the picture of LeMay and led the police to him. He was taken to Dade County jail in Florida but before he was brought to trial he managed to escape. Neither LeMay nor the money have been seen since.

Clean criminal

While he was under police surveillance Anthony Pino was seen taking a five-cent plastic cup. When he heard he was going to be questioned he then stole a pair of clean underpants in case the police conducted a body search.

Brodie, William

(1741–88)

Gambler and burglar

Brodie's double life was the model on which Robert Louis Stevenson probably based his story of Jekyll and Hyde.

William Brodie was born in Edinburgh during the middle of the 18th century. His father, Francis Brodie, was a wealthy wright and cabinet-maker, a member of the Town Council and also a Deacon of the Incorporation of Wrights (carpenters and other tradesmen). William Brodie followed in his father's footsteps, not only in business but also as a Deacon on the Town Council.

When Francis Brodie died in 1781 he left his son a small fortune and a large house in the Lawnmarket. By this time William Brodie was highly regarded in society; he mixed with all the right people and was a member of the exclusive Edinburgh club, the Cape Club.

Double life

But behind the image of a prosperous businessman Brodie had a secret life. He was a gambling addict and loved to frequent the inns and gambling dens in Edinburgh that stayed open during the night at the time. He frequently lost large sums of money and when he did win he invariably squandered it on one of his two mistresses.

By 1785 Brodie had spent most of his inheritance and was badly in need of money. To acquire it he turned to burglary while maintaining his veneer of respectability. He had two main advantages as a thief: no one ever thought of suspecting him and, due to his position in high society, he knew the layout of his acquaintances' houses and where the valuables were kept. Sometimes

he even copied the keys of clients who came to see him during the day.

In 1786 Brodie enlisted professional help in the form of three criminals named George Smith, Andrew Ainslie and John Brown, whom he knew from disreputable inns and gambling dens. Together they carried out a number of robberies, the most daring being the theft of the silver mace from Edinburgh University. They also stole £300-worth of lace from a shop in the city and, as a result, a King's pardon was offered to anyone who informed on an accomplice.

Flight abroad

On 5 March 1788 Brodie's gang broke into the Excise Office of Scotland. The robbery went hopelessly wrong and Brown decided to take advantage of the King's pardon. Smith and Ainslie were both arrested but Brodie, hearing what was happening, fled to Holland.

Brodie hoped to sail from Holland to America but a letter he wrote to a friend gave away his whereabouts and he was brought back to Scotland to stand trial. Before the trial Ainslie also turned King's evidence and when proceedings began on 27 August 1788 it was clear that the evidence against Brodie and Smith was overwhelming. They were both found guilty and sentenced to death.

Thousands of people turned up outside Edinburgh's St Giles High Kirk on 1 October 1788 to witness the once respectable Deacon Brodie being hung as a common criminal — on gallows which he himself had designed.

> **Literary inspiration**
> Before writing *Jekyll and Hyde* Robert Louis Stevenson wrote a play about Brodie's life. It was entitled *Deacon Brodie, or the Double Life* and was first produced at the Prince's Theatre in London on 2 July 1884.

Browne and Kennedy case

(1927)

Frederick Guy Browne and William Henry Kennedy

The murder of a policeman that led to significant advances in the science of forensic ballistics in Britain.

On the morning of 27 September 1927 the body of PC George Gutteridge was found outside the village of Howe Green in Essex. It was thought he had been killed while questioning a motorist. He had been shot four times and both of his eyes had been shot out. Earlier in the day the car of a local doctor had been stolen and this was later discovered in London. It had blood on the running-board and inside there was an empty cartridge case.

For four months the police made little headway but on 20 January 1928 they traced a stolen car to a known criminal named Frederick Browne and arrested him that evening. Browne had served several prison sentences for car-theft, carrying firearms and burglary. At the time of his arrest he was running a garage in Lavender Hill.

Arsenal discovered

When the police searched Browne's workshop and rooms they discovered four fully loaded revolvers and several types of cartridges. Five days after Browne's arrest the police in Liverpool apprehended one of his associates, William Kennedy. Kennedy pulled a gun on the policeman who tried to arrest him but, luckily for the officer involved, the safety catch was still on.

Kennedy, a persistent petty criminal, was taken to Scotland Yard where he made a full statement concerning the murder of PC Gutteridge. He claimed Browne had asked him to accompany him to Billericay in order to steal a car. After they accomplished this they were stopped and questioned by Gutteridge. Kennedy stated that Browne then shot the policeman and that he himself had nothing to do with the killing.

Crucial marks

On 6 February 1928 Browne and Kennedy were charged with murder and their trial began at the Old Bailey on 23 April. Apart from Kennedy's confession the main prosecution evidence was the ballistic evidence offered by the firearms expert Robert Churchill. He proved that one of the guns found in Browne's possession was the one that had fired the bullets that killed PC Gutteridge because the breech had been damaged and left a distinctive mark on every bullet it fired; this mark was on the bullets that killed Gutteridge. Churchill experimented with 50 other guns of the same make and none of them left these marks.

Due largely to the forensic evidence, Browne and Kennedy were found guilty of murder. It was a major step forward for forensic ballistics and contrasted favourably with the amateur ballistic evidence given in the celebrated American trial of Sacco and Vanzetti (see p202).

On 31 May 1928 Frederick Browne was hanged in Pentonville prison and William Kennedy was hanged in Wandsworth prison.

> **Forensic ballistics**
> This is based on a similar theory to fingerprinting since all gun barrels leave unique distinguishing marks. If a gun is suspected of being a murder weapon a firearms expert will use it to fire a test bullet which is compared with the crime bullet. If both the bullets have identical marks on them then it is indisputable that they were fired from the same gun.

Buckley, William

(c.1780–1856)

Convict

A convict who escaped from captivity in Australia and lived with an aborigine tribe for 32 years.

William Buckley was born near Macclesfield, Cheshire, and was brought up by his grandfather. After receiving a basic education he was apprenticed to a bricklayer. Being six feet, six inches tall and immensely strong, he was well suited to the job, but he soon tired of it and joined the Cheshire Militia and then the 4th Regiment. In 1799 he served in the Netherlands but was wounded in action and forced to return to England.

On his return, Buckley turned to crime and on 2 August 1802 he was imprisoned for receiving a roll of stolen cloth. The following year it was decided that he should be transported to Australia and in April 1803 he was taken to Port Philip, near Melbourne, Victoria. Buckley did not relish the thought of a life of captivity and shortly after his arrival he escaped with three of his fellow convicts.

One of the escapees was shot almost immediately but the other three made it to the far side of the bay from the convict settlement. Food was scarce and the men survived on berries and shellfish. After a few days Buckley's companions were so tired and hungry that they chose to give themselves up.

'Wild White Man'

Buckley laid low on the south Victoria coast and, just when he was on the point of starvation, he was befriended by a group of aborigines from the Watourong tribe who thought he was a reincarnation of their dead tribal chief. Because of his size and his appearance he became known as the 'Wild White Man'.

Buckley moved to the tribe's home at Bream Creek and lived happily there for 32 years. He learnt the aborigine customs and the language and he was given a wife, by whom he had a daughter. White visitors occasionally went to the village but Buckley was afraid to show himself in case he was sent back to the convict settlement.

Pardoned

In July 1835 a ship of white settlers arrived at Port Philip. Buckley overheard the aborigines plotting to rob the ship and kill those aboard. In an effort to save them he went to the ship, indicated what was planned, and gave himself up to the leader of the party J H Wedge. At first he could not communicate because he had forgotten how to speak English, but he was identified by a tattoo which bore his initials.

Once he had remembered his mother tongue Buckley proved useful as an interpreter and in return Wedge obtained his pardon from Lieutenant-Governor Batman. In December 1837 he moved to Van Diemen's land and settled in Hobart. He worked as a store-keeper and a gate-keeper before retiring on a state pension, which included £40 a year from the Victoria government. On 27 January 1840 he married a widow with two children, with whom he lived until his death in Hobart on 30 January 1856.

> **Wise words**
> Buckley offered valuable advice about the tribe with which he lived. His most sensible suggestion was that there should be no interference with the aborigine customs and language.

Bulow case

(1982–85)

Claus von Bulow

The case of a wealthy American socialite who was accused of trying to kill his wife with insulin injections.

In December 1980 Martha 'Sunny' von Bulow, the wife of the Danish-born socialite, Claus von Bulow, was admitted to a New York hospital in a coma. This was of considerable concern to her children from an earlier marriage, not least because they suspected their stepfather of trying to kill Sunny in an attempt to get his hands on her $75 million fortune, and then marry his mistress.

Lethal injections

After conducting some preliminary research the von Bulow children openly accused their stepfather of attempted murder, contending that Sunny's coma, and one she suffered a year earlier, was the result of von Bulow injecting her with insulin. Von Bulow was shocked by the allegations and he defended himself by saying that his wife's condition was the result of Sunny's dependence on barbiturate drugs and alcohol.

The press quickly dubbed the affair 'The Sleeping Beauty Case' and they revelled in this bizarre murder attempt — lingering over the sex, drink and drugs aspect of the case.

Unexplained needles

Claus von Bulow was arrested and sent for trial in 1982, amidst intense national interest. Many people found it hard to believe that this suave gentleman could try and murder his wife, while others developed an instant dislike for him. The key witness was Sunny von Bulow's maid who had found insulin and needles in von Bulow's cupboard. She asked him what they were for but he was unable to give her a reasonable explanation. Chiefly on this evidence von Bulow was found guilty and sentenced to 30 years' imprisonment.

Continuation

Shortly after the trial the conviction was overturned on a technicality. The media could not believe their luck when a second trial was ordered. It opened at Providence, Rhode Island, in April 1985. The entire trial was live on television and commentators treated it like a sporting event, weighing up the chance of an acquittal or a conviction.

Although some of the evidence was the same as in the first trial, vital information, such as facts about Mrs von Bulow's will, was ordered by the judge to be excluded. The defence made the most of the fact that several medical experts had stated that there had been no signs of insulin injections. This swayed the jury and on 10 June 1985, after 12 hours of deliberations, they found Claus von Bulow not guilty. In the courtroom he nearly fainted with relief and he then began his next battle — with his step-children over his wife's fortune.

Impartial jury
Due to the media hype it was almost impossible to find a jury that did not know about the case. When the jury was finally selected they were locked in their hotel rooms at night and not allowed to watch television or read the newspapers. They even had to be excluded from the legal arguments in court and in one three-day period they only spent three hours in court.

Bundy, Theodore Robert

(1946–89)

Convicted murderer

One of America's most prolific mass murderers who killed between 20 and 40 women.

Ted Bundy was born in a single mothers' home in Vermont. His mother was aware of the stigma of this and when her son was four she moved to Tacoma in Washington where she married Johnnie Bundy. The family were from a lower middle-class background and Ted grew up being ashamed of his social position. To compensate, he turned to shoplifting to obtain the luxury goods that his family could not afford.

In 1972 Bundy completed a degree in psychology at the University of Washington and began applying for law school. At first he was unsuccessful and worked for the Republican governor's office. Throughout this period he never felt fully at ease with himself and girlfriends complained of his excessive violence during love-making.

Murder spree

In January 1974 Bundy could contain his powerful but perverted sex drive no longer and he went on a four-year orgy of murder. On 31 January a student from the University of Washington disappeared from her rented room, leaving bloodstains on her pillow and her nightdress. In the next six months six young, attractive female students disappeared in the Seattle area.

On 14 July 1974 a woman at a picnic table by Lake Sammanish was approached by a man with one arm in a sling who asked her if she could help him lift his boat. She refused but another woman offered her assistance and was never seen alive again. On 7 September 1974 the remains of three bodies were found near the lake.

A man named Ted

Bundy used his sling ploy on a number of occasions to entice women into his car — a battered Volkswagen. Since he was handsome and charming they were usually willing to help. Some who refused reported to the police that they had been approached by a man named Ted. Bundy was reported as a suspect, but he was only one of over 2000.

In September 1974 Bundy moved to Salt Lake City to take up a place at the University of Utah's Law School. During October he committed at least three murders — all female students who were raped and either strangled or beaten to death. On 8 November he tried to abduct another student, Carol DaRonch, but she managed to escape. This did not deter Bundy; he only moved his murderous operation to Colorado. Between 12 January and 4 July 1975 five women disappeared or were found murdered and raped in the Colorado area.

Extradition and trial

On 16 August 1975 Bundy was questioned by police in Salt Lake City after he had been seen acting suspiciously. When his car was examined it was found to contain hair matching that of one of the murder victims in Colorado. He was charged with murder and extradited to Colorado in January 1977, after serving a short prison term for the kidnapping of Carol DaRonch.

During Bundy's trial he conducted his own defence, delaying the proceedings as often as possible. On 7 July 1977 he escaped from custody and remained at large for eight days until his recapture. Six months later he was more successful; on 30 December 1977 he escaped and this time fled to Florida.

New identity

Bundy assumed the name of Christopher Hagen and settled near the campus of Florida State University. On 15 January 1978 he rampaged through the Chi Omega sorority house, killing two female students and severely injuring three others. After these killings Bundy stole a van and went on the run.

Bundy's last victim was a 12-year-old girl whom he murdered on 7 February in Tallahassee, northern Florida. Three days later, in Pensacola, a policeman checked the licence plate of Bundy's car and discovered it was stolen. When he was approached, Bundy tried to escape but he was overpowered and arrested.

Televised trial

The authorities decided that it would be difficult to find 12 unprejudiced jurors in Tallahassee so Bundy's trial was moved to Miami. It took place during July 1979. Television cameras were allowed into the courtroom and millions of people across America watched the drama unfold, finding it hard to believe that the articulate, good-looking Bundy could be a mass murderer. He conducted his own defence and despite a polished performance he was found guilty of murder and sentenced to death. One of the most damning pieces of evidence were teeth marks found on the buttocks of one of the victims from the Chi Omega sorority house. When impressions were taken of Bundy's teeth they were found to match.

After 10 years of appeals and stays of execution Ted Bundy was executed in Florida on 24 January 1989. He is known to have murdered at least 20 people but the true number is probably much higher.

Enigma
Unlike most serial killers Bundy was of high intelligence and did not show any of the normal signs of being a mass murderer. He was well liked by people who knew him, who described him as entertaining and amusing. After his conviction he admitted that, 'Sometimes I feel like a vampire', and also claimed, 'What's one less person on the face of the earth anyway?'

Judicial praise
Following Bundy's trial Judge Cowart told him, 'Take care of yourself young man. It's a tragedy to this court to see such a total waste of humanity. You'd have made a good lawyer. I'd have loved to have you practise in front of me. I bear you no animosity, believe me. But you went the wrong way, partner'.

Burdell case

(1857)

Dr Harvey Burdell

The murder of a prominent New York dentist which led to sensational claims at the subsequent trial.

Dr Harvey Burdell was a tall, bearded gentleman who conducted a profitable dental business from his consulting rooms in Bond Street, New York City. Due to this, and the rooms that he let above his consulting rooms, he had acquired a considerable personal wealth by the beginning of the 1850s. However, his business deals were frequently less than legal and by 1857 he had fallen into debt and owed money to several people.

Frenzied attack

On 29 January 1859 Dr Burdell was seen going into his house in Bond Street. Although it was 10.45pm several people recognized the dentist. A few minutes later a cry was heard from Burdell's consulting room. Nothing was done at the time, but the next morning the dentist's bloodstained body was found on the floor. He had been strangled and stabbed several times in the neck and chest.

Since there was no sign of a forced entry into the house the police concluded that the murderer was one of the occupants of the rooms that Burdell rented, two of which were let by Mrs Emma Cunningham, who had in turn sub-let them to a dealer in hides named John J Eckel and a minister's son named George Snodgrass. All three were arrested and charged with murder, despite the fact that there was an almost total lack of evidence against them.

Sensational revelation

Before the trial Mrs Cunningham made a claim on Burdell's estate, announcing that she had married him in secret before he died. This helped generate enormous interest in the case and when the trial began she then told an astonished courtroom that she was pregnant with Burdell's child. Possibly distracted by this information the jury found Mrs Cunningham not guilty and the charges against Eckel and Snodgrass were dropped.

Mrs Cunningham continued to press her claim to Burdell's estate but she refused to be examined by a doctor to prove whether she was really pregnant or not. She did eventually appear with a child but was then charged with fraud when it was discovered that she had paid an unmarried mother $1000 in return for her newborn baby.

Still unsolved

The question of Dr Burdell's murderer remained unsolved. When it was ascertained how badly in debt he was (his possessions had to be sold to pay some of his creditors) a theory was advanced that the murderer was one of the people to whom he owed money. A man named Lewis later admitted to the crime but he was hanged for another murder before this could be verified.

Circus act
When Emma Cunningham failed to obtain Dr Burdell's estate she turned to the circus proprietor P J Barnum in an attempt to make money. For $25 a week she allowed him to display the child she had bought for $1000. Barnum was only too pleased to do so and exhibited it under a banner claiming, 'The Bogus Burdell Baby'.

Burgess, Guy Francis de Moncy

(1911–63)

Spy

A contemporary of Maclean, Philby and Blunt and for several years an undercover Soviet agent.

Guy Burgess, the son of a Royal Navy officer, was born in Devonport, Hampshire. He went up to Trinity College, Cambridge in 1930 and here he found fellow believers in his Communist views, including Kim Philby, Donald Maclean and Anthony Blunt. He was a gifted scholar and looked set for a brilliant academic career. However, after obtaining a first class in Part I of his honours degree his academic interest waned.

Change of views

After a visit to the Soviet Union Burgess's political views seemed to have mellowed and he no longer professed to being an ardent Communist. After failing to join the Civil Service he took a job with *The Times* newspaper and then joined the BBC in 1936. By this time he had already been recruited by Soviet intelligence agents and was regularly passing on classified information. While working for the BBC he made a number of influential political contacts, including a future Minister of State at the Foreign Office, Hector McNeil.

Drink problem

In 1939 Burgess joined Department D of the Secret Intelligence Service, where he was later joined by Philby. This was disbanded in 1941, when Burgess returned to the BBC and helped write war propaganda. Throughout his career he made no attempt to hide his homosexuality and this alienated him from his work-mates. He was also prone to violent bouts of drunkenness and

received a number of official reprimands.

In 1944 Hector McNeil invited him to join the Foreign Office, where he served until 1950, continually passing information to the Soviets. In November 1950 he was posted to Washington as second secretary of the British embassy. It was a surprising decision, not only because of his less than distinguished career but also because he made no secret of his anti-American feelings. Kim Philby was also serving in Washington at this time and for a while Burgess lived in his house.

Exposed

A year after his appointment the Americans were tiring of Burgess's personal habits and his antagonistic behaviour. He was recalled to London in 1951 for 'serious misconduct' and asked to resign. It is unclear how much information he had given to the Soviets at this stage but he himself must have been worried about his situation. When Kim Philby relayed the message that the authorities were on the trail of Donald Maclean, Burgess decided to join him. He had intended to spend a holiday on the continent but instead he defected with Maclean on 25 May 1951 and the two men left the country on the steamer *Falaise.*

Nothing was heard of Burgess and Maclean until they appeared at a news conference in Moscow in 1956. Guy Burgess died in Moscow on 30 August 1963.

Strained relations

Although Burgess did not pass as much vital information as Philby or Maclean his actions did little for relations between Britain and America. At one point Washington even threatened to exclude Britain from their atomic research information.

Burke and Hare

William Burke (1792–1829) and William Hare (1790–c.1860)

Murderers

Two of Scotland's most notorious criminals who killed the helpless and destitute and then sold their bodies to a local medical school.

William Burke was born in Cork and moved to Scotland in 1818 where he worked as a cobbler, a baker and a labourer. He met a prostitute named Helen McDougal and for several years they wandered aimlessly around southern Scotland before settling at the Beggar's Hotel in Edinburgh.

In 1827 Burke and Helen McDougal

VIEW IN EDINBURGH.
TAKEN ON THE SPOT.

Dr Robert Knox

moved into Log's Lodging House in Tanner's Close in Edinburgh's West Port. It was here that they teamed up with William Hare, an extremely unpleasant character who had lived in Londonderry before moving to Scotland. When the owner of the lodging house died Hare not only took over the business but he also went through a form of marriage with Log's widow, Maggie Laird.

An idea is born

On November 1827 a Highlander named Old Donald died of natural causes in the lodging house. He owed nearly £4 in rent and Hare had heard that anatomists were willing to pay good prices for bodies which they could use for dissection. After asking around, Burke and Hare discovered that a famous anatomist named Dr Robert Knox of Surgeon's Square would be prepared to buy the body. The two men were paid £7 and 10 shillings, no questions asked, and encouraged to bring along more bodies if they could.

Although Burke and Hare were both greedy men they were unwilling to take to grave-robbing to provide Knox with bodies. Since surgeons were only officially allowed one body a year for dissection, body-snatchers (or resurrectionists) were in high demand and the medical students themselves sometimes stole bodies for their teachers. However the penalties for this were severe and the graveyards were well guarded.

Lethal landlords

Rather than become resurrectionists Burke and Hare chose to kill people themselves and then sell the bodies to Knox before they could even be buried. They were aided in this enterprise by Helen McDougal and Maggie Laird.

Over the next few months the owners of the lodging house in Tanner's Close enticed a variety of helpless and destitute people into their rooms, plied them with drink and then murdered them by placing a pillow over their faces. They made sure that the people they killed would not be missed, and Dr Knox paid between £8 to £14 for each body, turning a blind eye to the methods used in obtaining them.

A victim is recognized

In April 1828 Burke and Hare murdered a young prostitute named Mary Paterson. She was an attractive girl and well-known around town. After her body was delivered to Dr Knox several of his students recognized her and raised questions about how she had died. When Knox asked Burke the reply was that she had died of drink, which was partially true because she had been made senseless with whisky before her murder.

In the summer of 1828 Burke and Helen McDougal moved to new lodgings, but the murderous partnership continued. Their penultimate victim was a well-known figure named Daft Jamie, a simple but kind-hearted man. He put up a considerable fight but was eventually delivered to Dr Knox. Again the victim was identified by several people but no one said anything since they did not want the supply of bodies to cease.

Final death

On 31 October 1828 Burke met another potential victim. It was an old beggar-woman from Ireland named Margery Docherty. He introduced himself and, claiming family connections, invited her back to his lodging house. She did not even survive the first night and Knox had another specimen for the dissection table.

The murder of Margery Docherty proved to be the undoing of Burke and Hare. At the time of her death there was a couple named Mr and Mrs Gray staying in the lodging house. When Mrs Gray noticed that the Irish woman was missing she was told that she had been thrown out for making advances towards Burke. This did not satisfy her and when she investigated a pile of straw at the bottom of a bed she found Mrs Docherty's body.

King's evidence

Despite efforts by Helen McDougal to stop her, Mrs Gray went to the police; Burke, Hare and their female accomplices were all arrested. The case against them was not strong and although it was thought that they had killed a minimum of 16 people they were only charged with the murder of Margery Docherty. In an attempt to gain a conviction the Crown offered Hare and his wife their freedom if they turned King's evidence. They readily accepted, the irony being that Hare was undoubtedly the more evil of the partnership.

The trial of William Burke began on 17 December 1828 and the courtroom was packed with the citizens of Edinburgh, all eager to see this apparent monster. Although the evidence was far from convincing he was found guilty on Christmas Eve and sentenced to death. Helen McDougal, who claimed she knew nothing about what went on in the lodging house, received a 'not proven' verdict.

William Burke was hanged in Edinburgh on 28 January 1829. There was a record crowd of over 25 000 and people who had windows in view of the scaffold charged record prices for the use of their premises. William Hare fled to London where he died blind and impoverished. Dr Knox was never prosecuted but he was forced to leave Edinburgh because of adverse public opinion.

Criminal's rhyme

The exploits of Burke and Hare were immortalized by a popular rhyme:

Up the close and doun the stair
But and ben wi' Burke and Hare.
Burke's the butcher, Hare's the thief.
Knox the boy that buys the beef.

Cruelty to animals

After committing a double murder Burke and Hare tried to transport the bodies to Dr Knox in a herring box. Unfortunately, the horse that they were using refused to move after only a few yards. In desperation they were forced to hire a man with a wheelbarrow to take the bodies to Surgeon's Square. The unfortunate horse then had its throat slit by its owners.

Butler, Robert

(c.1845–1905)

Convicted murderer and thief

A habitual criminal in Australia and New Zealand who also showed considerable literary talents.

Robert Butler was born in Kilkenny, Ireland, and emigrated to Australia when he was 14. He spent 13 of the next 16 years in prison for offences ranging from vagrancy to highway robbery. He spent much of his time in confinement educating himself and he read widely, including biographies of Napoleon, and Frederick of Prussia.

About 1875 Butler tired of Australian prisons and decided to move to New Zealand. In contrast with his earlier activities he chose to set up a school but old habits died hard and after a few months he was accused of theft and fled to Dunedin. Several burglaries occurred in the next couple of weeks and Butler, convicted of being the perpetrator, was sentenced to four years' imprisonment.

Journalistic criminal

Butler was released in February 1880 and having shown considerable literary skills he was given a job on the *Dunedin Daily Star*. Although he was a talented journalist he claimed that the effort made him feel like committing suicide. He walked off the job and returned to his former ways. On 13 March 1880 the house of a Dunedin solicitor, Mr Stamper, was broken into and then set on fire. The next day a similar incident happened at the home of the Dewar family, except this time the Dewars and their young baby were murdered.

Butler was an immediate suspect for the triple murder and was arrested on 15 March.

He confessed to the Stamper burglary but denied any knowledge of the Dewar murders. However, when some of Butler's bloodstained clothes were found in some bushes near the Dewar house he was charged with the triple murder.

Butler defended himself at his trial and he used his intellect to such good effect that after three hours of deliberation the jury found him not guilty of murder. However, for the Stamper burglary he received a severe sentence of 18 years' imprisonment. He spent the next 16 years in a New Zealand prison and on his release, an embittered man, he returned to Australia.

Continued trouble

The Australian police hounded Butler once they heard he had left New Zealand and he was arrested and charged with burglary and highway robbery. He again defended himself and gained an acquittal for the highway robbery but was convicted of burglary. He received another brutal sentence, 15 years, which was later reduced to 10 years.

In 1904 Butler was released and again made a brief attempt at journalism. However, his treatment by the authorities had made him too cynical to hold down a steady job and instead he roamed the country as a tramp. On 23 March 1905 he reached Tooringa, Queensland. While trying to rob an old man he shot and killed him and was arrested that evening. He was later convicted of murder and hanged.

Honest words

Before his execution Butler made no hypocritical attempt to be consoled by religion: 'Instead of the 'depart Christian soul' of the priest, I only hope for the comfort … of the last friendly goodbye of anyone who cares to give it'.

Cagliostro, Count Alessandro
(1743–c.1795)

Con man and charlatan

A trickster who flourished in the Age of Reason by telling people what they wanted to believe.

Count Cagliostro was the assumed name of Giuseppe Balsamo, born into a peasant family in Palermo, Sicily. He was an unruly and purposeless youngster and his one interest at school was chemistry and pharmacy, two subjects which he later exploited to good effect.

After being expelled from a local monastery he took to a life of petty crime in Palermo, even to the extent of forging his uncle's will. Eventually the police ran Cagliostro out of town. He then travelled to Malta where he befriended a local alchemist and persuaded him to part with a laboratory for making gold, as well as several valuable letters of introduction.

Accomplished con man

With his basic scientific knowledge and a shrewd understanding of human nature Cagliostro was able to embark on a career of deceit. He promoted himself as an alchemist and a miracle worker and travelled to a number of major cities, including Madrid, Lisbon, Warsaw, St Petersburg, Basel, Vienna, Venice and London.

Wherever Cagliostro based himself he made sure he learnt the local customs, so he understood the nature of the people he was about to con. He did this in a lavish style, using every trick in the book and inventing a few of his own — selling a miracle-cure elixir, pretending to make gold, telling fortunes, and dabbling in the occult. It was all a fraud but he did his research thoroughly and knew that people wanted to believe what he was telling them. Things did not always run smoothly though and after a barren spell with cynical audiences in London in 1772, he had to turn to house-painting for a living.

Cagliostro was aware of the possibilities of making money from religion and to this end he founded a new branch of freemasonry, under the name of the 'Grand Egyptian Lodge'. He exploited the secrecy involved in the religion but his main concern with the whole operation was to sell his elixir.

The Queen's necklace

Despite his career as a charlatan Cagliostro found his way into criminal history with his involvement in the Affair of the Queen's Necklace. One of his victims, the Cardinal Archbishop de Rohan, was in love with Marie-Antoinette, so Cagliostro and two accomplices persuaded him, with the help of forged letters, to buy her an extremely expensive necklace. He agreed, but the necklace never did reach the Queen — Cagliostro and his friends tricked him and pocketed the precious piece of jewellery themselves.

Cagliostro was arrested after the escapade with the necklace and spent six months in the Bastille before fleeing to Rome. Here his tamperings with religion soon got him into trouble and he was tried by the Inquisition and condemned to death as a freemason. This was commuted to life imprisonment and he spent the rest of his life confined in the Chateau de Saint Leon near Rome.

Showman

Cagliostro went to great lengths to impress his audiences: he plagiarized rituals from ancient Egypt and on one occasion he even claimed he was a contemporary of Christ, and had predicted His crucifixion.

Capone, Alphonse (Al)

(1899–1947)

Gangster

America's most celebrated gangster and racketeer, who ruled Chicago in the 1930s with an iron grip.

Al Capone's parents immigrated to America in 1893 and he was born in Brooklyn, New York, six years later. He was a pushy and temperamental child and after leaving school in the fourth grade he organized teenage gangs. He joined the vicious Five Points Gang and during a raid on a brothel-saloon he was slashed across the left cheek. The resulting mark earned him the notorious epithet 'Scarface'.

Rise of Scarface

One of Capone's youthful associates was Johnny Torrio, who in 1910 moved to Chicago. At this time the whole city was run by various gangs and Torrio soon established himself as a leading light with one of Chicago's most influential racketeers, 'Big Jim' Colosimo. But Torrio was ambitious and he was not content to wait patiently to take over from Colosimo. He formed a plan to hasten his rise to power and the first part of it was to invite Al Capone to Chicago.

Capone arrived in Chicago in 1918 and Torrio gave him a job as a bouncer at one of his brothel-nightclubs. His wage was $75 a week but within a couple of years he was running a chain of brothels for Torrio and earning over $1000 a week. In 1920 the hierarchy changed dramatically when Colosimo was assassinated. The killer was never identified but it was strongly rumoured that Al Capone had been involved in the killing. This left Torrio in control of one of the largest crime empires in America.

Illegal windfall

On 17 January 1920 gangsters like Torrio and Capone were delighted to hear that the US government had introduced Prohibition — the banning of the manufacture and sale of alcohol. The gangsters knew that people would still want to drink and they reasoned that they could make enormous profits from helping them fulfil this desire. As soon as the law was passed lavish bootlegging operations were set up by the gangsters. Illicit distilleries appeared all over the country, lorry loads of whisky were imported from Canada, and secret drinking parlours (speakeasies) began to flourish.

Although the authorities claimed they would be unceasing in their pursuit of the bootleggers, more often than not the police and the judges were taking substantial bribes and turning a blind eye. Only 10 days after the law had been introduced three agents from the Treasury Department's Prohibition Unit were indicted in Chicago on charges of accepting bribes and selling confiscated liquor. An Anti-Saloon League was set up, claiming that Prohibition was in America's best interests but they had to admit that there was 'rampant lawlessness, increasing by leaps and bounds'.

Capone in control

Since Torrio was a shrewd businessman who preferred to discuss problems rather than solve them with the barrel of a gun, his bootlegging business flourished and within a couple of years of the introduction of Prohibition his organization was making several million dollars a year from the sale of alcohol. Capone, who had already been given total control of the criminal activities in a neighbouring town, watched these developments with interest. In 1925 Torrio survived an assassination attempt by a rival gang and decided to retire and move back to Italy. He left his empire to Capone, saying, 'It's all yours Al'.

Capone made his headquarters in the Chicago suburb of Cicero and his reign contrasted dramatically with the diplomatic approach of Torrio. He would not tolerate any insubordination and he dealt ruthlessly with people who crossed him — on one occasion killing three men with a baseball bat.

The Big Shot

Capone quickly established himself as the crime king of Chicago and earned himself the title 'The Big Shot'. He lived up to his image: he attended opening nights at the theatre; he went to the opera; he bought a luxurious house in Miami; and he went to the races, where he bet millions of dollars, safe in the knowledge that he owned the bookmakers. He also moved his headquarters to the luxurious Lexington Hotel, where he took over the top two floors.

One of Capone's trademarks was how he dealt with rival gangs. From 1925 to 1930 there were approximately 500 gang deaths in Chicago, the majority at the instigation of Capone. It was almost a weekly occurrence for a gangster to be gunned down in a Chicago street or restaurant and the police seemed unable, or unwilling, to stop the blood-bath. Several attempts were made on Capone's life (including one when a rival gang tried to poison his soup), but he always escaped unharmed.

Prohibition profits

Rather than seeing himself as a gangster, Capone preferred to think that he was providing a public service at a time of Prohibition. He once remarked, 'Someone has to throw some liquor on that thirst, why not me?' He did this with meticulous efficiency and the Chicago Crime Commission estimated that at the height of his power he was

Al Capone

earning $60 million a year, two-thirds of which came from the sale of illegal alcohol. The FBI thought that this was a conservative estimate and put the figure at $120 million, $75 million of which came from alcohol. Some of this money was paid in bribes to the vast network of police, politicians and judges who were virtually Capone's employees.

Naturally, rival gangs were envious of Capone's power and wealth and one of them, an Irish gang from the North Side, made several attempts at assassinating him. The Big Shot was infuriated and in a rage he ordered the execution of the gang boss, Dion O'Banion. This did not satisfy his appetite for revenge and he vowed to teach the upstart gang and their new leader, 'Bugs' Moran, a lesson once and for all.

Bloody Valentine's Day

On 13 February 1929 Capone circulated a rumour to the Moran Gang that a shipment of illegal liquor would be delivered to a garage on the North Side of Chicago the following day. So on St Valentine's Day five of Moran's gang arrived at the appointed rendezvous, only to be met by five of Capone's henchmen who lined them up against a wall and machine-gunned them to death. Two innocent bystanders were also killed and over 200 spent cartridges were found at the scene of the crime. No one was arrested for the outrage and Capone had the perfect alibi — he was in Florida at the time.

Bugs Moran avoided the St Valentine's massacre only because he was late for the meeting but afterwards he swore vengeance against Capone, and for once in his life Scarface lost his nerve. He feared that the entire North Side would be on his trail and as a last resort he crossed the state line and was arrested in Philadelphia for a minor firearms offence. He spent a comfortable year in prison but when he returned to Chicago, in March 1930, he found a very different atmosphere. The country was in the grip of a depression and both the authorities and the public were fed up with the antics of Capone and his associates.

Tax evasion

The FBI worked tirelessly trying to convict Capone but in the end it was the Inland Revenue Department who helped bring him to trial. They discovered that he had never completed a tax return and in June 1931 he was indicted for tax evasion. He offered the authorities a $4 million bribe but this was rejected and in October he was brought to trial. A new jury was introduced shortly before the verdict, as Capone had bribed the original one, and they found the gangster guilty. He was sentenced to 11 years' imprisonment and fined an insignificant $80 000.

Al Capone was paroled on 19 November 1939. He was a broken man and turned his back on his former career, choosing to live quietly in Florida. The most notorious gangster in American history died of paresis of the brain, the result of an earlier bout of syphilis, on 25 January 1947.

Fortunate con man

The con man Victor Lustig even had the audacity to try and con Al Capone. He waited outside his headquarters until he was taken inside to meet the gang leader. He then put an ingenious plan to him which involved investing money on Wall Street and doubling it within 60 days. As ever, the prospect of easy money appealed to Capone and he gave Lustig $50 000 on the spot. The con man then disappeared. However, he must have realized that he was endangering his life because he returned to Capone and admitted that the whole thing had been a fraud. Capone was impressed by his honesty and instead of having him killed he handed him $5000 and gave him a job in his organization as a counterfeiter.

Justification

Capone always tried to justify his actions by claiming that he was only giving people what they wanted: 'All I ever did was to supply a demand that was pretty popular ... I've never heard of anyone being forced to go to a place to have some fun'.

Casement, Sir Roger David

(1864–1916)

Traitor

An Irish nationalist who sought support from Germany during World War I.

Roger Casement was born at Kingstown, County Dublin, Ireland. In 1895 he entered the British consular service and his first appointment was to Portuguese East Africa (Mozambique). He remained there until 1898 when he moved to Angola for two years. From 1901 to 1904 he was stationed in the Belgian Congo and from 1906 to 1911 he served in Brazil. He had an intuitive understanding of the inhabitants of these countries and achieved worldwide acclaim when he revealed the atrocities that the native workers in the Congo, and the Putumayo River region of Peru, suffered at the hands of the white traders. In recognition of his work he was knighted in 1912.

Converted nationalist

Casement retired from the consular service in 1912 because of ill health and returned to his native Ireland. His years abroad had made him aware of the importance of self-determination and he became a strong supporter of Irish Nationalism. He did not see why Ireland should have to fight in the war that was looming on the continent and saw it as a good opportunity to achieve independence from England.

In 1913 he formed the Irish National Volunteers and the following year he visited New York in an attempt to generate support for his cause. The Americans were indifferent and Casement's next port of call was Berlin in November 1914. He mistakenly thought that the Germans would view Irish independence as a blow against Britain, and so be willing to send an expeditionary force to Ireland. He was equally unsuccessful when he tried to persuade Irish prisoners of war to return and fight for a free Ireland.

Captured submarine

However, Casement was undeterred and decided to return to Ireland in April 1916, as the Easter Rebellion was being planned. He travelled in a German submarine, but it was spotted by a British patrol boat and when they put ashore at Tralee he was arrested, charged with treason and taken to London.

Before Casement's trial, in June 1916, Bernard Shaw urged him to make a rousing speech supporting Irish nationalism. He declined and instead his defence was that he had not technically committed treason because he was not within the King's realm at the time. This argument was rejected and on 29 June 1916 he was found guilty and sentenced to death.

Incriminating diaries

Many influential figures in Britain felt that Casement should be reprieved in view of his distinguished career in the British consular service. However, as support for a reprieve was growing, Casement's secret diaries, which pointed to his own homosexuality, were circulated to those people responsible for commuting the sentence. They were so shocked by these revelations that the sentence stood and Casement was hanged at Pentonville prison on 3 August 1916.

Authentication
In 1959 the Home Office allowed an independent inspection of the controversial diaries. Various experts agreed that they were genuine, but Casement could have copied them from another source.

Cato Street conspiracy

(1820)

Arthur Thistlewood

An attempt by a group of conspirators to assassinate the members of the British Cabinet.

Arthur Thistlewood was born in Lincolnshire in 1770. He studied to be a land surveyor but this did not interest him and he went to America and France instead. It was during this time that he developed his fervent revolutionary beliefs and when he returned to England in 1794 one of his contemporaries commented that he was, 'firmly persuaded that the first duty of a patriot was to massacre the government and overturn all existing institutions'.

Spencean member

Thistlewood married in 1804 but when his wife died shortly afterwards he gravitated towards London, with the vague idea of putting his theories into action. He joined the Spencean Society, a group devoted to revolutionizing the class system in Britain. Through his activities with the Society Thistlewood became known to the police and the government and he was noted as being a potentially dangerous character.

Spa Fields Riot

In December 1816 the authorities' suspicions were confirmed when Thistlewood was instrumental in organizing a huge public meeting at Spa Fields. He hoped it would develop into a full-blown revolution but the government were kept well informed as to the conspirators' plans and the meeting was broken up with little difficulty. Thistlewood went into hiding but he was captured in May 1817 and charged with treason. Surprisingly the judge ruled that a verdict of not guilty should be returned and so Thistlewood was free to continue with his revolutionary activities. He rejoined the Spenceans with renewed vigour and began dreaming up wild schemes for the overthrow of the government.

In 1818 Thistlewood was imprisoned for a year for challenging the former prime minister, Viscount Sidmouth, to a duel. He was released in 1819 and immediately embarked on his most ambitious plan yet — galvanizing the economic unrest in Britain into open rebellion. Some of his contemporaries were not happy with his violent methods and he was left with only four loyal supporters.

Assassination attempt

Despairing of a full rebellion Thistlewood settled on the assassination of the British cabinet. When he heard that the members of the cabinet were meeting for dinner on 23 February 1820 at the Earl of Harrowby's house in Grosvenor Square, London, he decided that this was an ideal opportunity. Thistlewood arranged a final rendezvous at a house in Cato Street, but the government's informants had been doing their job and on the evening of 23 February Thistlewood and his fellow conspirators were arrested.

Although Thistlewood escaped from captivity for one day he was soon recaptured. He and four others were convicted of high treason and hanged at Newgate on 1 May 1820. They were decapitated after death, but spared the indignity of quartering.

> **Last words**
> Thistlewood went to his death defiantly, declaring, 'Albion is still in the chains of slavery. I quit it without regret. My only sorrow is that the soil should be a theatre for slaves, for cowards, for despots'.

Chamberlain case

(1982)

Alice Lynne Chamberlain

Australia's most sensational criminal case that has become known as the 'Dingo Baby Murder' case.

In August 1980 a young Australian family from the Queensland mining town of Mount Isa went to Ayers Rock in the Northern Territory. Michael Chamberlain, 36, and his wife Lindy, 32, were both members of the Seventh Day Adventist Church and they were travelling with their three children, seven-year-old Aidan, four-year-old Reagan and nine-week-old Azaria.

On 17 August the Chamberlains spent the day walking around Ayers Rock. Shortly after a spectacular sunset Lindy put Azaria to bed in her tent and went to help her husband prepare the evening meal. Minutes later the campers nearby heard Lindy crying, 'A dingo has got my baby'. She had gone to check on Azaria only to see a dingo making off from the tent. She turned back to find that her baby had disappeared. That night dozens of campers searched the surrounding area for a sign of Azaria but she seemed to have vanished completely.

National interest

A week later Azaria's torn and bloodstained clothing was found near the base of Ayers Rock, and three miles from a dingo's lair. However, there were no signs of the baby. Speculation began to mount as to what had happened and soon an inquisitive public and media had constructed a number of theories. It was rumoured, with no foundation, that the name Azaria meant 'sacrifice in the wilderness' and that Lindy had killed her baby and then made up the story about the dingo.

In February 1981 an inquest was held at Alice Springs. In an effort to end the rumours and innuendoes that were sweeping the country, the coroner, Denis Barritt, delivered his findings before live television cameras. Over two million people heard him conclude that Michael and Lindy Chamberlain were entirely blameless for the disappearance of their daughter and that she had indeed been killed by a dingo. He added emphatically, 'I find that the name Azaria does not mean and never has meant 'sacrifice in the wilderness'.

New evidence

Despite the findings of the inquest the police were not satisfied. They called in two forensic experts, Dr Kenneth Brown from Adelaide, and Professor James Cameron from London, to re-examine the evidence. They concluded that the tear marks in Azaria's clothing had been made by a sharp object, such as a knife, and not by a dingo's teeth. When bloodstains were found in the Chamberlain's car, inside their tent and on a camera bag the case was re-opened. The findings of the first inquest were quashed and a second inquest was ordered. It opened in February 1982 and it was found that the Chamberlains had a case to answer and they were committed for trial in Darwin.

The trial of Michael and Lindy Chamberlain began in Darwin on 13 September 1982. She was charged with the murder of Azaria and he was charged as an accessory after the fact. By now the case had drawn incredible attention from around the world and a separate room with closed-circuit television had to be used to accommodate all the foreign journalists. The drama was heightened when it was discovered that Lindy was now seven months pregnant.

Expert opinion

The prosecution, led by Ian Barker, QC, alleged that Lindy Chamberlain had cut her daughter's throat in the front seat of the family car and then buried the body. He called on the forensic experts to testify that the blood found in the tent was that of a newborn baby, but not in sufficient amounts to suggest that the child had been taken by a dingo. It was also claimed that there were no saliva stains on the baby's clothes, as would be consistent with a dingo carrying the baby in its mouth.

The Chamberlain's defence introduced its own forensic evidence which contradicted that of the prosecution, and several witnesses were called who said they had seen dingoes around the camp on the night Azaria disappeared. Another witness reported that his four-year-old son had been attacked by a dingo only a month earlier. On a personal level witnesses described how Lindy had a 'new mum' glow about her. The blood inside the car was explained by a hitch-hiker picked up by the Chamberlains in 1979, who had been bleeding from a head wound.

Unanimous verdict

The trial lasted seven weeks, during which time the media conducted its own trial. In his summing-up Mr Justice James Muirhead said, 'We are not treading in the ground of unequivocal, unchallenged scientific opinion ... On the contrary, the scientific opinion on these vital issues is divided'. After six hours of deliberation the jury returned verdicts of guilty against Michael and Lindy Chamberlain. He was given an 18-month suspended sentence while she received life imprisonment with hard labour. Many people were shocked by the severity of the sentence, and the dubious nature of the evidence, suggesting that the media had influenced the verdict.

In April 1983 an appeal by the Chamberlains was dismissed by the Federal Court in Sydney. Then, in January 1986, Azaria's matinée jacket was found at Ayers Rock. Lindy was released from prison, pending yet another inquiry. This time the forensic evidence of James Cameron was discredited. This led to a Royal Commission, which concluded there were serious doubts about Lindy Chamberlain's guilt. In June 1987 the Chamberlains were pardoned, but their convictions stood.

The Chamberlains continued their campaign to prove their innocence and on 15 September 1988 their convictions were quashed by the Australian Court of Appeal. They followed this with a A\$4 million claim for compensation. In August 1991 they received A\$9000 as the first part of their compensation. The Seventh Day Adventist Church, who paid much of the their legal fees, received A\$395 000. The fight for compensation continues at the time of writing.

Court ordeal
While giving evidence during her trial Lindy Chamberlain broke down several times. On one occasion she turned on the prosecutor saying, 'You are talking about my baby, not some object'. When asked if she had deliberately smeared blood in the family tent she replied vehemently, 'No, that's pure fabrication'.

Birth in prison
Shortly after her conviction Lindy Chamberlain gave birth to a daughter named Kahlia. The baby was taken from her almost immediately but two days later she was released on bail, pending her first appeal. She was reunited with her daughter at an Adventist Church college.

Chatterton, Thomas

(1752–70)

Literary forger

A precocious literary forger who became distraught when his own work was poorly received.

Born in Bristol, Thomas Chatterton blossomed into a highly intelligent young boy. By the time he was eight he was an insatiable reader and would spend hours on his own, giving preference to his books over food or sleep. His favourite haunts were a dusty attic in his house and the nearby Redcliffe cathedral, where his uncle was the sexton.

Practical joke

From an early age Chatterton was accustomed to old documents because there were seven chests at Redcliffe containing medieval manuscripts. Some of these found their way into the Chatterton household. Thomas spent hours copying heraldic symbols and in 1767 he produced a forged document that proved his neighbour was descended from a Norman knight. The neighbour accepted this, until the hoax was discovered at the Heralds' College in London.

On 1 July 1767 Chatterton was apprenticed to a law firm in Bristol. Although the work was mundane and the hours long he managed to continue his self-education and learnt about heraldry, metaphysics, astronomy, medicine and antiquities. During this period he also continued a project that he had initiated two years earlier — the forgery of the work of a 15th-century monk named Thomas Rowley. Drawing on all his knowledge he produced a variety of documents, including poems, prose, letters, diaries, drama and drawings. He claimed that he had found all of these in the chests at Redcliffe cathedral.

Rejection

People in his native Bristol were satisfied that the Rowley manuscripts were genuine and at the age of 16 Chatterton acquired a certain fame for his part in their discovery. Seeking even more recognition he then sent some 'genuine' Rowley poems to James Dodsley, a publisher in London, and the antiquarian and novelist Horace Walpole. Dodsley ignored the offer but Walpole expressed an interest. Chatterton then revealed that he was a clerk to an attorney and this seems to have changed Walpole's attitude. He immediately denounced them as forgeries and returned them to their sender.

Early death

Chatterton was incensed by this behaviour and as word spread through Bristol he was forced to admit to the forgeries. Life then became intolerable for him and he left Bristol for London on 24 April 1770, determined to make a name for himself in his own right. He sold some of his work to various magazines but he received very little payment. This lack of recognition, coupled with his rejection by Walpole, was all too much for Chatterton. On 25 August 1770 he committed suicide by taking poison (although there is one school of thought that claims he died of venereal disease). He was 17 when he died, after a brief, but remarkable, literary career.

Paternal talent

Chatterton's father was a church sexton and also a skilled numismatist — he collected several hundred Roman coins during his lifetime. His one great claim to fame is the fact that he had such a wide mouth that he was able to put his clenched fist in it.

Chessman, Caryl

(1921–60)

Kidnapper

A case that raised serious questions about the use of the death penalty in the United States.

Caryl Chessman was brought up in California and from an early age he was in trouble with the police for a variety of minor offences and he served several prison terms. In January 1948 Chessman was accused of a series of sex attacks on two young women. The offender had stopped the women in their cars, taken them to his own car and then forced them to perform oral sex. He then released them unharmed. The attacker was known as the 'Red Light Bandit' because of a red light he had on his car.

Astonishing charge

There was some doubt as to whether Chessman was the 'Red Light Bandit' — the process of identification was not foolproof — but even more incredible was the crime with which he was charged. Rather than being charged with a sex offence Chessman was accused of kidnapping with intent to cause bodily harm. This was an extremely serious charge because, since the Lindbergh case, California had introduced the death penalty for kidnapping. In July 1949 Chessman was found guilty by a Los Angeles jury and, to everyone's horror and amazement, he was sentenced to death.

While on death row Chessman mounted a campaign to have his capital sentence commuted to life imprisonment. His cause was taken up by people in all walks of life and his case attracted an international following. Seven dates were set for his execution and he survived them all by lodging various appeals.

Reformed character

While he was in prison Chessman not only educated himself but he also wrote three books about his experiences on death row: *Cell 2455 Death Row*, which became a bestseller, *The Face of Justice*, and *Trial by Ordeal*. A film was also made about him and a record entitled *Ballad of Caryl Chessman* became a big hit.

As Chessman's time in prison dragged on it became clear that it was inhumane to keep a man on death row for so long. The Vatican newspaper *L'Osservatore Romano* commented that it was an 'excruciatingly slow agony' and suggested that he had already expiated his guilt.

Shameful execution

In 1960 Chessman appeared on the cover of *Time* magazine and his case symbolized the call for the abolition of capital punishment in both Britain and America. Unfortunately it was all to no avail and, after his final appeal failed, Caryl Chessman was executed in the gas chamber of San Quentin on 8 March 1960. He had spent 11 years on death row and the day after his execution newspaper editorials around the world were exclaiming their revulsion at this sorry episode in American legal history.

Wrong number
The final irony in the Chessman case occurred a few minutes before the execution took place. A judge in San Francisco was preparing to grant a 30-minute stay of execution so another of Chessman's pleas could be heard. But his secretary telephoned the wrong number for San Quentin prison and by the time she got through the execution was already in progress.

Christie, John Reginald Halliday

(1898–1953)

Convicted murderer

The 'Monster of Rillington Place', whose quiet manner hid a dark and murderous temperament.

Reginald Christie was born in Yorkshire and he soon showed himself to be neurotic, a hypochondriac and a petty thief. When he left school he was employed by the Halifax police and then in a carpet factory, but he was sacked from both for pilfering. His sex drive was as feeble as the rest of his health and one girlfriend dubbed him 'Reggie–no–dick'.

In May 1920 Christie married Ethel Waddington and after three years of mundane jobs and petty crime he left her and moved to London. From 1924 to 1933 he served three prison sentences. Ethel visited him in prison and in 1933 she moved back with her husband. In 1938 the couple moved into the ground floor of 10 Rillington Place, off St Mark's Road, London.

Perverted murderer

At the beginning of World War II Christie sent his wife to Sheffield and then embarked on a bizarre succession of perversion and murder. In August 1943 he met Ruth Fuerst, a student nurse from Austria. He invited her back to Rillington Place and strangled her while they were having sex. A year later he befriended Muriel Eady, a 32-year-old canteen worker. She also went to Rillington Place, where Christie gassed her, had sex with her and then strangled her. Both of the bodies were buried in the garden at Rillington Place.

Christie's wife returned at the end of the war and the killings suddenly stopped, probably because of her presence in the house.

In March 1948 Timothy Evans and his wife, Beryl, moved into the top floor of 10 Rillington Place. Evans was 24 and worked as a van-driver. He was poorly educated and was an excitable, boastful character. On 10 October 1948 the couple had a baby daughter, Geraldine, and for the next year they lived an uneventful existence. When Beryl became pregnant in October 1949 she decided to have an abortion and asked Christie's advice on some medical matters. A month later she disappeared. On 30 November 1949 Timothy Evans walked into a police station at Merthyr Tydfil, South Wales,

No 10 Rillington Place

63

and announced, 'I want to give myself up. I have disposed of my wife'.

Wrongful execution?

When the police first searched Rillington Place they found nothing, but on 2 December they discovered the bodies of Beryl and Geraldine Evans in the wash-house in the garden. They had both been strangled. Evans was arrested and tried for murder on 11 January 1950. He made several confused and contradictory statements, alternating between accusing Christie of the crimes and admitting to them himself. Christie was one of the main prosecution witnesses and Evans was found guilty of the murder of his daughter. He was hanged on 9 March 1950 and went to the gallows claiming, 'Christie done it'. There was no public outcry at the execution as the crime was considered a sordid domestic affair.

Murder spree

Three years after Evans's execution Christie embarked on another murder spree. It began on 14 December 1952 when he strangled his wife as she lay beside him in bed. There was no motivation for this but Christie later claimed that she was choking and since he could not bear to see her suffer, he killed her. He hid her body under the floorboards of the front room.

Now that he was on his own again Christie was free to indulge his peculiar sexual habits. From 6 January to 6 March 1953 he took three prostitutes, Hectorina MacLennan, Kathleen Maloney and Rita Nelson, back to Rillington Place. He then proceeded to gas them and strangle them. He also had intercourse with them while they were unconscious or dead. After putting all three bodies behind a wall in the kitchen, Christie sub-let his three rooms and moved to a down-and-outs' hostel in King's Cross.

Ghastly discovery

On 23 March 1953 the new tenant at 10 Rillington Place noticed a strange smell in the kitchen and that the wallpaper was loose. When he tore it off and peered into

the gap he was faced with a dead body. When the police searched the premises they discovered the ghastly secret of this nondescript house: the four bodies in the house and the two skeletons that had been buried in the garden 10 years earlier.

It took the police a week to find Christie and when they did he made several long, rambling statements, admitting to the murders of not only the six corpses in the house but also Beryl Evans. At one point he remarked, 'The more the merrier'.

Christie's trial for the murder of his wife began at the Old Bailey on 22 June 1953. His defence was based on a plea of guilty but insane. As he gave evidence the defendant certainly seemed confused and uncertain but after 85 minutes the jury found that he was guilty and sane. Reginald Christie was hanged at Pentonville Prison on 15 July 1953, by the same executioner who had hanged Timothy Evans three years earlier.

Posthumous pardon

Following Christie's execution and his claim that he killed Beryl Evans there was considerable concern that there had been a miscarriage of justice and that an innocent man had been hanged. In 1966 a public inquiry was held, which concluded that it was 'more probable than not' that Evans had killed his wife but that he did not kill his daughter. Since he had been convicted and executed for his daughter's murder Timothy Evans was given a free and posthumous pardon. However, no one will ever be sure of what exactly happened in 10 Rillington Place during November 1949.

Portrait

The artist Philip Youngman Carter painted a portrait of Christie and it proved to be a harrowing experience: 'I would say that the man was the nearest thing I have ever encountered to unadulterated evil. Two days' association with the picture made me almost physically sick, and the woman cleaning my studio, who had no idea about the subject of the portrait, asked me to put it away while she was working because it was frightening'.

Chudleigh, Elizabeth

(1720–88)

Bigamist

An outrageous socialite who married secretly during her twenties.

Born in Dorsetshire, Elizabeth Chudleigh grew up to be a ravishing beauty and she had her first love affair when she was 15. In 1740 she and her mother moved to London and three years later she was appointed Maid of Honour to Augusta, Princess of Wales.

After attracting the attention of several men at Court, Elizabeth met and married Augustus John Hervey, a lieutenant in the navy, and the grandson of the Earl of Bristol. The wedding took place at Lainston House near Winchester on 14 August 1744. It was kept a closely guarded secret because Hervey did not have good prospects and Elizabeth did not want to lose her place at Court.

Talk of the town

Hervey spent most of his time at sea and when he was at home the couple quarrelled. By January 1747 it was clear that the marriage was over in all but name. Elizabeth was glad of the freedom that this allowed her and she behaved scandalously around Court, taking many lovers and behaving outrageously at balls and social events.

In 1759 Elizabeth heard that the Earl of Bristol was seriously ill. Never one to miss an opportunity she took steps to enter her wedding in the church register at Lainston, so that when the Earl died, and her marriage was made public, she would become the Countess of Bristol and inherit a sizable fortune. Unfortunately her plan was foiled because the Earl recovered and lived for another 10 years.

Undeterred, Elizabeth continued with her riotous lifestyle, taking lovers both in Britain and abroad. In 1769 she was proposed to by the wealthy Duke of Kingston. Before accepting, she obtained a church decree against her legal husband Hervey, saying that he had falsely claimed that a marriage had taken place. On 8 March she became the Duchess of Kingston.

Secret uncovered

For four years the Duke and Duchess frequented numerous balls, parties and fêtes. When the Duke died, on 23 September 1773, he left his entire estate to Elizabeth. His sister and her family were shocked and took the will to Chancery. During these proceedings it was discovered that Elizabeth Chudleigh had been, and still was, married to Augustus Hervey, who was now the Earl of Bristol.

The Duchess of Bristol, as she officially was, was sent for trial in front of her peers at Westminster Abbey from 15 to 22 April 1776, an extravagant affair. Elizabeth Chudleigh was found guilty, but spared the traditional fate of being branded on the hand. Instead she was given a severe warning.

After her trial Elizabeth escaped to Europe where she continued to call herself the Duchess of Kingston, and live off the Kingston estate. She toured the courts of Europe in her customary scandalous fashion and died in 1788 of a burst blood vessel.

Outrageous attire

At a masked ball in 1749 Elizabeth Chudleigh arrived as Iphigenia, in a dress that revealed more than it covered. It caused an uproar and one commentator muttered, 'She was so naked that you would have taken her for Andromeda'.

Collier, John Payne

(1789–1883)

Literary forger

A literary editor who tried to outdo his competitors by forging his own 'unique' Shakespearean manuscripts.

John Collier was born in Leeds and although he never attended school or college, he began authorship before he was 16. In 1809 he joined *The Times* and worked for them as a reporter until 1821. He was then employed by the *Morning Chronicle* where he worked as a parliamentary reporter and a literary critic until 1847.

Despite his journalistic talent Collier gradually became known as one of the leading editors of Elizabethan and Jacobean literature and memorabilia. He founded two societies that specialized in reprinting early texts and he was the director of the Shakespeare Society (founded in 1840). An amiable man, he was also a prodigious worker.

Editorial competition

At this time there was great competition between editors to produce the definitive version of Shakespeare's work. Between 1842 and 1844 Collier had edited a version in eight volumes. It was well received by the literary world but there were a number of respected editors who were also preparing volumes at this time and Collier knew they would supersede his own work. To try and prevent this he announced that he had discovered a 1632 Shakespeare folio containing hundreds of unique corrections in the margin.

Collier's discovery was known as the Perkins folio, because the name Tho Perkins appeared on the binding. It was claimed that the corrections had been written by the 'Old Corrector' who was supposed to have been a contemporary of Shakespeare. When he was questioned as to where he had acquired the folio, Collier replied that he had bought it from an antiquarian bookseller, who had since died.

Collier's rivals were furious at what they believed was a blatant forgery but when he published *Notes and Emendations to the Plays of Shakespeare* in 1852, it sold 4000 copies in six months. It was a triumph for Collier and some of his rivals grudgingly included the additional information in their own work.

The 'Old Corrector' unmasked

Collier was careful not to let the original folio out of his custody, but in June 1853 he lent it to his literary patron, the Duke of Devonshire. The Duke died soon afterwards and his son lent the folio to Sir Frederick Madden, Keeper of Manuscripts at the British Museum. Due to an incident many years earlier Collier had made an enemy of Madden, which was to cost him dearly. After examining the folio, Madden took great pleasure in announcing that it was a blatant forgery: the alleged 17th-century handwriting had been included very recently, and the notes had been traced in ink over a pencil original. Collier put up very little defence against the charge of forgery.

Despite being branded a forger Collier continued his phenomenal editorial output. John Collier died at Maidenhead on 17 September 1883.

Vague admission
The closest Collier got to admitting to the forgery of the Perkins folio was when he wrote, 'If the proposed emendations are not genuine then I claim them as mine ... no edition of Shakespeare can now be published without them'.

Cotton, Mary Ann

(1832–73)

Convicted murderer

Regarded as Britain's most prolific female mass murderer, who killed for financial gain or simple elimination.

Mary Ann Cotton was born into a mining family in the Durham pit town of Low Moorsley. She trained as a nurse and she was considered a good-natured woman and a devout Methodist.

In 1852 Mary Ann married a labourer named William Mowbray and the couple moved to Devon. They had five children but four of them died. The couple then settled in the Sunderland area and had three more children. But their ill fortune continued and they all died. This was followed by the death of Mowbray himself.

Mary Ann seemed unperturbed by her husband's death and in August 1866 she remarried, this time to an engineer named George Wood. The marriage lasted 14 months, when Wood went the same way as William Mowbray. Mary Ann restricted the mourning period to one month, and then moved in with a widower named James Robinson, and his three children.

Trail of death

Between 21 April and 2 May 1867 two of Robinson's children died, as did Mary Ann's one surviving daughter by her marriage to Mowbray. Robinson himself survived — after refusing to take out life insurance. The couple had two children, one of whom died, while the other was given away when the marriage broke up.

Soon after murdering her own mother Mary Ann met Frederick Cotton and married him bigamously (she never bothered to divorce Robinson). The couple moved to West Auckland in County Durham and shortly afterwards Cotton's sister died; the newly-weds inherited £60 from her estate.

The Cottons celebrated their first wedding anniversary on 17 September 1871. Two days later Frederick died of suspected gastric fever. Mary Ann took a new lover, Joseph Natrass, but he too died the following year, as did another of her children and also Frederick Cotton's son Robert.

Diligent doctor

On 12 July 1872 Mary Ann's seven-year-old stepson Charles Edward Cotton died of what she claimed was gastro-enteritis. Although the doctor who examined him was suspicious he did not have time for a thorough post-mortem and he told an inquest that he could find nothing to suggest poisoning. However, he kept the contents of the boy's stomach and when he had time to examine them at his leisure he discovered significant amounts of arsenic.

Although Mary Ann Cotton was only charged with the murder of Charles Edward Cotton, the other deaths were allowed to be used as evidence against her and this proved to be decisive. On 8 March 1873 the jury took an hour to find her guilty of murder. The Home Secretary refused to commute the death sentence and Mary Ann Cotton was hanged in Durham Prison on 24 March 1873.

> **League table**
> Twenty-one people connected with Mary Ann Cotton died during her lifetime and it is thought she was responsible for at least 15 of the deaths. She and Dennis Nilsen share their total of mass murders in Britain — one behind Burke and Hare, who were attributed with 16.

Cream, Dr Thomas Neill

(1850–92)

Convicted murderer

A poisoner who had a tendency for leading the police straight to the crimes he committed.

Thomas Neill Cream was born in Glasgow in 1850 but emigrated to Canada with his parents while he was still a child. He qualified as a doctor from Montreal's McGill College in 1876 and set up practice as an abortionist. He was a highly unethical practitioner with a voracious sexual appetite. After he performed an abortion on a girl he had made pregnant he was forced, at gunpoint, to marry her. He left her after one day to continue his medical studies in Britain and when he returned after a year he found that his wife had died of consumption.

Adultery and murder

In 1880 Cream moved to Chicago where he again worked as an abortionist, and also turned to blackmail. He soon became involved with Mrs Julia Scott, the wife of one of his patients, and in 1881 her husband died after taking one of Cream's remedies. The doctor was not suspected but he wrote to the police, accusing a chemist of putting too much strychnine in Scott's pills and ordering that his body be exhumed. When this was done it was discovered that he had been poisoned with strychnine. However, the chemist could not have been responsible so Cream was arrested and sentenced to life imprisonment.

Cream served only 10 years of this sentence and when he was released in 1891 he left America, arriving in England on 1 October. To feed his sexual appetite he was soon inhabiting the disreputable areas of Lambeth in London and on some evenings he would see up to three different prostitutes.

Lust for poison

But sex was not Cream's only motivation for visiting prostitutes; he liked to give them pills which he claimed would help clear up their complexions. In reality the pills contained strychnine and Cream would have fantasies as he imagined the girls dying excruciating deaths. During October 1891 he poisoned Matilda Clover and Ellen Donworth, although in Matilda's case the cause of death was attributed to her alcoholism.

In the same month another prostitute, Louise Harvey, met Cream and spent the night with him. However, when he offered her his skin pills she pretended to take them and then threw them away. Cream was unaware of this and as far as he knew she died a painful death after he left her.

Following his spate of poisoning, Cream once again demonstrated his desire to publicize his actions. Under assumed names he wrote to two respectable members of London society, Lord Russell and Dr William Broadbent, accusing them of murdering Matilda Clover and demanding money from them for his silence. Under a third alias he wrote to the coroner who was to hear the Donworth case, claiming that he had information about the murder and that he was prepared to sell it for £300 000. It was treated as a hoax.

Two more murders

At the beginning of 1892 Cream became engaged and returned briefly to Canada and America. He was back in Britain by March, and on 12 April two young prostitutes in Lambeth, Emma Shrivell and Alice March, were found in excruciating pain. Before they died they said they had been given pills by a man named Fred who had a squint and a large moustache.

At the inquest of Emma Shrivell and Alice Marsh it was recorded that the girls had died of strychnine poisoning. This caused a sensation and a rumour quickly started that the Lambeth Poisoner was in fact Jack the Ripper, returning after his last murder in 1888.

Relishing the uproar he had caused, Cream then accused a young doctor, Walter Harper, of the Shrivell and Marsh murders. When Harper's father learnt of this he went straight to the police and they began a very thorough investigation of Dr Neill Cream.

Exhibitionist is caught

Cream was eager to help the police and he showed them a letter that had been sent to Alice Shrivell and Emma Marsh, warning them of Dr Harper, who, it was claimed, had murdered Matilda Clover and Louise Harvey. It was a fatal error: since it had been recorded that Matilda had died of natural causes only her killer would have known she had been murdered. Her body was exhumed and found to contain large quantities of strychnine.

The most puzzling aspect of the letter was the reference to the death of Louise Harvey, since the police had no record of this. They eventually discovered her, alive and well, in Brighton and she told them of her meeting with Cream.

'Fire away'

Cream was arrested on 3 June 1892 and charged with blackmail and murder. He was arrogant and overbearing when he was taken into custody, saying, 'You have got the wrong man. Fire away'. His trial began at the Old Bailey on 17 October 1892 and the evidence against him was overwhelming. There were eye-witnesses in the form of Louise Harvey and two prostitutes who had seen him with Matilda Clover, a chemist testified that he had bought nux vomica (from which strychnine is extracted), and seven bottles of strychnine were found in Cream's lodgings.

The jury took just 12 minutes to find Neill Cream guilty of murder and there was general relief when this vile man was hanged at Newgate prison on 15 November 1892. As he ascended the scaffold he announced to a startled crowd that he was Jack the Ripper. However, this was impossible because at the time of the Ripper murders Cream was serving a life sentence in America.

Eye problem

Following Cream's death an optician wrote to The Times claiming that his moral degeneracy might have been avoided if his squint had been corrected at an early age.

Identical twin

The celebrated advocate Sir Edward Marshall Hall once defended Cream against a charge of bigamy by claiming that he had been in prison in Australia at the time. He later discovered that Cream had never been to Australia although a man fitting his description had been in custody there. When he heard this Marshall Hall became convinced that Cream had a double in the underworld and that the two men supplied alibis for each other when necessary.

Murder of Cora Crippen

(1910)

Hawley Harvey Crippen

A mild-mannered man who was the first murderer to be apprehended through the use of wireless.

Hawley Harvey Crippen was born in Michigan in 1862 and he received a medical training in Cleveland, London and New York. In 1893 he married Cora Turner, whose real name was Kunigunde Mackamotzki, in Jersey City. Crippen was

Ethel Le Neve

an obsequious and staid husband who indulged most of his wife's extravagant whims, which included lessons to train as an opera singer although it soon became clear that Cora had little or no talent in this area.

In 1900 the Crippens came to London. Since Hawley did not have the necessary qualification to practise as a doctor in England he became manager of Munyon's, a patent medicine firm. Cora occupied herself by pursuing a career in music halls — a vocation for which her enthusiasm outstripped her inadequate talent. She spent a great deal of her husband's money on lavish costumes and in cultivating her music hall friends. Crippen accepted this uncomplainingly.

A submissive life

In 1905 the Crippens moved to 39 Hilldrop Crescent. They had frequent fierce rows, usually instigated by Cora, and they slept in separate bedrooms. Despite the fact that they entertained frequently at home their private life was rather squalid, with most of it being spent in a dingy kitchen, the windows of which Cora forbade to be opened.

Crippen found continuing consolation in the form of his secretary, Ethel Le Neve, with whom he began an affair in 1907. Cora discovered this liaison in December 1910 and threatened to leave her husband and take all the money in the couple's joint bank account.

On 31 January 1910 the Crippens entertained two of Cora's music hall friends, Mr and Mrs Martinetti. During the course of the evening Cora had a fierce argument with her husband in front of their guests. The following week Crippen contacted Cora's friends and acquaintances to tell them that she had left for America to tend to a sick relative. He then pawned some of his wife's jewellery for £195. Shortly afterwards Ethel Le Neve was seen frequently in

Crippen's company and in March she moved into 39 Hilldrop Crescent and began wearing Cora's clothes and jewellery.

Near-perfect crime

At the end of March Crippen informed Mrs Martinetti that Cora had died in America. For the next three months he played the part of a mourning husband. One of the people who came to offer his condolences was a friend of Cora's, Mr Nash. He was suspicious of Crippen's manner and reported the matter to Inspector Dew at Scotland Yard. Dew subsequently interviewed Crippen and searched 39 Hilldrop Crescent but found nothing amiss and thought little more of the incident.

However, Crippen was disconcerted by the appearance of the police, possibly thinking that Ethel would break down if questioned, and he made preparation to leave the country. He wound up his business affairs, vacated his home and bought some boy's clothes to be worn by Ethel as a disguise. On 9 July 1910 Crippen and Ethel left London for Antwerp.

On 11 July Inspector Dew went to Crippen's office to ask a few routine questions, and was astonished to discover that the doctor had fled. There followed an extensive search of Hilldrop Crescent and on 13 July Dew found a pile of human flesh in the basement. All the bones and vital organs had been removed and it took some time to identify the remains as those of Cora Crippen. The post mortem revealed that she had been poisoned with hyoscine — a drug readily available to Dr Crippen. Dew wasted no time in circulating descriptions of Crippen and Ethel Le Neve.

Capture by wireless

The fleeing couple left Antwerp on 20 July aboard the SS *Montrose*, bound for Quebec. Having read the description of Crippen and Le Neve, the captain of the *Montrose* was suspicious of a Mr John Robinson and his 16-year-old son, who seemed unnaturally affectionate together. He sent a lengthy wireless message to his company expressing his doubts. This was the first time the wireless played a part in criminal detection.

Once Dew received this information he boarded a faster vessel than the *Montrose* and embarked upon a chase that was to keep the nation enthralled for a week. On 31 July Dew caught up with the *Montrose* and arrested both Crippen and Le Neve just before they reached Canada.

During the voyage back to Britain Dew and Crippen had a number of long conversations and Dew developed a modicum of respect and liking for this polite, unassuming man, who nevertheless received a hostile public reception on reaching Liverpool.

Calm defendant

Crippen was tried on 18 October 1910 and found guilty of murder three days later. Le Neve was tried for being an accessory after the fact but she was found not guilty. Throughout his trial Crippen showed remarkable poise and calm, even when the remains of his wife were passed around in a soup bowl.

Hawley Harvey Crippen was hanged in Pentonville Prison on 23 November 1910 and his name has since passed into criminal folklore. The simplest explanation as to why he was driven to murder was his love for Ethel Le Neve; the only time he broke down in prison was when he received her letters.

Tabloid claim

After her trial Ethel Le Neve emigrated to Australia where she is alleged to have told a newspaper that Crippen killed his wife because she had syphilis.

Theft of the English Crown Jewels
(1671)

Colonel Thomas Blood

An audacious robbery that was carried out by a man who was involved with adventure and intrigue all his life.

Thomas Blood was born in Ireland about 1618. Little is known of his early life except that his father was a blacksmith who owned an ironworks. During the Civil War Blood was a firm supporter of Oliver Cromwell and fought with the Parliamentarians. He soon became known for his fearlessness and daring and was much admired by those who fought with him.

After marrying Miss Holcroft in Lancashire Blood returned to Ireland in about 1648. As a reward for his services during the Civil War he was presented with substantial tracts of land and forfeited estates, which provided him with a handsome private income of £500 a year. However, with the accession of Charles II in 1660 and the Restoration, his lands were taken from him and he lost his income. Enraged, he became an increasingly devoted republican and Presbyterian

Intended kidnap

In 1663 Blood conceived a bold plan designed to strike at the Duke of Ormonde, the royal authority in Ireland. He intended to seize Dublin Castle and take Ormonde, who was the lord-lieutenant there, hostage. The operation was planned for either the 9th or 10th March 1663 but when Blood heard that Ormonde had discovered the proposed date he decided to bring the attack forward to 5 March. As with many of Blood's plans it was ingenious in theory but complete chaos in practice. Before the attack

had even begun most of the conspirators were arrested and Blood himself only just managed to escape. Several of the captured men were put to death, including Blood's brother-in-law.

Following the debacle at Dublin Castle Blood went into hiding in the Irish hills, seeking help from old Cromwellians. He managed to avoid detection for several months, due to a mastery of disguise and the fact that he kept moving constantly, but he was eventually forced to leave the country and fled to Holland.

Roving conspirator

Blood's adventurous nature prevented him from being idle for long and he was soon back in Britain, plotting more intrigues. He associated with the Fifth Monarchy men and then moved north to join forces with the Covenanters in Scotland. He fought with them at the Battle of Pentland Hills on 27 November 1666, where over 500 men were killed, and then returned to England.

In November 1670 William of Orange came to England and the Duke of Ormonde visited London to pay his respects. Blood decided this was the perfect opportunity to avenge his friends executed by Ormonde following the attack on Dublin Castle. With five associates he apprehended the Duke's coach as it was travelling along St James's Street and dragged the startled Duke from it. The idea was to take him to Tyburn and hang him from a common gibbet. However, as the conspirators were making their way to Tyburn they were overtaken by a horseman who managed to rescue the Duke. Blood, who had ridden ahead to prepare the gibbet, was furious when he heard the news.

Theft of the Crown Jewels

Thomas Blood's most daring escapade was

saved for near the end of his life: in 1671 he hatched a plan to steal the Crown Jewels of England. Three weeks before the theft itself he arrived at the Tower of London with a woman whom he claimed was his wife. He introduced himself to Talbot Edwards, the Keeper of the Crown Jewels, and asked if he and his wife could see the priceless treasures. Edwards readily agreed and after showing them around he was concerned to see Mrs Blood faint. His wife attended to her and she recovered quickly.

Less than a week later the Bloods returned to the Tower to thank Mrs Edwards for her kindness. They gave her a present of four pairs of white gloves and suggested that the two families should meet socially — Blood claimed to have a nephew who he thought might make a good match for the Edwards's daughter. The meeting was arranged for 9 May 1671.

Frenzied robbery

On 9 May Blood arrived at the Tower as planned. He brought three friends with him and told Edwards that his wife and his nephew would be arriving shortly. To pass the time he suggested that Edwards showed the Jewels to his friends. As soon as they entered the room in which the Jewels were kept Edwards was attacked and gagged. When he tried to raise the alarm the four men beat him with mallets and then stabbed him, although not fatally. Blood grabbed the Crown, crushed it flat and then hid it under his cloak. One of his colleagues put the Orb down his baggy trousers. They tried to cut the Sceptre in half but as they were doing so the alarm was raised.

Blood and his men escaped from the Tower but a hue and cry followed almost immediately. The man with the orb down his trousers found it was handicapping his progress and discarded it, disappearing into the crowd. Blood made for his horse, but as he was mounting it the Crown slipped from his cloak and he was captured as he tried to retrieve it. As he was taken into custody he remarked, 'It was a bold attempt, but it was for a crown'.

Following his arrest Blood refused to talk to anyone except King Charles II himself. This haughty gesture paid off and the King agreed to see him. Instead of sentencing him to death for treason Charles was so impressed by this daring rogue that he not only pardoned him but he also reinstated his lands in Ireland and his £500-a-year income.

Thomas Blood died on 24 August 1680 from natural causes.

Critical ballad

Not everyone shared Charles II's view that Blood was a lovable rogue. A ballad published shortly after his death concluded:

Here lies the man who boldly hath run through
More villanies than ever England knew;
And ne'er to any friend he had was true.
Here let him by all unpitied lie,
And let's rejoice his time was come to die.

Dahmer, Jeffrey Lionel

(1960–   )

Convicted murderer

A gruesome case of mass murder, perversion and cannibalism.

Jeffrey Dahmer was born in Milwaukee, Wisconsin and moved with his family to Bath Township in Ohio when he was eight years old. He spent much of his spare time in the woods near his house, catching small rodents and experimenting with ways of mutilating their bodies.

When Dahmer was 14 he began drinking heavily and developed a paranoia about rejection. Shortly after graduating from high school he murdered a young hitchhiker. He dismembered the body, crushed the bones and scattered them around the neighbouring gardens.

Downward spiral

A week after Dahmer's first murder his parents were divorced. He joined the US Army in January 1979 but less than two years later he was discharged for excessive drinking. When he returned home he went to live with his grandmother in West Allis, Wisconsin. In 1985 he found a job as a labourer at the Ambrosia Chocolate Company in Milwaukee. The following year he was arrested for urinating in public and put on probation for a year.

As soon as his probationary period ended Dahmer again succumbed to the urge to kill: between September 1987 and March 1988 he murdered three young men, dismembered them and dissolved their bodies in acid. He then moved out of his grandmother's house and rented an apartment at Oxford Apartments, Milwaukee.

When Dahmer was not at work he spent much of his time in the gay bars of Milwaukee. He was convicted of sexual assault on a 13-year-old boy in January 1989, but this did not deter him and the killings continued — by May 1991 eight young men had been lured to Oxford Apartments and murdered.

Fatal error

On 27 May 1991 14-year-old Konerak Sinthasomphone was found staggering naked and bleeding, along the street near Dahmer's apartment. When the police arrived, however, Dahmer claimed that the boy was his homosexual lover and, incredibly, the policemen believed him and left his apartment. It was a fatal mistake: Sinthasomphone was killed later that evening and another four murders followed during the next four months.

On 22 July 1991 another young man, Tracy Edwards, managed to escape from Dahmer's gruesome residence. This time there was no escape for the murderer. When the police arrived at the apartment they made a horific discovery — the remains of at least 11 people, including bodies stuffed into a barrel, heads squeezed into the fridge and skulls stacked in a filing cabinet. Dahmer soon admitted to acts of dismemberment, necrophilia and cannibalism.

At his trial in February 1992 Dahmer lodged a plea of guilty but insane to the charge of 15 murders. The insanity plea was rejected and Jeffrey Dahmer was sentenced to 15 life sentences, ensuring that he will never be eligible for parole.

Forgiveness plea
After his conviction Dahmer asked for forgiveness, telling he judge, 'I take all the blame for what I did'. He expressed a wish that Ohio had the death penalty so that he could be executed for the 'holocaust' he had created.

Dampier, William

(1652–1715)

Buccaneer

A short-tempered buccaneer who became a respected explorer and author.

William Dampier was born in Somerset and commanded his first vessel, a Weymouth trader, when he was only 16. After several excursions at sea he went to Jamaica in 1674 to be the assistant manager of a plantation. This proved to be too passive for him and in 1675 he sailed to Mexico where he spent several riotous months with the local logwood cutters. For two years Dampier alternated between being with these hard-living men, and buccaneering on the surrounding seas.

Successful expeditions

By 1679 Dampier had returned to Jamaica and a year later he joined a large buccaneering expedition that was planning to attack Panama City and then undertake a piratical cruise in the Pacific. As they were approaching Panama they were met by eight Spanish ships and in a battle that lasted several hours the buccaneers emerged victorious. They soon quarrelled, however, and Dampier and 50 other men broke away from the main party. For a year they continued their buccaneering escapades along the Mexican and Panama coasts.

In 1683 Dampier joined another large piratical expedition, this time passing around Cape Horn into the Pacific. As with the earlier adventure the buccaneers were successful initially but then quarrelled and split up. Dampier joined Captain Swan on his ship the *Cygnet* and they sailed towards the East Indies. They arrived at Guam just before the crew carried out their decision to kill and eat Swan and Dampier.

Deserted

Dampier and several of his men left Swan in the Philippines in 1686 and for the next year and a half they explored the seas from New Holland to China, making sure that it was a profitable experience for themselves. In May 1688 Dampier's quarrelsome temper got him into trouble with his crew and he was left deserted on Nicobar Island in the Indian Ocean. He managed to sail to Sumatra and subsequently decided to give up buccaneering.

Dampier returned to England in 1691 and seven years later he published *Voyage Round the World*. Significantly, he glorified his own buccaneering exploits and the book went on to be a bestseller. As a result he was commissioned to undertake a major voyage of discovery. He was given command of HMS *Roebuck* and did some valuable exploration work around Australia, New Guinea and the South Seas. His buccaneering instincts never fully left him though and after one voyage he was severely reprimanded for cruelty towards one of his crew.

After one of Dampier's final voyages a crew member wrote a scathing account of his conduct and he was never fully trusted again. William Dampier died in 1715, shortly before he was due to receive a large sum of money for a commercial voyage to the West Indies.

> **Final resort**
> 'It was well for Captain Swan that we got sight of land before our provision was spent. For I was afterwards informed the men had contrived first to kill Captain Swan and eat him when the victuals was gone, and after him all of us who were accessory in promoting this voyage'. Entry in Dampier's 1686 diary.

Deeming, Frederick Bayley

(c.1854–92)

Convicted murderer

Murderer, bigamist and con man, Deeming had a habit of cementing his victims underneath floors.

Little is known of Frederick Deeming's early life, except that he was born in Lancashire. In 1883 he left his wife and sailed to Australia. Although he worked as a gasfitter his real talent lay in fraud. He knew how to impress people with flamboyant gestures and after narrowly avoiding imprisonment in 1888 he moved to South Africa.

His wife and four children joined him and, pretending to be the manager of a diamond mine, he perpetrated a number of frauds on jewellers in Cape Town, Durban and Johannesburg. He also swindled a rich financier out of £2800 after selling him fictitious goldmines.

Plausible criminal

By this time the police were on Deeming's trail and he decided to return to England, settling briefly in Hull and Beverley in Yorkshire. During his stay he underwent a bigamous marriage and swindled a jeweller in Hull out of £285. The proceeds of this helped pay for a trip to South America but when he reached Montevideo he was arrested and sent back to England. On 16 October 1890 he was sentenced to nine months' imprisonment.

When Deeming, using the alias Williams, was released, he decided that his first wife and children were becoming too cumbersome. He rented a cottage at Rainhill, near Liverpool, and then invited his family to join him. In July 1981 he murdered them and then buried them under the kitchen floor and cemented it over. He then married for a third time and with his new bride he left for Australia again.

Antipodean murder

On their arrival in Melbourne the new Mrs Deeming became suspicious of her husband. She had good reason to worry because at Christmas 1891 she was murdered and cemented into the bedroom floor. Deeming, who made no profit from any of his murders, then moved to Sydney where he met his next potential victim, a Miss Katie Rousfell.

Eight weeks after Deeming moved to Sydney an agent visited his former house in Melbourne. He was concerned about a strange smell in the bedroom and when he investigated he discovered a female body. Using clues found in the house the police traced the killer's steps back to England and his cottage at Rainhill. After digging up the kitchen floor they found the bodies of Deeming's five earlier victims.

Frederick Deeming was arrested at Southern Cross on 11 March 1892 and sent for trial in Melbourne. He was defended by Alfred Deakin, a future Prime Minister of Australia. He entered a plea of insanity, throwing several fits to back up his claim. None of this held any sway with the jury and he was found guilty. He was executed in front of a crowd of 10 000 people on 23 May 1892.

> **Continued interest**
> After his death, part of Deeming's skeleton was used to try and show that he was more closely related to anthropoid apes than modern man. It was also claimed that he could have been Jack the Ripper. This was an impossibility however, since he was in prison at the time of the Ripper murders.

DeSalvo, Albert Henry

(1931–73)

Murderer and convicted rapist

The 'Boston Strangler' who turned to rape and murder to try and satisfy his insatiable sex-drive.

Albert DeSalvo was born in the Massachusetts town of Chelsea. His father was a violent man who beat his wife and six children. On one occasion Albert watched his father break his mother's fingers one by one. His parents were divorced in 1944 and DeSalvo was soon in trouble with the police for breaking and entering, a skill that he put to deadly effect in later years.

When he was 17 DeSalvo joined the army and served in Germany. He was a talented boxer and won the US Army middleweight boxing championship. While he was in Germany he also met and married Irmgard, a girl from Frankfurt. It was not a happy marriage and Irmgard was soon complaining about her husband's constant demands for sex — up to six times a day.

Measuring Man

DeSalvo was discharged from the Army in 1956 and settled in Boston. A year earlier he had been charged with the molestation of a nine-year-old girl but the case was not pursued. It was the first sign of his sex-drive that was later described by doctors as 'uncontrollable'. As his wife became more and more reluctant to fulfil his sexual needs DeSalvo began looking elsewhere. He persuaded women to let him into their flats, on the pretence that he was from a modelling agency. He would then take their measurements, molesting them in the process. Some of the women slept with him willingly, thinking he would be able to get them a model-ling contract, but others complained to the police. As these attacks spread the perpetrator became known as the 'Measuring Man'.

On 17 March 1960 DeSalvo was arrested after a burglary. When he was questioned he admitted to being the 'Measuring Man' but was only convicted of breaking and entering. He was sentenced to two years' imprisonment, but more importantly his case was filed under breaking and entering rather than as a sex crime.

Green Man

DeSalvo spent 11 months in prison and was released in 1961. He still had an urgent craving for sex and this time he adopted a more aggressive persona — the 'Green Man', so-called because of his bright green trousers. He used a similar method to that of the 'Measuring Man' but this time once he had gained access to a woman's apartment he tied her up and raped her. The police estimated that a minimum of 300 women were attacked in this way.

At the same time as the 'Green Man' attacks an even more sinister spate of crimes began occurring in Boston. The first took place on 14 June 1962 when a middle-aged seamstress was found strangled and raped. A cord had been tied in a gruesome knot under her chin and her legs had been left spreadeagled in an obscene pose.

Boston Strangler

Over the next 18 months there were another 12 murders committed in a similar fashion. The killer chose women's apartments apparently at random, gained entrance by posing as a workman, and then strangled and raped his victims, leaving them with a crude bow around their necks and their limbs arranged provocatively. On occasions he even left messages for the police.

As the 'Boston Strangler' murders increased the citizens of Boston organized their lives around taking precautions against this maniac killer. Despite this the killings continued. At one stage the police even called in a psychiatric team to try and create a profile of the killer.

In October 1964 a young woman was sexually assaulted in her apartment. After the attack the assailant apologized and left. From the description that the woman gave the police they were able to conclude that the 'Green Man' was the same person as the 'Measuring Man'. Albert DeSalvo was arrested and taken for questioning. He was charged with a variety of offences including engaging in unnatural acts, but because his original charge sheet classified him under the breaking and entering section, no one thought to link him to the Strangler murders.

Remarkable confession

After initial questioning DeSalvo was judged to be mentally ill and was taken to the Bridgewater Mental Institute in Massachusetts. It was here that he stunned the police and the psychiatrists alike by admitting to the 13 Strangler murders. At first the police were sceptical but the more that DeSalvo revealed about the killings the more convinced they became that he was telling the truth. His confession ran to over 50 hours of tape and 2000 pages of transcript. All the facts were checked and most of them were found to be correct.

Despite the fact that DeSalvo had confessed there was still a very delicate situation as far as his prosecution was concerned. He had to be examined to see if he was sane at the time of the crimes. If it was found that he was not then he would be committed to an institution. If it was found that he was sane then his lawyer was duty-bound to forbid him to repeat his confession in court. Without the confession there was no case, as the police had virtually no hard evidence.

No Strangler trial

After many days of negotiating a compromise was reached: DeSalvo would only stand trial for the Green Man offences and not those of the Strangler. Whatever the outcome everyone agreed that he would never again be a free man. His trial began on 30 June 1966. Almost a year later DeSalvo was sentenced to life imprisonment for a variety of sex offences and burglaries. He served his sentence at Walpole State Prison and in 1973 he was stabbed to death by a fellow inmate who was never identified.

Motive

DeSalvo's motive for his 13 murders has never been conclusively discovered, although the most popular theory is that he had a grudge against middle-class women. In one of his many interviews after his arrest he told a psychiatrist, 'I'm not educated but I was able to put something over on high-class people. I know they look down on people from my background, but I outsmarted them'.

Despard, Edward Marcus

(1751–1803)

Conspirator

An Irishman in the British army, who became embittered against the government and instigated a plot to overthrow it.

Edward Despard was born in Queen's County, Ireland and he followed five of his elder brothers into the army. He entered as an ensign and in 1772 he was promoted to lieutenant and sent with his regiment to Jamaica. He proved to be a talented engineer and in 1779 he distinguished himself on an expedition to San Juan.

Effective captain

In 1781 Despard was promoted to captain and given command of Rattan Island, where several English logwood-cutters were stationed. Despard proved to be an effective captain and in 1783 when the Spanish granted the peninsula of Yucatan to the logwood-cutters, he was given command of the new territory. Initially he was a success but after a couple of years the old settlers began to complain that Despard was favouring the logwood-cutters. They filed a number of complaints against him and although the charges where dismissed by the Secretary of State for the Colonies, Despard was ordered back to Britain in 1790.

Resentment

It was not until 1792 that the charges against Despard were finally thrown out and by this time he was beginning to develop a strong dislike of English authority. This was heightened when in 1798, after an intense campaign to obtain compensation, he was imprisoned for two years without any charge being brought against him.

Despard was released from prison in 1800 and by this time his dislike of the English had turned into a bitter hatred. He began using his considerable abilities to form a plot against the English government. He planned to persuade some of the soldiers of the guard to join his cause and then seize the Tower of London and the Bank of England, before assassinating the King on his way to the opening of Parliament. It was a ridiculous plan but Despard never had a chance to put it into action: he was surrounded by government spies and on 16 November 1802 he was arrested along with 40 Irish labourers and soldiers.

Treason

Despard and 12 of his fellow conspirators were tried on 7 and 9 February 1803 in London. The evidence of numerous informers was overwhelming against the erstwhile army captain and he was found guilty of high treason and sentenced to death. Before his execution he refused to attend chapel or receive the sacrament and on 21 February 1803 he was drawn on a hurdle to the county jail at Newington. After a long speech on the scaffold he was hanged and then beheaded. His remains were given to his widow and then buried in St Paul's churchyard.

Nelson's testimony
During Despard's trial Lord Nelson was called to give him a character reference. 'We served together in 1779 on the Spanish main; we were together in the enemies' trenches and slept in the same tent. Colonel Despard was then a loyal man and a brave soldier'. Unfortunately for Despard, this did little to help him.

Dillinger, John Herbert

(1903–34)

Gangster

One of a new breed of gangsters in the 1930s and labelled 'Public Enemy Number One'.

John Dillinger was born in Indianapolis and, following the death of his mother when he was four, he was brought up by his father. It was a stern education as John Dillinger senior was a strict disciplinarian who beat his son frequently. In 1920 the Dillingers moved to the country town of Mooresville. The 17-year-old John hated the tranquillity of the country and craved action. In 1923 he tried to find it in the Navy but he deserted from the USS *Utah* after only a few months. In April 1924 he married Beryl Hovis but it was a short-lived union.

Although Dillinger could be a charming and entertaining companion his criminal instincts were never far from the surface. While playing for a baseball team, run by an ex-convict, he was persuaded to take part in the robbery of a Mooresville grocer. It was a badly planned and poorly executed affair, and Dillinger was arrested. He was persuaded to plead guilty in the hope of receiving a light sentence. He was horrified when he was subsequently given a 10 to 20-year sentence.

Criminal education

Dillinger served his sentence in the Indiana State Prison at Michigan City; far from reforming him it only served to turn him into a hardened and embittered criminal. He was a fast learner and questioned his fellow convicts constantly. When he was released in 1933 he formed his own gang, picking a number of highly intelligent criminals whom he had met in prison; a series of spectacular bank robberies began.

Unlike Al Capone, and other gangsters of this type who rarely took an active part in robberies themselves, Dillinger adopted a 'hands-on' approach to his activities. The increased availability of the motor car was a godsend for him; his favoured approach was to rob a bank and then drive across the state border so he woud be free from prosecution if he were caught.

Modern Jesse James

The Dillinger Gang performed their first bank robbery on 17 July 1933, at Daleville. In the following four months they repeated the operation at five banks, in Ohio and Indiana, and their escapades were soon receiving widespread attention. Dillinger was portrayed as a daring, athletic, well-dressed gangster and, rather than be horrified at this, the public viewed him as a dashing hero. The authorities were not so impressed, the FBI was strengthened, and a special 40-man 'Dillinger Squad' was formed by the Chicago police.

In September 1933 Dillinger was caught during another bank robbery, and imprisoned at Lima, Ohio. However, it proved difficult to keep him in prison and he was released by three of his gang members posing as prison officials. A further spate of bank robberies in Tucson, Florida and Indiana were undertaken and although Dillinger rarely used his gun gratuitously, a policeman was killed during a raid on a bank in East Chicago.

Hero and villain

By the end of 1933 Dillinger was a national figure and J Edgar Hoover, the director of the FBI, labelled him 'Public Enemy Number One'. Shortly after this he was captured in Tucson, Arizona, and extradited to Indiana where he was imprisoned in the Crown Point prison. Determined to

80

make his stay a short one, on 3 March 1934, using a home-made wooden gun coloured with black shoe polish, he forced the guards to free him from his cell. He then took a deputy sheriff and a mechanic hostage and escaped in a stolen car. When he later released his hostages he shook hands with them as they left.

This latest escape only served to increase Dillinger's popularity and he took advantage of it by forming a new gang. This time his accomplices were more concerned with violence than with cunning. They included the volatile and savage 'Baby Face' Nelson and the temperamental Homer Van Meter, one of Dillinger's closest advisers. The new gang continued where the old one had left off and the banks in the vicinity were under the constant threat of attack.

As Dillinger's status grew, the authorities became more and more anxious to capture him. On one occasion the FBI thought they had cornered him at a lodge in Northern Wisconsin. However, they fired at the wrong car, killing an innocent man, and Dillinger again escaped. One of his gang members was killed during the shoot-out.

Effective reward

Having had a narrow escape Dillinger decided to try and change his appearance. He had crude plastic surgery on his face and tried to burn off his fingerprints with acid, but neither action had much effect. There was now a $10 000 reward on his head and the FBI, the Dillinger Squad and the Indiana State police were all moving in.

It was the reward that proved to be Dillinger's downfall. The temptation was too great for a brothel madame friend of his named Anna Sage. On 22 July 1934 she arranged to go with him to the Biograph Cinema, in Chicago. The FBI had been informed by Anna and as the couple left the cinema Dillinger was approached by a number of agents. He made a move to draw his gun but was heavily outnumbered and died in a volley of bullets. Members of his gang claimed later that it was not Dillinger who died but rather a double who had been put in his place. There is no evidence to support this though.

The death of John Dillinger was not only

John Dillinger

the end of an era in American gangster history, it also signified the emergence of the FBI as a major investigative force. Before they killed 'Public Enemy Number One' they had been treated with a certain amount of contempt by county police and the general public.

Termination of a gang
Several members of the Dillinger Gang died shortly after their leader. Two of them, Harry Pierpont and Charles Makely, tried to escape from Ohio State Prison, in 1935, using guns carved from soap. Makely was shot dead but Pierpont was recaptured and sent to the electric chair a few weeks later. Homer Van Meter was shot during a gun battle with police, as was 'Baby Face' Nelson when he confronted a number of FBI men.

Dodd, William

(1729–77)

Financial forger

A popular and literary-minded preacher who resorted to forgery to help pay his debts.

William Dodd was born at Bourne, Lincolnshire, the son of a vicar. At university at Cambridge he showed an aptitude for mathematics but it was literature that really interested him. After graduating he went to London and wrote humorous plays and poems. In 1751 he married Mary Perkins, the daughter of a verger, and shortly afterwards his friends persuaded him to give up his literary career and join the church instead.

Prolific preacher

On 19 October 1751 Dodd was ordained deacon and became curate at West Ham, Essex. He soon proved to be an immensely popular preacher. All walks of society, including royalty, came to hear his sermons and he was particularly effective in raising money for charities.

Dodd still maintained his literary output and he wrote several edifying books and also became chief writer of the *Christian Magazine*. In 1763 his talents were recognized when he was made king's chaplain. He was also appointed as tutor to Philip Stanhope, Lord Chesterfield's nephew.

Despite his apparently exemplary lifestyle Dodd had an outgoing personality that attracted him to a variety of society activities in London. He had a weakness for dinner parties and flirting with high-society ladies. He frittered away his wife's legacy and he was struck off the list of chaplains in 1774 when his wife tried to buy into a profitable church post.

Forged banknote

After a brief period abroad, where he was well received by his former pupil, who was now Lord Chesterfield, Dodd and his wife returned to London. Their financial situation had not improved and so, in an attempt to maintain his affluent lifestyle, Dodd turned to forgery. He employed a stockbroker named Robertson to dispose of a bond worth £4200, signed by Lord Chesterfield. Robertson was successful in obtaining the money but a solicitor became suspicious of the bond and checked with Chesterfield, who denied any knowledge of the bond; it soon became clear that Dodd had forged the signature.

After he had been discovered Dodd paid back £3000 and promised security for the remainder. This was satisfactory for the parties involved but the mayor insisted that Dodd be brought to justice. He was tried on 22 February 1777 and found guilty. Forgery was still a capital offence at this time and the former chaplain was sentenced to death.

The public were horrified at Dodd's sentence and thousands of people signed petitions (one had over 23 000 signatures) calling for a reprieve. A number of influential figures also campaigned on Dodd's behalf but it was all to no avail. The king rejected a reprieve on the grounds that other forgers had already been put to death. On 27 June 1777 William Dodd joined their number when he was hanged at Tyburn in front of a huge crowd.

Plea

Before he was sentenced Dodd addressed the court, 'I am desirous to recompense the injury I have done to the clergy, to the world and to religion ... For these reasons, amidst shame and misery, I yet wish to live'.

Dominici, Gaston

(1877–1965)

Convicted murderer

The murder of an English family in Provence, which resulted in a trial consisting of lies, accusations and counter-accusations.

In August 1952 a distinguished biochemist, Sir Jack Drummond, his wife, Lady Drummond, and their 11-year-old daughter, Elizabeth, were driving through Provence on a camping holiday. On 4 August they had reached the vicinity of the village of Lurs and they pitched their tent near a river bank. The nearest property, Grand'Terre, a farmhouse owned by the 75-year-old Gaston Dominici, was 150 yards away. In the morning the bodies of the three Drummonds were found by one of Dominici's sons, Gustave. Sir Jack and Lady Drummond had been shot and Elizabeth had been beaten to death.

Family suspected

Commissionaire Edward Sebeille from Marseilles was assigned to the Drummond case and he immediately suspected that the Dominicis knew more about the murders than they admitted. He made little progress at first, except for the discovery of the murder weapon. Later, after exhaustive questioning, Gustave Dominici eventually admitted that Elizabeth Drummond had still been alive when he found the two other bodies. He was imprisoned for two months for failing to give aid to a person in danger of dying.

After Gustave's admission Sebeille became convinced that the solution to the case lay within Grand'Terre. For the next year he frequently visited the Dominici farmhouse, sometimes unannounced, and

questioned Gaston, Gustave, and an elder brother Clovis. All of them were moody and uncommunicative and they revealed no useful information.

On 13 November 1953 Sebeille made progress. After another bout of intense questioning Gustave confessed that his father had murdered the Drummonds. Clovis backed him up and Gaston himself confessed a few days later. He said that he had been watching Lady Drummond undressing and tried to approach her. Sir Jack had intervened and a struggle followed, during which Gaston had shot the biochemist. In a panic he then shot Lady Drummond and beat Elizabeth with the butt of his rifle.

Suicide attempt

After Dominici had confessed he took part in a reconstruction of the crime, and tried to commit suicide during the course of it by jumping off a railway bridge. During his trial in November 1953 at Digne Assize Court he made several confessions, retractions and accusations. Gustave also withdrew his accusation against his father and claimed that Clovis suspected their neighbour.

Despite the great confusion surrounding the evidence the jury found Gaston Dominici guilty and he was sentenced to death. Because of his age this was commuted to life imprisonment. He was released in 1960 and died five years later. There is still doubt that he was solely responsible for the death of the Drummond family.

Family feud
Understandably, Gaston Dominici was not particularly impressed by his sons' behaviour in turning him in. He cursed them freely as he was giving his confession and as he left the court he exclaimed, 'My sons — what swine!'.

Dougal, Samuel Herbert

(1846–1903)

Convicted murderer

A rogue and womanizer who murdered a spinster for profit and then buried her body in a moat of clay.

Samuel Dougal was born in the East End of London and grew up ill-educated, but totally irresistible to women. As a result of his womanizing he became heavily in debt and as an escape he joined the Royal Engineers in 1866. He served with them until 1887, during which time he visited Ireland, Wales and Canada, and married twice. Both of his wives died from alleged oyster poisoning and Dougal profited handsomely in each case.

After being discharged Dougal married for the third time, in 1892, only to desert his wife two years later. In 1896 he lost his service pension when he was convicted of forging cheques. He was sentenced to 12 months' hard labour. On his release he found himself short of funds, a situation which he found intolerable. He found a post as a clerical assistant but this was too tedious for him and he returned to London in 1898. It was here, while staying at a boarding house in Bayswater, that he met his saviour in the form of Miss Camille Cecile Holland, a 55-year-old spinster who had a substantial inheritance of over £7000.

Calculating charm

Dougal wasted no time in seducing Miss Holland and soon persuaded her to buy an old farmhouse near Saffron Walden, Essex, where they could live. Dougal christened the property Moat House Farm and he and Miss Holland moved in, ostensibly as husband and wife, at the beginning of 1899.

Two days after their arrival at Moat House Farm Miss Holland caught Dougal trying to seduce one of the servants. She was horrified and ordered him out of the house. He ignored her and the maid became suspicious when Miss Holland disappeared a few days later. She herself left shortly afterwards, expressing an intense dislike for Dougal.

Extended holiday

Dougal explained the disappearance of his 'wife' by saying that she had gone on a yachting expedition. The villagers noticed that this did not upset him unduly and they were shocked when he started entertaining a string of young ladies at his farm.

In January 1903 the police tired of Dougal's story of a yachting expedition. They investigated his recent financial transactions and discovered a cheque signed by Miss Holland. Realizing the game was up, Dougal tried to escape but he was caught after trying to pass suspicious banknotes. He was initially charged with forgery and then the police tried to find the hapless Miss Holland. For five weeks they searched Moat House Farm, concentrating on the surrounding moat that was filled with viscous clay.

On 27 April 1903 the police found the decomposed body of Miss Holland in the clay-filled moat. Dougal was charged with her murder and convicted on 23 June 1903. He was hanged at Chelmsford prison on 14 July 1903, confessing to his guilt while on the scaffold.

> **Provocative lessons**
> During Miss Holland's absence Dougal caused uproar with his behaviour. This included having simultaneous affairs with a mother and her three daughters and giving bicycle-riding lessons to naked women.

Dover, Thomas

(c.1660–1742)

Adventurer

An adventurer and privateer who discovered the real-life Robinson Crusoe.

Thomas Dover was born at Barton-on-the-Heath, Warwickshire around 1600 and baptized on 6 May 1662. He attended Magdalen Hall, at Oxford University, where he graduated with a BA in 1684. Shortly after this he suffered from a serious dose of smallpox but recovered sufficiently to return to Oxford to take his MB (Bachelor of Medicine).

By 1687 Dover had qualified as a doctor and begun to practise in Bristol. In August 1708 he was persuaded to join a group of adventurers in a voyage around the world. Two ships were involved, the *Duke* and the *Duchess*; Dover was second in command overall and captain of the *Duke*. Despite his medical experience he had no official medical post.

Original Robinson Crusoe

The most notable event of the voyage occurred on 2 February 1709. The privateers had reached the island of Juan Fernandez off the coast of South America, in the Pacific Ocean. When Dover went ashore he discovered Alexander Selkirk, a shipwrecked Scottish sailor who had survived alone on the island for four years and four months. Dover took him onto the *Duke* and eventually returned him to England. When Daniel Defoe heard this story he used it as the basis for *Robinson Crusoe*.

In April 1709 Dover and his fellow privateers reached the Peruvian city of Guaaquil. They wasted no time in plundering its treasures and showed the villagers little mercy.

They slept in the church so they could keep an eye on their spoils. It was an unpleasant experience for them because they were kept awake by the smell of recently buried bodies, that had been the victims of an epidemic of plague which proved to be contagious; when the privateers returned to their ships 180 men were struck down over the next two days.

Spanish prize

Calling on his medical training Dover ordered the ships' surgeons to bleed the men in both arms and, remarkably, only eight of them died. The rest recovered to such an extent that in December 1709 a valuable prize in the form of a Spanish ship of 21 guns was captured. Dover took command and sailed it to England via the Cape of Good Hope.

When he arrived home Dover had not only satisfied his desire for adventure but had also accumulated a small fortune and was in effect a millionaire. His success was to be one of the cornerstones on which the fraudulent South Sea Bubble was based 10 years later. His privateering escapade did not interfere with his professional advancement; in 1721 he was admitted to the College of Physicians and he maintained a highly successful practice in London until his death in 1742.

Strong medicine
When Dover was suffering from smallpox his friend suggested an original cure: 'I had no fire allowed in my room, my windows were constantly open, my bedclothes were ordered to be laid no higher than my waist. He made me take 12 bottles of small beer, acidulated with spirit of vitriol, every 24 hours'.

Dreyfus, Alfred

(1859–1935)

Alleged traitor

An attempt to punish an act of treason that led to a shameful episode in French justice.

Alfred Dreyfus was born at Mulhouse in Alsace. His family were well off and Jewish — a fact that was to have a profound effect on his life. When Alsace and Lorraine became German territory after the Franco–Prussian War in 1870, the Dreyfus family emigrated to France where Alfred joined the army. He was a successful soldier and advanced quickly through the ranks. In 1889 he married and four years later he joined the General Staff as a Captain.

Act of treason

Dreyfus's arrival at the General Staff coincided with the discovery that an alarming number of secrets were being passed to the Germans and the Italians. The authorities were extremely concerned and even went to the trouble of employing people to rake through the wastepaper baskets at the German and Italian Embassies in Paris. On 26 September 1894 the ploy paid off: a charlady found a *bordereau*, or memorandum, in a wastepaper basket in the German Embassy. It contained five pieces of military information that the writer was offering to sell to the Germans.

Although the *bordereau* was unsigned the French authorities were determined to find a culprit, and find one fast. They quickly settled on Captain Dreyfus. The evidence against him was flimsy to say the least — the secrets on offer concerned artillery and Dreyfus was an artillery officer. A greater factor against him was that he was Jewish, since various factions of the military were strongly anti-semitic.

Farcical trial

The court-martial of Captain Dreyfus took place in December 1894 and it was a complete farce. When one handwriting expert claimed that Dreyfus had not written the *bordereau*, another one was found who was persuaded to say that he had. One witness stated that an unnamed source who was 'an honourable person' had told him that Dreyfus was a traitor, and Major Henry, deputy chief of counter-espionage, presented a wealth of damning evidence that was in fact forged. One of the most incredulous pieces of evidence was from a witness who swore on oath that, 'the Jew went pale' when accused of treason.

On 22 December 1894 the French Army found its scapegoat and Dreyfus was found guilty. On 17 January 1895 he was sent to Devil's Island, in the French penal colony of Cayenne, French Guiana.

Culprit still at large

Although Dreyfus was out of the country the leaks still continued. In July 1895 Colonel Georges Picquart was appointed head of counter-espionage and he soon intercepted a secret document that was heading for the German Embassy. It had been sent by an officer named Walsin Esterhazy and when Picquart examined his handwriting he noticed that it was almost identical to that on the *bordereau*. When he told his superiors they were dismissive, 'What has it got to do with you if a Jew is on Devil's Island?', and he was transferred to North Africa. Esterhazy was later tried at a court-martial but it was only a token gesture and he was acquitted.

J'accuse

Dreyfus's family campaigned ceaselessly for a retrial and then, in 1898, the writer Emile Zola published a letter entitled *'J'accuse'*, in the newspaper *l'Aurore*, which accused the authorities of a massive cover-up over the Dreyfus case and lambasted some of the country's highest officials. For his trouble Zola was charged with criminal libel and sentenced to a year's imprisonment. He appealed twice and was eventually forced to flee the country.

Following the publication of Zola's letter France tottered on the brink of civil war as various factions became pro- or anti-Dreyfus. Those in favour of the man on Devil's Island were the republicans, the anti-clericals, the Protestants and the Jews. Those against him included the army, the monarchists, the Catholics and the anti-Semites. The bitterness split families and ended life-long friendships.

Forgeries discovered

In August 1898 the War Office decided that Picquart was becoming too troublesome and initiated his prosecution. This meant a close scrutiny of all his papers and it soon became clear that his assistant, Major Henry, had forged nearly all the original evidence against Captain Dreyfus. Henry was arrested and after confessing to the forgeries he committed suicide by cutting his throat. Esterhazy realized that he would be found out and so fled to England where he lived until his death in 1934.

Although it was now painfully clear that Dreyfus had been convicted of a crime he did not commit, the authorities dragged their feet in their efforts to confirm his innocence. It was not until September 1899 that Dreyfus was brought back to France for a retrial. It took place at Rennes and the verdict caused astonishment around the world. Dreyfus was found guilty on a majority verdict, but with 'extenuating circumstances'. The President of France obviously thought that there could not be extenuating circumstances for treason and instead he issued a pardon for Dreyfus.

Innocence proved

Despite his pardon Dreyfus was not totally satisfied. He went on campaigning to prove his complete innocence and achieved this in 1906 when the Rennes verdict was quashed. He was restored to the Army with the rank of major and fought with distinction in World War I. He eventually rose to the rank of lieutenant-colonel and the commander of the Legion of Honour.

Spymaster knew the truth
1917 saw the death of Major-General Max von Schwartzkoppen who had been the spymaster at the German Embassy in Paris. Esterhazy had given him 162 secret documents and before he died he was heard to say, 'Frenchmen, listen to me! Dreyfus is innocent. Everything was intrigue and falsification! Dreyfus, I tell you, is innocent!'

Humiliation
Following Dreyfus's court-martial he was subjected to ritual degradation. He was taken to the parade ground of the Military Academy, surrounded by troops, had his officer's insignia ripped off and his sword broken in two and thrown to the ground. He was then marched around the square to confront the jeering soldiers. Throughout this ordeal he kept shouting, 'I am innocent'.

Family against family
The writer Marcel Proust was a firm supporter of Dreyfus's case while he was on Devil's Island. His father, however, who was a personal friend of several government ministers, was firmly anti-Dreyfus, and when Proust started organizing a petition on the Captain's behalf he refused to speak to his son for a week.

Duval, Claude

(1643–70)

Highwayman

A highwayman who is remembered for his charm and good looks, but in reality he was far from chivalrous.

Claude Duval was something of a rarity in the 17th century — a French highwayman operating in England. He was born in Normandy in 1643 and when he was 14 he moved to Paris where he was employed in the service of the Duke of Richmond. He moved to England with Richmond at the Restoration and, due to the increased wealth in the country, he soon took to the profitable business of highway robbery.

Ladies' man

Duval quickly became notorious throughout England, not only for his daring feats of robbery but also for his amazing success with ladies of high fashion. His extreme good looks, insolent charm and overpowering sensuality ensured that 'maids, widows and wives, the rich, the poor, and the vulgar' fell for this swashbuckling character.

Due partly to his amorous adventures Duval gained a reputation for being a chivalrous and well-mannered robber. One of the most common stories told about him concerns an incident when he held up a coach in which a lady and gentleman were travelling with £400 in cash. As Duval approached, the lady began playing a tune on a flageolet. Never one to miss an opportunity, the highwayman invited the lady to dance a coranto with him on the heath. When they finished, Duval demanded payment for the dance but only took £100.

Glorified image

A more realistic assessment of Duval's character can be seen from an incident reported in the *Newgate Calendar*. On one occasion he held up a coach on Blackheath and after he relieved the ladies of their money he saw a baby feeding from a bottle. Since it was made of silver he took it from the child and only returned it when one of his companions reminded him of his reputation for gallantry.

By 1669 Duval had a high price on his head and he chose to return briefly to France. He would have been well advised to stay there because shortly after he returned to England he was arrested at the Hole-in-the-Wall tavern in London. He might have escaped his captors if he had not been hopelessly drunk.

Duval was sentenced to death on six charges of highway robbery. While he was awaiting execution he was visited by dozens of respectable ladies who petitioned the King for a pardon. They were not successful and on 21 January 1670 Duval was hanged at Tyburn. His body was laid in state outside St Giles and such a crowd came to see it that a judge's order had to be passed to stop the demonstration.

One of the reasons for Duval's favourable reputation was a biography written by William Pope shortly after his death. Pope intended to show his exploits in an ironic light but in subsequent histories this was missed and so the legend of a chivalrous highwayman grew.

> **Duval's Epitaph**
> Here lies Du Vall: Reader if male thou art
> Look to thy purse; if female to thy Heart ...
> Old Tyburn's glory, England's illustrious thief
> Du Vall, the ladies joy, Du Vall the ladies' grief.

Ellis case

(1955)

Ruth Ellis

The last woman to be hanged in Britain, for the murder of her racing-driver lover.

Ruth Ellis

Ruth Neilson was born into a lower middle class background in the Welsh town of Rhyl in 1926. Her family moved to Basingstoke in 1933 and at an early age Ruth determined that she was not going to remain poor.

Ruth worked in London as a photographic model and then became a hostess at the Court Club in Mayfair. It was a glamorous existence and she was soon earning a good wage from her duties at the club and also from working as a call-girl.

Jealous wife

In November 1950 Ruth married George Ellis. The marriage proved to be a disaster; Ellis was an alcoholic and Ruth an obsessively jealous wife. The couple parted after a year and Ruth went back to hostessing. In 1953 she was installed as the manageress of the Little Club, Knightsbridge.

While Ruth was running the club she met David Blakely, a racing-driver whose easy lifestyle matched her own. The couple started an on-off affair and when Ruth became pregnant Blakely offered to marry her. She turned him down.

A fast life

In the summer of 1954 Blakely went to race at Le Mans. During his absence Ruth missed him and she decided that she would accept his proposal. However, once Blakely returned from the continent he told her he no longer wanted to get married. Although the couple lived together their relationship deteriorated into a catalogue of endless drinking sessions, bitter fights and mad drives around London to check on each other's whereabouts.

On Easter Sunday Ellis discovered that Blakely had spent the weekend with some friends instead of with her. Drunk and seething with jealousy she followed Blakely to the Magdala pub in Hamstead carrying a Smith and Wesson revolver; when Blakely emerged from the pub she fired indiscriminately at him. He died a few minutes later.

Ruth Ellis was tried at the Old Bailey and on 21 June 1955 she was found guilty of murder. Despite a vigorous campaign to obtain a reprieve she was hanged on 13 July 1955, the last woman to suffer this fate in Britain.

> **Low self-esteem**
> At the age of 13 Ruth Ellis described herself as, 'as plain as hell'. She later remedied this by dying her hair peroxide blonde, always appearing heavily made-up, and spending lavishly on glamorous clothes.

Fahmy case

(1923)

Marguerite Laurent Fahmy

A sensational trial following the shooting of an Egyptian playboy prince.

Prince Ali Kamel Fahmy Bey held the nominal post of attaché at the French Legation in Cairo. He was a vain, vicious young man who was accustomed to getting his own way in everything he did. In the summer of 1922 he met Marguerite Laurent, a Parisian divorcee of great beauty, and in December 1922 the couple were married.

East meets West

The Fahmys moved from Paris to Cairo in 1923 but the marriage was a failure from the beginning. Fahmy had an evil streak and he forced his wife to perform several abnormal sexual deeds, which she despised. For her part Marguerite never came to terms with her husband's behaviour and although she became a Moslem she was unable to understand the Oriental way of thinking.

In July 1923 the couple arrived in London and booked into the Savoy Hotel. On 9 July Fahmy and his wife had a violent argument in the hotel restaurant. Later, when the band leader asked Marguerite if she would like a tune played she replied, 'I don't want any music — my husband has threatened to kill me tonight'.

Fatal struggle

At 2am that night a porter saw Prince Fahmy and his wife emerge briefly into the corridor. Seconds later he heard three shots from their room. When he went to investigate he found Fahmy lying on the floor, suffering from gunshot wounds to the head. He was taken to hospital but died shortly afterwards.

The trial of Marguerite Fahmy, charged with wilful murder, began on 10 September 1923. She was defended by Sir Edward Marshall Hall, the most sought-after defence lawyer in the country. He established that Fahmy had treated his wife with cruelty, both physically and psychologically.

Brilliant defence

The heart of the defence was that Mrs Fahmy had accidentally shot her husband after he had attempted to strangle her. Marshall Hall put Mrs Fahmy in the witness-box and showed her to be a fragile creature who knew nothing about the workings of the weapon that killed her husband. In a highly theatrical and effective display Marshall Hall described the last moments of Fahmy's life, acting out the words as he spoke them: 'As he crouched ... like an animal she turned the pistol and put it to his face, and to her horror the thing went off'. As he finished the advocate pointed the pistol at the jury and then dropped it to the floor with a clatter.

Marshall Hall's display was so impressive that the jury took less than an hour to find Marguerite Fahmy not guilty of murder or manslaughter. The verdict was met with cheering in court and Madame Fahmy went on to pursue a career in films.

Edward Marshall Hall
After the trial Marshall Hall became a celebrity and received letters of congratulation from around the world. One of these was addressed 'Marshall Hall, the Greatest Lawyer on Earth'. It reached him safely.

Fauntleroy, Henry

(1785–1824)

Financial forger

A respected banker who raised forgery to an art form and embezzled thousands of pounds.

Henry Fauntleroy's father was one of the founders of Marsh, Sibbald and Company, a private bank in London, . In 1800, when he was 15, the young Fauntleroy began work at the bank as a clerk. When his father died, in 1807, he was made a partner immediately. He had a natural aptitude for this type of work and it was not long before he was managing most of the bank's affairs himself. He worked tirelessly and impressed everyone at the bank.

Secret life

When Fauntleroy was not at work he entertained himself with a variety of mistresses. He married in 1809 but his wife soon left him and he was free to entertain his lovers at his various homes. He spent lavishly on these women, and it subsequently came to light that it was not always his own money that he used.

In 1815 Fauntleroy lent a substantial amount of the bank's money to a speculative builder. Unfortunately the venture failed and the money was lost. Fearing that if this became known the bank would have to close, Fauntleroy set about trying to repair the damage by forging documents which authorized clients' stock to be transferred into Marsh, Sibbald and Company's account.

Following the success of his first forgery Fauntleroy then began using the system for his own personal gain. His standard fraud was to sell stocks by forging signatures of clerks and bank officials on transfer documents and then pocket the money himself. He kept a note of all these transactions and paid the stockholders the correct dividends so they did not become suspicious. In total he made £170 000 in this way.

Deception uncovered

In 1824 a colonel died, leaving £46 000 invested in three per cent annuities for his family. When the executors of the will tried to locate the money they could only find £6000 — the rest had been sold off and embezzled by Fauntleroy. Following this his entire web of forgery and deceit was revealed.

Fauntleroy was arrested on 10 September 1824 and, after trying to bribe the police, his trial began at the Old Bailey on 30 October. Despite a claim that he was trying to help save the bank he was found guilty and sentenced to death. His case was not helped by widespread newspaper reports concerning his string of mistresses.

The public were horrified at the thought of Fauntleroy being put to death and strenuous efforts were made to gain a commutation of the sentence. One man, an Italian named Edward Angelini, even offered to take Fauntleroy's place on the scaffold. All these efforts were in vain, however, and Henry Fauntleroy was hanged on Ludgate Hill on 30 November 1824, in front of a crowd of 100 000 people.

Popular myth
One of the stories circulated about Fauntleroy after his death was that he cheated the hangman's noose by inserting a silver pipe in his windpipe. The myth went on to claim that he then fled to Europe where he lived to an old age.

Fenwick, Sir John

(c.1645–97)

Conspirator

A Jesuit conspirator who took part in an unsuccessful plot to assassinate William III.

John Fenwick was born in Northumberland and he served in the army as a colonel of foot, colonel of the 3rd guards and major general. Following his father's death in 1677 he became the Tory Member of Parliament for Northumberland, being returned for the last time in 1685.

From an early age Fenwick was a devoted supporter of James II and when in 1688 William of Orange was persuaded by the opponents of James to overthrow him, Fenwick began a long campaign against the new king. In 1689 he went to the north of England to try and galvanize the king's opponents but he only succeeded in getting himself arrested. He was committed to the Tower on 13 May 1689 but released six months later.

Overthrow hopes

During 1691 William received a number of military reverses on the continent and this gave Fenwick and his supporters hope that they might be able to topple him. Fenwick became openly arrogant and took to swaggering around Hyde Park in London — one of the paths that he took was soon known as Jacobite walk. His self-confidence even extended to being impertinent to Queen Mary II in public.

In 1695 Fenwick decided that direct action was required against William and with two fellow conspirators, Sir George Barclay and Robert Charnock, he hatched a plot to assassinate the king. Due partly to Fenwick's vain and over-optimistic manner the plot was a hopeless failure and Barclay and Charnock were captured.

Double-cross

Fenwick managed to escape and went into hiding. He followed the trial of the other conspirators closely and saw that there were only two witnesses. Hoping to escape he went to the witnesses, offering to bribe them if they would leave the country. They took the money, but then reported Fenwick to the authorities. He was arrested on 13 June 1696.

Fenwick knew that his only hope was a free pardon; in exchange for this, he offered a comprehensive statement about the Jacobite conspiracies. King William declined to grant a pardon until he saw the confession. This proved to be a sensible move because Fenwick's statement only implicated his political enemies and mentioned nothing about his own involvement with the Jacobites. The Whigs were furious and brought in a bill of attainder against Fenwick. Despite the fact that the chief witnesses had disappeared the House of Commons passed the bill by 189 votes to 156 and the Lords passed it by 68 to 61.

Convicted of high treason, John Fenwick was beheaded on Tower Hill on 28 January 1697.

> **Trial doubts**
> Fenwick's trial was unsatisfactory, not least because there should have been two witnesses for a treason trial. Afterwards the Bishop of Bristol remarked, 'The course of his life has been such that he has few friends; but the method of punishing him being out of the common road, and such as has not been often used, and, when it has, been condemned by those who have judged coolly, is what some are startled at'.

Ferguson, Robert

(c.1637–1714)

Conspirator

Nicknamed the 'Plotter' he took part in several conspiracies, and frequently swapped sides.

Robert Ferguson was born near Alford, in Aberdeenshire. It is likely that he was educated at Aberdeen University and he left Scotland about 1650. He went to Godmersham, in Kent, where he made his living at the local vicarage. In 1662 he was expelled and in January 1663 he was imprisoned for raising money for ejected ministers. He was released on a bond for good behaviour and took up writing religious and political literature.

On 15 May 1680 Ferguson published a pamphlet referring to allegations that Charles II had married his mistress Lucy Walters, the mother of the conspirator the Duke of Monmouth. Ferguson contended that this was a fabrication intended to discredit Monmouth and divert attention from the activities of the Duke of York, who had recently converted to Catholicism.

Rye House Plotter

In 1682–3 Ferguson was instrumental in arranging the Rye House Plot, which was designed to kill Charles II and the Duke of York and put Monmouth on the throne in their place. As it transpired the plot misfired because the conspirators got their timing wrong. Ferguson claimed this was deliberate because he favoured a rebellion rather than an assassination. In the event neither occurred.

After the failure of the Rye House Plot Ferguson fled to Holland but returned a few months later to engage in more conspiracies on Monmouth's behalf. He became his legal advisor but was suspected of treason and on 4 June 1683 a sentence of outlawry was passed against him for his part in the assassination plot. Thanks to his devious nature he succeeded in avoiding capture, and in 1685 he accompanied Monmouth to the West Country in his attempt to seize the throne. When it became clear that the attempt was doomed Ferguson did not wait around to the bitter end, but instead fled to Holland again.

Jacobite convert

Always willing to change sides, Ferguson now offered his dubious services to William of Orange. He wrote some pamphlets on his behalf but when the Prince made an expedition to England he felt that he was not given the position of authority that he deserved. When William was invited by the Whig to accept the throne in 1688, Ferguson turned his back on him and became a passionate supporter of the Jacobite cause. He used his conspiratorial talents on behalf of the deposed James II in an attempt to return him to power. As with his other intrigues he was unsuccessful.

In 1692 Ferguson was arrested for aiding the Jacobites and during the next 10 years his name was linked with numerous plots. In 1704 he was arrested for treason but his case never came to trial. He subsequently faded into relative obscurity and died in 1714 after several years of terrible poverty.

> **Unflattering description**
> A 1683 proclamation describes Ferguson as, 'A tall lean man, a great Roman nose, thin jawed, heat in his face, speaks in the Scotch tone, stoops a little in the shoulders; he hath a shuffling gait that differs from most men, and he wears his periwig down almost over his eyes'.

Ferrers, Laurence Shirley, 4th Earl

(1720–60)

Convicted murderer

An eccentric earl who was the last nobleman to die a felon's death in England.

The Ferrers family were descended from the Plantagenets and Laurence Shirley was born in 1720. He matriculated at Oxford University in 1737 but he preferred socializing to studying and left without taking a degree. In 1745, on the death of his uncle, he became the 4th Earl Ferrers. He had some difficulty in coming to terms with his station in life and tended to drink heavily to avoid his responsibilities.

A wayward earl

Ferrers married in 1752 but he behaved so badly towards his wife that in 1758 she applied to parliament for redress and was granted a separate maintenance, to be raised out of her husband's estates. At this time the Ferrers estates were vested in a trustee, John Johnson, who was the Earl's steward. Ferrers was furious at this and tried, unsuccessfully, to evict Johnson from his farm on the estate.

Ferrers was prone to bouts of extreme passion and one of these occurred when his brother, Walter, with his wife, visited him at his home Stanton-Harold. During dinner Ferrers argued with Walter, tried to murder his servant and threatened to kill his sister-in-law. It was this type of behaviour that led to a plea of 'occasional insanity of mind' at his trial.

Death of a steward

Following the incident over the farm Ferrers reverted to treating Johnson in a perfectly affable manner. When Ferrers asked him to his house on 18 January 1760 Johnson had no reason to be suspicious. However, when he reached the house he found it was empty save for Ferrers. The Earl invited his steward into his room, then locked the door, ordered him to kneel down and shot him.

While he was awaiting trial Ferrers was jailed in the Tower of London and his position afforded him certain privileges; he could receive visitors at will and the food and drink he obtained was far superior to that of other prisoners.

Clearly sane

Ferrers was tried by his peers in Westminster Hall on 16 April 1760. Although he entered a plea of occasional insanity of mind he cross-examined the witnesses in such a competent fashion that this plea was rejected and he was found guilty of murder and sentenced to death.

The 4th Earl Ferrers was hanged at Tyburn on 5 May 1760. He wore a dazzling white suit and when questioned about his choice of attire he replied, 'This is the suit in which I was married, and in which I will die'. There was a romantic notion that he was hanged with a silken cord but it seems more likely that a functional hemp rope was used.

> **Curtailed longevity**
> Ferrer's body was taken in a coffin lined with white satin to Surgeons Hall. An incision was made from the neck to the bottom of the breast and the bowels were removed. When the surgeon examined them he declared that he had never seen a body that showed greater potential for a long life.

Fish, Albert Howard

(1870–1936)

Convicted murderer

A man suffering from extreme sexual perversion who committed a number of crimes, including cannibalism.

Albert Fish's family had a history of mental abnormality and when he was five he was placed in an orphanage. At 15 he left school and worked as a grocer's assistant, a painter and then a decorator. In 1898 he married and had six children. Twenty years later his wife left him and he married three more times, never bothering to get a divorce. Although Fish was a frail and innocuous looking man he was a sado-masochist.

Cannibal

On 3 June 1938 Fish offered to take 10-year-old Grace Budd to a children's party in New York state. Grace never reached the party; Fish took her to an empty house in Greenburgh, Westchester County, where he strangled her and cut her body into two pieces. Over the next nine days he ate pieces of her flesh, cooking them with carrots and onions. He later claimed that this kept him in a state of continuous sexual excitement.

Over the next six years Fish travelled through 23 states committing a variety of offences from grand larceny to sending obscene letters. He was also involved in over 100 incidents of sexually perverted acts with children.

Sick letter

On 11 November 1934, six years after the murder of Grace Budd, Fish wrote a letter to her family. It began, 'Grace sat in my lap and kissed me. I made up my mind to eat her'. Fish knew that the letter could be traced and he was not surprised when he was arrested, in December 1934. He made a full confession, claiming, 'I am not insane. I am just queer'.

Whatever Fish's own opinion it was left to the psychiatrists to decide the question of his sanity. The man who examined him was Dr Frederick Wertham. He decided that not only did Fish have a highly developed case of sexual perversion but that he was also suffering from 'religious insanity'. He believed that he needed to purge himself and that he was driven to torment and kill children as part of this process. Wertham was convinced that Fish was insane.

In March 1934 Fish was tried for the murder of Grace Budd. When details of his sexual arousal during acts of cannibalism were read out in court the jury gasped with horror. However, the defence of insanity was not accepted as this would have saved him from execution. He was found guilty and Albert Fish was electrocuted at Sing Sing Prison on 16 January 1936. Dr Wertham thought he was connected with at least 15 other child murders.

Short-circuit
The first attempt to electrocute Albert Fish was unsuccessful and the charge failed. Experts agreed that it had been short-circuited — by the 29 needles that Fish had inserted under his scrotum over a period of years.

Role model
Fish was a great admirer of the German mass murderer and cannibal Fritz Haarmann, who killed a minimum of 27 young boys during World War I. He then ate their flesh and what he did not use he sold to the local meat market.

Fraser, Simon, 12th Lord Lovat

(c.1667–1747)

Conspirator

An unscrupulous traitor who was always willing to switch his allegiances.

A descendant of Sir Simon Fraser, high sheriff of Tweeddale, Simon Fraser was born in Tomich, Ross-shire. He attended Aberdeen University where he exhibited an incongruous mix of wild living and a love of classical studies. In 1696 he persuaded his cousin, Lord Lovat, to bequeath his estates to his father, Thomas Fraser, thus ensuring that they would eventually pass to him.

Simon Fraser's plans were nearly thwarted when the daughter of the 10th Lord Lovat assumed the title of Baroness of Lovat. To solve the problem he decided to marry the heiress. Things went terribly wrong and in a fit of anger he forced her mother, the dowager Lady Lovat, to marry him instead. This infuriated her kinsmen, the Murrays of Atholl, and Fraser was arrested and charged with treason.

Partial pardon

In 1699 Fraser succeeded his father as 12th Lord Lovat and the following year he obtained a pardon from William III. However, it was not a complete reprieve and he was tried for the 'rapt' of Lady Lovat. He decided not to appear for his trial and instead fled to France in 1702.

Fraser met a number of influential Jacobites while in France and in 1703 he returned to Scotland on a mission for them. He was supposed to tour the Highlands and rally Jacobite supporters but instead he communicated his brief to the Duke of Queensberry, the head of the Scottish ministry, and when he returned to France he was imprisoned for 10 years by disgruntled Jacobites.

Fraser returned to Britain in 1715 and at the outbreak of the Jacobite Rebellion of that year he judged that his own interests would be best served if he was seen to take the government's side. He did this so effectively that by 1733 he had obtained a full pardon and gained full possession of the Lovat title and estates.

Changeable supporter

Fraser was not content with this and in 1739 he swung back to the Jacobites. In 1740 he was secretly created Duke of Fraser, by James Edward, the Old Pretender. However, Fraser's allegiance to the Jacobites was again short-lived. Although he sent his son to join Bonnie Prince Charlie, he proclaimed that his own loyalties lay with King George II.

True to his nature Fraser again changed sides after the Jacobite victory at Prestonpans. This proved to be a bad choice and following their defeat at Culloden in 1746 he was captured and taken to London where he was found guilty of treason. His fickle nature could not save him from execution and he was beheaded at the Tower of London on 9 April 1747.

Last request
Before he died Fraser asked that pipers from John O'Groats house in Edinburgh should be invited to play at his funeral and that he be buried at Kirkhill. Neither happened and he was buried at the Tower.

Fatal accident
Before Fraser's execution the scaffold collapsed, killing a number of people. The accused man remarked, 'The more mischief the better the sport'.

Frith, Mary
(c.1584–1659)

Highwaywoman and receiver

The match of any highwayman and a respected receiver of stolen goods.

Mary Frith, or Moll Cutpurse as she became known, was born in London, the daughter of a shoemaker in the Barbican. Although she received an adequate education she grew up as a tomboy who had little regard for authority. One of her acquaintances of the time remarked, 'A very tomrig and rumpscuttle she was and delighted and sported in boys' play and pastimes'.

Reactionary

When she was a teenager Moll was put into domestic service. However, housekeeping and babysitting were totally alien to her and she hated every minute of it. At the first opportunity she left her employer and embarked on a much more exciting career. She dressed as a man, smoked a pipe and joined the street criminals as a pickpocket. With her quick wits and sharp reflexes she was an immediate success and she was soon accepted by her male contemporaries.

Moll was ambitious and she soon became disenchanted with the derisory sums that she was paid by fences for the goods that she acquired. To counteract this she set up as a receiver herself. She bought a shop in Fleet Street where she sold the items that she

---

Theatrical heroine
In 1611 a comic play entitled *The Roaring Girl* was written about Moll Cutpurse, referring to her booming voice. It proved to be a popular success.

---

stole. She quickly acquired a reputation for fairness and other pickpockets went to her, knowing that they would receive a higher rate than elsewhere.

Good reputation

Although she dealt with stolen goods Moll was scrupulously fair when it came to returning them (for a price) to their rightful owners. It was common practice to advertise stolen goods and Moll always gave the original owner first refusal. In this way she gained the respect of both the robbers and their victims. After a few years in business Moll was the most important receiver in London and everyone came to her first. If she was ever slighted she did not hesitate to use her sharp tongue or, if necessary, her equally sharp sword.

In 1612 Moll was convicted of a petty offence and compelled to do penance at St Paul's Cross. Onlookers were impressed when she began to cry bitterly but they may not have been quite so sympathetic if they had known she had just consumed three quarts of sack and was hopelessly drunk.

Highway hobby

In addition to her activities as a fence Moll was one of the rare breed of female highway robbers. This seems to have been as much for the excitement as for profit and she invariably travelled with a specially trained dog. On one occasion she is reported to have robbed General Fairfax on Hounslow Heath. After shooting him through the arm and killing two of his horses she escaped, only to be captured at Turnham Green. She was sent to Newgate prison but bought her freedom with £2000. Moll Cutpurse died at her house in Fleet Street on 26 July 1659.

Gloucester, Humphrey, Duke of

(1391–1447)

Traitor

Appointed protector of the English throne during the reign of the infant Henry VI, he was ambitious for power.

The youngest son of King Henry IV, Humphrey was made a knight on 11 October 1399, the day before his father's coronation. He was educated at Balliol College, Oxford, and proved to be a very learned young man. In contrast with this he had a depraved social life and as a result suffered terrible health.

In 1413 his brother became King Henry V and on 7 May of the same year Humphrey was made great chamberlain of England. A year later he was created Duke of Gloucester and Earl of Pembroke. He served gallantly with his brother's army in France in 1416 and as a reward for his services he received substantial lands in Wales and several more titles.

Thoughts of power

From 1417 to 1420 Gloucester was once again serving his brother in France, and making a notable reputation for himself as a soldier. Towards the end of 1420 he was sent back to England to take over from the Duke of Bedford as regent. He had to fulfil this task again in 1421 when Bedford went to France, and he enjoyed his position of power.

Henry V died on 31 August 1422, leaving the infant Henry VI as his heir. Before his death he warned Gloucester not to put his own ambitions before those of the nation. Gloucester disregarded his advice and connived to be left in England as the protector and defender of the kingdom, while Bedford, the official regent, was engaged in combat in France.

New rival

In the autumn of 1422 Gloucester married Jacqueline of Bavaria. It proved to be a disastrous match both politically and personally and the following year he took a mistress, Eleanor Cobham. After an abortive attempt to help Jacqueline conquer the Netherlands Gloucester returned to England with his health ruined and deeply in debt. He was not heartened when he discovered that his uncle, Henry Beaufort, had become chancellor and assumed much of the power over the running of the country. They quarrelled violently and in 1425 their supporters rioted in the streets of London.

Treason in Wales

For the next 10 years Gloucester tried to gain a stronger grip on the throne. Due to political ineptitude he never achieved this and by 1440 his career was on a downward spiral. When Henry VI assumed his full responsibilities he was suspicious of Gloucester's intentions. In February 1447 Parliament were told that the erstwhile protector was stirring up a revolt in Wales. When Gloucester attended Parliament a week later he was arrested and charged with high treason. However, he was never brought to trial because he died of natural causes on 23 February 1447.

Literary interest
Gloucester was extremely well-read and he was one of the first Englishmen to appreciate classical Greek and Roman literature. Patron of numerous English and Italian Humanists, he donated much of his library to Oxford University.

Great Train Robbery

(1963)

Bruce Reynolds and others

A daring robbery carried out with military-style efficiency and which is still the largest robbery from a train anywhere in the world.

At the beginning of 1963 a London gang leader, Bruce Reynolds, obtained information about the movements of large sums of money from Glasgow to London. It involved the transfer of HVPs (High Value Packages), on a Royal Mail train, from Scottish banks to the central banks in London. They were always carried overnight and they could contain several million pounds. Reynolds and his gang did some preliminary inquiries to make sure it was not a police trap and then they decided to rob the mail train. It was the beginning of the Great Train Robbery.

The first firm

Reynolds's gang was one of the most successful and respected 'firms' in the south-west of London. They were all professional thieves, some of whom had participated in a 1962 robbery near London Airport which netted them £62 000. In addition to Reynolds the gang consisted of Buster Edwards, a man with a cunning criminal mind; Gordon Goody, a careful planner;

Scene of the crime

Roy James, a highly talented racing-driver and a getaway driver; Jim Hussey, an amiable man who was useful for his sheer strength; Jimmy White, a lock-breaker; Charlie Wilson, an experienced thief; and John Daly, whom Reynolds considered to be lucky. Reynolds himself was suave, intelligent and imaginative. He had a liking for the high-life and was often to be found in exclusive nightclubs.

Once the gang had chosen their target they set about planning the robbery. They knew the route the train would take and quickly came to the conclusion that they could not rob it while it was in a station. This meant that they had to stop it at a deserted point as near to London as possible. This immediately presented a problem because none of the gang knew how to stop a train. Then Buster Edwards came up with a controversial idea: he knew of another gang who specialized in robbing trains and one of them was an expert in manipulating railway signals. Although it was uncommon to work with another firm it was eventually agreed to approach them.

The second firm

The second firm consisted of Roger Cordrey, the expert at changing signals; Robert Welch, an all-rounder in the criminal world; and Thomas Wisbey who was the gang leader. When they were approached they agreed to help as long as they received equal shares.

Once the two gangs had joined forces they set about looking for the best place to perform the robbery. They eventually decided on Bridego Bridge, 50 miles from London, near the small village of Cheddington. They knew that the HVPs were in the second carriage from the engine so they planned to stop the train a quarter of a mile before the bridge, uncouple the first two carriages, drive them a quarter of a mile to the bridge and empty out the HVPs.

Precise planning

For several weeks the gang planned and practised the operation meticulously, learning how to uncouple coaches, working out

the exact time the mail train would be at Bridego Bridge, checking the security on the coaches which carried the HVPs, and finding a hideout. They eventually settled on an old farmhouse called Leatherslade Farm, 30 miles from the bridge. They bought the farmhouse and planned to stay there for about four days after the robbery, until the immediate outcry had died down.

The only remaining problem was how to drive the train a quarter of a mile after it had been stopped. Reynolds opted for a professional train-driver to be brought in, which involved recruiting another criminal, Ronnie Biggs. Although Reynolds was contemptuous of his abilities as a thief he knew Biggs could provide a train-driver, so he was added to the gang.

Smooth operation

On the evening of Wednesday 7 August 1963 the gang gathered at Leatherslade Farm. At seven o'clock the Royal Mail Train left Glasgow for London. Having made their final preparations the gang left the farm in two landrovers and a three-ton army truck. Most of them wore army uniforms because there was an army base nearby. As planned, the train came into view at 3.03am. Roger Cordrey had done his job and changed the signals from green to red and the driver stopped the train a quarter of a mile before Bridego Bridge.

When the train stopped, the fireman, David Whitby, stepped down to try and telephone the signal box. But the lines had been cut and when he returned he was apprehended by Buster Edwards and Bob Welch. By this time Roy James had uncoupled the coaches and they were ready to move the train. As they got into the cab the driver, Jack Mills, tried to stop them and he was struck with a cosh by Edwards. The driver that Ronnie Biggs had brought along was too nervous to drive the train so Mills was forced to do it in his concussed state.

The Royal Mail carriage was quickly broken into and the HVPs moved along a human chain to the waiting vehicles. When there were still six sacks left, Reynolds shouted, 'That's enough', and the gang made for the vehicles. In total the Great Train Robbery took only 24 minutes.

Hideout

The gang got safely back to Leatherslade Farm and began to count the money. It was a long task and when they had finished they had reached a staggering total of £2 631 684. Including various accomplices the money was to be split 17 ways which meant that each man received at least £150 000.

The original idea had been to remain at Leatherslade until Sunday 11 August. However, on the afternoon of Thursday 8 August the gang heard on the radio that the police, led by Malcolm Fewtrell of Buckinghamshire CID, knew the gang had used army trucks and that they were probably hiding within 30 miles of Bridego Bridge. When the gang heard this they decided to leave on Friday 9 August.

Capture

On Tuesday 13 August the police found the gang's hideout and as Fewtrell commented, 'The whole place was one big clue'. They found the fingerprints of Reynolds, Welch, Wisbey, Hussey, Biggs, James, Daly and Wilson. Later the same day they arrested Roger Cordrey in Bournemouth. By the end of December the majority of the gang had been arrested, but Reynolds, Edwards and White were still missing, as was £2 million.

The trial of the captured train robbers began on 20 January 1964 at Aylesbury. Except for Cordrey they all pleaded not guilty. During the course of a two-month trial that generated worldwide interest John Daly was released due to lack of evidence and Ronnie Biggs was sent for re-trial. The judge spent six days on his summing-up and the jury then took two days to reach the verdict: the Great Train Robbers were guilty on all counts. Ronnie Biggs was also found guilty at his re-trial.

Harsh sentences

Sentencing of the robbers took place on 15 April 1964. They expected severe sentences but everyone was stunned when Justice Edmund Davies announced that Charlie Wilson, Ronnie Biggs, Tommy Wisbey, Bob Welch, Jim Hussey, Roy James and Gordon Goody would serve 25 years for conspiracy to rob the mail and 30 years for armed robbery. Roger Cordrey was sentenced to 20 years because he pleaded guilty and three associates received 52 years between them. In total the Great Train Robbers were sentenced to 307 years in prison.

On the run

After the robbers were imprisoned, Charlie Wilson escaped in August 1964 and Ronnie Biggs did the same in July 1965. Biggs eventually settled in Brazil while Wilson went to Canada, joining Reynolds, Edwards and White on the run. After hiding out in Britain Edwards and Reynolds fled to Mexico, but Edwards and his wife June could not adapt to the lifestyle and returned home and surrendered. Despite expecting a relatively light sentence Buster Edwards received 15 years for robbery and 12 years for conspiracy. Jimmy White was caught in 1966 and sentenced to 18 years. Reynolds and Wilson were both arrested in Canada in 1968, and Reynolds received a 25-year sentence. Only Ronnie Biggs eluded capture.

The men who perpetrated one of the most famous crimes in history only served approximately 10 years of their harsh sentences and most of them were released in the 1970s.

Where are they now?

Buster Edwards went back to his old profession as a flower-seller.
Bruce Reynolds was released in 1978 but sent back to prison in 1984 for supplying amphetamines.
Gordon Goody moved to Spain and was arrested in 1986 for complicity in a drugs racket.
Bob Welch went to work in a London car business.
Charlie Wilson moved to Spain and was shot dead in 1990.
Jimmy White returned to his former trade of painting and decorating.
Roger Cordrey set up a business in the west of England.
Tommy Wisbey and Jim Hussey were imprisoned in 1989 for cocaine trafficking.
Roy James was involved in a VAT fraud in 1982 but the case collapsed and it is thought he now lives in Spain.
Ronnie Biggs lives in a wealthy suburb of Rio de Janeiro.

Gunness, Belle

(1859– c.1908)

Suspected murderess

A widow who enticed men to her farm with promises of matrimony and then robbed and killed them.

Belle Poulsdatter was born near Trondheim, Norway, and spent the early years of her life touring the country with her father's magic show. In 1883 she decided to emigrate to America.

Shortly after arriving in America, Belle met and married Mads Sorenson and the couple settled in Chicago. They had two children but in 1900, when two separate life insurance policies were due, Sorenson died. Despite whisperings of poisoning Belle collected the insurance money and bought a new house in Austin. This mysteriously burnt down and again the insurance company had to make a pay-out to Belle.

Second dead husband

In 1902 Belle moved to a farm, at La Porte, Indiana, and remarried, this time to a Norwegian named Peter Gunness. Her run of bad luck seemed to be continuing when, within a year, he suffered a fatal accident. Another payment of insurance money was of some comfort to her however.

Shortly after Gunness's death Belle gave birth to a son. She now had four children to look after as she had previously adopted a friend's child and was now faced with the problem of running the farm and raising her family on her own.

In an attempt to find a husband Belle placed matrimonial advertisements in the local newspapers, ending them with 'No triflers please'. She asked her prospective suitors to bring substantial sums of cash with them. Although a number of men

visited her they seldom stayed long and the neighbours presumed that they had disliked the intimidating Belle.

Unidentified body

On 27 April 1908 Belle visited her lawyer and told him that an ex-employee of hers, Ray Lamphere, who was in love with her and resented being sacked, was threatening to kill her and burn down the house. Sure enough, that night her house was raised to the ground. The decapitated body of a woman was found inside but there was no proof that it was that of Belle Gunness.

When the police searched the farm at La Porte they found a total of 14 bodies buried in the garden — men who had been prospective suitors and others who had worked, briefly, on the farm. It was agreed that Belle had killed them, some with strychnine and some with an axe, but no one discovered what became of her after the fire. Lamphere was tried for her murder but acquitted, mainly because the jury did not believe the body found in the house was that of Belle.

Despite numerous attempts to locate Belle Gunness she was never seen after 1908 and the burnt body in her house was never identified.

Denture identification

A set of dentures were found in Belle Gunness's house and a gold miner named Louis Shultz offered to sift through the ashes to try and find the gold caps that Belle was supposed to have. This attracted huge crowds and he eventually found the caps. This did not help identify the body though because the dentures could have been put there by Belle herself.

Gunpowder Plot

(1605)

Guy Fawkes and others

The most famous conspiracy in British history, when a group of Catholic sympathizers tried to blow up the Houses of Parliament.

The Gunpowder Plot was initiated by a group of fervent Catholic supporters shortly after the accession of James I to the throne in 1603. It had been hoped that he would relax the severe penal laws against Catholics and for the first six months of his reign he appeared to be doing this. But this only worried the Protestant zealots and so the King returned to the harsh laws that had been instigated by Elizabeth I.

One man who was particularly angered by the actions of the King was Robert Catesby, who had possessed considerable wealth until he fell foul of Elizabeth and had to sell his estate. He then turned to his Catholic religion and, believing that nothing but supremacy would suffice, swore himself to removing the oppressive Protestant regime.

Plot takes shape

In 1604 Catesby joined forces with Thomas Winter and John Wright and went to Flanders in the hope of securing Spanish support for Catholic relief in England. The official response was cool and so the three men decided to take matters into their own hands; the Gunpowder Plot was born.

The first thing that the conspirators needed was someone to carry out the practical side of their plan. While they were in Flanders they found just the man they were looking for, Guy Fawkes. Born in 1570

Fawkes had been brought up in Yorkshire. His parents were Protestants and he was brought up as such. Following his father's death Fawkes's mother married Dionis Baynbrigge of Scotton and the family moved to Scotton, where they were neighbours to a number of influential Catholic families. Fawkes was greatly impressed by this and soon became a convert to the Catholic faith.

Brave soldier

In 1593 Fawkes travelled to Flanders where he joined the Spanish army as a soldier of fortune. In 1595 he was present at the capture of Calais by the Spanish, under Archduke Albert, and according to one of his contempories he was, 'sought by all the most distinguished in the Archduke's camp for nobility and virtue'. His courage and coolness even attracted the attention of Sir William Stanley, the leader of the English Catholics in exile.

After Fawkes's exploits with the Spanish the Gunpowder Plot conspirators realized that he was the man to be entrusted with the main task of their conspiracy — the destruction of the Houses of Parliament with the King and his Lords inside it. In April 1604 Fawkes was approached by Thomas Winter and shortly afterwards he returned to England where he was told about the conspiracy by Catesby, Winter and Thomas Percy. Afterwards a private ceremony was held during which everyone was sworn to absolute secrecy.

Vital cellar

On 24 May 1604 Percy, with Fawkes disguised as his servant, rented a room in a tenement next to the Houses of Parliament. The conspirators planned to tunnel through the basement into the adjoining cellar, which was located directly below the House of Lords. For several weeks they endeavoured to dig through 11 feet of solid stone, only to discover that the cellar space was available for lease to the general public. Much relieved, they rented one of the cellars.

By May 1605 five more conspirators had been recruited: John Wright's brother Christopher, Robert Keyes, John Grant, Thomas Winter's brother Robert and a servant named Bates. This group helped fill the cellar with 36 barrels of gunpowder which were covered with rocks and iron bars, to increase the destruction from the explosion, and then hidden under a heap of coals and wooden faggots.

After visiting Flanders, to update Sir William Stanley, Fawkes returned to London in August 1605. It was then that he learned that Parliament would meet on 5 November. Due to his military experience he had been chosen to detonate the gunpowder and during the next two months he made sure that the explosives were dry and in order. The intention was for him to light a 15-minute fuse and then board a boat headed for Flanders. Shortly before the execution of the plot three more country gentlemen joined the conspirators: Sir Everard Digby, Ambrose Rookwood and Francis Tresham.

Fatal letter

While the conspirators waited they became increasingly nervous and began worrying about their Catholic friends who would be in the House of Lords on 5 November. It was decided that individuals could contact their friends — while avoiding specifics — to try and persuade them to miss the opening of Parliament. As a result of this an anonymous letter was sent to Lord Monteagle warning him that, 'they shall receive a terrible blow, the Parliament, and yet they shall not see who hurts them'. Monteagle's suspicions were raised by this and he took the letter to higher authorities. By 31 October 1605 it had been deduced that a plot was in operation and on 4 November when the Lord Chamberlain checked the cellars he found Guy Fawkes, who claimed he was just watching the cellar for his master, Thomas Percy.

Fawkes was not arrested after this first discovery and he immediately warned the other conspirators. Some of them prepared to leave the country but Fawkes was ordered to go back and finish his task. When he returned to the cellar on 5 November he was met by Sir Thomas Knevett and a party of soldiers. After a quick search the 36 barrels of gunpowder were discovered and Guy Fawkes was arrested.

Brutal torture

Despite being interrogated personally by the King Fawkes refused to name his fellow conspirators. He was taken to the Tower of London and very nearly tortured to death. Eventually, on 9 November, he broke down and told the authorities everything. Six of the conspirators were soon arrested and the remainder were killed trying to escape.

Guy Fawkes and the six others were tried in Westminster Hall on 27 January 1606. There was never any doubt about the verdict and on 31 January the seven men were executed at Westminster. Guy Fawkes's name has lived on in the form of the traditional fireworks celebrations of 5 November.

Barbaric executions

Some members of the House of Commons believed that the conspirators should suffer a more painful death than the traditional hanging, drawing and quartering that was the punishment for treason. Considering this consisted of being hanged until they were semi-conscious, then being disembowelled and their entrails burnt before their eyes and then being hacked into four pieces, it is difficult to imagine what could have been more painful.

Sign of torture

Guy Fawkes's changing signature revealed how he was weakened by his torture. When he was first arrested he signed his name boldly as 'Guido Fawkes' but by the end of his ordeal he was only able to write a shaky 'G' and a line that tapered into nothing.

Haigh, John George

(1909–49)

Convicted murderer

A rapacious killer who thought he could escape detection by dissolving the bodies of his victims in a drum of acid.

John Haigh was born at Stamford in Lincolnshire in 1909. His parents belonged to a religious sect, the Plymouth Brethren, which disapproved of any frivolous light entertainment, so Haigh grew up as a solitary child. Music was his favourite pastime and he sang in the school and the cathedral choirs.

On leaving school he was apprenticed briefly to a motor engineer but he chose a less strenuous way of making a living. In 1934 he was sentenced to 15 months imprisonment for conspiracy to defraud a hire purchase company. In 1936 he came to London and worked briefly for a man named Donald McSwann. A year later he was again imprisoned, this time for four years for obtaining money by false pretences.

Haigh continued his career of petty crime and in 1941 he was sentenced to 21 months for stealing household goods. He used his time to study the effects of sulphuric acid on mice and when he was released he vowed that he would give up the risky, unprofitable business of petty criminal.

Graduation to murder

In 1945 Haigh was living in London when he met Donald McSwann again. McSwann was running a highly profitable amusement arcade and on 9 September 1944 Haigh invited him to his basement workshop. As his guest was admiring the impressive array of equipment Haigh murdered him with a blow from a hammer. He spent the rest of the night feeding the body into a vat of sulphuric acid. In the morning he poured the resultant sludge down a basement manhole.

Although Haigh took over the amusement arcade his greed soon got the better of him and he turned his attentions to McSwann's parents. He had already convinced them that their son had gone to Scotland to escape the war. However, when they visited him in July 1945 they suffered the same fate as their son. Using forged documents Haigh obtained over £4000 of the McSwann family's money, including the freehold in four properties and their gilt-edged securities.

In debt again

Due to bad investments and Haigh's addiction to gambling this money lasted barely three years and in February 1948 he lured Dr Archie Henderson and his wife Rosalie to his new workshop at Crawley, south of London. They were supposed to be there to discuss a land deal but instead Haigh murdered them and dissolved them in his acid bath.

By now Haigh was beginning to feel safe from detection and in February 1949 he embarked on another murder. He was staying at the residential Onslow Court Hotel, in Kensington, and he was again in debt. Another of the hotel guests, a wealthy widow named Mrs Olive Durand-Deacon, frequently spoke to Haigh during dinner and one evening she suggested a business venture that involved marketing artificial fingernails. Haigh was extremely interested in Mrs Durand-Deacon, but not because of her cosmetics idea.

Acid victim

On 18 February 1949 Haigh invited Mrs Durand-Deacon to his Crawley workshop to discuss business. As soon as she was in the workshop Haigh shot her, fed her into the vat of acid and then went to a restaurant to have a cup of tea and poached eggs on toast.

Over the next two days Haigh made several trips to Crawley, to ensure that Mrs Durand-Deacon was dissolving satisfactorily and also to sell her jewellery and her Persian lamb coat. By now the staff and residents of Onslow Court were becoming worried about Mrs Durand-Deacon's disappearance and one of them suggested that the police were informed. Haigh agreed and co-operated fully with the police. He then went back to Crawley and emptied the sludge into the yard next to his workshop.

Suspicion aroused

After their first visit the police were suspicious of Haigh's glib manner, so they investigated further and found out about his workshop. On visiting the premises they discovered the sludge in the yard. Haigh was arrested on 28 February and during questioning he said, 'Mrs Durand-Deacon no longer exists. No trace of her can ever be found. How can you prove murder if there's no body?' Unfortunately for Haigh, his theory was hopelessly inaccurate; when the sludge from Crawley was examined it was found to contain 28lbs of animal fat, two gall stones, part of a foot, 18 bone fragments and a set of dentures that were identified by a dentist as belonging to Mrs Durand-Deacon.

Haigh admitted to the murders of the McSwann family and the Hendersons, and also three other people who he had met by chance in London. On 18 July 1949 he was tried for the murder of Mrs Durand-Deacon.

Sane and guilty

The defence was based on a plea of insanity following Haigh's claim that he drank the blood of his victims after he had murdered them. There was no evidence of this however and the only witness called by the defence had to admit that Haigh knew he had done something that was 'punishable by law' and so therefore he could not claim to be insane.

The jury spent just 17 minutes to decide that John George Haigh was sane and guilty of murder. Before sentence was passed the prisoner was asked if he had anything to say. In his usual glib manner he replied, 'Nothing at all'. He was hanged at Wandsworth Prison on 6 August 1949.

Dr and Mrs Archibald Henderson

> **Trickster**
> Before he turned to murder one of Haigh's swindles involved posing as a small-time solicitor who was winding up a client's estate. He pretended to be disposing of a block of shares from the estate and offered them to anyone who gave him a 25% deposit. He made over £3000 from this scheme before he was caught in 1937.

> **Contempt of court**
> Before Haigh's trial the *Daily Mail* published sensational material about the case. Since they had already been warned not to by Scotland Yard, the newspaper was fined £10 000 for contempt of court and the editor, Silvester Bolam, was sentenced to three months' imprisonment.

Hatry, Clarence Charles

(1888–1965)

Financial forger

A financial genius who resorted to forgery to try and save his career.

Clarence Hatry was born in Hampstead and was a sensitive but inventive child. When he was 18 he inherited his father's business, which proved not to be a blessing at all, for in 1906 the business collapsed, leaving liabilities of £8000.

This early failure did not discourage Hatry and he quickly established himself as an insurance broker. With the capital he raised he started buying and selling companies. He had a talent for this that bordered on genius; one of his greatest achievements was buying Leyland Motors for a reported £350 000 and then selling it within a day for nearly twice that figure.

In addition to buying and selling businesses Hatry also established his own companies, one of these being the Commercial Bank of London. His favourite financial ploy was to form combines — one large company embracing several small ones — and then sell them off. Using these methods he had accumulated a personal fortune of over £2 million by 1920.

Mechanics of money-making

Although Hatry was ambivalent towards his wealth (it was the mechanics of making money that really interested him), he still enjoyed the lifestyle of a millionaire. He had several opulent houses, the world's second largest yacht and a number of racehorses. However, he did not covet money just for its own sake and in 1921, during an economic slump, he used some of his personal fortune to inject capital into his various business ventures.

In 1929 one of Hatry's companies, Corporation and General Securities Ltd, made a bid for United Steel. It was an ambitious scheme but Hatry and two business associates, Edmund Daniels and an Italian named John Gialdini, managed to raise 90% of the money they needed. Their cause was not helped by the election of a Labour government in May 1929, which led to a nervous stock exchange.

Forged bonds

Hatry and his associates were £900 000 short of the money they required so they decided to issue unauthorized stock bonds — a crime amounting to forgery. The bid failed and private investors in Corporation and General Securities lost £15 million.

Hatry appeared voluntarily before the director of public prosecutions and admitted to the forgeries. He was tried at the Old Bailey and on the fourth day of the trial, 25 January 1930, his counsel advised him to change his plea to guilty, which he did only to be sentenced to 14 years' imprisonment. This was considered to be extremely harsh and in 1939 he was released on the advice of the Home Secretary.

On his release he reasserted himself as a financier but since people were now wary of him, he never again reached the heights of his earlier years. He died in a London hospital in 1965.

Critical leaders

The *Sunday Observer* was in no doubt about Hatry's sentence: 'False sentimentality about this sentence is contemptible. Humble rascals get seven years for smaller offences. In this case a man who gets 14 years leaves some of his victims to ruin and misery for life'.

Heath, Neville George Clevely

(1917–46)

Convicted murderer

An ex-RAF Captain who committed two sadistic murders in 1946.

Neville Heath was born at Ilford. He attended a Catholic school and developed a reputation for bullying and cruelty to animals. For several years he followed a pattern of petty, but not violent, crime. He joined the RAF in 1936 but was dismissed in 1937 for theft. During the next eight years he was convicted of various offences including robbery and the unlawful wearing of RAF uniform and decorations. He also served in the South African Air Force but he was court-martialled in 1945 for undisciplined conduct.

In 1946 Heath was living in London and on 15 June he used his considerable charm to persuade Yvonne Symonds to spend the night with him at his hotel, the Pembridge Court Hotel, Notting Hill. The next day she returned to her home in Worthing in high spirits, for Heath had proposed to her.

Sadistic murder

Four days later Heath was again socializing in London, this time with Mrs Margery Gardner, an aspiring film actress recently separated from her husband. She and Heath spent the night at the Panama Club in South Kensington and after midnight they returned to the Pembridge Court Hotel, considerably under the influence of drink.

After an apparently peaceful night the chambermaid went into Heath's room at the hotel and found the horribly mutilated body of Margery Gardner. She had been beaten ferociously with a metal-tipped whip and her body had been sexually mutilated, although there was no sign of intercourse.

The police soon discovered that Heath, using the alias of Bill Armstrong, had stayed the night with Margery Gardner and a nationwide man-hunt was ordered. Due to the sadistic nature of the murder the police knew that they had to act quickly.

Plausible killer

On 21 June Heath travelled to Worthing to see Yvonne Symonds. She had read of the murder of Margery Gardner and was concerned that the police wanted to interview Heath. He tried to reassure her but she was worried by his intimate knowledge of the murder. He told her that it had been the work of a sexual maniac. The next day Yvonne saw in a newspaper that the police were looking for Heath. He claimed it was a mistake and that he would return to London to clear things up.

Not satisfied with this Heath then wrote to the police officer in charge of the investigation, Chief Superintendent Tom Barratt. In his letter he claimed, 'I booked in at the hotel last Sunday, but not with Mrs Gardner ... Mrs Gardner asked if she could use my hotel room until two o'clock and intimated that if I returned after that I might spend the rest of the night with her. When I returned I found her in the condition of which you are aware. I realized that I was in an invidious position, and rather than notify the police I packed my belongings and left'. Heath also claimed to have found the whip with which she was beaten and promised to send it to the police, which he never did.

Second outrage

Following this remarkable statement Heath went to Bournemouth where he stayed at the Tollard Royal Hotel under the alias of Group-Captain Rupert Brooke. On 3 July he met an ex-WRN, Doreen Marshall, and they dined together that evening. Afterwards Heath insisted on walking her to her hotel. She was never seen alive again but by the time her body was discovered Heath was under arrest for Margery Gardner's murder.

The manner of Heath's arrest shows he either had a scant regard for danger or that he was not aware of his predicament. On 5 July he telephoned Bournemouth Police Station saying that he had dined with Doreen Marshall, who had now been reported missing, on the night of 3 July. To make matters worse he went to the police station the following day. Although he was still using the name Brooke, one of the police officer noticed his likeness to the description of Heath they had been given from the earlier killing. He was detained and when the police searched his hotel room they found a tightly knotted blood-stained handkerchief and some of Doreen Marshall's hair. The police also found a cloakroom ticket which produced a suitcase containing the riding crop from the first murder. On 6 July 1946 Heath was charged with the murder of Margery Gardner, and two days later the mutilated body of Doreen Marshall was found.

Question of sanity

The trial of Heath generated widespread interest and it was reported in Europe and in America. The only real issue was whether the defendant was insane or not. The defence claimed that at the time of the murders Heath was suffering from temporary insanity and as such could not be held responsible for his actions. In his summing-up the judge pointed out various aspects of the case that indicated that Heath was well aware of what he was doing. The jury agreed with him and found George Clevely Heath guilty of murder. He made no appeal and was hanged at Pentonville Prison on 26 October 1946.

McNaughton Rules
The rules governing criminal insanity in England are based on the McNaughton Rules, which were drawn up after Daniel McNaughton murdered Robert Peel's private secretary in 1843. The rules state: '1 A man is presumed sane until the contrary is proved and 2 It must be clearly proved that at the time of committing the act, the accused was labouring under such a defect of reason as not to know the nature of the act, or that he was doing wrong'.

Hillside Strangler murders

(1977–9)

Kenneth Alessio Bianchi

A mass murderer who was a multiple personality and claimed to know nothing of the murders he committed.

Kenneth Bianchi was adopted by Nicholas and Frances Bianchi a year after his birth in Rochester, New York, in 1951. Frances Bianchi was an over-protective mother and Ken grew up as a sensitive and sickly child. Nicholas Bianchi died when his son was 13 and this had a traumatic effect on Ken.

Ken Bianchi married in 1971 but his wife left him after only eight months. This devastated him and a few years later he decided to move to Los Angeles to stay with his cousin Angelo Buono. At first he was thrilled by the freedom of California and the uninhibited lifestyle of his cousin. He enjoyed the drugs and the prostitutes but since he was essentially a home-loving person he soon craved stability.

Bianchi got what he wanted when he found a job, rented his own apartment and met Kelli Boyd. Kelli was a quiet, unassuming girl and within weeks of being introduced to Bianchi, in November 1976, they moved in together. Although Kelli found Bianchi a loving man she was annoyed at his immaturity and his inability to save money. She was also concerned about the frequent visits he made to Buono.

The Hillside Strangler

In October 1977 the Los Angeles police found the naked body of a strangled prostitute on a hillside near the Ventura freeway. In the next two months nine more women were found in similar circumstances, all of them strangled and naked. By the end of

1977 the citizens of Los Angeles were living in fear of the Hillside Strangler.

In February 1978 Bianchi and Kelli had a son named Sean. But their relationship was breaking up and in March Kelli moved back to her home in Bellingham, Washington. Bianchi persuaded his wife to let him join her, and in May 1978 he moved to Bellingham. He immediately became more responsible, found a good job with a private security firm and joined the Sheriff's Reserve.

Jekyll and Hyde

On 12 January 1979 two young women were found strangled in Bellingham. When inquiries were made the name of Ken Bianchi kept coming up. He was arrested for questioning and members of the Los Angeles police force were sent to interview him. It was decided to question him under hypnosis and this provided a remarkable result. In a changed voice, Bianchi claimed to be a man called Steve, who admitted to the Hillside Strangler murders and also implicated Angelo Buono.

It took five years to arraign Bianchi in court on a charge of murder. Despite the wait he was found guilty and sentenced to five life sentences. Buono was charged with one murder and sentenced to life imprisonment. Bianchi claimed that it was Steve who committed the murders and that he knew nothing about them.

Ken and Steve
During questioning under hypnosis a remarkable transformation came over Ken Bianchi. 'I'm not Ken. You can call me Steve. I hate Ken … he tries to be nice. I hate nice! I hate Ken!' The doctors claimed he was a multiple personality but the police remained sceptical.

Holmes, Henry Howard

(1860–96)

Convicted murderer

One of America's first mass murderers, who built his own 'castle of death' to dispose of his victims.

Herman Webster Mudgett was born in the small New Hampshire town of Gilmanton. He was a scholarly child but had morbid tendencies, which included setting a neighbour's cat on fire. When he was 18 he eloped with a farmer's daughter and then went to study at the universities of Vermont and Michigan successively, where he began to use his talents for criminal rather than academic activities. He took out a life insurance policy on one of his friends, stole a corpse from the dissecting room of the university, identified it as his friend and then pocketed the insurance money. The simplicity with which he was able to defraud the insurance company was duly noted by Mudgett.

Mudgett left university as a Doctor of Medicine but soon turned to crime. He was a handsome man and as he had already left his wife he had little difficulty in attracting women, many of whom he would swindle and then desert. For six years he conned his way through Minnesota and New York.

Bigamous swindler

In 1885 Mudgett, now using the name Henry Howard Holmes, settled in the Chicago suburb of Wilmette. He wasted no time in bigamously marrying Myrtle Belknap, the daughter of a wealthy Chicago family. The marriage lasted just as long as it took Holmes to swindle Myrtle's father. He then left his latest wife and moved into a chemist shop, which he had acquired from a widow who had mysteriously disappeared shortly after employing Holmes.

The chemist shop prospered and Holmes began diversifying. He bought the land opposite his shop and began building a monstrous Gothic-style, three-storey building. During its construction Holmes hired and fired a continuous stream of workmen, so that no one knew too much about the overall design. When it was completed it contained over 90 rooms and was dubbed by the locals 'Holmes's Castle'. In reality it was a huge chamber of death and torture. From the second floor upwards there were secret staircases, connecting hallways, trapdoors, asbestos-lined rooms equipped with gas jets, soundproof rooms with dissecting equipment, and vats of acid and quicklime.

Castle of death

Once his 'Castle' was completed Holmes began putting it to good use. It is estimated that he murdered 27 people in various ways in his sadistic home. Some were killed purely for financial gain, others were imprisoned to satisfy Holmes's sexual desires and then disposed of when he tired of them. Several of the murders were entirely gratuitous, in order to test the various gadgets of death with which he had surrounded himself.

Although Holmes made large sums of money from some of the people he murdered he was continually in debt and always looking to make a dishonest dollar. In June 1894 he tried to sell a drug-store that did not belong to him and he was imprisoned for three months. While he was in jail he met a notorious train robber named Marion Hedgepeth. At the time Holmes was planning to resurrect the insurance swindle that he had used at university and he promised Hedgepeth $500 if he could put him in touch with a crooked lawyer. This was duly done and after Holmes was released he took out a life insurance policy on an acquaintance named Benjamin Pitezel.

On the run

When the supposed body of Pitezel was found, charred beyond recognition due to an explosion, his wife believed Holmes's story about her husband being in hiding and that the corpse was one he had exhumed from a cemetery. The insurance company raised no questions and paid Holmes $10 000. Once he had his money he forgot about his promise to Hedgepeth and left Chicago with three of Mrs Pitezel's children, arranging to meet her in Detroit. Hedgepeth was furious and wrote to the insurance company telling them of the fraud. In turn the insurance company employed the respected Pinkerton Detective Agency to track down the elusive Mr Holmes.

By the time Holmes was run to ground and arrested in Boston on 17 November 1894, the three children he had been entrusted with were no longer with him. Some painstaking detective work followed and eventually the bodies of the two Pitezel girls were discovered in a garden in Toronto and the charred remains of their brother were found in an old stove in Indianapolis. Holmes then admitted that he had killed Pitezel and had then planned to dispose of the rest of the family.

Bodies discovered

After Holmes was arrested for the murder of Benjamin Pitezel the police discovered the grisly contents of his house in Chicago.

They had never seen anything like it. In addition to the macabre construction of the house they found human bones in a large stove and other human remains buried in quicklime under the cellar.

Holmes was only charged with the murder of Benjamin Pitezel and his trial began on 28 October 1895. It was one of the most widely publicized trials in America in the 19th century and there was little surprise, or sympathy, when the jury announced their verdict of guilty. While he was awaiting execution Holmes embraced the Catholic Church and confessed to killing 27 people. He later withdrew his confession but it did him no good and he was hanged on 7 May 1896.

Comprehensive burial

There were a number of attempts to obtain Holmes's body once he had been hanged. These were all thwarted by Holmes himself, who in his will ordered that his body should be encased in cement in his coffin. His lawyer went one better and had him buried 10 feet deep and then covered the coffin with a two-foot layer of cement.

Mass murderers

Holmes, with a minimum of 27 victims, is still one of America's most prolific mass murderers. Those who murdered a similar number are: Earle Nelson, 22 victims by 1927; Carl Panzram, 21 victims by 1928; Charles Whitman, 16 victims by 1966; and Dean Corll, 27 victims by 1973. One man who surpassed Holmes's record was John Wayne Gacy, who killed at least 32 people by 1979.

Houndsditch murders and the siege of Sidney Street

(1910–11)

George Gardstein and others

An example of how far revolutionary elements of London's immigrant population were prepared to go to achieve their aims.

During the first 10 years of the 20th century Britain experienced a massive influx of immigrants seeking safety from persecution in eastern Europe and Tsarist Russia. Thousands of these immigrants settled in the East End of London, a rundown area where jobs were scarce. On 23 January 1909 two political refugees from Latvia, Paul Hefeld and Jacob Lepidus, attempted an armed wage snatch outside a factory in Tottenham. Unfortunately things went disastrously wrong, the attempt was bungled and in the chase that followed a policeman and a young boy were shot dead and three policemen and 14 bystanders were injured. The two robbers finally shot themselves.

There was nationwide disgust at the Tottenham Outrage and feelings against the immigrant population ran high, not least because the refugees had used their guns so gratuitously.

London's revolutionaries

Although the British press conveniently labelled all immigrants involved in criminal activities as anarchists this was not always strictly true. Many of them were revolutionaries from Russia and the Baltic states who had fled to Britain following the abortive revolutions of 1905 and the subsequent brutal repressions. London was a popular choice for these refugees because of Britain's toleration of political exiles and also because of its proximity to the sea routes to the Baltic ports.

Once they reached London the revolutionaries' main concern was to obtain funds to continue the struggle for the liberation of their homelands. They achieved this by carrying out 'expropriations' (robberies of state or private funds). Since many of the immigrants had suffered brutally at the hands of their native police forces they had little respect for the British forces of law and order and the expropriations were invariably carried out by armed men who did not hesitate to use their weapons.

No 11 Exchange Buildings

At the beginning of December 1910 a group of Latvian revolutionaries were planning an expropriation when they discovered a wealthy jeweller's shop in Houndsditch. The house behind it, 11 Exchange Buildings, was vacant and available for rent.

The gang were all experienced revolutionaries who had been actively involved in the 1905 uprisings. They were led by George Gardstein and the other Letts included Yourka Dubof, William Sokoloff (known as Joseph), Jacob Peters, Fritz Svaars, Peter Piatkow (known as Peter the Painter) and John Rosen. By the evening of Friday 16 December all the arrangements for the robbery had been finalized and the gang began the task of drilling through the wall of No 11 Exchange Buildings into the jeweller's shop at 119 Houndsditch.

Unfortunately, the noise of the drilling soon attracted the attention of the neighbours and the police were called. They began making enquiries at the houses near the jeweller's shop. When they entered No 11 they were met by Gardstein standing at

The 'Sidney Street Siege' 1911

the top of a staircase. They had time to ask two questions before he opened fire. He was soon joined by another member of the gang and in the ensuing gunfire three policemen, Sergeant Bentley, Sergeant Tucker and Constable Choate, were shot dead and two others were wounded. In the confusion that followed the whole gang managed to escape but not before Gardstein was mortally wounded by a bullet from one of his own men. It was never known for sure who fired the shots that killed the policemen.

Trapped in Sidney Street

There was outrage at the Houndsditch Murders and a massive manhunt and undercover operation was organized to find the murderers. In the early hours of 3 January 1911 two of the suspected murderers, William Sokoloff and Fritz Svaars, were traced to a house at 100 Sidney Street, a block of eight three-storeyed houses, situated halfway along the street and opposite a large brewery.

Remembering the savagery of the Houndsditch attack the police were unsure of how to deal with the situation. As day broke Svaars and Sokoloff began firing on the police. What followed was a pitched battle between the two revolutionaries and the police, supported by about 20 Scots Guardsmen. Several of the policemen were unable to participate in the gun battle because they were fully occupied in restraining the large crowd that had gathered, undeterred by the bullets that were crashing into buildings on all sides of Sidney Street.

Churchill in charge

By noon the Home Secretary, Winston Churchill, had arrived on the scene. He was considering the use of artillery when this already dramatic situation was heightened still further by the sight of flames coming from No 100. Churchill was adamant that the fire brigade would not immediately put it out. As the house burnt there was the sound of two gunshots and when he was sure that the occupants were dead Churchill ordered the fire brigade and the police to enter the smouldering building. Inside they found the charred bodies of Svaars and Sokoloff, both decapitated and barely recogniszable. The Siege of Sidney Street was over but there was no proof that the two men had murdered the three policemen in Houndsditch.

Reaction

The Siege of Sidney Street caused amazement both in Britain and abroad. At home, people were shocked at the amount of firepower that had been employed on both sides, and Churchill was somewhat unfairly criticized for not having brought the men out alive. The international community were concerned that the incident might have an adverse effect on Britain's immigration policy and some sections of the international press also took great delight at the fuss that had been caused over the capture of just two men.

Although Dubof, Peters and Rosen were later arrested they were all acquitted and no one was ever convicted of the Houndsditch murders.

Peter the Painter

The name best remembered from the Houndsditch Murders and the Siege of Sidney Street is that of Peter the Painter. He is often regarded as the most notorious of the Lettish gang but he took little part in the Houndsditch robbery and none in the Siege. As someone remarked at the time, he would probably not have gained such notoriety if his nickname had been Albert the Greengrocer.

Hungerford massacre

(1987)

Michael Ryan

The murder of 16 people in a small English village, which shocked the nation.

To those who knew him, Michael Ryan was either a quiet unassuming loner, or a fantasist who invented stories about imaginary girlfriends in order to impress people. He was born in 1960 and lived in the town of Hungerford, a small market town in Berkshire. He had been unemployed for much of his life and he had no close friends, although his mother was strongly attached to him. His one great passion was guns — he owned five and belonged to two gun clubs.

On 19 August 1987 Ryan took three of his guns, a Kalashnikov AK47 semi-automatic rifle, an M1 carbine and a 9mm Beretta pistol, and went to Savernake Forest, nine miles from Hungerford. It is likely that he was thinking of committing a sexual attack but when his intended victim tried to run away he shot and killed her. By the time the police had reached the scene of the crime Ryan was back in Hungerford.

Rampage

After the first killing something snapped in Ryan's mind and this previously peaceful man went on a killing spree. Dressed in a combat jacket and a bullet-proof vest he roamed the streets of his home town, shooting on sight and at random. After he had slaughtered seven people, including two of his neighbours and a policeman, Ryan's mother Dorothy came into the street to try and stop him. His answer was to shoot her dead with four shots.

The killings continued, with the residents of Hungerford barely able to comprehend what was going on. After setting fire to the house where he had lived all his life Ryan made his way to the John O'Gaunt secondary school, where he barricaded himself into the English classroom. On the way to the school he claimed another seven victims as his savage spree continued. Once inside the building he held a 'lucid and reasonable' conversation with Police Sergeant Brightwell. They spoke for an hour and a half and Ryan said that he did not know how many people he had killed and that the death of his mother had been a 'mistake'. In a moment of considerable understatement he added, 'Hungerford must be a bit of a mess'.

Terror ends in suicide

Towards the end of his conversation with Sergeant Brightwell Ryan tied a white handkerchief to the barrel of his Kalashnikov and threw it on to a grass verge. The police thought he was going to surrender but instead he pointed the Beretta at his head and shot himself with a round that he had kept for that very purpose. Ryan's brief reign of terror had come to an end. The carnage of 16 dead and 14 wounded was by far the worst shooting incident in British history.

The reasons for Ryan's wild behaviour have never been fully discovered and following the massacre there was an in-depth review of the gun laws in Britain.

Inquest

At the inquest, Ryan's aunt said he was a 'very nice but lonely person ... but he felt much more important and much more powerful with a gun'.

Ireland, William Henry

(1777–1835)

Literary forger

A precocious teenager who produced forged works of Shakespeare, including two new plays.

William Ireland was born in London and throughout his formative years there was some doubt concerning his legitimacy. He was brought up by his father, an elderly antiquarian bookseller named Samuel Ireland, and William was desperately eager to please him. Although he was a poor scholar he was a keen devotee of the famous literary forger Thomas Chatterton.

In 1793 Samuel Ireland took his 17-year-old son to Stratford-upon-Avon, which was in the process of becoming a literary shrine to William Shakespeare. Samuel was so obsessed with everything connected with the famous playwright that William vowed to give him what he most wanted, a genuine Shakespeare document.

Forgeries accepted

Ireland's first forgery was a title deed, signed by Shakespeare, to some property near the Globe Theatre. Samuel Ireland was delighted when he received the document and he immediately accepted it as genuine, as did a distinguished scholar. Spurred on by this success William Ireland produced several more documents signed by Shakespeare. These included formal and personal letters, and amendments to plays, including *King Lear* and *Hamlet*. When questioned about their origin he would only say that they had been given to him by a wealthy gentleman with the initials M H.

In February 1795 Samuel Ireland could keep his discovery a secret no longer and he put all the documents on display at his London home. Most of the people who came to see them accepted them as genuine, including the Prince of Wales. James Boswell fell to his knees, exclaiming, 'I now kiss the invaluable relics of our bard!'

If William Ireland had left it at this then his forgeries may not have come to light for several years. But his next forgery proved to be his undoing. He claimed to have found two new plays by Shakespeare, *Vortigern and Rowena* and *Henry II*. At first they were accepted by the literary world and the lessees of the Drury Lane Theatre offered to produce both the new plays.

Disasterous opening

The opening night of *Vortigern and Rowena*, on 2 April 1796, coincided with the publication of a paper by a scholar named Edmond Malone who called into question the authenticity of the Shakespearian documents. The forgery soon became clear when the play was performed: it was so palpably not written by Shakespeare that the audience were soon in fits of laughter. It ran for one night.

In disgrace William Ireland admitted to his forgeries. His father was heartbroken and died in 1800, refusing to acknowledge the truth. William continued with his literary career but it soon became known that his ability to produce original work was moderate. He died in 1835, never regaining the fame he had found as a forger.

> **Calamitous performance**
> The producer of *Vortigern and Rowena* was so convinced that it was a forgery that he made sure the production was a farce, originally wanting to open the play on April Fool's Day. During the fifth act he laid special emphasis on the line 'And when this solemn mockery is ended', at which point the audience could contain their mirth no longer.

Jack the Ripper

(1888)

Unidentified murderer

The most famous unsolved murder case in British history, which has given rise to numerous theories as to the identity of Jack the Ripper.

Illustrated Police News 1889

On 7 August 1888 the body of a prostitute, Martha Turner, was discovered in the Spitalfields district of the East End of London. Although the murder of prostitutes was a fairly common occurrence in the squalid East End the ferocity of the attack stunned those who saw the body. Martha had been stabbed 39 times with a bayonet and a long-bladed knife. Despite this, little attention was paid to the murder and no one was aware that it was the beginning of three months of terror in the East End.

Three weeks later, on 31 August 1888, the mutilated body of another prostitute was found in Spitalfields. She was Mary Ann Nicols, known as Pretty Polly, and she had been disembowelled and her throat slit. The doctor who examined her body said, 'I have never seen so horrible a case'. He was able to ascertain that the killer was left-handed and, due to the nature of the mutilations, that he had some medical knowledge.

Possible sighting

As news of these savage murders began to spread a third killing took place. The victim was a 47-year-old prostitute named Annie Chapman and her body was found by a Spitalfields porter on 9 September. Not only had her throat been cut but her kidneys and ovaries had also been removed from her body. The only clue that the police had was a vague description of a man who was seen near the scene of the crime: tall, pale, and with a black moustache.

At the end of September the case had a new twist when the Central News Agency in Fleet Street received a letter that read, 'I am down on whores and shant quit ripping them till I do get buckled'. It was signed 'Jack the Ripper' and the sobriquet immediately caught the public's imagination. Meetings were held in the streets during which the police and the Home Secretary were criticized for their inaction, and questions were raised in the House of Commons. At one point the head of the Metropolitan Police, Sir Charles Warren, ordered the use of bloodhounds in an attempt to capture the Ripper. However, this ended in farce when the dogs got lost on Tooting Common.

Police thwarted

Despite intense police activity in the East End, the Ripper continued to strike undetected. On 30 September he slipped through a tight police cordon and committed two more murders. As with the previous killings they were both prostitutes, and they were both murdered in the Whitechapel district. The first, Elizabeth Stride, had not been mutilated, which led the police to believe that the Ripper had been interrupted during the attack. The second victim of the night, and the fifth altogether, was Catherine Eddowes, who had been butchered in a similar fashion to the earlier victims. On a wall near the body was a scrawled a message, 'The Juws are the men that will not be blamed for nothing'. This was the first substantial clue that the police had discovered; Sir Charles Warren was offended by the message and ordered it to be wiped off.

Hysteria

By now there was panic on the streets of London. Groups of vigilantes operated in Spitalfields and Whitechapel. For a few weeks it appeared that the Ripper murders had stopped, but on 9 November he struck again. The victim was 25-year-old Mary Kelly and her body was found in a house near the City. Her head had virtually been severed from her body, her heart had been placed on a pillow and her entrails had been draped over a window frame.

Mary Kelly was the last victim of Jack the Ripper and the murders ended as suddenly as they began. However, this did not help Sir Charles Warren and as a result of his failure to catch the Ripper he resigned shortly afterwards.

The theories

The inability of the police to catch Jack the Ripper has led to a variety of theories as to his identity. These include claims that he was a foreigner who was on the run from political troubles in his own country; a policeman; a midwife who was wreaking a sadistic revenge against prostitutes; a mad doctor whose son had died after contracting syphilis from Mary Kelly; and even that the killings were the result of a Black Magic ritual. It has also been suggested that the Ripper was Queen Victoria's eldest grandson, Prince Albert Victor, the Duke of Clarence. All of these theories have their supporters but there is no conclusive evidence.

Suspects

Several policemen working on the case had their own ideas about the Ripper's identity. Inspector Robert Sagar, who died in 1924, wrote in his memoirs, 'We had good reason to suspect a man who lived in Butcher's Row, Aldgate. We watched him carefully. There was no doubt that this man was insane and, after a time, his friends thought it advisable to have him moved to a private asylum. After he was removed, there were no more Ripper atrocities'.

Sir Melville Macnaghten, who became head of the CID in 1903, suggested three men who could have been the Ripper. They were a Polish tradesman who hated women, a Russian doctor, and a failed barrister named Montagu John Druitt. Of the three, Druitt is the most likely. He had medical connections and a history of mental instability. A few weeks after the death of Mary Kelly, Druitt committed suicide by throwing himself into the Thames. His death coincided with the end of the Ripper killings.

Whatever the truth about Jack the Ripper his identity is now safely hidden in criminal history.

Ripper ghosts

Although the area where the Ripper operated has changed considerably the ghosts of two of the victims have returned to the scene of the crime. Mary Ann Nicols has allegedly been sighted in Whitechapel, near where she was killed, and the screams of Annie Chapman have been heard in Spitalfields.

Centenary

In 1988 several books were published celebrating the centenary of the Ripper murders. However, little new evidence was advanced, except for the discovery in a policeman's notebook stating that the Ripper was a man named Kosminski.

James, Jesse Woodson

(1847–82)

Outlaw

The most notorious outlaw of the American West, who led a gang which specialized in bank and train robberies.

Jesse James was born near Kearney, Clay County, Missouri. His father was a baptist minister but died when Jesse was only four, so he and his elder brother Frank (born 1843) were raised by their mother Zerelda. She was a dominant but loving woman and her sons received a religious upbringing. In 1851 Zerelda remarried but was granted a divorce shortly afterwards. She tried again in 1857, this time marrying Dr Reuben Samuel.

Jesse and Frank James grew up in a period during which slavery was still commonplace and violent border disputes a way of life. They quickly conditioned themselves to this and became expert marksmen and horsemen.

Confederate sympathizers

When the American Civil War broke out in 1861 Zerelda James and her husband were enthusiastic supporters of the Southern cause. Jesse and Frank were only too pleased to follow suit. The authorities were aware of this and their home was twice raided by Union troops, on one occasion nearly hanging Dr Samuel. Jesse was outraged at this behaviour and in retaliation he and his brother joined the Confederate guerillas under the leadership of William Clarke Quantrill. They soon won the gang's respect and helped them in several daring attacks. They had no qualms about dealing violently with their enemies and on one occasion they shot over 30 federal militiamen

during an attack at Rocheport Road. In another incident, in September 1864, over 20 Union soldiers were murdered when Quantrill's gang attacked a train.

Gang leader

At the end of the Civil War, in 1865, the majority of Quantrill's gang surrendered, but the James brothers would not give themselves up to the authorities. One of the reasons was that Jesse had been severely wounded by Union soldiers while he was under a flag of truce. It took him nearly a year to regain his full strength and when he did he decided to make a career for himself outside the law. He gathered together a dozen men and formed what was to become the notorious James Gang. His brother Frank was included as were the widely feared Younger brothers.

On 3 February 1866 the James Gang rode into Liberty, Missouri, and committed what was reputedly the first daylight bank robbery in America in peacetime. This was to be the first of many similar robberies, from Iowa to Alabama and Texas. Unlike his successor, John Dillinger, Jesse James was not slow to use his gun: in one bank robbery a 16-year-old boy was murdered, in another a cashier was shot dead, and in a third, three civilians were slain. As the notoriety of the gang spread, the people of Missouri began to regard Jesse James as a hero, driven to crime because of his Southern allegiances. In contrast, the rest of the country branded him as an outlaw.

Early train robber

In 1873 Jesse James struck on the idea of robbing trains. His theory was first tested on 21 July 1873 when the gang held up a train on the Rock Island railroad at Adair, Iowa. They loosened a rail at a blind corner in an effort to stop the train and, when this proved to be a success, they disguised themselves as Klu Klux Klansmen and robbed the occupants of the train. Despite the ingenuity of the plan the gang only profited to the tune of $2000.

Jesse was not put off by their small haul from the Rock Island hold-up and he continued with the new challenge. Train robberies were reported in Texas, Montana Territory, Colorado and Arkansas. Although more people died during these attacks the gang made a considerable amount of money and they were never in danger of being caught. As a sideline the gang also robbed stage-coaches, stores and individuals. Whenever a crime was reported in a newspaper in association with the James Gang, Jesse would write to the newspaper and deny that he had been involved.

Thorn in the side

The organization that was most frustrated by the activities of the James Gang was the Pinkerton Detective Agency. Since their main source of income was derived from the protection of trains and mail coaches the crime wave that was spreading through the West was not good for their image. They offered a reward for Jesse James and had several agents on his trail. When one of these men was discovered by Jesse he was hanged from a tree, with an accompanying note which read, 'Compliments of the James Boys to the Pinkertons'.

After 10 years of successful criminal activity the James Gang had their first setback. On 7 September 1876 the gang raided a bank at Northfield, Minnesota, but for once their plans were shambolic. Before they could complete the raid they were surrounded; three of the gang members were killed and another three were captured. Jesse and Frank James were the only ones to escape and they had no hesitation in deserting their colleagues. For the next three years they deemed it wise to lie low.

Traitorous gang member

By 1879 Jesse had put together a new gang, but they never quite performed with the same gusto as the initial group. In 1879 they committed one train robbery, followed by another two in 1881. By now the authorities were becoming desperate to bring the James brothers to justice and in 1881 the governor of Missouri, Thomas T Crittenden, offered a $10 000 reward for them, dead or alive. It proved to be too tempting for one of the James Gang members, Bob Ford. He went to visit Jesse at St Joseph, Missouri, where he had been living under the name of Thomas Howard. On 3 April 1882, while he had his back turned adjusting a picture, Bob Ford shot Jesse James through the back of the head. He died instantly.

Following his brother's murder Frank James surrendered. He was brought to trial twice but on both occasions he was acquitted. He settled in Missouri and lived a respectable life until his death in 1915.

Characteristics

Jesse James was of medium height, well built but slim, with a narrow bearded face and piercing blue eyes. He had a good sense of humour and enjoyed a joke, but this was balanced by a quick temper. As he grew older he became more suspicious of those around him and even shot dead one man whom he thought had betrayed him. He claimed he became an outlaw because of the persecution he and his family suffered during the Civil War. He joined the Baptist Church in 1868 and maintained his Christian faith until his death.

Folk hero

A popular song was written shortly after the shooting of Jesse James:
Jesse James's lovely wife
Became a widder all her life,
Though her children they were brave.
Oh, the dirty little coward
That shot poor Mister Howard
And laid Jesse James in his grave.

Joyce, William (Lord Haw-Haw)

(1906–46)

Traitor

A propaganda expert who served Germany during World War II and was later tried in Britain as a traitor.

William Joyce was born in Brooklyn, New York. His father was originally from Ireland but had become a naturalized American citizen in 1894. In 1921 William went to England and later took a first class honours degree at London University. He felt at home in England and he saw the country developing into an imperial superpower. In 1933 he applied for a British passport, which was granted due to his false claim that he had been born in Ireland.

Fascist devotee

After being a member of the British Fascist Party and the Conservative Party, in 1933 he joined Sir Oswald Mosley's British Union of Fascists. He was an impressive speaker and organizer and within two years he had risen to the post of Director of Propaganda and Deputy Leader. However, in 1934 he fell out with Mosley and formed his own party, the British National Socialist League. He was convinced that fascism was the only way forward for Britain and on the eve of World War II he fled to Germany, hoping to impose a fascist state in Britain.

Initially the Germans were unimpressed by Joyce but they recognized his oratory talents and made him an English announcer in the Propaganda Ministry. Almost immediately he was a success. He made broadcasts to Britain, claiming what a wonderful way of life there was in Germany and that the Allied forces were going to suffer grave military setbacks. The British public were disconcerted by these broadcasts, particularly as Joyce had a hypnotic, educated English accent.

Lord Haw-Haw

Joyce continued to make his broadcasts, from Zeesen, Hamburg, Bremen and other locations, until 1945. At one point an English journalist gave him the nickname 'Lord Haw-Haw' on account of his accent. The name stuck and from that moment he became a figure of fun rather than a serious threat to public morale.

Once Germany had been defeated Joyce tried to escape to Holland. However, two alert border guards recognized his voice and arrested him.

Joyce was taken back to England and charged with high treason. His trial began at the Old Bailey on 17 September 1945. The first point to establish was whether he was a British citizen or not. The judge, Mr Justice Tucker, ruled that he was an American since he had been born there and his father was a US citizen. However, the prosecution argued that, because he was holding a British passport when he made his first broadcast, he owed allegiance to the British Crown. This argument was accepted and Joyce was found guilty and sentenced to death. There was considerable debate over the legality of the verdict.

Two appeals failed and on 3 January 1946 Joyce was hanged at Wandsworth Prison.

> **Treason law**
> The essence of the British treason law is the maxim *protectio trahit subjectionem, et subjectio protectionem* (protection attracts allegiance, allegiance attracts protection). It was argued that since Joyce was protected by the Crown when he held a British passport he therefore owed his allegiance to the Crown.

Murder of Emily Beilby Kaye

(1924)

Patrick Herbert Mahon

*An apparently charming man
who murdered his lover and then
hacked her to pieces.*

Patrick Mahon was born in 1890 of a prosperous middle-class family in Liverpool. He was handsome, charming and attracted women easily. In 1910 he married his childhood sweetheart, Jessie, who soon discovered that he was a philanderer and a swindler. In 1916 he was imprisoned for five years for attacking a woman with a hammer during a bungled robbery. On his release he obtained a job, thanks to his forgiving wife, as sales manager for a firm in Sunbury.

It was during a sales trip to London at the beginning of 1923 that Mahon met Emily Kaye, a 38-year-old secretary. She was an attractive, strong-willed woman and she set her sights on the dashing salesman. Never one to pass up an opportunity, Mahon began an affair with Emily Kaye.

Love experiment

The affair proceeded happily for a year but then Emily started hinting at marriage. Mahon was horrified and insisted that it remained a casual affair. In April 1924 Emily planned to rent a cottage so that the couple could undergo a 'love-experiment', during which time Mahon might be won over. She found the ideal place, a cottage called the Officer's House on the Crumbles, near Eastbourne.

The couple agreed to meet at the Crumbles cottage on 12 April. Before she went, Emily told her friends that she was engaged to Mahon and that they were going to emigrate to South Africa. Mahon obviously had other ideas because he stopped in London to buy a cook's knife and a small meat-saw. The last time Emily Kaye was seen alive was 14 April 1924.

By this time Mrs Mahon was becoming suspicious of her husband's comings and goings so she searched his clothes and found a cloakroom ticket for Waterloo station. It yielded a bag that contained blood-stained female clothing. The police watched the cloakroom and when Mahon came to pick up the bag on 2 May he was arrested.

Gruesome find

After interviewing Mahon the police visited the Crumbles cottage, where they made a gruesome discovery. Not only had Emily Kaye been murdered but her body had been crudely dismembered: her limbless torso was in a trunk, her heart and other organs were in a biscuit tin and hatbox, various other parts had been boiled in a saucepan and there were charred remains in the dining-room and sitting-room grates.

During his trial, which began on 15 July 1924, Mahon claimed that Emily had died as a result of a fall following an argument about their affair. He gave a dramatic performance but it did not prevent the jury from finding him guilty. Dubbed one of the wickedest men in Britain, Patrick Mahon was hanged on 9 September 1924.

Murder Bag

When the famous pathologist Sir Bernard Spilsbury arrived at the Crumbles cottage he was shocked to find one of the police officers using his bare hands to pick up bits of flesh. He consulted with Scotland Yard and thereafter a Murder Bag, with all the necessary equipment, was taken to the scene of every murder.

Keating, Thomas Patrick

(1917–84)

Art forger

The creator of over 2000 fake paintings, which he used to expose the pretensions of the highbrow art world.

Tom Keating was born in Forest Hill, London. When he was 10 he won a box of paints in a school competition and immediately became enthralled with drawing and painting. He left school when he was 14 and tried a variety of jobs before working for his father as a decorator. It was during this time that he expanded his artistic knowledge by learning how to mix paint.

In 1947, after being invalided out of the navy, Keating took an art course at Goldsmiths' College, in London. He had his heart set on teaching but after failing his exams he had to settle for working in a restoration studio in London. His failure at college led to him harbouring a grudge against what he saw as an elitist and uncaring art world.

Illusions shattered

At the restoration studio Keating was asked to make copies of various paintings. When he later discovered that they were being sold as originals it was the last straw and he decided to take his revenge against the hypocrisy displayed by art dealers and collectors.

Keating left the restoration studio and set himself up as a freelance restorer. He proved a moderate success at this but his talent lay in his hobby — the creation of fake paintings. Over the next 25 years he produced forgeries of the work of over 130 artists, including Rembrandt, Constable, Degas, Renoir and Turner. He later estimated that he had put over 2000 imitations onto the market.

Keating's intention was never to make a large profit from his work (he either gave the paintings away or sold them for moderate sums at small auctions), he only wanted to show that the so-called experts were not infallible.

'Joke' is revealed

It was not until 1976 that anyone questioned any of Keating's fakes. An art expert writing in *The Times* claimed that a series of water-colours by Samuel Palmer were not his genuine work. Keating immediately wrote to *The Times* and proudly admitted what he had done. He had no desire to escape detection, as he wanted to show the world how easily the experts could be fooled.

Keating was arrested, and tried at the Old Bailey for forgery. He quickly become a cult figure and there was widespread relief when the case against him was dropped because of his deteriorating health.

In 1982 Tom Keating was given his own television art show on Channel 4. He gave a highly polished performance and won a Broadcasting Press Guild award. In 1983 135 of his paintings were sold as Keating originals, fetching a total of £72 000. It was the first time in his life that he had a substantial amount of money. Unfortunately his health prevented him from enjoying it and he died in Colchester on 12 February 1984.

Sexton Blakes
Using his own form of Cockney rhyming slang Keating dubbed his work 'Sexton Blakes'. He also said that fooling the experts had been the greatest pleasure of his life; the thought of it made him helpless with laughter.

Kelly, Edward (Ned)

(1855–80)

Bushranger

Australia's most famous bushranger who was driven by a fierce hatred of the police.

Ned Kelly was born in 1855 at the township of Beveridge, 20 miles north of Melbourne. His father had been transported from Ireland for stealing pigs and from an early age Ned was bitterly anti-English, citing his father's transportation as an example of the injustices in the English legal system.

In 1860 the Kellys moved to Avenel in New South Wales and from 1866, when his father died, Ned was constantly in trouble with the police. The Kelly family were well known to the district troopers who had once been heard to pledge to 'send the Kellys to Pentridge (a notorious Melbourne jail) even on a paltry offence'. This heightened Ned's dislike of the authorities and he spent most of his teenage years as a horse-thief.

In 1878 a warrant was issued for the arrest of Ned and his younger brother Dan, on horse-stealing charges. A local policeman, Constable Fitzpatrick, who had a particular dislike of the Kellys, was sent to Mrs Kelly's house at Greta to see if her sons where there. When he reached the house he threatened Mrs Kelly with a gun, just as Dan entered the house. There was a brief struggle during which Mrs Kelly struck Fitzpatrick over the head with a shovel and Dan escaped from the house.

Driven into the bush

Following this incident Mrs Kelly was harshly sentenced to three years' imprisonment, due mostly to some very dubious evidence from Fitzpatrick who was later dismissed from the police force for being a 'liar and a larriken'. A warrant was issued for the arrest of Ned and Dan Kelly for attempted murder. It was these events that led to Ned Kelly commencing a life on the run in the bush.

Ned and Dan fled to the hills in the Wombat Ranges in Victoria, and they were joined by two other men, Steve Hart and Joe Byrne. The gang supported themselves by searching for gold and preparing to distil moonshine. In October 1878 a group of four policemen, Sergeant Kennedy and Constables Lonigan, Scanlon and McIntyre, were patrolling the hills in search of the Kelly Gang. Kelly spotted them first and planned to raid their camp at Stringybark Creek and seize their firearms. Unfortunately when they surprised the camp one of the policemen opened fire and in the ensuing gun-battle Lonigan, Scanlon and Kennedy were killed, while McIntyre alone managed to escape.

Kelly and his gang were now wanted for murder and a £1000 price was put on their heads. In an attempt to avenge their murdered colleagues the police launched the largest and most expensive man-hunt in Australian history. The gang had the advantage of knowing the country intimately and a wide network of sympathizers made sure that Ned and his companions were always a step ahead of the police.

Audacious robbers

Money was of vital importance to the Kelly Gang if they were to maintain a successful campaign against the police and so in December 1878 Ned masterminded a daring bank-raid at the township of Euroa, at the foot of the Strathbogie Ranges. They began by taking 20 people hostage at a homestead on the edge of Euroa, then calmly went into town and robbed the bank of £2000. The whole operation was spread over two days and during this time not a single shot was fired. The police were furious when they heard of the raid but the general public admired the audacity and the coolness of the gang.

Despite efforts by the police to trap them in Victoria the four men crossed into New South Wales and in February 1879 they carried out a raid at Jerilderie which was even more daring than the Euroa robbery. They walked into the police station, overpowered the town's two constables and put them in the lock-up with a solitary drunk. They then commandeered the local hotel and while Dan Kelly and Steve Hart held the town's population hostage Ned and Joe Bryne removed £2140 from the bank. Once again there was no violence and Ned even had time to tell his hostages his philosophy of life: a firm belief in Irish independence and a hatred of Saxon oppression.

End of the line

There was outrage from the authorities after the Jerilderie raid and the reward for the gang was increased to £2000 per head. Due to this they kept a low profile for a year, no doubt enjoying the ridicule that was being directed at the police for their inability to locate the gang. Then on 26 June 1880 Aaron Sherritt, a known police informer, was shot dead by Joe Bryne at Beechworth. It was the beginning of another of Ned's plans: he knew a large number of policemen would be sent once they heard of the shooting and he proposed to derail their train at Glenrowan, kill as many of them as possible and then raid one of the banks in the neighbouring town of Benella.

Following his usual tactics Ned rounded up the town's population and held them at the Glenrowan Inn. The gang then settled down to wait for the train. Unfortunately it was about 12 hours later than expected and by the time it arrived at two o'clock in the morning the local schoolmaster had managed to escape from the hotel and had warned the train and its occupants of the danger.

Cornered

The siege at the Glenrowan Inn lasted seven hours and it was a hopeless situation for Ned Kelly and his gang. Joe Bryne was the first to die and Ned himself was wounded as he faced the police in his homemade armour. When he was finally captured the armour was found to have been hit by 25 bullets. Unfortunately for Ned it was cumbersome and severely restricted his movements. The police ended the siege by setting fire to the Inn and when they entered the building they found the bodies of Dan Kelly and Steve Hart, both of whom had committed suicide rather than be captured.

Ned Kelly was tried in Melbourne for the murders of Constables Lonigan and Scanlon. He was found guilty and hanged on 11 November 1880 in Pentridge Gaol.

Legend
It is said to have cost £115 000 to capture a man who is now considered to be an Australian hero. In reality he was someone who had passionate beliefs and he considered himself justified in everything he did.

Brave to the end
Shortly before he was hanged Ned Kelly's mother visited him in his prison cell and told him, 'Mind you die like a Kelly, Ned'. This he did, and it is generally agreed that he 'died game' — an important aspect of the bushranger's code of conduct.

Assassination of President John F Kennedy

(1963)

Lee Harvey Oswald

A political assassination that stunned America and sent shock-waves around the world.

According to the findings of the Warren Commission, Lee Harvey Oswald shot and killed John Fitzgerald Kennedy, the 35th President of the United States of America, at 12.30pm on 22 November 1963. Kennedy was the youngest-ever president and the first Catholic to hold that office, and the fourth to be assassinated. He was an immensely popular leader and his death is still hotly debated, especially since the 1992 film *JFK.*

Portrait of an assassin

Lee Harvey Oswald was born in New Orleans on 18 October 1929. His father had died two months earlier and when his mother's second marriage failed he became difficult and unsettled. He dropped out of school when he was 16 and after a brief tour with the marines he obtained a compassionate discharge and went to Russia, in 1959. While he was there he married a 19-year-old Russian named Marina Nikolalaevna Prusakova and became a supporter of communism. He tried to obtain a resident's permit but when this was refused he and Marina returned to America on 14 June 1962, settling in Dallas.

Oswald was unhappy back in his home country and his wife became disconcerted when he bought a Männlicher-Carano rifle and a Smith and Wesson hand-gun. She later said that she thought he used the rifle in an unsuccessful attempt to kill a retired army general. In September 1963 Oswald was desperate to leave America and he visited the Russian embassy and the Cuban

consulate in Mexico City in an effort to enter either country. His requests were refused and he returned to America an angry and embittered man. He took a job in Dallas at the Texas School Book Depository.

On 21 November 1963 Oswald visited his wife in Irving, Texas, where she was convalescing after the birth of their second child. He then returned to Dallas, knowing that President Kennedy was visiting the city the following day.

American hero

When President Kennedy, and his wife Jacqueline, arrived in Dallas on 22 November it was in the knowledge that he was as well liked by the public as a man in his position could be. He had gained considerable respect for his treatment of Kruschev during the Cuban Missile Crisis (1962) and his civil rights reforms had won him many admirers. But most of all the public appreciated his clean-cut, all-American image. Despite this he had made a number of enemies — the communists, right-wing whites in the south, and the Mafia, against whom he campaigned vigorously.

Ignoring the obvious threats to his life President Kennedy was reluctant to adopt excessive security procedures. He did not allow police out-riders to accompany his motorcade, nor did he permit Secret Service bodyguards to sit with him in the rear of his car.

Fatal motorcade

The reason for the President's visit to Dallas was to boost the Democrats' ailing fortunes in the city. A highly publicized motorcade was organized and it set off through the streets of Dallas shortly after 11.30am. Kennedy and his wife were in the third car of the convoy, sitting in the back of their limousine with Governor John B Connally and his wife. Secret Service men occupied the two front seats. There was a huge crowd to see the President and despite earlier doubts they gave him a rapturous welcome.

As the presidential limousine passed the Texas School Book Depository on Elm Street, Lee Harvey Oswald fired two shots from a sixth-storey window. Both of them hit Kennedy, one of them passing through his neck and striking Governor Connally. The Governor recovered from his injuries but President Kennedy died shortly afterwards in Parkland Memorial Hospital.

Immediately after the shooting Oswald went downtown and committed a second murder, shooting a policeman at point-blank range. He then fled into a cinema, where he was eventually overpowered by the police.

Killer is slain

As the shock of the assassination began to sink in around the world, people began to debate who was ultimately responsible. Conspiracy theories were suggested in connection with the Russian and Cuban governments, the Mafia and the CIA. On 24 November the one man who knew the full answer was murdered. While Lee Harvey Oswald was on his way to a press conference in the Dallas police headquarters he was fatally shot by Jack Ruby, a nightclub owner with underworld connections. The ease with which Ruby performed the murder only served to increase speculation about a conspiracy.

The answer to the riddle of Kennedy's death probably died with Oswald but since then it has been the most hotly debated assassination of modern times. In 1979 a Select Committee of the House of Representatives declared that there was a high probability that two gunmen had fired at the President and that three bullets had been used, not two. However, the committee cleared the Russian and Cuban governments and the Mafia of any involvement, although they did say that individuals from the underworld could have been involved. They also concluded that it was likely that the President died as a result of some form of conspiracy. However, despite all the theories that have been put forward it is possible that Oswald acted alone.

Headlines announcing Kennedy's assassination

Moment of impact

Governor Connally spoke of the moment the shots were fired: 'I was hit ... I was knocked over, just doubled over by the force of the bullet ... I heard another shot. It hit with a very pronounced impact ... it made a very, very strong sound. Immediately I could see blood and brain tissue all over the interior of the car and all over our clothes'. Jacqueline Kennedy was more graphic at the moment of the shooting: 'They have killed my husband ... I have his brains in my hand'.

Committee's comments

The Select Committee of 1979 had serious concerns about the death of Lee Harvey Oswald: 'The committee was troubled by the apparently unlocked doors along the stairway route, and the removal of security guards from the area of the garage nearest the stairway shortly before the shooting'. Ruby was convicted of murder and died in prison 1967. His pistol sold for $220 000 in 1991.

Murder of Francis Saville Kent

(1860)

Constance Kent

A murder which resulted in an acquittal and then a very unsatisfactory confession.

Constance Kent had a difficult childhood; by the time she was 16 she had acquired a reputation as a strange child. This was not helped by the fact that her mother had been declared insane and then died in 1852. A year later her father, Samuel Kent, married his children's governess.

Jealousy leads to murder

The new Mrs Kent soon had three children and she devoted herself to them, at the expense of the children from Kent's first marriage. On the morning of 30 June 1860 it was discovered that three-year-old Francis Savile Kent was missing from his cot. A search of the grounds revealed the body of the boy, with his throat cut, in the outside privy. The local police were unable to solve the crime so Chief Inspector Whicher from Scotland Yard was sent for.

Whicher was immediately suspicious of Constance, on the evidence that her nightdress was missing and because she was known to be jealous of her half-brother. She was charged with murder but on 27 July 1860 she was released due to the lack of evidence. Two months later the Kents' nurse, Elizabeth Gough, was arrested but she too was released.

Confession from the convent

To avoid a scandal Constance was sent to a convent school in France immediately after the trial. She returned to England in August 1863, when she entered St Mary's Convent in Brighton. Two years later, in April 1865, Constance Kent made the shocking admission that she had murdered Francis Savile Kent five years earlier. It was a strange confession and it is thought that the Reverend at the Convent, Arthur Wagner, had put pressure on her to confess. Nevertheless, Constance was arrested again and on 21 July 1865 she was found guilty of murder. The death sentence was commuted to life imprisonment and on her release in 1885 she emigrated to Canada.

Despite her confession there was considerable doubt about the guilt of Constance Kent, with a number of people taking the view that evidence had been suppressed. This included information that the cause of death was strangulation, despite the fact that Constance insisted the murder weapon had been a razor blade.

Alternative explanation

A more popular explanation was that Samuel Kent killed his son. The theory was that he was having an affair with Elizabeth Gough, and one evening the boy saw them together. In a panic, Kent smothered his face and strangled him. He then took the body outside and mutilated it in the fashion of other knife attacks that had been taking place in the area at the time. Kent's evasive behaviour during the investigation suggests that this is the likely version of events.

Runaway

When Constance was 12 she dressed up as a boy and tried to run away to the West Indies with her brother. The local newspaper hailed her a 'little hero' but her family used it as evidence that she was abnormal.

Kidd, William (Captain Kidd)

(c.1645–1701)

Privateer

A seaman who was ordered to apprehend pirates and later became one himself.

William Kidd was born in Greenock but brought up on the east coast of America. Initially he lived in New York and spent much of his time with the local pirates, listening to their stories and observing their way of life.

In 1695 William III appointed the Earl of Bellomont governor of New England and New York. One of his first problems was to deter the pirates who raided his shores. Knowing that Kidd, now a respected sea-captain, had an intimate knowledge of the pirate's way of life he asked him to lead an expedition designed to round up and capture as many as possible. Sensing the likely financial gains, the venture was backed by a number of influential members of the British Government.

Pirate captain

At the beginning of 1696 Kidd and his company of 155 men sailed from New York in the *Adventure Galley*. The captain, thinking that the most profitable place to find pirates would be the Red Sea, headed for Madagascar. Once they arrived Kidd became decidedly over-zealous and rather than just capturing pirates he followed their example. After the British Government received a number of complaints, Bellomont ordered Kidd back to America. On his way he stopped at Gardiner's Island and buried a substantial amount of treasure from his most valuable prize, the *Quedah Merchant*.

Kidd tried to convince Bellomont that he had not been involved in piracy because all the ships he had taken were French and, since the two countries were at war, legitimate targets. He even handed over the passes from the French ships to prove his claim. But Bellomont was not convinced, as he had heard several accounts of vicious piracy, and sent Kidd back to England.

Scapegoat

When Kidd arrived in England the people who had financed his venture realized that it would be politically expedient if he were restrained from revealing the nature of their involvement. He was arrested and it was clear that he was going to be made a scapegoat. He was not only charged with piracy against six ships but also with the murder of one of the *Adventure*'s crew, whom he allegedly hit over the head with a bucket. The judge was strongly prejudiced against Kidd, and the French passes that he had produced when he arrived in America had now mysteriously disappeared. Kidd was found guilty of piracy and murder and was hanged at Execution Dock on 23 May 1701.

Although it is highly likely that Captain Kidd was involved in some piratical activities there is some justification in his claim that he only attacked legitimate targets. The French passes which went missing before his trial were discovered 200 years later in the Public Record Office in London.

Pirates or privateers?
During times of war private vessels were encouraged to plunder enemy merchant shipping under licence from their government. During peacetime, however, these privateering licences were revoked and the seamen involved reverted to the status of pirates, for which there were severe punishments.

Kray Twins

Ronald and Reginald Kray (1933–   )

Gangsters and convicted murderers

Identical twins who controlled the London underworld during the 1960s.

Ronnie and Reggie Kray were born on 17 October 1933 in the East End of London. Reggie was the older by an hour. Although they could be polite and charming they were ruthless with their contemporaries and were frequently getting into violent fights. They were known in the neighbourhood as the 'Terrible Twins'. In 1951 they became professional boxers at lightweight, and they invariably won their contests.

In 1952 the twins were called up for National Service but decided to go on the run instead. For the next two years they were constantly in trouble with the Army and spent much of their time in military prisons. They put these periods to good use and learnt as much about the criminal world as they could. When they were dishonourably discharged in 1954 they were ready to establish their criminal empire.

The Firm

The Krays set themselves up in a billiard hall in the East End of London. Ronnie, the dominant partner, styled himself on Al Capone, acquiring the title of the 'Colonel'. Reggie had a better mind for figures and he was responsible for the organization of their business. They ruled through fear and intimidation and soon the Krays' 'Firm' was in control of most of the East End.

In the summer of 1956 Ronnie Kray went on a revenge mission against a gang who had beaten up one of their associates. He arrived at a pub where he thought the gang would be and set about the first person he saw. He was subsequently arrested and sentenced to three years' imprisonment for causing grievous bodily harm.

With Ronnie in prison Reggie could carry on building the Kray empire. He bought a club in Bow and reopened it as the Double R. It was an immediate success and was frequented by celebrities of showbusiness and the criminal world alike. The Firm even set up an illegal gambling club next to the Bow police station.

Mental illness

While Ronnie was in prison it became clear that he was suffering from a mental illness and in February 1958 he was moved to an asylum in Surrey. Visitors were allowed and on one occasion Reggie arranged his brother's escape by swapping places with him. However, Ronnie's mother soon realized that he was in need of help; he was returned to custody, but responded to treatment and was released in 1958.

In February 1960 it was Reggie's turn to serve a prison sentence, for demanding money with menaces. During this period Ronnie acquired a new venue, Esmeralda's Barn in Knightsbridge. It was at this time that he began admitting to being homosexual.

During the 1960s the Krays ruled the criminal world in London. They lived a lavish lifestyle, opening successful clubs and mixing with celebrities from all walks of life. But they maintained their ruthless streak and were feared throughout the underworld. In 1965 the twins were charged with demanding money with menaces but the jury were so intimidated that the case collapsed.

Gang rivalry

The only serious threat to the domination of the Firm was the Richardson gang from

Reginald and *Ronald Kray* with their mother and grandfather

south London. At Christmas 1965 George Cornell, one of the Richardson henchmen, taunted Ronnie about his homosexuality and an all-out gang war was declared. In March 1966 Cornell was involved in a raid on a pub under the Krays' control. Seeking revenge, Ronnie found Cornell in the Blind Beggar pub in Bethnal Green and calmly shot him between the eyes. No witnesses were prepared to come forward and implicate Ronnie Kray.

Following the murder of Cornell, Ronnie taunted his brother about never having killed a man. Reggie was drinking heavily at this time and he was in the mood to respond to his brother's goading. In October 1967 he was having problems with a small-time villain named Jack 'The Hat' McVitie and decided that he would be a suitable victim. On 28 October McVitie was invited to a party in the basement of a rented flat. When he arrived, Reggie Kray put a gun against his head and fired. The gun jammed and McVitie struggled wildly for his life, but someone handed Reggie a carving-knife and, with Ronnie shouting encouragement, he hacked McVitie to death. The body was never found.

Undercover operation

Despite the fact that the Krays liked to think

they were above the law, their activities attracted an enormous amount of police attention. An extensive undercover operation, headed by Commander John du Rose and Detective Superintendent Leonard Read, was launched by Scotland Yard. One of the people interviewed made a statement of over 200 pages, enough to arrest Reggie and Ronnie. On 9 May 1968 68 policemen raided a house in Shoreditch where the Kray twins were staying.

Once the Krays were in custody 28 criminals were promised immunity if they gave evidence against them. Their trial was one of the longest and most expensive in British criminal history. It took place at the Old Bailey and lasted 39 days from January to March 1969. They were both found guilty of double murder and sentenced to life imprisonment of not less than 30 years.

Unsolved disappearance

In 1966 the Krays arranged for Frank Mitchell, nicknamed the Mad Axe Man, to escape from Dartmoor prison. They sent him to a hideout in East London and even provided a nightclub hostess to keep him company. He soon became troublesome though and he was disposed of. His body has never been found.

Kreuger, Ivar

(1880–1932)

Swindler and financial forger

An international swindler who was a trusted figure in European and American business circles.

Ivar Kreuger was born in the Swedish seaside town of Kalmar. From an early age he showed a propensity for swindling and his philosophy was the realization of the maximum results with the minimum of effort.

In 1900 Kreuger made his first visit to America and he soon realized that this was a place where people were always willing to lend money — a factor that was to play a vital part in his life. He worked in several engineering jobs and in 1908 he returned to Sweden to form the construction company Kreuger and Toll, which was an immediate success.

When his father died in 1913 Kreuger decided to take over the family match-manufacturing business. He set about revolutionizing the match business in Sweden and by the end of World War I his new company, the Swedish Match Company, had a virtual monopoly in its home country.

The Match King

But Kreuger was not prepared to rest on his laurels: he had his eyes on a worldwide match monopoly. He did this by offering loans to countries that had run into financial difficulties during the war. All that he asked in return was the monopoly for producing matches in these countries. In total, the Match King, as Kreuger became known, lent £100 million in return for match monopolies in over 13 countries.

The source of the money for these loans was America, where Kreuger soon became a respected financial figure. Companies invested heavily in him but what they did not know was that his impressive fortune was largely fabricated by complicated financial manoeuvering. Kreuger's favourite trick was to create a company and then transfer a large sum of money, on paper, to it from another of his businesses.

Resorts to forgery

In 1927 Kreuger lent the French government £15 million to alleviate a short-term financial crisis. Two years later he did a similar deal with the German government. Both of these loans were paid in instalments but in 1930 several of the countries who owed Kreuger money defaulted on their interest payments. Since this was his main source of income he was in serious difficulty; he knew if he failed with a payment of his French and German loans then his shaky empire would be exposed.

To try and raise the money Kreuger turned to forgery and fabricated 42 Italian Treasury bills worth a total of over £20 million. At first these were accepted as genuine but when they were revealed to be forgeries, Kreuger knew that his credibility was ruined; rather than face exposure he shot himself in Paris on 11 March 1932.

International swindles

One of Kreuger's favourite swindles was to transfer large sums of money between different banks. On the strength of the receipts that he obtained he then borrowed even larger sums. He also conned the central government bank of Sweden, by promising them goldmine stock as security for a loan. What the bank did not know at the time was that the stock had already been pledged to another bank.

Kurten, Peter

(1883–1931)

Convicted murderer

Known as the 'Monster of Düsseldorf', Kurten held the city in fear during a five-year reign of terror.

Born in Cologne-Mulheim, Germany, Peter Kurten moved to Düsseldorf with his family in 1894. His upbringing was an extremely unhappy one — his father was a violent drunk who used to beat his wife and abuse her sexually in front of his children. At an early age Peter Kurten was following his father's example and raping his sister frequently.

When he was eight Peter Kurten was introduced to the local dog-catcher, who had a habit of torturing the animals he caught. Kurten entered into this practice with great enthusiasm and he later claimed that the sight of blood gave him a sexual thrill. He was soon involved in acts of bestiality with sheep, goats and pigs, always stabbing them in the process.

In 1899 Kurten stole some money and ran away from home. He was soon in trouble with the law and was imprisoned for theft. In total, he spent 24 years of his life in prison.

Murderous fantasies

During his periods of imprisonment Kurten was able to indulge in his own perverse fantasies. He liked to imagine being responsible for acts of mass murder, such as blowing up a bridge with a train on it, killing hundreds of people in a huge fire, or giving arsenic-laced sweets to a class of school-children. He later admitted that these fantasies gave him immense sexual satisfaction.

On 25 May 1913 Kurten graduated from theft and arson to murder. He was in the process of robbing an inn at Cologne-Mulheim when he found a 10-year-old girl asleep in her bed. He raped her and then strangled her, finally stabbing her repeatedly.

Gruesome query

Shortly before his execution Kurten asked the police psychiatrist, Professor Karl Berg, 'After my head has been chopped off, will I still be able to hear, at least for a moment, the sound of my blood gushing from the stump of my neck? That would be the pleasure to end all pleasures'.

Psychiatric study

After numerous interviews with Kurten, Karl Berg wrote a classic study of the sexual killer: *The Sadist* (Heinemann, 1933). He concluded that his unhappy childhood could have been the major factor in the development of his sadistic character.

Peter Kurten

During World War I Kurten chose not to fight, and spent most of the war years in prison. In 1921 he was released and went to Altenburg, where he married and appeared to become a respectable citizen. He was quiet and well-mannered, had a job as a moulder, became an active trade unionist and dressed with meticulous care. Children in particular adored him.

Vampire tendencies

After living a seemingly harmless life for nearly four years Kurten and his wife moved to Düsseldorf in 1925. For the next five years he began enacting his fantasies. He attacked innocent strangers with scissors and knives, gaining sexual satisfaction by the sight of their blood. By 1929 there were 46 unsolved perverted crimes in Düsseldorf, including four murders. One of the distinguishing features of them was that the police believed the killer had drunk the blood of his victims.

During the summer of 1929 Kurten committed a variety of sexual attacks and murders. He did not mind how he killed his victims, usually stabbing or strangling them, or whether they were old or young, male or female. He killed one eight-year-old girl and also a 45-year-old businessman. By this time the citizens of Düsseldorf were in a state of panic and the case had created international interest. It was reminiscent of the fear induced by Jack the Ripper, a fact that would have pleased Kurten since the Ripper was one of his idols.

Increased activity

On the evening of 23 August 1929 two young girls were brutally murdered as they left a funfair and later the same night a servant-girl was stabbed but survived. Kurten was stepping up his attacks and the next three months saw a catalogue of murder and vicious assaults. His last known victim was a five-year-old girl whom he killed on 27 November, inflicting 36 wounds on her body. Even though the murders stopped the attacks continued.

In May 1930 a 21-year-old maid named Maria Budlick came to Düsseldorf looking for work. She was befriended by a man at the station but she became suspicious of his intentions. To her relief another man came to her assistance, but unfortunately for Maria her saviour was Peter Kurten. He took her back to his flat for something to eat and then, as he was walking her to her hostel, he raped her. Afterwards, he asked her if she remembered where he lived. Maria said that she did not and this appeared to satisfy Kurten, who left her where she was.

Maria wrote to a friend telling her of the incident but the letter was delivered to the wrong address and eventually opened by a Post Office worker. He took it to the police who immediately contacted Maria and asked her to take them to the house she had visited in Düsseldorf. By the time the police arrived Kurten had fled.

Quiet surrender

Kurten went immediately to his unsuspecting wife and told her that he was the Monster of Düsseldorf and urged her to turn him in so she could claim the reward that was on offer for his capture. She was disbelieving at first but finally agreed. When the police came for him Kurten surrendered with a smile, saying, 'There is no need to be afraid'.

The trial of Peter Kurten began on 13 April 1931 in a converted drill-hall at Düsseldorf's police headquarters. Every day thousands of people surrounded the building trying to see the man who had committed such atrocious crimes. He was charged with nine murders and seven attempted murders, although the number he actually killed was probably much higher. He admitted everything, claiming he was a sex maniac, a rapist, an arsonist, a vampire and a sadist. The verdict was a foregone conclusion and he was found guilty on all charges.

Peter Kurten was guillotined on 2 July 1931 at Cologne's Klingelputz Prison. The evening before he ate a last meal of veal and fried potatoes and enjoyed it so much that he asked for a second helping.

Lacenaire, Pierre-François
(1800–36)

Convicted murderer

A murderer who captured the imagination of the French public because of his literary ability.

Following his birth in Paris, Pierre-François Lacenaire became a gifted scholar and had the makings of a talented poet. He joined the French army but found life too tough, and deserted in favour of a career as a wine salesman. In 1830 he took to petty crime but was invariably caught and imprisoned for a few months at a time.

In December 1834 Lacenaire moved from small-time thieving to violent robbery. On 16 December a widow and her son were found hacked and stabbed to death in their flat in Paris. The man was a known homosexual but although the police detained a number of people they made no arrests.

Ill-conceived robbery

Two weeks later, a bank clerk carrying a large sum of money was attacked by two men. He managed to frighten them off and they fled empty-handed. Chief Inspector Canler of the Sûreté was put in charge of the case and he was soon convinced that the attempted robbery had been carried out by the same people who had murdered the widow and her son.

After weeks of meticulous detective work Canler arrested two men, Martin François and Victor Avril, who he thought had been involved with the crimes. He also wanted to interview a man he knew as Gaillard, but he had no clues as to his whereabouts. Fortunately for Canler, François and Avril solved his dilemma; in return for the promise of a light sentence they would divulge Gaillard's

real identity. They named him as Pierre-François Lacenaire and claimed that he was the mastermind behind the two crimes.

Poetic murderer

On 2 February 1835 Lacenaire was arrested in Beaune and taken back to Paris in chains. When they first saw him the police did not believe he was a criminal of any sort; he looked more like a literary figure fallen on hard times. At first he would not tell the police anything, but when he heard that Avril and François had betrayed the criminal's strict code of conduct he vowed revenge. He admitted to his crimes and implicated Avril in the two murders and François in the attempted robbery.

While he was in prison Lacenaire became more of a hero than he had ever been through crime. The French public were intrigued by this poetry-writing murderer and they came to see him in their hundreds. He did not disappoint his audience and while he was awaiting trial he wrote a creditable set of memoirs, in which he justified his actions by claiming he had been a victim of injustice since infancy.

Lacenaire's literary output did little to alter the course of his trial, which began in November 1835. He was found guilty and sentenced to death. Avril fared no better and François was sentenced to life imprisonment. Pierre-François Lacenaire was guillotined on 10 January 1836.

Malfunction
As the blade of the guillotine fell to severe Lacenaire's neck it became stuck in the groove. It had to be raised again, as Lacenaire lay staring into a basket which already contained Avril's head, and on the second attempt it completed the task.

Trial of Lady Chatterley's Lover

(1960)

Penguin Books

A sensational censorship trial at the Old Bailey that set the tone for the Swinging Sixties.

In 1955 the Labour MP Roy Jenkins sponsored a draft obscenity bill in Parliament. It was designed to look at and clarify the obscenity laws, following a spate of prosecutions of books that dealt openly with sex. In 1959 the Obscene Publications Act was passed. It stated that a book could be prosecuted as being obscene if, 'Taken as a whole its effect is such as to tend to deprave and corrupt'. However, there was a clause that provided immunity for genuine works of art, `If it is proved that publication of the article in question is justified as being for the public good on the ground that it is in the interests of science, literature, art or learning, or of other objects of general concern'.

In 1960 the Obscene Publications Act was given its first serious test. It was the year of the 75th anniversary of DH Lawrence's birth and 30 years since his death. To celebrate this double anniversary Penguin Books decided to expand their list of Lawrence titles, including the first full English version of the controversial and sexually explicit *Lady Chatterley's Lover*. The book had been on sale in Britain in its expurgated form since 1928 but a complete version had never been published. It was Sir Allen Lane, the Chairman and founder of Penguin Books, who took the decision to publish *Lady Chatterley's Lover*.

Peaceful offer

In August 1960 the Director of Public Prosecutions, Sir Theobald Mathew, was informed of Penguin's intention and he ordered the police to buy a copy. To make their task easier Penguin invited them to their offices and offered them as many copies as they needed. The police left with 12 volumes and on 19 August Penguin were served a summons under the Obscene Publications Act.

Amid intense public interest, the trial of Penguin Books and *Lady Chatterley's Lover* began at the Old Bailey on 20 October 1960. Although the Prisoner at the Bar was described as Penguin Books Limited, the dock was empty, giving the impression that it was the fictional Lady Chatterley herself who was on trial.

Wives and servants

The prosecution was led by Mervyn Griffith-Jones and he opened by reminding the jury

Lady Chatterley's Lover, Penguin Books

136

of the Obscene Publications Act and giving them the definitions of 'deprave' and 'corrupt'. His task was to prove that the book was not only obscene but that it could not be excused on the grounds of literary merit. He listed the 13 separate incidents of sexual intercourse and also added up the number of obscene words used in the book. He then suggested a method for the jurors to decide whether the work was obscene or not, 'Is it a book that you would wish your wife or your servants to read?'. A ripple of laughter echoed around the court, as people expressed their amazement at someone who was so out of touch with modern times.

The defence, led by Gerald Gardiner QC, opened by claiming that Lawrence's extensive use of four-letter words was designed to expose the hypocrisy with which society treated them. Gardiner went on to say that the book was a moral one that celebrated a physical love between two people, as opposed to the love of money or power.

Lady C at the Old Bailey

After the opening speeches the jury were instructed to read *Lady Chatterley's Lover*. Comfortable leather armchairs were provided for them at the Old Bailey and it took the slowest reader three days to finish the book.

When the trail resumed on 27 October the defence began calling witnesses. In such an important censorship trial experts were queuing up to defend *Lady Chatterley's Lover*. They included Dame Rebecca West, E M Forster, Dilys Powell, Cecil Day Lewis and even the outspoken Bishop of Woolwich. When Graham Hough, Lecturer in English and Fellow of Christ's College, Cambridge was asked whether sex was dragged into the book at every conceivable opportunity he replied, 'No man in his senses is going to write a book of 300 pages as mere padding for 30 pages of sexual matter'.

Support for Penguin

All of the witnesses agreed that although *Lady Chatterley's Lover* was not the best of Lawrence's novel it was nevertheless an important literary work. Almost as persuasive as the literary experts was Miss Sarah

Beryl Jones, Classics Mistress at Keighley Girls Grammar School. She testified that *Lady Chatterley's Lover* was fit to be read by her pupils and said, 'The book deals honestly and openly with the problems of sex — which are very real to the girls'.

In total the defence called 35 expert witnesses to defend the charge against Penguin Books. In face of this the prosecution's cross-examination became less and less enthusiastic. The final triumph came when Roy Jenkins made it clear that the Obscene Publications Act was not intended for use against this type of material.

Popular verdict

After the judge had curtailed the number of defence witnesses the prosecution declared that they would not be calling any witnesses. Even so, the verdict was not a formality. After three hours of deliberation, and to cheers and applause from the public gallery, the jury returned a verdict of Not Guilty against Penguin Books on 2 November 1960.

Whatever else the trial achieved it did wonders for the sales of *Lady Chatterley's Lover*. Penguin had printed 200 000 copies at a cover price of 3s 6d which were quickly sold out as people queued to get a copy of this sensational book. In all the book sold three million copies in the three months after the trial.

An ordinary case
As well as asking the famous question about wives and servants reading *Lady Chatterley's Lover*, Mervyn Griffith-Jones declared in another trial, 'It is a perfectly ordinary case of a man charged with indecency with four or five guardsmen'.

Changed times
Twenty-four years after the trial of *Lady Chatterley's Lover* a plumber in Sussex filed a complaint against his local video shop on the grounds that five pornographic videos he had hired were not explicit enough. He won his case and was awarded a £15 refund.

Lafarge, Marie Fortunée

(1816–51)

Convicted murderess

A young lady who was forced into an arranged marriage and then poisoned her husband.

Maire Fortunée Cappelle was born into a respectable Parisian family who had illegitimate connections to the reigning royal family. By the time she was 18 her parents had died and she was sent to live with a wealthy aunt, who considered her niece something of a burden and endeavoured to get her married off as quickly as possible. A local subprefect was suggested but he did not fit Marie's romantic notion of a handsome aristocrat and she promptly rejected him.

Arranged marriage

By 1839 Marie's aunt decided to take matters into her own hands and find a husband for her niece. She went to a matrimonial agency and chose a wealthy ironmonger named Charles Lafarge, from the Limousin district. When Marie met him she found him overbearing, coarse and entirely unattractive. In addition to this, far from being rich as he had told the agency, he was in fact bankrupt and found Marie's 90 000-franc dowry very attractive.

Despite Marie's protestations she was married to Charles Lafarge in August 1839, and went to live with him in his farmhouse at Le Glandier, just outside Limoges. This was a cause of further dismay for her: the place was a rat-infested shambles and her in-laws were rustic farmers. It did not conform to her romantic image of married life and, to make matters worse, she found her husband physically repellent and refused to consummate the marriage.

Poisonous cake

In November 1839 Charles Lafarge left for Paris to try and patent a new smelting process. Marie cheered up immediately and even baked a cake for her husband, which she sent to Paris. Lafarge became violently ill after eating it and had to return home.

Marie tended personally to her husband and dismissed her maid's enquiries when questioned about a white powder she was mixing with his food. The maid reported her suspicions to the Lafarge family but it was too late to save Charles and he died on 14 January 1840. Marie was suspected immediately and when arsenic was found in his stomach she was arrested.

Marie Lafarge's trial took place in September 1840 and it generated great interest among all levels of French society. The defence enlisted the help of a prominent Paris toxicologist, Professor Orfila, to try and prove that Lafarge had not been poisoned, but unfortunately for them he concluded that the cause of death was criminally administered arsenic. This was all the jury needed and Marie Lafarge was found guilty and sentenced to life imprisonment.

Marie Lafarge spent 10 years in prison and on her release in 1850 she wrote her memoirs, still maintaining her innocence. She died in 1851.

Married life

'The day after my marriage I was obliged to leave my family and all that was familiar to me. Upon arriving at Le Glandier, instead of the charming chateau I had been led to expect, I found a dilapidated ruin. I was so unhappy, I would have given anything in the world to get away'. Marie Lafarge's statement during her trial.

Landru, Henri Desiré

(1869–1922)

Convicted murderer

Dubbed the 'French Bluebeard', he was a mass murderer who killed at least 11 people, purely for financial gain.

Henri Landru was born in Paris into a loving family environment; brought up in a Christian school at Ile St Louis, he was a good scholar and sang in the local choir. When he left school he took a course in engineering and set himself up in various small businesses. Unfortunately his ventures invariably failed.

Instead of pursuing his business activities Landru chose a less scrupulous method of making money. He had a powerful effect on women and used this to exploit elderly widows. He would court them, obtain their money and possessions and then desert them. However, he was not so proficient at avoiding detection and by 1910 he had served seven prison sentences for fraud.

Advertising for a spouse

Towards the end of 1914 Landru, using one of his numerous aliases, ignoring the fact that he was married with four children, inserted a matrimonial advertisement in a Paris newspaper, *Le Journal*: 'Widower with two children, aged 43, with comfortable income, affectionate, serious, and moving in good society, desires to meet widow with view to matrimony'. It was answered by a widow named Mme Cruchet and in December 1914 she and her son went to stay with Landru in a villa he had rented at Vernouillet, on the outskirts of Paris. The Cruchets were last seen on 4 January 1915.

In May 1915 Landru's advertisement again appeared in *Le Journal* and this time there were three responses, from Mmes Laborde-Line, Guillin and Heon. They all knew Landru by a different alias and during the course of the summer they all disappeared, two at Vernouillet and one at Gambais, where Landru had rented another villa. One of the improvements he made when he first moved in was to install a large stove.

Disappearing widows

By 1918 another six women had answered Landru's advertisements, gone to stay with him at his villa at Gambais and were never seen again. But by this time the relatives of the missing women were becoming suspicious. In May 1918 the mayor of Gambais received a letter from a Mme Pelat, enquiring about the whereabouts of her sister, Mme Colomb, who had last been seen at Gambais with a man named Dupont. He may have ignored this if it had not been for a similar letter he had received a few weeks earlier from a Mlle Lacoste. She was enquiring about her sister Mme Buisson who had last been seen at Gambais with a man named Fremyet. The mayor suggested that the two women get together, and when they did they realised that Dupont and Fremyet were the same man.

The two women went to the police and the description of the man — small and bald, with a big red beard — was known to them as an engineer named Guillet. By coincidence, Mlle Lacoste spotted the man she knew as Dupont in a Paris street the day after she had gone to the police. He was followed and arrested the next day. It was soon revealed that his real name was Henri Landru. When he was searched a notebook was discovered, which contained meticulous entries about the women he had met over the years and their financial standings. In all there were 283 names.

Henri Landru and nine of his victims

Circumstancial evidence

The prosecution contended that Landru strangled the 10 women and the boy and then burnt the bodies in his stove. Financial gain was given as the motive, despite the fact that the accused only made small amounts from each of his victims. The defence claimed that the majority of the evidence was circumstantial, as indeed it was, and at one point Landru said to the judge, 'You say that some of these women have not been found. Perhaps they will turn up during the trial'.

The jury took an hour and a half to reach their verdict. Despite the lack of physical evidence Landru was found guilty, largely because of the entries in his notebook, and sentenced to death. He was guillotined on 25 February 1922, in the courtyard of the Versailles prison.

Villa of death

On 29 April 1919 the police searched Landru's villa at Gambais. In the ashes beside the stove they found 295 bone fragments as well as buttons and items of clothing. When neighbours were questioned they said that they frequently saw acrid, black smoke coming out of Landru's chimney.

It took the prosecution two and a half years to prepare a case against Landru. They had to check all the names in his book and they concluded that he had had relationships with at least 179 women. However, there were 11 names that the police could not trace — and Landru had written that he had taken them all to Gambais or Vernouillet. In each case he had bought a return ticket for himself but a single for his companion.

Landru's trial began on 7 November 1921 and he was charged with the murders of 10 women, and the son of one of the women. Throughout the trial the courtroom was packed with women curious to see this murderous 'Bluebeard'. Landru remained calm and composed throughout and on one occasion even offered his seat to some of the women standing at the back of the courtroom.

Guillotine

A French journalist described Landru's execution: 'The two gaolers hastily pushed Landru face foremost against the upright board of the machine. His body crumpled as they shoved him forward under the wooden block, which dropped down and clamped his neck beneath the suspended knife. In a split second the knife flicked down, and the head fell with a thud into a small basket. As an assistant lifted the hinged board and rolled the headless body into the big wicker basket, a hideous spurt of blood gushed out'.

The Landru woman

At the time of his execution Landru's lover was a woman named Fernande Segret. Sixty years after he died a film was made of his life and to everyone's amazement Fernande Segret turned up at the première. She sued the film company for 200 000 francs, but received only 10 000. She later committed suicide in a nursing home in Normandy, having said that she was tired of being pointed out as 'the woman in the Landru case'.

Lauder, William
(c.1680–1771)

Literary forger

A talented classics scholar who forged documents to try and prove that parts of Paradise Lost had been plagiarized from modern Latin poets.

William Lauder was educated at Edinburgh University, where he graduated with an MA on 11 July 1695. He took up teaching and he was only slightly hindered in his profession by the loss of a leg following a golfing accident. For a few months he was assistant to the professor of humanity at Edinburgh University but he then failed to find a satisfactory teaching post.

Critical talent

Lauder was a talented scholar and specialized in modern Latin poetry. In 1739 he published a collection of sacred Latin poems; also included in the volume was the work of Arthur Johnston, a poet writing in Latin. Due to the support of a number of professors at Edinburgh Lauder succeeded in having his work accepted as a textbook in Scottish grammar schools. This infuriated certain members of the establishment, who considered Lauder to be an inept critic and the work of Johnston to be sub-standard.

In 1742 Lauder applied for the rectorship of Dundee grammar school, but was rejected. In disgust he left Scotland and decided to try and make a living in London. Instead of trying to impress the literary world with his own work he chose to stun it by publishing an article, in 1747, in which he contended that much of Milton's *Paradise Lost* consisted of plagiarisms from modern writers of Latin verse.

Sides were quickly taken in the debate centring around Lauder and although Dr Johnson appeared to take his side, a large number of critics denounced his claims. Undeterred, Lauder published another article in which he gave examples of where Milton had borrowed from no less than 18 modern writers of Latin verse, most notably Masenius and Staphorstius.

Interpolations

In the spring of 1750 Bishop John Douglas announced that Lauder had interpolated numerous quotations into the works of the relevant Latin poets. It was then discovered that most of these quotations had been taken by Lauder from a Latin translation of *Paradise Lost*.

Immediately after his forgeries had been exposed Lauder was forced to sign a confession of guilt. Although it was dictated by Dr Johnson Lauder managed to claim that he never had any criminal motives and that the whole exercise was intended to poke fun at the followers of Milton.

Following his exposure, an embittered Lauder tried to make his own mark on the literary world. However, his reputation was ruined and he emigrated to Barbados. His luck did not change and he died in poverty in 1771.

> **Convivial daughter**
> Lauder had one daughter, Rachel. In contrast to her father she was warm-hearted and generous and after his death she became the landlady of the Royal Navy Hotel in Barbados. In 1786 the future William IV visited the hotel and during a drunken evening much of the furniture was smashed. However, he enjoyed his hostess's company to such an extent that he made sure she was amply compensated.

Leopold, Nathan and Loeb, Richard

(1904–71) and (1903–36)

Convicted murderers

Two Chicago teenagers who killed for the thrill of carrying out the 'perfect crime'.

Nathan Leopold was born in 1904 and Richard Loeb a year earlier. They both came from wealthy families and they had all the privileges that life could offer. In 1924 they were both studying law at Chicago University and subscribed to the Nietzschean theory of 'superman'. They carried out some minor thefts to prove they were above conventional laws and ethics.

Perfect crime

In May 1924 Leopold and Loeb decided to carry out a perfect crime. Their plan was to kidnap a rich teenager, kill him and then collect the ransom money. Before they underwent the kidnapping they hired a car and wrote a ransom note on a typewriter obtained from an earlier theft.

On 21 May Leopold and Loeb went in search of a kidnap victim. They met 14-year-old Robert Franks, whose father they knew to be a millionaire. They invited Franks into the car and then killed him by striking him with a chisel and stuffing a cloth into his mouth. They took the body to an area of waste ground called Hegewich, poured acid on it and dropped it into a drain. Mr Franks received the ransom note, but before he could act he had been told that his son was dead.

The main clue was a pair of spectacles that were found at Hegewich and which were traced to Nathan Leopold. It was also discovered that the ransom note had been written on the same typewriter as some

work done by Leopold. He gave his alibi for 21 May as Richard Loeb but this only threw suspicion on them both. The Leopolds' chauffeur added to these suspicions when he stated that he had seen the two boys cleaning blood from the back of a hired car.

Not the perfect crime

When Leopold and Loeb were interrogated separately they broke down and confessed to the crime, although they blamed each other for striking the fatal blow. Their trial began on 23 July 1924 and they were defended by one of the greatest advocates of the day, Clarence Darrow. Darrow's aim was to avoid the death penalty and to this end he lodged a plea of guilty, so that the judge and not a jury would pass sentence. It was a brilliant move and after a highly technical trial that lasted nearly three months (the prosecution still had to prove their case), the judge sentenced Leopold and Loeb to life imprisonment for murder and 99 years' imprisonment for kidnapping.

In 1936 Richard Loeb was stabbed to death during a homosexual riot in Chicago's Joliet prison. Nathan Leopold remained in prison, eventually being released in 1958. He then took a masters degree, married, and worked for the San Juan Health Department. He died in August 1971.

Repercussions
The people of Chicago believed the death penalty should have been passed for such a callous crime. The trial judge, Judge Calverly, had to have police protection for several months afterwards and the local press made sure that no one forgot Leopold and Loeb and their crime.

Assassination of President Abraham Lincoln

(1865)

John Wilkes Booth

The killing of the 16th President of the United States, carried out by an actor who was a supporter of the South during the Civil War.

John Wilkes Booth was born on 10 May 1838, the ninth of the 10 children of Junius Brutus Booth, a drunken and eccentric actor. Several of the family followed in their father's footsteps and one of his sons, Edwin, became one of the most famous actors of the period. John showed some early potential as an actor but this was offset by an emotional instability and an irrational, vain temperament.

John Booth made his acting debut in Baltimore in 1856. His performance drew criticism from the audience and critics alike, but undeterred he joined a touring Shakespeare company and performed in Richmond, Virginia and several other southern cities. Here his style was more appreciated and he was never short of work, his fame reaching a peak during a tour of the Deep South in 1860.

Ardent Confederate

It was during this period that Booth was converted to the Southern cause and he became a vigorous supporter of the Confederates at the outbreak of the American Civil War in 1861. He had a particular dislike of Abraham Lincoln, who had been elected to the presidency in 1860 vowing to abolish slavery. Being a confirmed racist and a supporter of slavery (he was a member of an organization that had hanged an Abolitionist in 1859), Booth was infuriated by Lincoln's stance and began planning how he could reverse this trend.

Bungled attempts

In 1863 Lincoln proclaimed all the slaves in the southern states to be free. This was the final straw for Booth and the following year he began to formulate a plan for kidnapping the President, and holding him ransom in exchange for Confederate prisoners held by the North. By January 1865 he had recruited half a dozen fellow conspirators and he was ready for his kidnap attempt. His management was woeful, however, and three attempts ended in abject failure, mainly because Lincoln changed his plans at the last moment and Booth was unable to adapt his own strategy.

Victory assassination

On 11 April 1865 the Civil War ended in victory for the North. While Washington DC was in a state of celebration Booth decided that now only the assassination of Lincoln would suffice. He discovered that the President would be attending the Ford's Theatre, 10th Street, Washington DC on 14 April, to see a comedy entitled *Our American Cousins*. Again he gathered his fellow

Assassination of President Lincoln

conspirators and told them their mission, ordering his men to kill various members of Lincoln's party while he himself assassinated the President.

At 6pm on the evening of 14 April Booth, who was well known to the staff, entered the Ford's Theatre. He made his way to the State Box where Lincoln and his party would be sitting and inserted a piece of wood in the outer door so it could be jammed shut from the inside. He then went to a nearby bar to await his moment. Fortunately for him the President's bodyguard deserted his post when the play began and Booth saw him drinking in the same bar.

Fatal vision

Booth returned to the theatre shortly after 10.15pm. The play was in the second scene of its third act and the President looked tired as he watched the proceedings. A few days earlier he had mentioned that he had dreamt about his death several times and he had even seen his own murdered corpse in the White House.

After briefly watching the play Booth made his way to the State Box, entered unnoticed, and jammed the door shut behind him. He then aimed his eight-ounce, single-shot derringer pistol at the back of Lincoln's head. He fired from a distance of four feet and the bullet entered the President's head past his left ear and lodged behind his right eye. He was in a coma until the early morning but died at 7.22am on 15 April 1865. The attempts on the other members of Lincoln's party were less successful: the man assigned to kill the Vice-President got drunk on the night in question and was asleep in bed, while the man entrusted with killing the Secretary of State only succeeded in inflicting a stab wound.

Escape

After he had executed his attack Booth cried 'Sic semper tyrannis' (such be the fate of tyrants) and leapt out of the State Box onto the stage. Despite landing heavily and breaking a bone in his left leg the panic in the theatre enabled him to escape down an alleyway and he fled on his waiting horse. His luck held and, together with another of the conspirators, named Herold, he managed to make his way to Virginia. For 12 days Booth and Herold evaded the authorities but on 26 April 1865 they were eventually surrounded in a barn near Bowling Green, Virginia. Herold surrendered, and was later executed with two other conspirators, but Booth refused to move from his hiding place. In order to flush him out the barn was set on fire. No one emerged and when the soldiers moved in they found a badly distorted body that had been shot through the neck. It was later identified as that of Booth and the official cause of death was suicide.

Following his assassination Lincoln became a national hero and he has since become regarded as one of America's finest presidents.

Spate of confessions

There was some doubt in the public's mind as to whether the body found in the barn in Virginia was that of Booth. Confessing to being the 'real' Booth became a popular pastime and over 40 people claimed that they were the assassin of Abraham Lincoln. One of them, John St Helen (or Daniel George) bore a close resemblance to Booth and his mummified body was displayed at carnivals all over America.

Claim to fame

On the evening of the assassination someone remarked to Booth that he would not be as famous an actor as his father. He retorted, 'When I leave the stage I will be the most famous man in America'.

Lindbergh kidnapping

(1932)

Bruno Richard Hauptmann

The kidnapping of a young child that caused outrage throughout the United States.

In May 1927 Charles A Lindbergh, an American of Scandinavian decent, became the first person to make a non-stop transatlantic flight between America and Europe. He was a national hero and on his return to the States he became a semi-recluse, moving into a large mansion near Hopewell, in the Southland Mountains of Hunterdon County, New Jersey. He lived here with his wife Anne Morrow Lindbergh. In 1930 the couple had a son, Charles A Lindbergh Jnr.

Illegal immigrant

Four years before Lindbergh made his historic flight, a poorly educated German named Bruno Hauptmann entered the United States. He was born in Saxony on 26 November 1899 and after a basic education he became a carpenter at the age of 14. He served in the German Army during World War I and then pursued a career of small-time burglary. In 1919 he was convicted of breaking and entering and in 1922 arrested for possession of stolen goods, but subsequently escaped before his trial. In 1923 he entered the United States illegally, settling in the Bronx, New York. However, he remained fervently pro-German and his idol was the German wartime flying ace, Richthofen.

On 1 March a crime was committed that shocked America: 20-month-old Charles A Lindbergh Jnr was kidnapped from his upstairs nursery at the Lindbergh mansion. The kidnapper had used a crude home-made ladder to gain access to the second-storey nursery and then made off with the

Bruno Hauptmann

son of one of the nation's greatest heroes.

Fervent activity

A crude ransom note was left after the kidnapping, demanding $50 000 for the baby's safe return. There were no other clues and no fingerprints were discovered. The Lindberghs hurriedly tried to raise the ransom, while trying to contact the kidnapper. The police also made numerous enquiries, including interviewing a number of known underworld criminals, but no leads were uncovered.

On 6 March 1932 the Lindberghs received a second ransom note, increasing the figure to $70 000. Shortly afterwards, Dr

John F Cordon, a retired teacher, wrote to the *Bronx Home News* offering to act as a go-between. The offer was accepted by both the Lindberghs and the kidnapper, who communicated with Cordon through newspaper columns. During this period Cordon adopted the alias of 'Jafsi'.

Contact

After several communications with the kidnapper Dr Cordon met with another go-between named John, at Woodlawn Cemetery, New York, on 13 March 1932. To establish his authenticity John gave Dr Cordon a child's sleeping suit that was later identified by Mrs Lindbergh as belonging to her son. John told Cordon to bring the ransom money to St Raymond's Cemetery, where he would be told of the baby's whereabouts. This he duly did and in return for the ransom money (he persuaded John to take only $50 000) he was told that the baby could be found on a boat named *Nellie*, moored near Martha's Vineyard, Massachusetts.

When Lindbergh heard this news he rushed to the appointed place but there was no sign of the boat or his son. To make matters worse Cordon said that because it had been dark in the cemetery he was unable to identify John.

Tragic discovery

On 12 May 1932 a lorry driver discovered the decomposed body of Charles Lindbergh just five miles from the Lindbergh's home. The body was identified by Mrs Lindbergh and the baby's nurse, Betty Gow. The nation was horrified and a massive man-hunt was undertaken.

The only real clue was the serial numbers of the ransom money that had been handed over. They were helped by the fact that some of the money was in the form of gold certificates, which were withdrawn from circulation in 1933 when America left the gold standard.

On 15 September 1934 one of the withdrawn certificates was presented at a petrol station in the Bronx. The attendant checked the serial number and discovered it was one of the notes from the Lindbergh ransom. He noted the number of the man's car and

contacted the police. When the car was traced it was found to belong to Bruno Hauptmann. He was arrested and the police found over $11 000 of the ransom money in his flat.

Despite protesting his innocence, and claiming that he had been given the money by a friend who had since returned to Germany, Hauptmann was charged with kidnapping and murder. His trial took place at Flemington, New Jersey, from 2 January to 13 February 1935.

Substantial evidence

In addition to the ransom money there was a significant amount of damning evidence against Hauptmann: it was shown by a handwriting expert that he had written all the ransom notes; Cordon's telephone number was found written in a cupboard in his flat; witnesses identified him as being near the Lindbergh house around the date of the kidnapping; and Dr Cordon claimed to recognize him as the man he met in the graveyard. The police also discovered that part of the ladder used in the kidnapping had come from a floorboard in Hauptmann's flat.

On 13 February 1935 Bruno Hauptmann was found guilty of murder and sentenced to death. A year of delays and a temporary reprieve followed before he was electrocuted at Trenton State Prison, New Jersey, on 3 April 1936. Doubts have since been raised about the validity of his conviction.

Opportunists

Before the discovery of Charles Lindbergh Jnr's body there were a number of people who tried to exploit the family's plight. One man, Gaston B Means, was jailed for 15 years for obtaining money by false pretences from Evelyn Walsh Maclean, after claiming that he was able to contact the kidnapper. Another, John Hughes Curtis, the president of a boat-building corporation, received a 12-month term for leading the Lindberghs on a wild-goose chase for a non-existent boat that was supposed to be connected with the kidnapper.

Lucan case

(1974)

Richard John Bingham, 7th Earl of Lucan

The disappearance of an English nobleman, following a murder at his estranged wife's home, has become one of the greatest mysteries of modern times.

On 7 November 1974 the tranquillity of London's Lower Belgrave Street was disturbed when Lady Veronica Lucan ran into The Plumber's Arms pub. She had bloodstains on her face and was crying hysterically, 'Help me, I've just escaped from a murderer'.

Lady Lucan was taken to hospital and

then interviewed by the police. She told them that she had been spending that Thursday evening with her children at her home near Buckingham Palace. At nine o'clock the nanny, Sandra Rivett, asked Lady Lucan if she would like some tea. Thursday was Sandra's usual night off but this particular week she had taken the Wednesday off instead.

Murdered nanny

When Sandra had not returned after 20 minutes Lady Lucan decided to investigate. She went to the kitchen, where she saw a man hunched over the dead body of the nanny. The man then attacked her but she managed to break free and her attacker fled. She told the police that she was sure the man was her estranged husband, Lord

Lord and Lady Lucan

Lucan. When the police went to Lady Lucan's house they found the body of Sandra Rivett in a mail-bag; she had been beaten to death with a heavy, blunt object.

'Lucky' Lucan

Following the discovery of Sandra Rivett's body the police immediately began a hunt for Lord Lucan. Born Richard John Bingham in 1934 he had inherited his title in 1964. He lived a flamboyant, high-society lifestyle and his friends nicknamed him 'Lucky' due to his addiction to gambling.

In the early 1970s the Lucans' marriage was on the rocks and they separated in 1973. Lord Lucan applied for custody of their children but he lost and custody was given to his wife. He was deeply upset by this and friends said that shortly before the murder he had been in a depressed and bitter mood.

The police soon discovered that Lucan had driven to a friend's house after the murder and told his version of events. He claimed that he had been passing his estranged wife's house when he saw someone attacking Lady Lucan: 'I let myself in with my own key and rushed down to protect her. I slipped on a pool of blood and the attacker ran off. My wife was hysterical and accusing me of being her attacker'.

Abandoned car

By the time Lucan's friend informed the police of the nobleman's whereabouts he had already fled. On 9 November 1974 the police learned that Lucan had sent two letters from Uckfield, Sussex. But again there was no trace of him and the following day the police discovered Lucan's car at the port of Newhaven, whence there are regular crossings to France. Inside the car were bloodstains and a length of the same lead pipe that had been used to kill Sandra Rivett. Several of Lucan's aristocratic friends were questioned as to his whereabouts but all the police inquiries drew a blank.

In June 1975 an inquest was held into the death of Sandra Rivett. Although Lord Lucan had still not been found a verdict of murder was brought in against him. This resulted in legislation being passed in 1977 that made it impossible to name anyone as

a murderer until they had been charged and tried under normal legal procedure. Lucan's family tried to have the legislation applied retrospectively but this was denied and the charge of murder still stands.

Public fascination

After seven years of fruitless police investigations stretching from Africa to America, Lord Lucan was legally declared dead; to this day his whereabouts are debated. Several books have been written about the case: *Trail of Havoc* by Patrick Marnham, claims that Lucan hired a killer to murder his wife and then fled when the plan went wrong; in *Lucan: Not Guilty*, Sally Moore argues that there was an official cover-up following the case, because the real murderer was a policeman.

Difference of opinion

The two policemen who led the search for Lucan had their own theories about what happened. Superintendent Roy Ransom claimed: 'He killed the nanny by mistake, thinking he could dispose of his wife and get the custody of the children he loved. When he realized his error, he killed himself in a remote spot, like a lord and a gentleman'. Superintendent Dave Gerring disagreed: 'Lucan is still in hiding somewhere and he is the only man who knows the full story. He is a lord and a gentleman, but he is still a gambler. And he is gambling on the odds that no one will ever find him'.

Daring disappearance

On 24 November 1971 an American calling himself D B Cooper pulled off a vanishing trick even more dramatic than that of Lord Lucan. He hijacked a Northwest Airlines Boeing 727 from Seattle at 20 000 feet and took $200 000. He then ordered the pilot to fly to Reno, Nevada, and went to the back of the plane to wait. However, when the plane landed Cooper was nowhere to be seen. After checking the 'black box' it decided that he must have parachuted out of the plane while it was flying over the densely wooded American West. Despite an intensive search no sign of D B Cooper or his money has ever been found.

Luciano, Charles

(1897–1962)

Gangster

One of the most influential figures in organized crime in America during the 1930s.

Originally Salvatore Lucania, Charles Luciano was born in Sicily and immigrated to New York City in 1906 with his family. He immediately became involved with mugging, shoplifting and extortion and in 1916 he was sentenced to six months' imprisonment for peddling heroin. When he was released he joined forces with a number of up and coming young gangsters and he soon gained the nickname 'Lucky' because of his uncanny ability to avoid arrest.

In 1920 Luciano became involved with Joe Masseria, one of New York's top crime bosses. His organizational ability ensured that he rose quickly through the ranks and he became one of Masseria's most trusted lieutenants. He kept an eye on all aspects of the business but specialized in narcotics, prostitution, slot-machines, loan-sharking and protection.

Narrow escape

Luciano made several enemies and in October 1929 he was the victim of an assassination attempt. However, he lived up to his nickname and, despite being stabbed repeatedly with an icepick and having his throat slit, he survived.

From 1930 to 1931 Masseria was engaged in a debilitating gang war with a rival gang boss, Salvatore Maranzano. Luciano considered this to be bad for business and to solve the problem he had Masseria assassinated on 15 April 1931. Six months later he order the execution of Maranzano. The result was that Lucky Luciano was now the most influential criminal boss in New York.

Looking to his business interests, Luciano joined forces with the other crime bosses in New York to form a crime syndicate, also known as Murder Incorporated. It proved to be immensely powerful and few people who got on the wrong side of it, either criminals or law enforcers, lived for long.

Tenacious prosecutor

In 1936 New York special prosecutor Thomas E Dewey made a concerted effort to catch Luciano. While the crime boss was in Florida Dewey found three prostitutes willing to testify against him. Despite intimidation from the syndicate the women kept their word and Luciano was convicted of compelling women to become prostitutes and received a 30 to 50-year prison sentence.

Prison life did little to curb Luciano's criminal activities and he continued to run the crime syndicate as efficiently and as profitably as before. In 1942 the Navy came to him for his help in tightening security around New York Harbour. The crime boss obliged willingly and in return his sentence was commuted in 1946 and he was released. After a brief visit to Italy he went to Cuba where gang leaders from all over America came to pay their respects. However, hostile public opinion forced the Cuban government to deport him and he returned to Italy where he settled in Naples, but he had to worry constantly about police surveillance. Lucky Luciano died of a heart attack in Naples on 26 January 1962.

Murder Inc.

It is thought that Murder Incorporated was responsible for over 1000 killings in its first five years of operation. The fees ranged from $1000 to $5000. One killer is believed to have committed over 500 contract murders. The bodies were rarely found.

Lustig, Victor
(1890–1947)

Con man

An audacious trickster who sold the Eiffel Tower on two separate occasions.

Born in the Czechoslovakian town of Hostinne, the self-styled Count Victor Lustig soon realized that he had a talent for depriving the rich and greedy of their money. He learnt card-sharping in Paris and after deciding to emigrate to America, using a total of 24 aliases he spent several years crossing and re-crossing the Atlantic to disburden his fellow passengers of their wealth. After World War I he became bored with the easy pickings in America and returned to Paris.

In March 1925 Lustig was sitting in his room at the plush Crillon Hotel when he saw a newspaper article saying that the French government was worried about the cost of maintaining the Eiffel Tower. There was even a suggestion that it may have to be dismantled and rebuilt. This was all Lustig's sharp mind needed and he began planning the con of a lifetime.

Greedy and gullible

Lustig's first move was to obtain some headed notepaper from the French Ministry of Posts and Telegraphs, the department responsible for the maintenance of the Eiffel Tower. Using the notepaper he invited five top Parisian businessmen to a secret meeting at the Crillon Hotel. When they were assembled he told the stunned men that the Eiffel Tower was in such a perilous state that it would have to be pulled down and used for scrap. He asked them to submit tenders for the contract, adding that, naturally, the project was to be treated with the utmost secrecy.

After meeting the businessmen Lustig decided that André Poisson was the most likely dupe. He informed Poisson that he had been 'lucky' enough to win the contract, adding that he needed a bribe to get the project smoothly through government channels, which seemed natural to the gullible businessman, who gave Lustig the money for the contract and the bribe.

Double-take

Lustig left immediately for Vienna and waited for the outcry that he thought would follow. To his amazement nothing happened and he realized that Poisson had been too embarrassed to go to the police. So he did what anyone in his position would do — he went back to Paris and tried exactly the same con again. As with Poisson it worked, except that this time the victim did go to the police.

The master con man returned to America where he became involved in counterfeiting for Al Capone. This proved to be his undoing and in 1936 he was jailed for distributing $134 million in counterfeit bills. He served 11 years of a 20-year sentence and died in Springfield Prison, Missouri, in March 1947.

Lustig's 10 con commandments

1 Be a patient listener.
2 Never look bored.
3 Have the same political views as your subject.
4 Agree with your subject's religious views.
5 Hint at sex talk.
6 Never discuss illness.
7 Never pry into someone's personal circumstances.
8 Never boast.
9 Never be untidy.
10 Never get drunk.

MacGregor or Campbell, Robert (Rob Roy)

(1671–1734)

Freebooter

A legendary Scottish freebooter who fought passionately to protect himself and his clan.

Robert MacGregor was born at Buchanan, Stirlingshire. His father was Lieutenant-General Donald MacGregor of Glengyle, the younger brother of the chief of the Gregor clan. Ten years before Robert's birth the restrictive laws that had been in force against the 'wicked clan Gregor' for nearly a century, were repealed. However, since their lands were not restored this had little effect, other than to encourage their freebooting activities.

Robert received a good education and for several years he lived as a grazier at Balquhidder. Initially he suffered at the hands of reivers (cattle-rustlers) from the north who travelled south in order to steal cattle and plunder the lands, but, being a quick learner, in 1691 he wasted no time in forming a band of armed followers who not only protected his land, but also indulged in some reiving of their own. Robert also helped protect the farms of his neighbours, for which he expected a generous fee.

Appearance of Rob Roy

In 1693 the penal laws against the MacGregors were reintroduced, thus effectively making them outlaws. In response Robert adopted Campbell as a surname and took to signing his name 'Rob Roy' (Gaelic for Red Robert). He also indulged in one of his most prolific periods of freebooting.

By the end of 1693 Rob had not only become the nominal head of the clan Gregor but he had also acquired new lands at Inversnaid and Craigroyston in the

Trossachs, near Loch Lomond. It was an area that lay between the lands of the rival houses of Argyll and Montrose. Rob shrewdly played his warring neighbours against one another and he won the particular approval of James Graham, 1st Duke of Montrose. Although still pursuing his freebooting activities, Rob was also concerned with legitimate business deals and one of his projects involved bringing black cattle from the highlands and selling them at a handsome profit to the lowland farmers. He persuaded Montrose to lend him a substantial amount of money to finance this project but he soon found that the business was not as profitable as he had first thought and he began to slip into debt. His solution in 1711 was to take Montrose's money and retreat to the Western Isles.

In the dock

Montrose promised Rob his protection if he returned. He did so in 1712, only to be sent before the court of session in Edinburgh, being described as 'a noutour bankrupt' who keeps 'a guard and/or company of armed men in defiance of the law'. Rob's own explanation for his disappearance was that he feared for his life as a result of the banning of the Gregor clan. He did not wait to stand trial and went into hiding.

While Rob was on the run Montrose tired of his behaviour and took revenge by plundering his house and evicting his wife and children, who were forced to wander homeless in the middle of a severe winter; his wife was so distraught that she composed a piece of pipe music entitled 'Rob Roy's Lament'.

Vengeful homecoming

Rob sought refuge in the highlands and was given shelter by John Campbell, 1st Earl of

Breadblane. He also won the support of the Duke of Argyll, who wisely thought it would be best to have as many fighting men on his side as possible. Once he had reassembled a sufficient force of clansmen Rob returned to the Trossachs to seek his revenge on Montrose. He seized a fort at Inversnaid and ravaged Montrose's lands. In 1714, following the death of Queen Anne, the country was thrown into considerable confusion, thus leaving Rob free to continue his campaign against Montrose.

Rob Roy was a supporter of the Jacobite cause and in 1715 he took a band of his supporters to Sherriffmuir to aid the Earl of Mar. However, when he discovered that his benefactor the Duke of Argyll was in opposition he took no active part in the battle but stood watch for the booty. In April 1716, he returned to Craigroyston to continue his vendetta against Montrose. Shortly after his arrival his homes at Craigroyston and Glengyle were destroyed and in revenge he kidnapped Montrose's estate factor, Graham of Killearn, and stole all the money that had been collected in rents.

Local hero

Rob Roy was aided in his exploits by the local people, who warned him of the actions of Montrose and his men; in return the freebooter shared some of his plunder with them. However, this underground network was unable to help him on 4 June 1717 when Rob was captured by another of his enemies, the Duke of Atholl. His captivity was short-lived though, for he soon escaped from prison.

For the next few years Rob Roy, possibly with the help of the Duke of Argyll, continued his feud with Montrose. For much of this time he lived in caves or woods and became a folk hero, with numerous tales being told of his exploits and his narrow, and daring, escapes from capture.

Peace treaty

In 1719 Rob challenged Montrose to settle the dispute by single combat. The duke declined and, sensing things were getting out of hand, Argyll effected a reconciliation between the two men in 1722. Argyll advised Rob to send a letter to General Wade saying that he only sided with the Jacobite rebels in order to provide information about their activities. The authorities must have realized that this was a blatant lie because in 1726 Rob Roy was arrested and taken to Newgate prison in London. In January 1727 he was ordered to be transported to Barbados but he received a pardon shortly before the ship sailed.

Rob Roy returned to Balquhidder where he renounced his former ways and led a quiet life. On one occasion he was forced to fight a dual to settle a dispute between the Maclarens and the MacGregors, but he had lost some of his youthful dexterity and was wounded in the arm. Rob Roy MacGregor died on 28 December 1734, shortly after converting to Catholicism.

Novelist's description
In Sir Walter Scott's highly romanticized version of Rob Roy's life, in which he labels him as a Scottish Robin Hood, he offers this description of the freebooter, 'His stature was not of the tallest, but his person was uncommonly strong and compact. The greatest peculiarity of his frame were the breadth of his shoulders and the great and almost disproportioned length of his arms, so remarkable, indeed, that it was said he could, without stooping, tie the garter of his highland hose, which are placed two inches below the knee. His hair was dark red, thick, and frizzled, and curled short around the face. His fashion of dress showed of course the knees and upper part of the leg, which was described to me as resembling that of an highland bull, hirsute, with red hair, and evincing muscular strength similar to that animal'.

Maclean, Donald Duart

(1913–83)

Spy

A British spy who worked for the Soviet Union and gave them vital information about atomic research in America.

Born in London, Donald Maclean was the son of the Liberal MP Sir Donald Maclean and he had a privileged upbringing. In 1931 he went up to Trinity College, Cambridge, where he studied modern languages and sought to dominate the University Socialist Society. During this time he made friends with Guy Burgess, Anthony Blunt and Kim Philby and the four became firmly committed in their views against capitalist democracy.

Before Maclean graduated from university he told his family that he was going to Russia to teach. However, in 1933 he gave up his political activities and decided to join the Diplomatic Office instead. This sudden change of heart was explained by the fact that he had been recruited by the NKVD, the forerunner of the KGB.

Rapid promotion

In 1938 Maclean was posted to the Paris embassy. Here he met and married Melinda Marling and the couple moved back to London, where Maclean was promoted to the post of Second Secretary and served in the General department until 1944. His superiors at the Foreign Office were so impressed by his work that in 1944 he was promoted to First Secretary to the British Embassy in Washington.

Maclean served in Washington for four years and during this time he obtained classified information relating to the development of the atom bomb. Towards the end he had access to the American Atomic Energy Commission and passed some vital information to the Soviets.

Behind the image of a suave diplomat Maclean was a homosexual and a heavy drinker, frequently causing havoc when he went on binges. After moving to Cairo in 1948 his problems increased and in 1950 he was recalled to Britain. Following psychiatric help he seemed to make a full recovery and was appointed head of the American Department of the Foreign Office.

Hasty flight

Incredibly, at the time of Maclean's new appointment MI5 already suspected him of earlier leaks from Washington. By May 1951 the authorities were ready to question him, but he was warned of their intentions by Kim Philby. On 25 May 1951 Maclean, along with Guy Burgess, left Britain.

Nothing was heard of Maclean or Burgess for five years, until they appeared at a news conference in Moscow in 1956. They declared their longstanding allegiance to Communism but denied they had ever been spies. By this time Maclean's wife had joined him but later had an affair with Kim Philby.

Donald Maclean became a respected Soviet citizen and taught courses in international relations as well as working for the Foreign Ministry. His wife and family returned to the West in 1979 and he died in Moscow on 6 March 1983. As well as passing on atomic secrets he is known to have furnished the Soviet Union with information about the formation of the North Atlantic Treaty Organization (NATO).

International affairs

In 1970 Maclean published *British Foreign Policy since Suez*. It was widely acclaimed and as a result he was awarded a doctorate from the Institute of World Economic and International Relations.

Maitland, William

(c.1528–73)

Conspirator

Secretary to Mary Queen of Scots with plans to bring about an alliance between Scotland and England.

William Maitland of Lethington studied at St Andrews University. After graduating he continued his education on the continent and was renowned for his intellect and his erudition. In 1558 he was appointed secretary to the Catholic, pro-French queen-regent, Mary of Lorraine. This did not suit his purposes and he joined the Protestant lords against the regent in an attempt to expel the French from Scotland.

Secretary Lethington

When Mary, Queen of Scots assumed power in Scotland in 1560, Maitland took it upon himself to try and create an alliance between Scotland and England by persuading Elizabeth I to name Mary as her successor. The Queen of Scots approved of his actions and in 1560 she appointed him as her secretary. He became known as 'Secretary Lethington' and impressed the English court with his wit and learning whenever he went to visit Elizabeth. This was intentional because he wanted Elizabeth to accept his plan, reasoning that she would not have an heir and that his own influence would be increased considerably if Mary acceded to the English throne.

Plans thwarted

It soon became clear to Maitland that Elizabeth was not going to do as he wished. In order to try and push the English queen into a corner he then entered into negotiations for the possible marriage between Mary and Don Carlos of Spain. It was a match that Elizabeth could not afford and she countered it by suggesting a much less dangerous liaison with Robert, Earl of Leicester. However, these suggestions were unacceptable to the single-minded Queen of Scots and she rejected them.

Maitland continued his plotting and scheming and in 1566 he incurred Mary's wrath when he was a party to the murder of her favourite, David Riccio. He was also instrumental in the murder of Mary's husband, Lord Darnely, with whom Maitland had argued and saw as an obstacle to his proposed alliance. He also thought it was not in Mary's interest when it was suggested that she marry James Hepburn, 4th Earl of Bothwell. He joined with a coalition of Protestant and Catholic nobles who forced Bothwell to leave Scotland.

Lost cause

When Mary was taken to England in 1568 Maitland remained in Scotland and continued to try and restore her to her rightful place. With this in mind he took possession of Edinburgh Castle in 1571, thus alienating himself from James Stewart, Earl of Moray, the regent for the infant James VI. He remained a firm supporter of Mary and her cause until he was forced from the Castle by Moray, aided by the English. Before Maitland was put on trial for treason he died in prison in Leith in 1573.

> **Favourite**
> Despite his numerous intrigues Maitland was devoted to Mary, Queen of Scots. On one occasion he showed a sign of his esteem by sending her an oval ornament of gold, enamelled with Aesop's fable of the mouse saving the lion from the net.

Mandelbaum, Fredricka

(c.1825–c.1890)

Receiver of stolen goods

An intimidating woman who was one of the most successful 'fences' that New York City has ever seen.

Although little is known of Fredricka Mandelbaum's date of birth or parentage she soon made a name for herself in New York as a petty criminal and a pickpocket. By 1862 she had graduated to receiving and selling stolen goods and the police had her on their files as a suspected 'fence'.

Mandelbaum, who became known in the criminal world simply as 'Marm', was an intimidating woman in both size and character. She weighed over 15 stone and no one with an interest in self-preservation crossed her. She set up business at 79 Clifton Street, where she lived with her husband and three children, and it was here that she entertained members of the criminal fraternity, receiving their spoils and then selling them on at a handsome profit.

Criminal instructor

But Marm was not only interest in lining her own pockets; she took a genuine pleasure in educating others in the ways of the underworld. She provided a safe house for criminals on the run and her clients included the colourfully-named Shang Draper, Pete 'Banjo' Emerson and Lena 'Black' Kleinschmidt. Once they were back on their feet she gave them money for their next operation; in this way she financed most of the bank robberies in New York over a 20-year period.

One of Marm's greatest pleasures was giving courses in advanced burglary techniques. Her speciality was pickpocketing

and she formed a squad of highly efficient female pickpockets who stole thousands of dollars from unsuspecting New Yorkers. They were invariably well dressed and demure — and utterly ruthless in their pursuit of profit.

Dubious lawyers

Marm was well known to the police and for two decades they tried to catch her redhanded. The fact that they rarely did was attributed to the lawyers 'Big Bill' Howe and 'Little Abe' Hummel whom she retained for $5000 a year. They shared her view on crime and ensured that her interests were well looked after.

By 1884 Marm had been in the business for over 20 years and handled between $5 and $10 million worth of stolen goods. Her luck eventually ran out when she was caught with the proceeds of a silk robbery. Even Howe and Hummel were unable to prevent her being charged but they did advise her to jump bail. She was only too eager to take their advice and in December 1884 she signed over everything to her daughter and fled to Canada. She died in obscurity shortly before the end of the century.

The Garrotters

While Marm's gangs of pickpockets were roaming the streets of New York, London had its own female menace. They were called garrotters and worked in groups of two or three. They attacked their victims from behind with a scarf, rifling their pockets while they were incapacitated. A *Punch* rhyme sums up their activities:
The old 'Stand and deliver's all rot.
Three to one; hit behind; with a wipe round the jowl, boys,
That's the ticket, and *Vive la Garrotte*.

Mandeville, Geoffrey de, Earl of Essex

(?–1144)

Traitor

An English nobleman who turned to open brigandage after his attempts to gain the throne failed.

Little is recorded of Mandeville's early life except when he succeeded his father as the constable of the Tower of London in 1130, a position of considerable power at the time. In 1140 he supported the English king, Stephen, in quelling some of his rebel noblemen and for this he was rewarded with the title of the 1st Earl of Essex.

Mandeville enjoyed his new title and the power in Essex which it allowed him. He exercised great influence over his estates of Pleshy and Saffron Walden and was not averse to using violence and intimidation to get his way.

In June 1141 Empress Matilda, also known as Empress Maud, came to London to promote her claim for the English throne. Essex was briefly won over to her cause when she confirmed him as the hereditary sheriff, justice and escheator of Essex. It soon became clear that this would be the full extent of his power if he stayed with Matilda so he deserted her, liberated the imprisoned King Stephen and received a pardon for his treason.

Secret plotting

In addition to a pardon Mandeville insisted on becoming sheriff and justice of London and Middlesex. This was granted, thus making him one of the most powerful figures in the south of England. However, his ambitions were not satisfied and in early summer 1142 he met Empress Matilda in Oxford. In return for the promise of his support he

made her a number of outrageous demands that would have to be met once she was queen but, since Matilda was never able to displace Stephen, this never happened.

Although Mandeville was wise enough to keep his conspiratorial activities a secret from the King, Stephen became suspicious of the powerful earl. During court at St Albans in September 1143 Mandeville was accused of treason by a group of fellow noblemen and, much to his surprise, Stephen agreed with them and ordered his arrest. Instead of hanging him the king forced him to give up his estates of Saffron Walden and Pleshy and, most importantly, his control over the Tower of London.

Outlaw

When the emasculated Mandeville was released he was in a furious rage, 'like a vicious and riderless horse, kicking and biting'. He travelled to the fenland around Ely and established himself at one of his forfeited properties, Ramsey Abbey. Now that he knew his pretensions to the throne were at an end he gave way to his baser instincts and spent the rest of his life plundering the fenland and committing numerous atrocities. When Stephen heard of this he besieged him in his fortified abbey but the King was no match for the wild Mandeville. In August 1144 Mandeville lay seige to Burwell Castle, during which he was struck on the head; he died from his wound on 16 September 1144.

Successful heir
Empress Matilda was unsuccessful in her attempts to remove Stephen from the throne and she died in 1167. However, her son took up the family cause and in 1154 he became Henry II, the first Plantagenet king of England.

Manson family murders

(1969)

Charles Manson

Horrific killings carried out by members of Charles Manson's 'Family' sect.

Charles Manson was born in Kentucky in 1934 and although he claimed his mother was a Flower Child in reality she was a prostitute. When he was still a toddler she was imprisoned for five years for armed robbery and subsequently Manson grew up in various institutions. This had an adverse affect on his character and at the age of 13 he committed his first crime, an armed robbery. Four years later he committed a homosexual rape and by the time he was 18 he was listed as 'dangerous with assaultive tendencies'.

In 1954 Manson was sent to live with relations in West Virginia. He met and married a 17-year-old waitress and although she bore him a son and moved to California with him, the marriage ended in divorce in 1958. Manson was still unable to integrate happily in society and in 1960 he was imprisoned for 10 years for a variety of offences including procuring, fraud and theft.

The Family

After enjoying the company of various criminals in prison, and learning to play the guitar, Manson was released in 1967. He was terrified of the outside world and gravitated towards the Haight-Ashbury district of San Francisco, the centre of the hippy community in the city. Manson revelled in this atmosphere of free love and drug experimentation and he quickly set up a commune of which he was indubitably the leader. His first followers were Mary Brunner and Lynette Fromme, who were joined by Susan Atkins and Patricia Krenwinkel.

Manson had an incredible power over the Family and they looked up to him as a God-like creation. On one occasion Susan Atkins said, 'Now I have visible proof of God, proof the Church never gave me'. Manson wore his hair long, grew a beard in the style of Jesus, kept his followers high on hallucinogenic drugs and ordered them to take part in group sex. As Manson's reputation grew, people, particularly woman, drifted in and out of the Family, all of them falling for Manson's charismatic power.

In the autumn of 1967 Manson decided that he want to be 'bigger than the Beatles' in his musical capacity. He bought a Volkswagen bus and took the Family on a tour of the southern states. Despite making an unprofitable record and a film, Manson did not achieve the recognition that he felt he deserved and he returned to California.

Ranch commune

Back in California Manson set up a new commune at the Saphn ranch, 30 miles from Los Angeles. The Family now numbered over 20 people and it was during this period that Manson began drawing up a death list of 'pigs' whom he wanted to eliminate for various reasons. The death of these people, who included Warren Beatty and Julie Christie, was to occur during the day of reckoning, which Manson had given the code-name 'Helter Skelter', taken from a Beatles record.

By the summer of 1969 the Saphn ranch was being used for various criminal activities and the number of Manson's followers had risen to over 40. However, their leader was beginning to bore of their passive adoration and turned his attention to murder for his kicks. On 25 July 1969 he sent Susan Atkins, Mary Brunner and a musician named Bobby Beausoleil, to rob the house of another musician, Gary Hinman. When they failed to find any money Manson himself came to the house and after cutting off Hinman's ear with a sword he ordered his followers to murder him. This they did by stabbing him and leaving him to bleed to death.

Helter Skelter

A week after the Hinman murder Beausoleil and Mary Brunner were arrested for other offences. When he heard of this Manson declared, 'Now is the time for Helter Skelter'. On 8 August 1969 Manson sent Susan Atkins, Patricia Krenwinkel, Tex Watson, a former American football star, and Linda Kasabian to the house of a record producer who was on his death list. However, the record producer had since moved and instead the house was inhabited by Roman Polanski's young wife Sharon Tate. On 8 August she was entertaining her former lover and friend Jay Sebring, a coffee heiress Abigail Folger and her lover Wojiciech Frykowski.

After ransacking the Polanski house the Family members tied up their four victims and then murdered them. First Atkins stabbed Sebring to death in the garden as he tried to escape, then Watson shot Frykowski. Abigail Folger was then stabbed a number of times by Atkins and finally Sharon Tate was attacked by Atkins, Krenwinkel and Watson. Despite the fact that she was eight and a half months pregnant she was shown no mercy and was stabbed 16 times. Before they left, Manson's followers daubed 'Pig' and 'War' in blood on the walls.

Executions ordered

Manson was not content with this and two days later he ordered Watson, Krenwinkel,

and Leslie van Houten to murder a supermarket owner, Leno LaBianca, and his wife Rosemary. In total the couple received 53 stab wounds between them and this time 'Death to Pigs', 'Rise' and 'Healter Skelter' (sic) were daubed on the walls.

In October 1969 Atkins, who was in custody for a minor offence, boasted to a cellmate that she had taken part in the Sharon Tate killings. The police heard about this and on 1 December Watson, Krenwinkel and Kasabian were arrested for the murders. Then Atkins, van Houten and Manson himself were arrested on the same charges. After an extraordinary trial in 1970 Charles Manson was found guilty of nine murders. He was sentenced to death but this was commuted to life imprisonment when the death penalty for murder was abolished by the Californian Supreme Court. Manson was unrepentant about his activities and later said, 'If it takes fear and violence to open the eyes of the dollar-conscious society, the name of Charles Manson can be that of fear'.

Sentences

Several of the Family were charged along with Charles Manson: Tex Watson was found guilty of seven murders and had his death sentence commuted to life imprisonment; Susan Atkins was sentenced to life imprisonment for Gary Hinman's murder, and also the Tate and LaBianca murders; and Leslie van Houten and Patricia Krenwinkel were given life terms for the Tate and LaBianca killings. Mary Brunner and Linda Kasabian both gave evidence for the prosecution and no charges were brought against them.

Manuel, Peter Thomas Anthony
(1927–58)

Convicted murderer

Regarded by his trial judge as 'very bad but not mad', Manuel committed several murders for no apparent reason.

Peter Manuel was born to Scottish parents who had emigrated to New York in the 1920s. During the Depression they moved back to Scotland and Manuel was brought up in Glasgow. From an early age he was involved in crime and by the time he was 16 a probation officer said that he had the worst record he had ever seen for someone of his age.

Manuel served several prison sentences. including terms for theft, indecent assault and rape. In January 1956 he committed his first murder. He met a 17-year-old girl in East Kilbride and for no apparent reason took her into a wood and beat her to death.

On 16 September 1956 Manuel and two accomplices went on a robbery spree in Glasgow. After the first break-in Manuel decided to continue alone and broke into a house owned by the Watt family. He became bored with the idea of robbery and instead turned to murder. Mrs Marion Watt, her daughter and her sister were all shot dead in cold blood. Nothing was taken and there was no sexual interference with the bodies.

Wrongful arrest

After the Watt killings Manuel was questioned (as he was after every major crime) but it was William Watt who was arrested and accused of the murders of his own family. He spent two months in custody and then Manuel had the audacity to approach

him with an offer to find, and kill, his family's murderer. Mr Watt declined.

On 8 December 1957 Manuel took a trip to Newcastle and again he performed a motiveless murder, this time of a taxi-driver. This was followed by the murder of a 17-year-old girl he had never met before, Isabelle Cooke.

Manuel celebrated the New Year of 1958 by breaking into the Glasgow bungalow of Peter Smart and his family. After taking a mere £25 he shot dead Peter Smart and his wife and son. Before leaving he calmly fed two tins of salmon to the cat.

Identifiable notes

When Manuel tried to spend the money he had taken from the Smart household he was seen using a new blue £5 note. This was the type taken during the triple murder and Manuel was arrested. Following the discovery of house-breaking equipment at his home, Mr Manuel senior was also arrested and his son agreed to talk on the condition that his father was released.

Manuel admitted to the murders but offered no reasons or excuses. His trial took place in May 1958 and he was charged with eight murders. He conducted his own defence and the judge complimented him on his knowledge of the legal system. It did him little good though and he was found guilty on seven counts of murder. Peter Manuel was hanged at Barlinnie Prison in Glasgow on 11 July 1958.

Morbid calm

During questioning, Manuel offered to show the police where he had buried the body of Isabelle Cooke. When he reached the spot he announced, 'This is the place. In fact, I think I'm standing on her now'.

Murder of James Maybrick

(1889)

Florence Elizabeth Maybrick

The poisoning of an English businessman that led to considerable changes in the English legal system.

On 27 July 1881 Florence Chandler, a Southern belle from Alabama, married an English cotton merchant, James Maybrick. It had been a whirlwind romance and some friends were worried at the disparity in ages: Maybrick was 42, his bride barely 18.

The couple settled in Liverpool and not only did Maybrick prove to be a dour and uninspiring husband but he was also a hopeless hypochondriac. He was continually swallowing pills and powders, including strychnine and arsenic, which he claimed was an aphrodisiac.

Double adultery

Maybrick also kept a mistress and by 1888 he had fathered five children by her, while he also had two legitimate children. When Florence discovered her husband's infidelity she refused to sleep with him. When this had no effect she took a lover of her own, Alfred Brierley, a business friend of Maybrick. In March 1889 Florence and Brierley spent a weekend together in London and when she returned home Maybrick confronted her and struck her in the face.

During the following month Mrs Maybrick bought a dozen flypapers, each containing a grain of arsenic. She claimed she wanted to extract the arsenic to prepare a face-wash, a common practice at the time. On 27 April James Maybrick fell ill and, despite exhaustive attempts to cure him, he died on 11 May 1889.

Maybrick's brother, Michael, who had never liked Florence, suspected her of tampering with his medicine and ordered her to stay in the house while he and the servants searched the premises. In all they found enough arsenic to poison 50 people. There was no proof that it belonged to Mrs Maybrick though and when the body was later exhumed there was less than half a grain of arsenic in it — two grains would be a fatal dose. Despite this Mrs Maybrick was arrested and charged with the murder of her husband.

Public support

Mrs Maybrick's trial began on 31 July 1889 and it was an unsatisfactory affair from beginning to end. The medical experts could not agree on the cause of death and the defendant herself was not allowed to give evidence. The most extraordinary aspect of it was the biased summing-up of the judge, Mr Justice Stephen. He seemed to have convinced himself of Mrs Maybrick's guilt and he placed greater emphasis on her adultery with Brierley than the crime for which she was being tried.

Florence Maybrick was found guilty of murder and sentenced to death. There was outrage throughout Britain and America: newspapers were deluged with letters and a petition containing over 100 000 signatures was prepared in support of her. Since there was no avenue of appeal until the establishment of the Court of Appeal in 1907, the Home Secretary intervened and commuted the sentence to life imprisonment. She served 15 years and died in Connecticut in 1941.

Maybrick judge

The Maybrick trial judge, Justice Stephen, who was criticized from all sides for his attitude during the trial, retired soon after the case and died in a lunatic asylum.

Merrett, John Donald

(1908–54)

Forger, smuggler and murderer

An impetuous and dashing character who committed three murders within a period of 28 years.

Donald Merrett was born at Levin, New Zealand, and came to England in 1924 with his mother. He went to school at Malvern but it soon became clear that all he wanted to study was the opposite sex. His mother took him out of school and went with him to Edinburgh where he studied art at Edinburgh University.

Merrett enjoyed a hectic social life in Edinburgh and he funded his activities by forging his mother's signature on her cheques. When the bank queried the size of her overdraft he decided that drastic measures were called for. On 17 March 1926 Merrett rushed up to the maid and announced, 'Rita, my mother has shot herself'. Mrs Merrett was lying on the sitting-room floor and she died on 1 April 1926.

When the police found the cheques that Merrett had forged they charged him not only with forgery but also with his mother's murder. He was tried at Edinburgh in February 1927 and although there was a strong case against him the jury returned a verdict of Not Proven. He spent eight months in jail for forgery.

New identity

When he was released Merrett took the name of Ronald John Chesney and went to Hastings to stay with a family friend, Mrs Mary Bonnar. Within a few weeks he had eloped with her daughter, Vera. A year later, in 1929, Merrett inherited £50 000 and settled £8500 on his young wife. She was to use the interest for living expenses and the capital would return to Merrett in the event of her death.

Over the next 10 years Merrett led a reckless, spendthrift life. He took to crime to supplement his inheritance and turned his hand to theft, blackmail, smuggling and fraud. After World War II, during which he served in the Royal Naval Volunteer Reserves, Merrett based himself in Germany and engaged in more criminal activity, including gun-running.

Murder for profit

By 1954 Merrett had squandered most of his inheritance and was desperately in need of money, when he remembered his wife's capital. On 3 February 1954 he flew to London to visit Vera. They had an enjoyable night drinking gin and then Merrett returned to the continent. A week later he returned to London, travelling on a false passport, plied Vera with gin and then drowned her. As he was leaving, Vera's mother saw him. To silence the old lady he beat her to death.

The police soon realized that Chesney and Merrett were the same person, but before they could apprehend him his body was found in a forest near Cologne on 16 February 1954. He had committed suicide. An inquest decided that he was responsible for the deaths of Vera Chesney and her mother.

Incriminating volume
While imprisoned in Italy during World War II Chesney was recognized as John Merrett by a prisoner who had read of the death of his mother in a volume of the *Notable British Trials* series. Merrett brushed aside the suggestion but in later years his wife had read the same book and had similar suspicions.

Murder of PC Sidney Miles

(1952)

Derek William Bentley and Christopher Craig

The murder of a policeman that led to one of the most controversial sentences in post-war Britain.

Derek Bentley and Christopher Craig were both born in south London, Bentley in June 1933 and Craig in May 1936. Bentley was of below average intelligence and compensated by taking up body-building. Craig was dyslexic but a talented sportsman. Guns were his passion and by the time he was 16 he owned over 40 pistols and revolvers.

On 30 October 1952 Craig's elder brother, Niven, was convicted of armed robbery and sent to prison for 12 years. Craig, who idolized his brother, bitterly resented the sentence and was still seething three days later when he went to visit Derek Bentley.

The two teenagers went to West Croydon where they planned to rob a wholesale confectioner's warehouse. However, while they were climbing over the fence they were spotted and the police arrived 15 minutes later, by which time Bentley and Craig were on the flat roof of the confectioner's warehouse.

'Let him have it Chris'

Six policemen confronted the two intruders and Derek Bentley was quickly overpowered by PC Fairfax. He broke free though, shouting, 'Let him have it, Chris'. Craig then began firing with a revolver. Bentley was recaptured and as the shooting continued PC Sidney Miles, who was one of the last to appear on the scene, stepped onto the roof. Seconds later, Craig shot him through the head. He died instantly.

When his ammunition ran out Craig continued to hurl insults at the police and then he threw himself off the top of the warehouse. He later claimed he was trying to kill himself, but he only succeeded in fracturing his spine, wrist and breastbone.

Common purpose

The trial of Bentley and Craig began at the Old Bailey on 9 December 1952. Although Bentley had been under arrest 15 minutes before PC Miles was shot they were both charged with murder, as the law states that an accomplice is as guilty as the person who fires the shot if there is a 'common purpose'. Therefore the prosecution had to prove that Bentley knew Craig had a gun. He denied this vehemently but his shout of, 'Let him have it, Chris' was a damning piece of evidence.

Despite some contradictory evidence from the police Bentley and Craig were found guilty. Craig, at 16, was too young to hang but Bentley was sentenced to death. His appeal was dismissed and despite protests from all factions of society Derek Bentley was hanged in Wandsworth jail on 28 January 1953.

There was considerable consternation following the hanging of a teenager who had not committed murder and the case did much to hasten the abolition of hanging. In 1991 the case was reopened and Christopher Craig announced that Bentley did not shout the vital words, 'Let him have it Chris'.

Outrage

On the morning of Bentley's execution a crowd of 5000 protested outside Wandsworth prison. They shouted 'Murder' and sang 'Abide with me'. When the notice of death was hung on the prison gate it was torn down and smashed.

Molineux, Roland Burnham

(1868–1917)

Poisoner

A respectable member of New York society, he was accused of trying to maintain his position with the aid of murder.

Roland Molineux was an affluent pharmaceutical factory manager in New York. His one main hobby was athletics and he was a member of the exclusive Knickerbocker Athletic Club, founded in 1895. He liked to think that he was one of the mainstays of the club and his manner frequently antagonized the other members.

In the spring of 1898 Molineux and another member at the Knickerbocker Club, Henry C Barnet, were both courting the same young lady, Blanche Cheseborough. On one occasion Molineux proposed to her but she was indifferent and seemed to prefer the attentions of Barnet.

Poisons through the post

In October 1898 Barnet received a package of medicine through the post. Believing that it was a laxative he took the powder, only to become seriously ill. Initially, Barnet's doctor thought that his patient had diphtheria but he discovered the powder to contain cyanide of mercury. Barnet died before he could tell the doctor who had sent him the poison.

On 29 November 1898, less than three weeks after Barnet's death, Molineux married Blanche Cheseborough. Rumours abounded that he had poisoned Barnet but there was no proof of this. When Molineux returned to the Knickerbocker Club he had a dispute with one of his long-time adversaries, Harry Cornish. As a result Molineux resigned from the club in a fury.

Retaliation

On 23 December 1898 Cornish received a bottle of Bromo-Seltzer through the post. He considered it a strange Christmas present, particularly as he rarely took medicines, but he liked the bottle and took it home for his landlady, Mrs Katherine Adams. On 28 December Mrs Adams complained of a headache and Cornish gave her some of the powder. She commented about the strange taste of the medicine, and minutes later she was dead. The contents of the bottle were found to contain mercury cyanide.

When the police investigated the members of the Knickerbocker Club they soon decided that Molineux was a prime suspect for the murder of Mrs Adams, reasoning that he was attempting to kill his rival Cornish. When his handwriting was found to match that on the parcel addressed to Cornish he was arrested.

When the trial began, on 2 August 1899, several handwriting experts testified against Molineux. It was also shown that he had ordered a consignment of cyanide mercury for supposed use in his factory. However, the prosecution made the mistake of using information relating to the death of Henry Barnet. Because of this a second trial was ordered, even though the defendant was found guilty, at which Roland Molineux was acquitted in November 1902.

Downhill path

Following his acquittal Molineux never regained his former position. In 1903 his wife divorced him; in 1913 he married for the second time but a year later he entered a mental asylum, where he died on 2 November 1917. Blanche Cheseborough married her divorce lawyer.

163

Theft of the Mona Lisa

(1911)

Vincenzo Perruggia

The theft of the world's most famous painting, which caused uproar in the art world and gave rise to several swindles.

Vincenzo Perruggia, a petty criminal with a dislike of the French, first had the idea of stealing the Mona Lisa, the *Gioconda*, in 1910 while he was working as a glazier in the Louvre. He was one of the men entrusted to put the famous painting behind glass and when he had completed the work he knew how to remove it quickly from its protective covering.

Although Perruggia knew how the painting could be stolen he needed greater backing to profit from the theft. Using his own underworld connections he teamed up with Eduardo de Valifierno, a con man, and Yves Chaudron, an art forger. Between them they formulated a plan for stealing the Mona Lisa and then making a handsome profit from their haul.

Lady goes missing

On Monday morning 21 August 1921, when the Louvre was closed to the public, Perruggia donned his overalls and walked into the museum. He marched unchallenged to where the Mona Lisa hung, took it from the wall, cut the canvas from the frame and hid it in his overalls. A few minutes later a group of workmen passed the space where the painting should have been and one of them joked, 'They have taken it away in case we steal it'. It was not until the next day that the authorities realized what had happened. The Chief Curator of the Louvre was dismissed immediately.

There was uproar in the art world when news of the theft became known and Perruggia, Valifierno and Chaudron took advantage of the confusion. They approached six wealthy American art collectors and offered each one the missing Mona Lisa for a bargain price of $300 000. They all readily accepted, unaware that the paintings they were given were fakes painted by Chaudron. Initially they were too embarrassed to admit their folly.

No trace

While the thieves were making a fortune an intensive search was undertaken for the lady with the enigmatic smile. It was suggested that the painting had been taken by a tourist, a hoaxer, a sensation-seeking journalist, or a gang wishing to trade it for another painting. Suspicion even fell on the painter Pablo Picasso, but the Mona Lisa remained in hiding.

Two years after the original theft the three gang members quarrelled over money and Perruggia went to Italy, taking the painting with him. In Florence he invited a local art dealer to his hotel, later renamed the Gioconda, and the man was amazed when Perruggia produced the Mona Lisa. It was soon returned to the Louvre and put under the heavy security which it enjoys to this day.

Double dupe

In 1927 the curators of the Cleveland Museum of Art were perturbed to discover that one of their most prized possession, a wooden Madonna and Child, supposedly carved in the 13th century, was in fact a fake made in the 1920s by an Italian art restorer named Alceo Dossena. They immediately replaced it with a $120 000 marble statue, only to discover that it too was a Dossena fake.

Monmouth, James Scott, Duke of

(1649–85)

Conspirator

A claimant to the English throne who took advantage of the anti-Catholic feelings of the time.

Born in Amsterdam, the future Duke of Monmouth was the illegitimate son of King Charles II and his mistress Lucy Walter. Since Lucy had been banished from England for claiming to be the King's wife, her son James was brought up in Paris. Although he was slightly effeminate he was a strikingly handsome young man who had a regal bearing from an early age. In 1662 James was brought to England and he quickly established himself as a firm favourite at court, particularly with his father. In recognition of this Charles created him Duke of Monmouth, Earl of Doncaster and Baron Tyndale on 14 February 1663. He was also made a Knight of the Garter.

Scandalous lifestyle

On 20 April 1663 Monmouth married Anne Scott, a wealthy Scottish heiress and the Duchess of Buccleuch. He added the Duke of Buccleuch to his titles and adopted his wife's surname. Although they remained married until James's death it was an un-conventional marriage. Monmouth had exotic sexual tastes and surrounded himself with whores, Negro slaves and eunuchs. He could be a charming and persuasive man when he chose to be but he was also prone to violent mood swings.

Although Monmouth himself may have been happy continuing with his indulgent lifestyle there were others in England who wanted to use him for their own purposes. Being a Protestant, his actions were monitored by a number of influential men who feared a return to Catholicism under the Stuarts. One of these men was Anthony Ashley Cooper, the Earl of Shaftesbury and the leader of the anti-Catholic Whigs.

Secret ambition

Outwardly, Monmouth showed no signs of disloyalty. In 1668 he was appointed captain of the Kings Guard and he served with distinction on the continent during the Anglo–Dutch War (1672–74). In 1678 he became captain general of all the armed forces in England. But behind this facade was a deep desire to become King of England. His cause was helped when Charles's brother and heir to the throne, James, Duke of York, announced his conversion to Catholicism. There was widespread panic that the Catholics were conspiring to capture the throne and numerous attempts were made to exclude the Duke of York from his royal inheritance.

Charles II acted swiftly. Realizing that Monmouth was being projected as a future monarch he banished him from England in September 1679. The young Duke was livid and against his father's wishes he soon returned and started building up a band of supporters. In this he was aided by the Earl of Shaftesbury, who orchestrated two semi-royal tours through the counties of England, promoting Monmouth as the future king.

Rye House Plot

In 1683 Monmouth and Shaftesbury helped devise the Rye House Plot. Its aim was simple; to kill Charles and the Duke of York and then install Monmouth on the throne. The plotters, who assembled at Rye House in Hertfordshire, planned to assault Charles and James when they were returning from the Newmarket races, and kill them. However, the plan backfired because the royal party left a hour later than was expected.

The conspirators were arrested and hanged, drawn and quartered. Although Monmouth had not taken an active part in the attempted assassination it was well known that he had been a party to its planning. Instead of ordering his son's execution Charles banished him from court again and the errant Duke moved to the Netherlands. The Duke of York was not so forgiving and he never forgot Monmouth's participation in the abortive plot.

Open rebellion

When Charles II died on 6 February 1685 and the Duke of York became King James II, Monmouth saw his opportunity for another thrust at the throne. On 11 June 1685 he landed at Lyme Regis, Dorset, with a band of 82 men. He quickly let it be known that he intended removing James II from power and delivering England from the grip of Catholicism. Seeing Monmouth as a romantic hero the common people of the West Country flocked to his banner and he soon had a force of over 4000 men. However, he was unable to rally any of the nobility to his cause.

Meagre force

When Monmouth reached Taunton he attended a ceremony during which he was proclaimed King of England. Although he began to act like a monarch he did not have sufficient forces to back up his claim. On 6 July 1685 his hastily assembled and ill-equipped army was faced with the superior forces of James II. The outcome was never in doubt and Monmouth and his supporters were routed. The defeated claimant to the throne tried to escape but he was captured hiding in a ditch near Bridgwater.

Monmouth was taken to London and put in the Tower of London. There was no question of his guilt and he pleaded to James for his life, on one occasion even promising to convert to Catholicism. But James still had the memory of the Rye House Plot fresh in his mind and he refused to show the usurper any mercy. James Scott, the Duke of Monmouth, was beheaded on Tower Hill on 15 July 1685.

Bloody Assizes

Following Monmouth's defeat his supporters were persecuted mercilessly. Undercover agents were employed to locate the rebels and hundreds of them were tricked into giving worthless confessions. The most atrocious character during this period of persecution was the sadistic Judge Jeffreys. He was led to believe that if he dealt efficiently with the traitors then he would be made Lord Chancellor. This was all the encouragement he needed and he presided over a barbarous courtroom in which it was almost unheard of for a defendant to be freed. On one occasion his summing-up consisted of these rantings: 'Thou villain! I think I see thee already with a halter around thy neck. Thou impudent rebel to challenge these evidences that are for the King. Hold up a candle so that I may see more clearly the countenance of this lying wretch about to die'.

Indelicate gift

When Monmouth arrived in Taunton the townsfolk were so overjoyed to see him that they presented him with 10 young virgins. Considering the Duke's sexual appetite it is debatable how long the ladies' virtue remained intact.

Moors murders

(1963–5)

Ian Brady and Myra Hindley

One of the 20th century's most horrific crimes, which involved the torture and mutilation of young children.

Ian Brady and Myra Hindley met in 1961 when they were both working for a medical supply firm in Gorton, Manchester. Brady, whose real name was Ian Duncan Stewart, had been raised in the Gorbals in Glasgow and moved to Manchester after he been in trouble with the Glasgow police. This had little beneficial effect on him and he became a teenage drunk and spent two years in borstal for theft. When he was released he became obsessed with the Nazis and read *Mein Kampf* avidly.

Nazi fascination

Myra Hindley, who was four years younger than Brady, was born in 1942 in Gorton, and grew up as a plain and somewhat unsociable girl. She became a Catholic convert in 1958 but three years later, when she met Brady, her life went on a downward spiral. They soon discovered that they shared a fascination with all things German, and Hindley was soon dressing in the style of a female guard at a Nazi concentration camp. The couple also indulged in various sexual perversions, including Hindley posing for pornographic photographs which they tried unsuccessfully to sell.

Hindley soon became as depraved a character as Brady and they started planning armed hold-ups as a way of making money. They bought guns and ammunition but never performed any of the robberies that they discussed. Instead they turned to torture and murder.

Myra Hindley

Disappearances

On 23 November 1963 12-year-old John Kilbride vanished after working in Ashton market. A year later, on Boxing Day 1964, 10-year-old Lesley Ann Downey went missing from near her home in Ancoats. Two other children also disappeared during this period: 12-year-old Keith Bennett and 16-year-old Pauline Reade. At first no trace was found of them and the police had no clues.

After Brady had indoctrinated Hindley the couple set about corrupting her 17-year-old brother-in-law, David Smith. Smith himself had a record of violence and Brady and Hindley were hopeful that they could turn him into a cold-blooded killer. They trained him in the use of firearms and on 6 October 1965 they committed a murder for his benefit; the victim was a 17-year-old homosexual named Edward Evans. Hindley, who was posing as Brady's sister, took Evans from a club in Manchester to her grandmother's house in Wardle Brook Avenue, where the couple were living. Once Evans was in the house Smith was made to watch Brady brutally murder him with a hatchet. Afterwards Brady commented, 'It's the messiest yet. It normally only takes one blow'.

Horrified witness

The murder of Edward Evans did not have the desired effect on David Smith. Rather than being impressed by this piece of brutality the youngster was horrified and the following day he telephoned the police. When they arrived at Wardle Brook Avenue they arrested Brady and Hindley and searched the house. By this time Smith had told them that Brady had boasted of several other murders and they decided to search the area of the Pennine Moors where he had been taken for target practice. On 16 October 1965 the body of Lesley Ann Downey was found. There were signs of sexual abuse and she had been buried in a shallow grave, between Greenfield and Holmfirth.

Two days later the police searched Myra Hindley's belongings. What they found was to spark off one of the most disturbing searches of modern times. In her prayer book they discovered two left-luggage tickets for Manchester station. This revealed two suitcases and inside were tape-recordings and photographic material that related to the murders of Lesley Ann Downey and John Kilbride. A massive search of the Moors followed and on 21 October 1965 the body of John Kilbride was found 400 yards from the grave of Lesley Ann Downey. He too had been sexually abused.

National disgust

The public outrage at these crimes was heightened by two facts: firstly it was thought that they must also be responsible for the disappearances of Keith Bennett and Pauline Read, and secondly because of the

perverted photographs they had taken of the children and the tape recordings. On one of these there were the pitiful screams and cries for help of Lesley Ann Downey shortly before she was murdered.

The trial of Brady and Hindley began on 19 April 1965 at Chester Castle. There was such animosity towards the two accused that the unprecedented step of surrounding the dock with 4" bullet-proof glass was taken. The trial catalogued how Brady and Hindley had persuaded the two young children to come back to their house and then tortured, sexually assaulted and murdered them. The courtroom was stunned.

On 6 May 1966, just two months after capital punishment had been abolished in Britain, Ian Brady was found guilty of all three murders and sentenced to three life terms, to run concurrently. Myra Hindley was found guilty of the murders of Edward Evans and Lesley Ann Downey and sentenced to two life terms, plus seven years for an accessory after the fact in the murder of John Kilbride. The judge described them as 'sadistic killers of the utmost depravity'.

Parole campaign

In 1985, following a campaign headed by Lord Longford, Myra Hindley applied for parole, claiming that she was a reformed character. There was a wave of protest and the Home Secretary, Leon Brittan, denied the application. Two years later both Brady and Hindley aided the police in a search for the bodies of Pauline Reade and Keith Bennett. Amidst intense media coverage the body of Pauline was found on the Moors but the search was called off before the remains of Keith Bennett were found.

> **Editorial comment**
> Following the discovery of Pauline Reade's body *The Daily Telegraph* commented, 'The time has come for a halt to police excavations, and to visits by the murderers to the Moors in the glare of publicity which could please only the least admirable of policemen. There must also be no more discussion of any kind about the possible release of Brady and Hindley. What they did was simply too dreadful for society to contemplate granting their freedom'.

Morgan, Sir Henry Johan
(c.1635–1688)

Buccaneer

A British pirate who operated in the West Indies and eventually became lieutenant-governor of Jamaica.

Born in Wales, Morgan was kidnapped at an early age in Bristol and sold as a servant in Barbados. When he obtained his freedom he made his way to Jamaica where he joined the local buccaneers. In 1666 the governor of Jamaica, Sir Thomas Modyford, commissioned one of the famous buccaneers of the day, Edward Mansfield, to undertake the capture of Curacoa. Morgan had his own ship to command but the mission was a failure and Mansfield was captured by the Spanish and put to death. The decisive and charismatic Morgan was unanimously elected as the new leader of the buccaneering force.

Forceful buccaneer

In 1667 Charles II signed a treaty with the Spanish and Thomas Modyford was ordered to withdraw all privateering commissions, which he was reluctant to do because the Spaniards in Cuba were threatening to invade Jamaica. In order to thwart them Modyford ordered Morgan to assemble a force and find out about the proposed invasion. Morgan sailed to Cuba with 10 ships and about 500 men; the buccaneers captured the town of Puerto Principe and discovered that a large force was being assembled for action against Jamaica.

Not satisfied with just gaining military information Morgan decided to head to the town of Puerto Bello where he had heard several Englishmen were being held captive. After fierce fighting Morgan and his men were able to scale the three forts in the town and capture the Spanish garrison, and for the next two weeks the buccaneers went on an orgy of torturing and pillaging. The town was sacked, contrary to Morgan's later claim that the town was left 'in as good condition as we found it', and the buccaneers eventually left when the president of Panama agreed to pay a ransom of 100 000 pieces of eight and 300 negro slaves.

Reprimanded and forgiven

Morgan returned to Jamaica with his plunder, in August 1668, only to be reprimanded for exceeding his commission which referred to shipping only. Morgan was unrepentant and Modyford soon forgave him, offering him another commission to carry out further hostilities against the Spanish along the coast of Cuba.

In March 1669 Morgan, with a force of only eight ships and less than 500 men, attacked the Venezuelan port of Maracaibo and Lake Maracaibo. As with Puerto Bello the town was sacked, and its inhabitants mercilessly tortured into revealing the hiding place of the town's treasures. Morgan's force then went to Gibralter, at the head of the lake, and for five weeks they continued their vicious looting and destruction.

Daring escape

When Morgan and his small fleet returned to Maracaibo they discovered that the Spanish had cut off their escape route. A few skirmishes followed and although Morgan was paid a handsome ransom for Maracaibo his fleet were refused a safe passage from the town. Morgan decided that some ingenuity was called for and assembled his men as if they were going to attack the town's fort from the land. Instead, under the cover of night, he weighed anchor and sailed past the Spanish, who had moved their cannons to the land side of the fort.

When Morgan returned to Jamaica he again incurred the wrath of Modyford for being over-zealous, but this was forgotten in 1670 when the queen regent of Spain ordered her governors in the Indies to make open war against the English. Modyford at once granted Morgan a commission to gather all the ships of war he could find into one fleet and put to sea for the security of Jamaica. This was exactly the type of commission that Morgan liked.

Invasion of Panama

On 14 August 1670 Morgan sailed from Jamaica and, after three months of ravaging the coast of Cuba, he decided to attack Panama, which seemed justifiable since their president had granted several commissions against the English. A few coastal towns were captured and then Morgan decided to take his force of 1400 men overland towards Panama city. At the beginning of January 1671 the Spanish met them on the 10th day of their march. Morgan was faced by a force of 3000 and several hundred bulls that the Spanish hoped would break the buccaneers' lines. Unfortunately this plan back-fired and the bulls did a U-turn, trampling the Spanish forces as they fled. That afternoon Morgan and his men were in possession of the city of Panama.

The capture of Panama was a great military and financial success for Morgan, and his mercenary nature was revealed when he divided the spoils between his men. It had been agreed earlier that everyone would receive an equal amount, but Morgan kept the lion's share for himself and rewarded his men with a pittance.

Recalled to England

Due to political manoeuverings in England Thomas Modyford was recalled in the summer of 1671. In April 1672 Morgan had to follow him to explain his buccaneering activities. He argued his case so successfully that he was sent back to Jamaica two years later, with a knighthood and a commission as lieutenant-governor of Jamaica.

When Morgan arrived back in Jamaica he gave up his buccaneering career and settled down to a life of respectability and responsibility. In addition to being lieutenant-governor he was also a senior member of the council and commander-in-chief of the forces. Since Jamaica was now safe from invasion Morgan even executed large numbers of men from his former profession. He died in his sleep in 1688 and was buried in St Catherine's Church in the town of Port Royal.

A pirate's wage

Although all of Morgan's buccaneering adventures were commissioned it was always made clear that there was to be no payment from the government for these expeditions. In his 1669 commission, which led to the invasion of Panama, Thomas Modyford concluded, 'as there is no other pay for the encouragement of the fleet, they shall have all the goods and merchandizes that shall be gotten in this expedition, to be divided amongst them, according to their rules'. Unfortunately for his men, Morgan always made sure that he received by far the largest share.

Muller, Franz

(1839–64)

Convicted murderer

The first person to be convicted of a murder on a British train.

Franz Muller was born in Saxe-Weimar, Germany, and moved to Britain in 1862 after failing at his chosen profession as a gunsmith. He settled in London and decided to become a tailor. He did not enjoy life in England, however, and made it widely known that he was going to leave his new home and emigrate to America. On 15 July 1864 he boarded the sailing ship *Victoria*, bound for New York.

Railway murder

Six days before Muller left for America two bank clerks boarded a commuter train at Hackney and went into an empty compartment. They immediately saw a hat, a walking stick and a bag. There was also blood on the seats. They alerted the police and later that evening the unconscious body of Thomas Briggs, a 70-year-old chief clerk at a London bank, was found near the railway line between Hackney Wick and Bow stations. He had been viciously assaulted and died a few hours later. Robbery was the obvious motive as his gold watch, gold chain and gold eye-glasses had been stolen.

Although the hat on the train was identified as not belonging to Briggs, the first clue the police received came from a jeweller with the inappropriate name of Mr Death. He told the police that on 11 July a man had exchanged a gold chain for a newer chain and a ring. His most obvious characteristic was that he spoke with a German accent. Then a cab driver came forward to identify the hat found on the train. He recognized it as belonging to Franz Muller, who had once been engaged to one of his daughters.

Chase to New York

When the police went to interview Muller they discovered he had already left for America. In a chase similar to that involving Dr Crippen, Scotland Yard's Chief Inspector William Tanner and Detective Sergeant Clarke boarded the steamship *City of Manchester* and headed after Muller to New York. Since their ship was considerably faster they arrived a couple of weeks before Muller's sailing ship. When he arrived he was met by a large, inquisitive crowd and Chief Inspector Tanner, who promptly arrested him. Briggs's hat and gold watch were found in his luggage.

Muller was extradited and his trial began at the Old Bailey on 27 October 1864. Because of his dramatic capture and the fact that he had committed the first ever railway murder there was enormous public interest in the case. None of this helped Muller and he was found guilty on 29 October and sentenced to death.

The German Society in London petitioned the Home Secretary to grant a reprieve and the King of Prussia even telegraphed Queen Victoria asking for clemency. All these pleas were rejected and Muller was hanged on 14 November 1864, in front of a riotous crowd outside Newgate prison.

Peep-holes
People were so concerned about travelling on trains after the Muller case that peep-holes, known as 'Muller holes', were inserted between compartments to give passengers added security. Eventually they were abandoned because people complained it restricted their privacy.

Musica, Philip

(1884–1938)

Financial swindler

An American-Italian who became one of the most effective swindlers of the 20th century.

Philip Musica was born in Italy and moved to New York with his family while he was still a child. His father was a barber who was involved in several dubious business ventures and he grew up in an atmosphere of dishonesty. In 1898 he spent five months in prison for bribing customs officers.

Prison did not deter Musica from a life of deception and he began selling stock in his United States Hair Company. With his new found wealth he became a pillar of the Italian community in New York; attending the opera, sitting on committees and giving generously to charities. Then, in 1913, he was arrested, along with his three brothers, for obtaining money on the worthless stock of the United States Hair Company.

Following his arrest Musica used his powers of persuasion and managed to avoid a prison sentence by offering to work as a police informer. This type of work suited him and he later became a counter-espionage agent for the attorney general.

New identity

At the end of World War I the notorious Philip Musica disappeared, to be replaced by the eminently respectable Frank Donald Coster, supposedly a doctor from Heildelberg University who had worked for two years in New York City. It was nearly 20 years before the truth about Dr Coster was discovered.

When F Donald Coster appeared in New York he was already the managing director of a flourishing pharmaceutical business, Girard & Co. In 1926 Coster went to Julian

Thomson, the head of a large investment bank, and, with the aid of doctored books, persuaded him to lend him enough money to take over the established pharmaceutical firm of McKesson & Robbins Inc. As a reward Thomson was made a director.

Drugs con

With his new company Coster was able to perpetrate one of the longest and most successful swindles in history. After putting himself in sole charge of the crude drug department he bought large quantities of drugs in Canada and then sold them through another company, W W Smith. However, the purchase and sale of the drugs was totally fictitious and the only genuine transaction was the commission paid to W W Smith. In reality this was just a single room that was occupied by Philip Musica's brothers. The amount of money paid in commission amounted to at least $18 million.

After several years of exceptional business Thomson became suspicious of the crude drugs department and the large profits it seemed to be making. He asked Coster to convert some of the stockpiled drugs into cash and, when he refused, Thomson took his suspicions to the police. Coster was arrested and during routine fingerprinting he was discovered to be none other than Philip Musica. The business community of New York was stunned, but before the shock had died down Musica committed suicide. His brothers were convicted and sent to prison.

Keeping the faith

Although Coster claimed to be a Methodist, Musica clung to his original religion; after his death a card was found in his wallet that read, 'I am a Catholic. In the case of accident, notify a priest'.

Neilson, Donald

(1936–)

Convicted murderer and kidnapper

Known as the 'Black Panther', he murdered four people, including a young heiress.

Donald Neilson, who changed his name from Nappey, was born near Bradford in Yorkshire. He was a juvenile delinquent who was usually morose and difficult. After completing his National Service he turned his hand to a variety of jobs, including taxi-driving, house repairs, plumbing and joinery. He was unsuccessful at them all and his failures only exaggerated the grudge that he already had against society.

Armed robbery

Neilson had violent tendencies from an early age and he soon turned to crime. He committed numerous house burglaries and then began attacks on post-offices. On 16 February 1972 he raided a sub-post-office in Heywood, Lancashire. However, the sub-postmaster interrupted him and tried to pull off the black hood that he was wearing. As he did so the raider's gun went off and the man escaped through the back door.

Over the next two years there were 15 similar raids on post-offices, with the perpetrator getting away with a total of over £20 000. On 15 February 1974 the man that had become known as the 'Black Panther', on account of his hood, raided another post office. During the course of the attack the sub-postmaster, Donald Skepper, tried to apprehend the intruder but he was shot cold-bloodedly and died in his wife's arms.

Panther murders

On 6 September the Black Panther struck again. This time the target was a sub-post-office near Accrington. Again the raid resulted in a fatal shooting, sub-postmaster Derek Astin being murdered in front of his wife and children. They later told the police that the gunman had been short, slim and wiry.

A third killing took place in November 1974. This time the location had moved to Worcestershire, and the village of Langley. The Black Panther followed a similar pattern to his previous two attacks; he tried to rob the post-office but when he was interrupted he was not slow to use the shotgun he carried; he killed Sidney Grayland, whose wife Margaret later recovered from her wounds.

New tactic

As the police stepped up their campaign to capture Britain's most wanted man the Black Panther decided to change his tactics. He realized that post-offices were becoming too closely watched, so as an alternative he turned to kidnapping. On 13 January 1975 he abducted 17-year-old Lesley Whittle from her home in Highley, Shropshire. He had researched his victim carefully and knew that she was the heiress to a large family fortune. A ransom note for £50 000 and a death-threat were left at the Whittle house.

Lesley's brother Ronald undertook to find his sister and twice followed the kidnapper's instructions, only to be frustrated when there was no sign of his sister or her abductor. On 15 January a security guard, Gerald Smith, questioned a suspicious looking man who was leaving a transport depot in Dudley, Worcestershire. Unhappy with the man's answers, Smith went to telephone the police, but as he did so he was shot six times in the back. He recovered from his injuries but died 14 months later, almost certainly as a result of his ordeal.

Wire noose that killed Lesley Whittle

Fourth victim

After this attack the police decided that Lesley Whittle had been kidnapped by the Black Panther. On 6 March a schoolboy found a note saying, 'Drop suitcase into hole' in a park near Kidsgrove. The police searched the area and on 7 March they discovered the body of Lesley Whittle, hanging from a wire rope in a drainage shaft. It was clear that the Black Panther had decided that the park, with its network of underground sewage tunnels, would be the ideal place to hide the body.

Although the capture of the Black Panther was a number one priority it was not until nine months later that he was taken into custody. On the night of 11 December 1975 two police officers, Tony White and Stuart Mackenzie, were driving through Mansfield Woodhouse in Nottinghamshire. As a matter of routine they stopped to question a man loitering outside a post-office. The inquiry became anything but routine when the man produced a sawn-off shotgun, took the two policemen hostage in their car, and ordered them to drive six

miles to the village of Blidworth. When they arrived the gunman asked for a piece of rope. White waited until the man's attention was diverted and then he tried to disarm him. The gun went off, slightly injuring White. Two men from a nearby fish and chip shop came to the policemen's aid and between them they managed to capture the gunman. When the police discovered that he was carrying two Black Panther hoods they realized the significance of their arrest.

Shaky defence

Once he was in custody it was revealed that the Panther was Donald Neilson. When his house in Bradford was searched the police found more Panther hoods, guns, knives, military clothing and house-breaking equipment.

Neilson was tried at Oxford in June 1975, for the kidnapping and murder of Lesley Whittle. His defence was that she had died accidentally after falling while she was tied up. He used a similar defence a month later when he was tried for the murders of the three sub-postmasters, claiming that on each occasion his gun had gone off by mistake. Donald Neilson was sentenced to life imprisonment for each of the four murders, with an additional 21 years for the kidnapping of Lesley Whittle.

Public retribution
Following the arrest of the Black Panther the members of the public who helped capture him took matters into their own hands; a photograph of Neilson, taken shortly after his arrest, shows that he had been severely beaten.

Mistaken identity
Although kidnapping is relatively rare in Britain another notable case occurred on 29 December 1969. Two brothers, Arthur and Nizamodeen Hosein, kidnapped Mrs Muriel McKay, thinking mistakenly that she was Mrs Rupert Murdoch, the wife of the Australian millionaire. They demanded £1 million but they were soon traced and captured. Mrs McKay was never seen again and the brothers were convicted of murder.

Nelson, Earle Leonard

(1897–1928)

Convicted murderer

A brutal killer who carried a Bible and murdered over 20 landladies across America.

Earle Nelson's mother died nine months after his birth and he was brought up by an aunt, Lilian Fabian. He was an introverted child and when he was 10 he was knocked down by a trolley car. He recovered but the blow had a lasting effect on his personality and he suffered frequently from blinding headaches. After the accident he spent most of his time brooding in his room or reading his Bible.

In 1918 Nelson was charged with the attempted rape of his neighbour's daughter. He was judged insane and committed to an asylum, but using his physical strength (he had particularly strong hands) he managed to escape three times in six months. He married in 1919 but he was intensely jealous and constantly accused his wife of having affairs; she soon suffered a nervous breakdown and left her husband.

Preying on landladies

For the next seven years Nelson disappeared from public view. On 20 February 1926 he reappeared at a house in San Francisco that had advertised a room to rent. As the landlady was taking him upstairs he strangled her and then performed necrophilia on the dead body. The following month he struck again, in San Jose, and the newspapers christened the murderer, 'the Dark Strangler'.

For over a year Nelson roamed across America, picking out rooms for rent and then strangling the landladies and sometimes stealing their jewellery. He committed these horrendous killings in California, Oregon, Washington, Iowa, Missouri, Philadelphia and New York. Due to the ferocity of the killings the press coined a new sobriquet, 'the Gorilla Murderer'. Nelson's peripatetic nature ensured that he was always one step ahead of the police. Because of his plausible manner and proclaimed interest in religion he was never suspected by his victims until it was too late.

Trapped in Canada

In June 1927 Nelson decided to move his activities to Canada, arriving in Winnipeg on 8 June. He rented a room and his landlady was impressed by her new lodger, as he had appeared on her doorstep carrying a Bible. That evening Nelson strangled a teenage girl who was staying at the same lodgings. The next day he killed a middle-aged woman and then left the city.

One of the most intense police searches in Canadian history ensued and Nelson was eventually captured near Regina. Despite his catalogue of horrors he was only charged with his final murder. He was tried in Winnipeg on 1 November 1927, found guilty four days later, and hanged at Winnipeg on 13 January 1928. It is believed he could have been responsible for more than the 22 murders with which he has been attributed.

Bible John

In 1968 and 1969 there were three murders in Glasgow, thought to be carried out by a man who had a liking for quoting from the Bible. He met his victims at dances and then strangled then. The only clue the police uncovered was that the murderer was called John. Despite one of Glasgow's biggest man-hunts Bible John was never caught.

Nevison, John
(1639–84)

Highwayman

A courteous and successful highwayman who gained the reputation as a latter-day Robin Hood.

John Nevison was born at Pontefract in Yorkshire and his schooldays were spent stealing apples and poultry. He then graduated to stealing his schoolmaster's horse and consequently fled to Holland. He enlisted in an English regiment in the Spanish army and fought in Flanders. He did not enjoy the regimented lifestyle of the army though and, following the Restoration, he returned to England and became a highwayman.

Polite robber

Nevison quickly became a familiar figure on the highways of York, Lincoln, Nottingham and Derby, and he was renowned for his gentlemanly behaviour and courteous manner. He made it a policy to rob only the rich and he gave some of his booty to the poorer members of the community. On one occasion he made £450 from a single hold-up, and decided to retire with this fortune. But he soon tired of his life of leisure and went back to a life on the road.

Nevison also ran a profitable protection

Modern Robin Hood

Nevison's polite manner earned him a reputation as a generous highwayman, as can be seen from this popular ballad:

> He maintained himself like a gentleman
> Besides he was good to the poor
> He rode about like a bold hero
> And gained himself favour therefore.

---

system in his native Yorkshire, which was designed to make him money but also give the local farmers genuine help. He levied a charge on local drovers and graziers and in return he ensured that they were protected from other robbers.

Single killing

In 1676 Nevison and some members of his gang were arrested, tried and convicted of robbery and horse-stealing. He avoided execution by promising to turn King's evidence, and then promptly refused to divulge any information. As a result of his silence he was sentenced to a life of military service but easily escaped and returned to his chosen profession.

In 1681, after five more profitable years, Nevison was doped by an innkeeper named Fletcher, who hoped to turn the highwayman over to the authorities. However, Nevison did not succumb to the potion and escaped, shooting Fletcher dead in the process, the only person he ever killed. When Charles II heard about the incident he offered a reward of £20 for his arrest.

Ride to York

Although he was arrested shortly after the shooting of Fletcher, Nevison escaped yet again and remained at large for another three years. His luck finally ran out on 1 March 1684 when he was arrested by Captain Hardcastle at a public house near Wakefield. This time there was no escape for Nevison and he was hanged at York on 15 March 1684.

During his career Nevison acquired the sobriquet of 'Swift Nicks' and many people believe it was he, and not Dick Turpin, who inspired the legend of the epic ride to York. Whatever the truth, Nevison was certainly a much more likeable character than the ruffian Turpin.

Nilsen, Dennis Andrew

(1945–   )

Convicted murderer

A loner who felt rejected by society and retaliated by becoming one of Britain's worst mass murderers.

Dennis Nilsen was born in Fraserburgh, Scotland. His father was a Norwegian soldier who drank heavily and frequently beat up his wife. The marriage ended in 1949 and Nilsen was sent to live with his grandparents. This was one of several incidents in his life when he felt a grave sense of rejection.

Nilsen enjoyed living with his grandparents and became strongly attached to his grandfather, Andrew Whyte. In 1952, when Nilsen was seven, Whyte died. Nilson was devastated and retreated into himself, refusing to mix with other children and spending his time reading or studying wildlife.

Social outcast

In August 1961 Nilsen joined the army and three years later he became an army cook. He enjoyed the freedom that his job afforded him and he travelled to Aden, the Persian Gulf, Cyprus and West Germany. He made few friends though and was regarded as a loner.

After 12 years in the army Nilsen went to London and joined the Metropolitan Police. However, the strict regulations irritated him and he only lasted a few months. He then worked briefly as a security guard before finally settling as a civil servant working at the Jobcentre in Soho near Leicester Square.

Emotional block

During this time Nilsen formed a strong emotional relationship with a girlfriend. They were well suited and spent long hours taking walks and reading poetry. At one point Nilsen realized that he was in love and considered proposing. However, his fear of rejection overcame him and instead of asking her to marry him he broke up with her.

In 1975 Nilsen met a young man named David Gallichan. They became close friends and in November 1975 they decided to live together in a flat at Melrose Avenue, Cricklewood. Although they lived as a domestic couple there was no evidence of a homosexual relationship and for the first time in his life Nilsen felt truly settled. He lived a quiet existence and the presence of Gallichan made him at peace with himself. Then, in May 1977, Nilsen's world fell apart when Gallichan announced that he was leaving and moving to Devon.

Floodgates open

Once Gallichan had left, all of Nilsen's resentment and hang-ups rose to the surface. His alienation soon manifested itself in murder. Towards the end of December 1978 he was on one of his frequent drinking binges and met an Irish labourer. He invited his new friend back to Melrose Avenue and they kept drinking. When the labourer eventually passed out Nilsen strangled him with a tie. After the killing Nilsen went through a strange ritual that followed all of his murders. He stripped the body and then cleaned it thoroughly before dressing it again. After this he took off his own clothes and covered himself with powder so that he too looked like a corpse.

The following morning Nilsen discovered that, 'I had a corpse on my hands'. He was unsure of what to do so he encased it in two plastic bags and hid it under the floorboards. It remained there for eight months until, on 11 August 1979, he burnt it on a bonfire at the bottom of his garden. In order to hide the smell of burning flesh he added a quantity of rubber gloves.

Pattern develops

Nilsen's second victim was a Canadian holidaymaker named Kenneth Ockenden, who accepted the offer of a night's accommodation. When he reached Melrose Avenue he watched television while listening to records on headphones. Nilsen considered this the height of bad manners and strangled his guest with a flex; unable to fit the whole body under the floorboards, he cut it up into pieces.

Nilsen moved from Melrose Avenue in October 1981; by this time he had killed a total of 12 men. They all followed a similar pattern — people whom he met while out drinking, or down-and-outs he encountered at work. He invited them back to his flat, sat drinking with them until they passed out, and then strangled them. Disposing of the bodies proved to be the biggest problem: he either burnt them on a bonfire straight away or else cut them up and stored them for up to a year before burning them.

When Nilsen left Melrose Avenue he moved to Cranley Gardens, in Muswell Hill. Between October 1981 and February 1983 another three men spent the night drinking with him but did not live to tell of their experience. He cut up the bodies and put the bits in sacks and even boiled the head of one victim in a large pot.

Flesh in the drain

On 8 February 1983 some of the residents of Cranley Gardens found that their drains were blocked. They called Dyna-rod and when the engineer investigated the drains outside Dennis Nilsen's house he recoiled in horror; he was convinced that the mass of white flesh he saw was of human origin. The police were contacted and the next day they questioned Nilsen. When asked where the rest of the body was he pointed to the wardrobe and said, 'It's in there, in two plastic bags'. He also confessed to a total of 15 or 16 murders.

Nilsen's trial began on 24 October 1983; he was charged with six murders and two attempted murders. On 4 November he was found guilty on all charges and sentenced to life imprisonment. Since he has been in prison Nilsen has taken up writing, but he has not been accepted by his fellow inmates — while in Wormwood Scrubs he was slashed across the face with a razor.

Self-contempt

Soon after Nilsen was sentenced the prison chaplain suggested to him that he might like to attend chapel and ask forgiveness for his sins. His reply was blunt and final: 'I'm a mass murderer, not a bloody hypocrite'.

Unpopular property

In November 1983 the house at Cranley Gardens where Nilsen lived was put up for sale. It attracted a large number of goulish sightseers but very few genuine buyers. It was eventually sold in 1984 for a sum well below the asking price.

Oates, Titus

(1649–1705)

Informer and perjurer

*The inventor of a fictitious
Catholic plot that led to the
deaths of 35 innocent men.*

Titus Oates was born at Oakham, the son of an Anabaptist preacher. Although his academic career was marked by frequent expulsions he was ordained into the Church of England and instituted to the vicarage of Bobbing, Kent, in 1673. The following year he joined his father as a curate at All Saints, Hastings. It was here that he began his career as a perjurer, trumping up a spurious charge against a local schoolmaster. The sham was exposed and Oates was thrown into prison.

In 1675 Oates escaped from Dover prison and joined the Navy as a chaplain. His deceitful character was soon exposed and he suffered yet another expulsion, but he soon overcame this setback and in 1676 became chaplain to the Protestants in the household of Henry Howard, 6th Duke of Norfolk.

Popish Plot

It was while he was in the service of the Duke of Norfolk that Oates first had the idea of inventing a story about a Catholic plot against the Crown. He found an accomplice in Israel Tonge, an erstwhile vicar who was devoted to discrediting the Jesuits. Oates offered to gather information about their activities and with this in mind he feigned conversion to Catholicism in March 1677.

In June 1677 Oates was admitted to the Jesuit seminaries of Valladolid and St Omer, only to be expelled shortly afterwards. He returned to London in 1678 and by this time he had a wealth of material for the 'narrative of a horrid plot'. Tonge was delighted with this and together they set about fabricating their story of a vast Catholic conspiracy.

Story believed

On 6 September 1678 Oates and Tonge went to a respected justice of the peace, Sir Edmund Berry Godfrey, and informed him of a plot which involved the overthrow of King Charles II in favour of his Catholic brother James, Duke of York. Godfrey believed the story and when Oates repeated it before the Privy Council it caused great excitement and fear throughout London.

Wave of terror

In October 1678 the possibility of a conspiracy was increased by the murder of Sir Edmund Godfrey. Catholic conspirators were blamed for the crime but it is likely that it was performed by Oates in an effort to gain credibility for his conspiracy theory. A witch hunt ensued and Oates was responsible for the judicial murder of over 35 men.

As a plot failed to materialize people began to doubt the allegations made by Oates. When James II acceded to the throne in March 1685 he put him on trial for perjury. He was convicted and then pilloried, flogged and imprisoned for life. He was set free during the Revolution of 1688 and died in obscurity in 1705.

> **Plot details**
> Oates claimed that the Catholic conspirators had three possible methods of killing Charles II: using the royal physician to poison him; hiring four Irish thugs to stab him to death; or using two Jesuits to shoot him with silver bullets.

Olive, 'Princess of Cumberland'
(1772–1834)

Imposter

A house-painter's daughter who claimed to be the legitimate daughter of the Duke of Cumberland.

Olivia Wilmot was born at Warwick on 3 April 1772. Her father, Robert Wilmot, was a house-painter and Olivia took an interest in art at an early age. When she was 17 she married her art teacher, John Thomas Serres. The couple quarrelled frequently and were separated in 1804.

Following the break-up of her marriage Olivia occupied herself with her painting and had exhibitions at the Royal Academy from 1804 to 1808 and at the British Institution in 1806. Through this she was introduced to members of the Royal Family and in 1806 she was appointed landscape-painter to the Prince of Wales. She also wrote various works of literature but her talent for painting was superior.

Royal aspirations

Olivia's experience with royalty left a big impression on her and she decided that she would like to have a title herself. In 1817 she did this by claiming that she was the illegitimate daughter of Henry Frederick, Duke of Cumberland and Strathearn, brother of George III.

Initially, Olivia's extravagant claim had little effect, so in 1820 she embellished her story by stating that she was the legitimate daughter of the Duke, in recognition of which she was rechristened Olive, daughter of the Duke of Cumberland. To keep up appearances she hired a carriage, placed the royal arms on it and had her servants dress in the royal livery.

Bizarre claim

Olive argued that Dr Wilmot of Oxford had married a sister of the king of Poland and their daughter had subsequently married the Duke of Cumberland. Olive claimed she was the result of this marriage. As a baby she had been given to Robert Wilmot (Dr Wilmot's brother), whose wife had just suffered a stillbirth; despite the imaginative nature of this claim some newspapers took up her cause, as did the famous genealogist Henry Nugent Bell.

While trying to live up to her title Olive ran up considerable expenses and in July 1821 she was arrested for debt. She asserted that, because of her title, she was exempt from arrest in civil cases. When this brought little response she produced an alleged will of George III's. It left her £15 000 as the daughter of his brother. There was considerable discussion as to whether the will was genuine or not. Olive's supporters presented a petition to Parliament on her behalf but in 1825 Sir Robert Peel, the Home Secretary, announced that her claim was baseless.

John Serres died in 1825, stating in his will that his wife's claims were spurious. Olive never regained her former prominence and died on 21 November 1834.

Daughter continues claim

One of Olivia Serres's daughters, Mrs Lavinia Ryves (1797–1871) took up her mother's cause but was unable to obtain the £15 000 that had supposedly been left by George III. In 1866 she petitioned the court to declare that her mother had been the legitimate daughter of the Duke of Cumberland. After much consideration it was declared that the documents before the court, over 70 of them, were all forgeries.

Orton, Arthur (The Tichborne Claimant)

(1834–98)

Imposter and perjurer

A butcher from Wapping who claimed to be the heir to a wealthy English estate.

Arthur Orton was born in 1834 and he soon displayed a taste for adventure. After learning the family trade of butchery, and travelling through South America, in 1852 he emigrated to Australia, where he worked as slaughterman, stockman, mail-rider, bushranger and horse-thief. He eventually settled in Wagga-Wagga in New South Wales under the alias of Thomas Castro.

In 1865 Orton's attorney saw an advertisement in an Australian newspaper asking for an information about the whereabouts of Roger Tichborne, the heir to the seat of Tichborne in England. Believing that Orton was the heir, the attorney contacted the author of the advertisement, the Dowager Lady Tichborne.

Lady Tichborne was surprised but delighted to hear that her son was alive because it was widely believed that he had drowned at sea in 1854. But, desperate to believe that he was living, she ordered him to return home immediately.

The claimant arrives at Tichborne

Arthur Orton, claiming to be Roger Tichborne, arrived in England on Christmas Day 1866. In many ways his claim was comical; Orton was a large, overweight man whereas the real Roger Tichborne had been slight and delicate, and he did not even know the christian names of the lady who was supposed to be his mother. Despite this, the ageing Lady Tichborne claimed that she recognized her son.

By this time Orton had captured the public's imagination and he had considerable support when he brought an action for possession of the Tichborne estate. The case lasted 102 days between May 1871 and March 1872 and by the end of it Orton had been exposed as a hopeless imposter. He was arrested for perjury and in 1874 he was found guilty after the longest trial in English criminal history — 188 days.

Orton was sentenced to 14 years' penal servitude and was released in 1884. He signed a confession saying that he had entered into the fraud for fun but decided to continue it when he was recognized by Lady Tichborne. He died in 1898, on April Fool's Day.

Prison diet
Prison had a noticeable effect on Arthur Orton: he weighed nearly $28^1/_2$ stone when he entered Pentonville Prison but on his release he tipped the scales at a mere 12 stone.

Ossianic poetry forgeries

(1760–63)

James Macpherson

The most audacious literary forgery of the 18th century, which involved passages of ancient Highland poetry.

James Macpherson was born at Ruthven in Inverness-shire and he attended King's College, Aberdeen and Edinburgh University. Although he educated himself to a high standard he never obtained a degree from either establishment.

Macpherson was an extroverted figure who sought recognition and fame. In 1758 he tried to achieve this when he published an ambitious poem entitled *The Highlander*. This, like some of his earlier works of poetry, was poorly received so he chose another method of gaining acceptance into the literary world.

Ancient poems

In 1760 Macpherson showed some friends in Edinburgh fragments of poetry that he claimed to have translated from extracts he had found in the Highlands. His friends were so impressed that they encouraged him to publish them. He agreed and in July 1760 Macpherson published *Fragments of Ancient Poetry, Collected in the Highlands of Scotland, and Translated from the Galic of Erse Language*. He claimed that it was a translation of the work of a third-century bard and warrior named Ossian.

In his preface to *Fragments* Macpherson hinted that there was a longer epic poem in existence and, since the reaction to his first work had been so favourable, a group of Edinburgh publishers agreed to finance Macpherson on a trip to the Highlands so he could try and unearth more works by Ossian. Realizing how his reputation was growing Macpherson agreed and in 1762 he published his translation of the epic Ossianic poem *Fingal*. It was hailed as a triumph and Macpherson was paid £1200.

Cool reception in London

After publishing *Fingal* Macpherson went to London, where he was met with a very lukewarm reception. Several people believed that his Ossianic poem was a forgery; Samuel Johnson in particular was very damning of him and his work. When asked if any living man could have written the Ossianic poems he replied, 'Yes, sir, many men, many women and many children'.

Undeterred by his critics Macpherson translated another epic Ossianic poem in 1763. It was entitled *Tempora* and this was more roundly criticised as being a forgery. However, there was no conclusive proof and Macpherson himself refused to be drawn into a debate about the poems' authenticity. He also refused to part with his original manuscripts. Part of the animosity towards the poems stemmed from the 1745 Rebellion and an English dislike of anything connected with the Highlands .

Macpherson died in 1796 and a year later the Highland Society of Scotland appointed a committee to investigate the authenticity of the poems. In 1805 the committee concluded that they were forgeries and that Macpherson had, 'liberally edited his originals and inserted passages of his own'.

> **Literary hit**
> Despite the rumours of forgery the Ossianic poems were extremely popular and gained Macpherson the fame and wealth that he desired. They were translated into most European languages and it was said that Napoleon carried a pocketbook version of the poems with him at all times.

Palmer, William

(1825–56)

Convicted murderer and poisoner

An inveterate gambler who poisoned as many as 14 people in an attempt to pay his debts.

William Palmer was born in Rugeley, Staffordshire. His father died when he was 12 and after he left school he was apprenticed to a firm of chemists in Liverpool. Although he was intelligent he preferred to direct his attentions to women and gambling. He was sacked for stealing from his employer.

Palmer's mother settled his debts and sent him to work for a local surgeon named Edward Tylecote. Palmer worked for him for five years and in addition to the medical knowledge he gained he also stole from his employer and fathered 14 illegitimate children. Eventually Tylecote became fed up with Palmer's behaviour and sacked him.

Fascination with poison

The next stage of Palmer's education was as a 'walking pupil' at Stafford Infirmary. His main interest at the hospital was in the study of poisons and he left after a patient died in mysterious circumstances. He went to St Bartholomew's Hospital in London where he spent a debauched year and only just managed to graduate as a doctor. His one area of expertise was again toxicology.

In August 1846 Palmer returned to Rugeley and set up practice as a GP. The locals were suspicious of him and his moderate business did little to help pay his debts at the local race-track. The patients he treated did not always survive and several of his illegitimate children died after visiting Palmer's surgery.

Mounting debts

By 1847 Palmer was becoming desperate for money. He was heavily in debt, to a London lawyer named Thomas Pratt and also to a firm of money-lenders named Padwick and Wright. He realized that he was not going to win a fortune on the horses, so he decided to marry. His wife, Ann Brookes, had a substantial private income and her mother had property worth over £12 000; Palmer made sure that the money would pass to him if his mother-in-law died. In 1848 he invited her to stay at Rugeley; she was dead within 10 days of arriving at the Palmers' house.

There were other mysterious deaths connected with Palmer, including that of his own uncle and four of his five children, but there was little proof that he was a murderer. To reinforce his alleged innocence Palmer always allayed suspicion after a mysterious death by calling on a second opinion from another doctor. He was very specific in his choice, a local doctor named Bamford who was over 80 and was quite happy to agree with anything that Palmer said.

Despite receiving some of the money from his mother-in-law's estate it was not as much as Palmer had hoped and his financial situation was getting worse all the time. In January 1854 he was getting desperate and took out three life insurance policies on his wife, for a total of £13 000. In September Mrs Palmer fell ill and although her husband treated her personally she died shortly afterwards. Palmer consoled himself with the money that the insurance companies paid out, albeit reluctantly, and he paid off some his debts to the money-lenders.

Suspicious insurers

Realizing that he had hit on an effective plan for subsidizing his gambling and

183

William Palmer

did not escape his attention that Cook pocketed nearly £2000 as a result of his victory. To celebrate, Cook held a supper party for his friends and at one point he complained of a funny taste in his brandy. Shortly afterwards he became violently ill and although Palmer took it upon himself to treat the man he was unable to save him and he died on 20 November. Palmer then forged a document to show that Cook owed him £4000.

On 23 November John Cook's stepfather arrived in Rugeley and demanded a post-mortem. Remarkably, Palmer was allowed to attend it and he did his best to destroy the contents of Cook's stomach. When they were finally examined they were found to contain small traces of antimony, but not enough to kill a man. An inquest was held, which returned a verdict of wilful murder. Palmer was arrested and taken to Stafford jail.

Prince of poisoners

William Palmer's trial began at the Old Bailey on 14 May 1856. The prosecution contended that he had poisoned Cook with strychnine, despite the fact that none was found at the post-mortem. There was a wealth of unsatisfactory evidence from medical experts but the circumstantial evidence was overwhelming and the jury found Palmer guilty.

William Palmer, one of the most prolific poisoners in British criminal history, was hanged in public outside Stafford prison on 14 June 1855. Shortly afterwards his home town of Rugeley applied to the prime minister to change its name.

mistresses, Palmer then tried to insure the life of his brother, Walter, for a staggering £82 000. The insurance companies were more cautious this time and Palmer could only secure policies for £13 000. The caution was well placed because on 16 August 1855 Walter died after a drinking binge with his brother. Much to Palmer's annoyance the insurance companies considered Walter Palmer's death to have been under suspicious circumstances and refused to pay out on his policy.

By November 1855 Pratt and the money-lenders were threatening to sue Palmer, and the mother of one of his illegitimate children was blackmailing him. To cheer himself up on 13 November he went to the Shrewsbury races with a friend, John Parsons Cook.

A day at the races

As usual Palmer lost on the horses but he was delighted when Cook's own horse, Polestar, won the Shrewsbury Handicap. It

The Palmer Act

Due to intense hostility directed at Palmer in Rugeley a special act of parliament was passed allowing an accused person to be tried in London if it was thought they would not get a fair trial in their home county. This became known as the 'Palmer Act'.

Peace, Charles Frederick

(1832–79)

Thief and convicted murderer

A notorious house-breaker who was convicted of murdering his neighbour and attempting to murder a policeman.

Charles Peace was a small, ugly, selfish man who was born in Sheffield. He was apprenticed at a rolling-mill but left after an accident which cost him two fingers on his left hand. He turned to burglary, at which he was very skilful, being strong, agile and able to change his appearance at will. He also had an interest in amateur dramatics and music, sometimes carrying his house-breaking equipment in a violin case.

A burglar's life

From 1851 to 1872 Peace served four prison sentences for burglary, ranging from one month to six years. When he was not in prison he roamed from town to town, committing burglaries as he went, and enjoying his growing notoriety. In 1859 he married a widow named Hannah Ward, and in 1875 he moved to Darnall, just outside Sheffield. To create a respectable image he worked as a picture-framer and guilder.

Fatal affair

At the end of 1875 Peace embarked on an affair with one of his neighbours, Mrs Katherine Dyson. She encouraged his advances but her husband was not so enthusiastic and left a note in Peace's garden saying, 'Charles Peace is requested not to interfere with my family'. Peace ignored this request and on 29 November 1876 he went to the Dyson's house to see Katherine. Arthur Dyson intervened and in the ensuing struggle Peace shot him dead. Peace left Sheffield and moved to London.

Now with a reward of £100 on his head, Peace set up house in Peckham. Posing as a respectable citizen interested in music he carried out dozens of lucrative burglaries. This may have continued indefinitely if someone had not informed on him. On 10 October 1878 Peace's house was surrounded by police; he tried to shoot his way out of trouble but only managed to injure one constable before he was overpowered.

Identity revealed

On 19 November 1878 Peace, using the name John Ward, was convicted of attempted murder and sentenced to life imprisonment. During the course of the trial his real identity was revealed and he was taken by train to Sheffield to stand trial for the murder of Arthur Dyson. He tried to escape by jumping from the train but only succeeded in seriously injuring himself.

Peace was tried for murder on 4 February 1879, with Katherine Dyson as the main prosecution witness. The defendant was covered in scars and bruises but the jury were unsympathetic and took just 15 minutes to find him guilty of wilful murder. Charles Peace made a full confession and was hanged in Armley Prison on 25 February 1879.

> **Confession**
> Part of Peace's confession concerned a murder he committed in 1876, when he shot and killed a policeman named Cock. Two brothers, William and John Habron, were charged with the crime and William was sentenced to life imprisonment. After Peace's confession he was released and paid £1000 compensation.

Petiot, Marcel

(1897–1946)

Convicted murderer

A French doctor who admitted to killing 63 people during World War II.

Marcel Petiot was born in the French town of Auxerre. After beginning medical studies he joined the army in 1916 but was discharged in 1920 on psychiatric grounds. The following year he qualified as a doctor and in 1924 set up his own private practice in Villeneuve-sur-Yonne. It was a profitable business, based on selling illegal drugs and performing abortions.

In 1933 Petiot went to Paris. He opened a new practice and built up a loyal clientele who were eager for his dubious services. Outwardly he gave the appearance of being a respectable family man.

In 1940 the Germans entered Paris. At the same time Petiot bought a disused mansion at 21 Rue Le Sueur and set about renovating it. This included a large furnace in the cellar and a soundproof triangular room. Then Petiot started circulating rumours that he would, for a fee, help people escape to Spain or Cuba, but none were ever seen again.

Doctor of death

In 1943 the Gestapo arrested Petiot in connection with a number of Jews who had gone missing. He was held for several months but released without prosecution. When he went back to Rue Le Sueur his neighbours began complaining about the foul-smelling smoke coming out of his chimney. In March 1944 the police arrived, and discovered the remains of 27 bodies. Remarkably, they believed his story that they were all Nazi collaborators and did not arrest him.

Once Petiot's story was checked it became clear that none of the people found at Rue Le Sueur had been collaborators, but by this time the doctor had fled Paris. He was eventually arrested after writing a letter in which he claimed he was a leader of the Resistance.

Although Petiot said he had killed 63 people he was only charged with the murders of 27. His trial began on 18 March 1946. After seeing his death chamber and 47 suitcases filled with the belongings of his victims, the jury found him guilty. Marcel Petiot was guillotined in public on 25 May 1946.

Dr Marcel Petiot

Death chamber

It was never fully discovered how Petiot killed his victims. It is thought he either injected them with a deadly poison or put them in his triangular room and gassed them. When dead they were covered in quicklime and incinerated.

Philby, Kim (Harold Adrian Russell)

(1912–88)

Spy

The most effective British spy during the Cold War period.

Born on New Year's Day 1912 in Ambala, India, Kim Philby (nicknamed after the hero in Kipling's story) grew up to be greatly influenced by his father, Harry St John Philby. Harry was an eccentric officer in the Indian Civil Service who had considerable sympathies for the Arabs, and spent the last few years of his life exploring the Arabian desert. He warned his son against trusting the British 'Establishment' and Kim Philby later wrote that he felt he did not belong to any nationality.

In 1929 Kim Philby went to Trinity College, Cambridge, and he soon became involved with Guy Burgess, Donald Maclean and Anthony Blunt. He became an ardent Communist and during his summer vacations he travelled extensively in Europe, usually on a motorbike, witnessing the growing Nazi menace. What he saw only hardened his Communist views and he vowed to serve the cause by penetrating the British intelligence service.

Double-agent

In 1933 Philby was recruited by Russian intelligence. To create a cover he took an extreme right-wing stance in public. In 1936 he was employed by *The Times* to report on the Spanish Civil War and he took the side of Franco's fascist forces. At the end of the war he was decorated by Franco.

In 1940 he achieved his ambition of joining the British intelligence when he was employed by Department D of the Secret Intelligence Service (SIS), which covered sabotage, subversion and propaganda. Philby ensured that much of this information reached his Russian masters.

Department D was closed down in 1941 and Philby was then trained as an agent for the Special Operations Executive (SOE). He was a brilliant trainee but it was decided not to put him into the field because of his stammer. Instead, and to the delight of the Russians, he was assigned to Section V of the SIS. This was the counter-espionage department that was responsible for spy networks in foreign countries. Philby proved so effective in his post that at the end of World War II he was asked to head the newly re-opened Soviet counter-espionage section of the SIS. He could not believe his luck and he was soon able to tell Moscow everything that the British knew about their espionage operations.

Above suspicion

In 1946 a minor purge occurred in the SIS and all the undesirable elements were removed. Philby was not one of them and, ironically, he received the OBE in the same year. He also divorced his first wife and remarried.

Philby's career continued to flourish and in 1949 he was posted to Washington as a liaison officer between the SIS and America's Central Intelligence Agency (CIA). From the espionage point of view it was a prime posting because he had access to highly classified information from both Britain and America. He soon made his mark and was responsible for passing information to the Russians about a joint CIA/SIS operation in Albania. It was designed to destabilize the Communist regime there but, due to Philby, whenever guerillas were parachuted in they were met by Communist forces. Over 300 men lost their lives. At this time the head of CIA counter-intelligence had his doubts about Philby, but he kept them to himself.

Vital link

Due to his position, Philby was informed when it became known that British intelligence investigators were closing in on Donald Maclean, who was now back in London. In an attempt to warn Maclean of the impending danger he sent Guy Burgess, who had shared his house in Washington, to London. Not only did Burgess tell Maclean that he was suspected, he also chose to defect to the Soviet Union with him in 1951.

Following the disappearance of Burgess and Maclean British intelligence became highly suspicious of Philby, particularly as Burgess had lived with him. He was interrogated by members of the SIS and although he was not charged with any offence he was removed from his post in Washington.

The 'Third Man'

For several years the security forces tried to collect enough information to convict Philby of espionage and they even held an unproductive secret trial. Then, in 1955, Colonel Marcus Lipton MP named Philby as the third man in the Burgess and Maclean spy ring. Even under intense interrogation he refused to confess and the Foreign Secretary, Harold Macmillan, told the House of Commons that nothing could be proved against Philby. Despite this he was forced to resign.

In 1956 Philby was back working for the SIS, this time in Beirut, using the cover of a correspondent for the *Observer* and the *Economist*. He was well liked in Beirut and enjoyed his role as a foreign correspondent, although his use to the Russians as an espionage agent was undoubtedly diminished.

Defection

Philby remained in Beirut until 1963, by which time the SIS were convinced of his role as a secret agent. They sent a team to interrogate him and he was so unsettled by the experience that he decided to seek refuge in Russia. On 23 January 1963 he did not appear for a dinner date and six months later a Russian newspaper announced that Kim Philby had been granted political asylum in Moscow.

Philby settled readily into the Soviet way of life and he was rewarded for his services by being made a colonel in the KGB. He became a respected consultant and there are those who believed he helped in the rise to power of President Andropov. Kim Philby, the most effective and influential spy of his generation, died on 11 May 1988, and was buried in Kuntsevo with full military honours.

In his own words
In his book *My Silent War* (1968) Kim Philby wrote, 'There is still an awful lot of work ahead; there will be ups and downs … But as I look over Moscow from my study window, I can see the solid foundations of the future I glimpsed at Cambridge'.

A dissident's view
Vladimir Sakharov, who later fled to the West, said of Kim Philby, 'Contrary to what was believed in the West, Philby was no retired intelligence agent when he arrived in Moscow. In fact, he had become an important member of the KGB's inner circle'.

Foreign correspondent
During his time in Beirut Philby relished his role as a foreign correspondent. He mixed easily at the Normandy Hotel with his fellow journalists and to complete the picture he even ran off with the wife of a journalist on the *New York Times*. She later became his third wife and subsequently wrote a book entitled, *Kim Philby: The Spy I Loved* (1968).

Pigott, Richard

(c.1828–89)

Forger

An Irish nationalist who forged papers in an attempt to discredit the Irish Home Rule leader Charles Stewart Parnell.

Richard Pigott was born in County Meath and his first job was as an errand boy at the Belfast journal the *Nation.* He then moved on to be a clerk at the *Ulsterman,* a newspaper with extreme nationalist views. Pigott soon became an ardent supporter of Irish nationalism.

Pigott moved with the *Ulsterman* to Dublin in 1858 and became the manager of the newspaper under its new name, the *Irishman.* He approached his job with such enthusiasm that in June 1865 he was made editor and proprietor of the newspaper. Through a mixture of luck and good judgement he increased the circulation of the *Irishman* and in 1866 he opened two magazines, the *Shamrock* and the *Flag of Ireland.* All of his publications reflected his political opinions, which were becoming more and more extreme and because of which he fell foul of the law; in 1867 he was sentenced to 12 months' imprisonment for publishing seditious material. This did little to curb his activities and after declaring in court that he was a fenian he was sentenced to 6 months' imprisonment in 1871 for contempt.

Antagonism

Pigott's extreme behaviour and his lavish lifestyle did little to endear him to his fellow nationalists. Over the next few years the circulation of his publications dropped steadily. Due to this, and his own financial difficulties, he was forced to sell his three periodicals to a company headed by the Irish nationalist leader Charles Stewart Parnell, in 1881.

Pigott was furious at having to sell out to Parnell and he sought his revenge. Initially he concentrated on blackmailing various politicians but this was not as effective as he had hoped. In 1886 he sold various papers to the anti-Home Rule organization, the Irish Loyal and Patriotic Union. The information alleged that Parnell and other prominent Home Rule leaders had taken part in various outrages and that they had condoned the Phoenix Park tragedy.

Newspaper accusations

Although Parnell immediately denied the allegations there were a number of people who were inclined to believe them. In 1887 *The Times* published a series of articles entitled 'Parnellism and crime' which were based on the information supplied by Pigott.

At the inquiry, *The Times* was reluctant to divulge its sources but was eventually forced to call Pigott as a witness. Under severe cross-examination by Parnell's counsel, on 22 February 1889, it became clear that he had given forged material to the Irish Loyal and Patriotic Union.

The following day Pigott made a full confession to an MP and then vanished to the continent. He was traced to Madrid but before the police had a chance to arrest him he shot himself dead.

Scandal
Pigott's actions had little effect on Parnell's career and he continued promoting the Irish Nationalist cause, constantly frustrating Gladstone in Parliament. However, his career came to an end in 1890 following an adultery scandal with Mrs O'Shea.

Podola, Guenther Fritz Erwin

(1929–59)

Convicted murderer

The murder of a policeman that made British legal history when the killer subsequently claimed to be suffering from amnesia.

Guenther Podola was born in Berlin and joined the Hitler Youth during World War II. In 1952 he decided to leave Germany and emigrate to Canada. In 1958 he was convicted of theft and robbery and deported back to Germany. A year later, in May 1959, he again left his home country, this time choosing to live in England.

Gangster image

Podola settled in London and was soon a well-known figure in the nightclubs of Soho. He liked to promote a gangster image and adopted the name Mike Colato for this purpose. Although he had a few legitimate businesses, Podola's main source of income came from burglary and blackmail.

On 3 July 1959 Podola burgled the South Kensington flat of Mrs Verne Schiffman, stealing jewellery and furs worth £2000. Not content with this, he then tried to blackmail Mrs Schiffman by claiming to have compromising photographs and tapes, but she was not easily intimidated and went straight to the police. When the blackmailer next contacted her the police tapped the phone and quickly traced the call to a telephone box.

When the police, Detective Sergeants Purdy and Sandford, arrived, they found Podola still talking to Mrs Schiffman and arrested him. He tried to escape but was caught in a nearby block of flats. While Sandford was looking for assistance Podola pulled out a gun and shot Purdy, killing him instantly. He then ran off.

Four days later, on 16 July, the police tracked Podola to a hotel in Kensington. They knew he was armed and when he did not answer their command to open the door they burst in. At that moment Podola was standing behind the door and he was knocked unconscious as it fell on top of him. He was taken into custody in a very dazed state.

Alleged amnesia

After his arrest Podola was taken to St Stephen's Hospital, claiming that he could not remember anything. He was examined by six doctors; four believed he was suffering from amnesia, and two thought he was faking.

Podola's trial began at the Old Bailey on 10 September 1959. The first nine days were taken up with complicated medical and legal arguments about Podola's alleged amnesia. The jury took three and a half hours to decide that it was not a genuine case of amnesia and that he was therefore fit to stand trial. A new jury was installed for the murder trial and they found him guilty.

Guenther Podola was not only the first person in Britain to claim amnesia as a defence against a capital charge but was also the last person to be hanged for killing a policeman. His execution took place at Wandsworth prison on 5 November 1959.

Amnesia

It was laid down in the Podola case that the accused could be tried if he understood what was going on — as Podola could. The judge who heard the appeal commented, 'Even if the loss of memory had been genuine, that did not of itself render the appellant insane'.

Porteous riots

(1736)

Captain John Porteous

The actions of a brutal law-enforcer in Edinburgh that led to a public lynching by an angry mob.

John Porteous was born near Edinburgh and as a youth he was apprenticed to a tailor. He later moved to the city, where he graduated to the position of master-tailor. However, he preferred good company to hard work and, after some initial success, his business began to suffer. Alarmed at this, his wife went to the city provost, a family friend, to ask for help. The provost pulled some strings and Porteous was appointed Captain of the City Guard.

The City Guard at this time was in effect the local police force and consisted of three companies of men, each with 25 members. As Captain of one of these companies Porteous received a salary of £80 and also a prestigious scarlet uniform.

Personality change

Following his new appointment Porteous changed from being a tailor accustomed to good living into a brutal law-enforcer. He soon became known and disliked throughout the city for his harsh methods and his severe treatment of offenders. He took particular pleasure in raiding brothels, including several which he himself frequented, and exposing the eminent citizens whom he found there. On one occasion he was sent to keep the peace at a church meeting where trouble was expected. Rather than ensure tranquillity he instigated a riot, during which two ministers were killed, one by Porteous's own hands.

One of the activities that the authorities most wanted to clamp down on at this time was smuggling, which was highly prevalent in Scotland. In March 1736 two smugglers, Andrew Wilson and George Robertson, were sentenced to death for robbing an Excise Officer in Fife. They were imprisoned in Edinburgh's Tolbooth prison and immediately launched a daring, albeit unsuccessful, escape. This only increased their popularity in the eyes of the general public.

The execution of Wilson and Robertson was set for 14 April 1736 and, as was customary, the condemned men were allowed to attend a church service three days before the sentence was carried out. As they entered the church Robertson broke free and escaped into the crowded city streets. Wilson held back the City Guards who were escorting them and Robertson was able to make good his escape. He later settled in Holland where he ran a successful tavern.

Snub

Outraged at Robertson's escape, the city magistrates and Captain Porteous were determined that Wilson would be executed without further incident. The magistrates ordered five companies of the Welsh Fusiliers to line the streets from the Tolbooth to the gallows in the Grassmarket. Porteous was furious at this decision, considering it an insult to his City Guard. He was in a foul mood as he took control of his men for the day.

The hanging of Andrew Wilson took place as planned on 14 April, in front of a large and unruly crowd. Following the execution there was a minor disturbance as angry onlookers threw mud and stones at the City Guard. It was not a sinister act of civil disobedience but it incensed Porteous and he reacted in his usual over-zealous fashion. He ordered his men to, 'Fire, and be damned', and he himself began firing his rifle into the crowd. His officers were at first reluctant to follow suit so they fired over the heads of the mob. This act of mercy had the unfortunate effect of killing and injuring people who were watching events from the high tenement windows.

Carnage

After the initial attack the crowd turned on the City Guard and chased them to one of the city gates. The troops kept firing as they retreated and when the casualties were recovered there were nine dead and dozens wounded. Several of the wounded required amputations because the soldiers had fired at their feet. The citizens of Edinburgh were outraged at this brutality and, in an effort to placate them, Porteous was stripped of office and arrested for murder.

The trial of Captain Porteous took place at the High Court of Judiciary in Edinburgh on 6 July 1736. He was charged with ordering his men to fire, 'without any just cause or necessary occasion'. There was considerable debate about whether he had acted on his own initiative or whether he had been under orders from the city magistrates. A total of 44 witnesses were called and the jury found Porteous guilty by a majority of only one vote, but it was enough to sentence the former Captain to death.

Suspected reprieve

While Porteous was in prison awaiting execution, set for 7 September 1736, several of his influential friends began trying to obtain a reprieve. They petitioned the regent, Queen Caroline, and on 2 September news reached Edinburgh that the Queen had granted a six-week stay of execution. It was widely thought that this was the prelude to a reprieve and a pardon, so people began taking matters into their own hands.

The morning of 7 September passed without incident but by the evening a group of men had gathered outside the West Port, one of the gates into the city. They seized the gate, locked it and then made their way to the other city gates to secure them. This left the city virtually in their control because the City Guard was stationed on the outside of the city gates.

The group of men then made their way to the Tolbooth prison where Porteous was being held. They captured the town drum and as they made their way through the city streets their numbers were swelled by enthusiastic supporters. The mob tried to knock down the door of the Tolbooth but when this failed they set fire to it instead. They found Porteous inside and proceeded to drag him, still in his nightclothes, to the Grassmarket.

Lynching

Once the mob reached the Grassmarket they numbered well over 1000 and they were in complete control of the city. Then, shortly before midnight, they hanged Captain Porteous from a dyer's pole, some of them hacking at the body with an axe. Once Porteous was dead the mob dispersed with great calm and organization, indicating that it was a carefully planned operation. Several people and organizations were suspected, including the Jacobites and the Covenanters, but the ringleaders were never apprehended.

Southern outrage

The authorities in London were horrified at the events in Edinburgh and tried in vain to find the culprits. A motion was put to the House of Commons that the Lord Provost of Edinburgh should be imprisoned, the city gates be destroyed and the City Guard be disbanded in disgrace. None of this was allowed to happen and the only punishment that befell Edinburgh was a £2000 fine. It was left for the law-makers in London to shake their heads in disbelief at the defiant actions of their northern cousins.

Portuguese banknote case

(1924–5)

Alva Reis and others

One of the most ingenious and profitable swindles of the 20th century.

On 4 December 1924 a reputable Dutch businessman named Marang van Ysselveere walked into the London offices of the printing firm Waterlow & Sons, who printed the banknotes for the Bank of Portugal. He met with the chairman, Sir William Waterlow, and explained that he was the head of a Dutch syndicate that had been asked by the Portuguese Government to try and restore the ailing economy of their colony Angola. They intended to do this by increasing the money supply with £3 million worth of Portuguese currency.

Marang stressed to Sir William the importance of secrecy in their operation and gave him letters of authorization from the Portuguese Minister at the Hague and the head of the Bank of Portugal. All seemed above board and Sir William agreed to print 600 000 notes of 500 escudos each. Before the printing began Sir William wrote to the head of the Bank of Portugal, acknowledging the receipt of his letter. The letter never arrived.

Con man

Despite his impressive manner everything about Marang was a fraud. All the documents that he presented to Sir William were forgeries and he insisted that all correspondence from the printing firm was delivered by hand by himself or his associates. One of these men, Alva Reis, was an ambitious Portuguese businessman who was the mastermind behind the scheme.

The printing of the money went smoothly and it was handed over to Marang in seven trunks. Getting it into Portugal was no problem as he had arranged for a diplomatic passport. The biggest difficulty was in disposing of the money, as the sum was too vast to put into circulation without it being noticed. To overcome this Reis decided to open his own bank. The first application was rejected but the second one was accepted and in July 1925 the Banco Angola e Metropole began trading.

Throughout 1925 the Banco Angola flourished, despite the fact that several other banks in the country went out of business. Its success raised questions about forgeries but twice their banknotes were examined and found to be genuine.

Issue withdrawn

On 4 December 1925 it was noticed that foreign currency was being bought with an unusually large number of 500 escudos bills. They were declared genuine, but the Bank of Portugal withdrew the entire issue from circulation. Minute examination revealed that although they had been printed on genuine plates they had not been properly authorized.

Alva Reis and several of his associates were arrested and given long prison terms. Marang escaped to Holland and never returned to Portugal. It is thought that the men behind the Portuguese banknote fraud made millions of pounds.

> **Disgrace**
> Following the disclosure of the fraud Waterlow & Sons were disgraced. They were sued by the Bank of Portugal for contributory negligence and after a long legal battle the Bank was awarded £569 421 plus costs. This was later reduced to £300 000 but then the House of Lords increased it to £610 392, one of the largest awards made to that date.

Pritchard, Edward William

(1825–65)

Convicted murderer

A highly unpleasant doctor who was the last man to be publicly hanged in Scotland.

Edward Pritchard was the son of a naval captain and he grew up in Hampshire. In 1846 he joined the Navy as an assistant surgeon. Soon afterwards he met and married Mary Jane Taylor, the daughter of an Edinburgh silk merchant. After leaving the Navy in 1851 Pritchard and his wife moved to Hunmanby, Yorkshire, where he set up practice as a doctor.

It soon became clear to the inhabitants of Hunmanby that Dr Pritchard was a singularly unpleasant character. He was vain, arrogant, unfaithful, impudent and a habitual liar. He used his membership of the Freemasons as a means of advertising his business, which only served to alienate him from the community even more. By 1858 his behaviour had necessitated his departure from Hunmanby.

Exaggerated claims

After a year travelling abroad, the Pritchards settled in Glasgow. Events were similar to those in Yorkshire and Dr Pritchard became widely disliked in a remarkably short period of time. He tried to ingratiate himself by giving boastful lectures about his travels and spuriously claiming that Garibaldi was one of his personal friends. He applied for a prestigious medical post using the names of several famous English doctors as his testimonials. None of them had heard of him and he did not get the post.

On 5 May 1863 there was a fire at the Pritchard household, during which a maidservant died. The girl had made no attempt to leave her bed and it was rumoured that Pritchard was responsible for her death. A year later Pritchard and his wife moved to Sauchihall Street.

Slow poisoning

Pritchard wasted no time in seducing a 15-year-old servant, and made a promise to marry her. Conveniently, in November 1864 Mrs Pritchard was taken ill. She recovered after a visit to Edinburgh but on her return to Glasgow she fell ill again. On 8 December 1864 Pritchard bought a large dose of aconite. He made three similar purchases over the next three months.

When Mary Jane Pritchard's mother, Mrs Taylor, heard of her daughter's condition she decided to tend to her personally. Shortly after her arrival she too fell ill and died on 25 February 1865. Dr Patterson, the doctor who attended the two women thought that they were being poisoned but, incredibly, considered it unethical to interfere.

On 18 March 1865 Mrs Pritchard finally succumbed to her illness and died. However, an anonymous letter was written to the police, thought to be from Dr Patterson, suggesting that Pritchard had poisoned his wife and mother-in-law. The two bodies were examined and found to contain large quantities of antimony and aconite.

Dr Pritchard was arrested and sent for trial in Edinburgh. He was found guilty and hanged in Glasgow on 28 July 1865. What proved to be the last public execution in Scotland was watched by 100 000 people.

Emotional display

When his wife died Dr Pritchard gave a dramatic display of affection. He cried, 'Come back, my dear Mary Jane. Don't leave your dear Edward'. He then lifted the coffin lid and kissed the corpse on the lips.

Profumo affair

(1962–3)

Stephen Ward

A sex scandal that rocked the British government and led to the resignation of the Secretary of State for War.

At the beginning of the 1960s Stephen Ward was a successful osteopath, a talented artist and a leading light on the social circuit in London. One of his favourite haunts was Murray's Cabaret Club, where he met Christine Keeler and Mandy Rice-Davies. Both were extremely attractive and promiscuous. Keeler was born in the Thames Valley and after an unhappy childhood she moved to London when she was 16 and found a job at the Cabaret Club. She was soon joined by Rice-Davies, who had been born in Wales and brought up in the Midlands. The two women became friends and they revelled in the social scene in London.

Swinging Sixties

Ward was attracted by the glamour of Keeler and Rice-Davies and thought that they would be useful for one of his sidelines — obtaining women for wealthy businessmen. He had a brief and volatile affair with Keeler and in 1960 he provided both her and Rice-Davies with accommodation in Comeragh Road. There were often numerous men at the flat, some of whom paid for sex with Keeler and Rice-Davies, others who seemed to be transient boyfriends.

In the summer of 1961 Ward held a party at his cottage on the Cliveden estate. The glamorous Keeler and Rice-Davies were present, as were the Conservative Secretary of State for War, John Profumo, and an assistant Russian Naval Attaché, Captain Eugene Ivanov. The two men were attracted to Keeler and they both had short affairs with her. To Christine Keeler it was just another brief fling but for Profumo it was to have lasting consequences.

Rise and fall

John Dennis Profumo was born in 1915 and educated at Harrow and Oxford. After becoming a Conservative MP in 1940 he held several government posts before becoming Secretary of State for War in 1960. His brief indiscretion with Keeler may never have come to light if it had not been for a violent quarrel between two of her lovers.

On 28 October John Edgecombe and Aloysius 'Lucky' Gordon, who lived with

Christine Keeler

Keeler at her new flat at Bryanston Mews, Marylebone, quarrelled violently about their flatmate. Gordon's face was slashed and he needed 17 stitches. Shortly afterwards Keeler left the flat. Edgecombe was livid and on 14 December he went to Stephen Ward's flat at Wimpole Mews, where he expected to find Keeler. She would not let him in and in retaliation he fired several shots through the door. He was arrested and sentenced to seven years' imprisonment.

Worrying allegations

The shooting generated little interest, but then Keeler began to tell her story. She spoke of her promiscuous lifestyle and the fact that she had had affairs with Profumo and Captain Ivanov. The rumours could not be suppressed and it was not long before Profumo was being asked questions in the House of Commons. There was considerable concern that he had shared a lover with a Russian diplomat and the issue became a matter of national security. On 22 March 1963 he told the House that there had never been any impropriety between himself and Christine Keeler. It soon became clear that this was a blatant lie and a week later John Profumo resigned.

Society trial

Profumo's resignation was swiftly followed by the trial of Ward, Keeler and Rice-Davies. It opened on 22 June 1963 and Ward was charged with living off immoral earnings, while the two women faced related charges. The press had a field day.

The prosecution quickly established that Ward had a lurid side to his veneer of respectability. They showed that one of his flats was used for sex and whipping sessions with Keeler, Rice-Davies and several unnamed prominent citizens. However, proving that the girls were prostitutes and that Ward was living off their earnings was not so easy.

Dynamic performances

Keeler was the first witness to be called and the public gallery was packed to see this much talked-of young lady. She gave an electrifying performance, admitting that she had a free and easy lifestyle but denying that she was a prostitute. On the occasions that she did have sex for money, she said, it was in order to pay back money that Ward had lent her.

Mandy Rice-Davies was the next witness. She had already provided the tabloids with a memorable headline at the magistrates court: when confronted with the fact that Lord Astor had denied her claim that they had slept together she replied, 'Well he would, wouldn't he?' She stunned the court by telling them that in Ward's flat it was quite normal for people to have sex while he was watching. She was reprimanded for 'going on talking without reason for doing so'; she gave no hint that Ward lived off any of her earnings, immoral or otherwise.

As the trial progressed Ward appeared to be under great strain. On 30 July 1963, halfway through the judge's summing-up Ward took an overdose and was rushed to hospital. The trial continued and he was found guilty of the charges relating to Keeler and Rice-Davies. This proved to be irrelevant because Stephen Ward died on 2 August 1963.

Postscript

John Profumo left politics and in 1975 he was awarded the CBE for services to charity. Christine Keeler served a short prison sentence and in the 1980s she wrote her autobiography and collaborated on the film *Scandal*, which dealt with the Profumo affair. Mandy Rice-Davies moved to Israel after the trial and opened two nightclubs named Mandy. She married twice and eventually moved back to London where she too wrote her autobiography.

Rachman

One of Rice-Davies's boyfriends was the notorious slum landlord, Peter Rachman. Born in Poland he moved to Britain in 1946 and he was soon letting flats to prostitutes for exorbitant sums. By 1953 he had property all over London and was charging poor West Indians excessive fees for staying in his flats. Rachman enjoyed a lavish lifestyle on these earnings but he was eventually taken to a rent tribunal by his tenants. He died in 1962, leaving nothing.

Rann, John

(?–1774)

Highwayman

An elegant highwaymen who was known as 'Sixteen-string Jack' because of the 16 silk strings attached to his buckskin breeches.

Jack Rann was born into a humble family who lived in a small village near Bath. His education was virtually non-existent and for a while he made a living as a pedlar, before gaining employment as a footman and a coachman. The paltry wages that this afforded led him to abandon his employment and he became a pick-pocket before taking up the more lucrative business of highway robbery.

As well as working with other highwaymen Rann was involved with a local prostitute named Eleanor Roche, whom he used to sell the proceeds from his illicit raids. Although he was unconcerned that she had to take all the risks of dealing with a fence he did accept the consequences when she was caught for trying to sell a stolen watch. He stood trial with her but they were both acquitted due to a lack of evidence.

Frequent arrests

1774 was not a good year for Rann and he was arrested seven times for offences ranging from highway robbery to burglary. Whenever he appeared in court he dressed with great elegance, usually in a pea-green suit and his characteristic 16 silk strings. Invariably, the witnesses against him could not believe he was the same man who, in his working attire, was supposedly a notorious highwayman. On his first six appearances in court he was acquitted.

Rann had little fear of the law and on one occasion, after a brawl in a public house during which he lost a ring, he admitted to being a highwayman and remarked, ''Tis but an hundred guineas gone, which one evening's work will replace'. On another occasion, after he had not been recognized at a turnpike, he told the tollman to inform the bailiffs that he was heading for London if they wanted to try and catch him.

Cheerful to the last

The Bow Street Runner, John Clarke, pursued Rann diligently for two years and was responsible for his seventh arrest in 1774. Rann was so confident of being acquitted again that he organized a celebration supper and invited seven prostitutes to attend. Unfortunately Eleanor was not one of them because she had been sentenced to transportation for receiving stolen goods. For once Rann's optimism was misplaced and he was found guilty of highway robbery and sentenced to death. He threw his party anyway and was reported as being remarkably cheerful.

Jack Rann was hanged at Tyburn on 30 November 1774. True to his profession as a 'Knight of the Road' he was calm and composed before his execution and went to the gallows in a new pea-green suit and a ruffled shirt.

Morbid curiosity

On one occasion Rann attended a public execution at Tyburn. He managed to push his way to the front of the crowd and explained to one of the constables on duty, 'Perhaps it is very proper that I should be a spectator on this occasion'. The irony was that it was another highwayman who was being hanged.

Read, Mary

(c.1692–1721)

Pirate

A rare case of a female pirate who operated in the West Indies with Anne Bonney.

Mary Read's origins are uncertain but it is likely she was born in Plymouth, an illegitimate daughter to unknown parents. She had a habit of dressing in boy's clothing and when she was 13 she became a footboy to a French noblewoman. However, her tomboy temperament led her to seek more active employment and she joined a man-of-war as a powder-monkey.

Male disguise

After six years at sea Mary, still disguised in male clothing, joined an infantry regiment in Flanders, fighting the French. After this she transferred to the cavalry as a Light Dragoon. While she was serving here she fell in love with a Flemish trooper. To the amazement of the rest of the regiment she revealed her true identity and married the astonished trooper. They opened a tavern in Breda, Brabant, but this business venture was curtailed when Mary's husband died suddenly.

Shortly after her husband's death Mary went back to sea. Using her previous male disguise she joined a ship bound for the West Indies. During the voyage, however, the ship was captured by English pirates under the captaincy of Jack Rackham. Mary joined the pirates without a second thought and was delighted that there was another female member of the crew, Anne Bonney.

Brave and skilful

Although both Mary and Anne wore men's clothes while aboard the pirate ship it was only for convenience, since the crew all knew of their real identities. Mary thrived on the ship and she became known for her bravery and swordsmanship. On one occasion she took the place of her lover, who had been challenged to a duel, and killed her opponent with clinical efficiency.

After several months of successful piratical adventures in the West Indies' Rackham's ship was captured off the Jamaican coast in October 1721, by a ship specifically commissioned by the Governor of Jamaica for the task. The crew were caught unawares and, after a brave resistance, Mary and Anne were captured with the rest and sent for trial.

Pregnancy plea

Mary Read and Anne Bonney were tried at San Jago de la Vega on 28 November 1721. They were both found guilty of piracy and sentenced to be hanged. However, they both put in pleas of pregnancy and as a result of this they escaped the gallows. Mary died in prison shortly afterwards, on 4 December 1721, while giving birth to her child. Anne Bonney survived for many years but the rest of the pirate crew were not so lucky and Rackham and his men were all hanged.

Mutual affection

It is possible that Mary Read and Anne Bonney were lovers for a short period. When they first met Mary was still dressed in men's clothing and it is thought that Anne made a pass at her thinking she was a man. Nothing developed from the relationship because if Rackham, who was Anne's lover, had thought they were having an affair he would have killed them both.

Rosenberg espionage case
(1951)

Julius and Ethel Rosenberg

A husband and wife spy team whose case became a cause célèbre around the world.

Julius Rosenberg was born in New York on 12 May 1918, the son of Jewish immigrants from Russia. He was an ardent Communist from an early age and while studying electrical engineering at City College in New York he became a card-carrying Stalinist militant. In 1936 he met Ethel Greenglass and soon converted her to his views. The couple were married on 18 June 1939.

Julius Rosenberg was soon singled out by the Soviet espionage network in America. The network was run by Anatoli Yakovlev who had arrived in America in 1944, ostensibly as vice-consul in New York. One of the first people he recruited was Rosenberg and initially he was asked to work on obtaining information concerning American radar secrets. He did this so successfully that he was then sent undercover to concentrate on atomic espionage. Although his wife was not as active as Rosenberg she certainly knew what he was involved with and helped him whenever she could. It is doubtful whether she was recruited as a fully-fledged agent though.

Recruiting powers

Rosenberg quickly proved his worth to Yakovlev and became a 'principal agent'. This meant he was responsible for recruiting more people to the network. His methods for this were steady and unimaginative; he usually chose family members, or friends who shared his own views. One of his first recruits was his wife's younger brother, David Greenglass who had been a member of the Young Communist League of America

and in spite of this had been given technical training by the army. In July 1944 he was posted to the Manhatten District Project at Oak Ridge, Tennessee and Ethel Rosenberg made sure that he passed on as much classified information as he could.

The fourth member of Rosenberg's network was Harry Gold, whose family had emigrated from Switzerland to America while he was still a child. He became committed to Communism while at university and in 1935 he was recruited into the network. He specialized in the theft of industrial chemical secrets.

Atomic secrets

At the end of 1944 David Greenglass was transferred to an atomic research base at Los Alamos. Rosenberg was delighted and persuaded him to divulge various atomic secrets. Much of the information was relayed through Harry Gold; although he and Greenglass only met briefly the meeting was to have disastrous consequences.

In 1945 Greenglass gave Rosenberg various sketches connected with the atomic bomb. Although the work was of dubious quality it was enough to give the Russians a fair idea of the workings of the bomb. Later,

Advertising the Rosenberg clemency train

199

when President Truman told Stalin officially about the existence of the bomb the Russian leader did not seem at all surprised.

Domino effect

In 1947 the FBI interviewed Harry Gold and seemed satisfied that he was not involved in espionage. However, they changed their opinion in 1950 when the British spy, Klaus Fuchs, was arrested and named Gold as his go-between. Gold in turn named Greenglass, as a result of their one meeting, and then Greenglass was only too pleased to implicate his sister and brother-in-law.

Julius and Ethel Rosenberg were arrested and charged with espionage. At their trial, which began in March 1951, Greenglass gave evidence against the Rosenbergs, detailing how he stole atomic secrets for Julius Rosenberg to give to the Russians. Gold also testified against the Rosenbergs and in May 1951 they were found guilty of espionage. The evidence against Julius Rosenberg was reasonably conclusive but the grounds for convicting his wife were less satisfactory. Some people argued that she had only been charged in an effort to make him confess. Despite their testimonies, Greenglass and Gold were also convicted and sentenced to 30 and 15 years' imprisonment respectively.

Harsh sentence

The Rosenberg trial caused a certain amount of interest around the world but it was the sentence that turned the case into a *cause célèbre*. The Espionage Act (1917) states that the death penalty can only be applied for spying in wartime. Judge Irving Kaufman had the unenviable job of deciding whether this could still be applied during periods when Russia was America's ally. He ruled that it could and that the law applied equally to men and women. Subsequently, the Rosenbergs were sentenced to death, the date of execution being set for 26 May 1951.

Tide of protest

World opinion was appalled at the sentence and it was generally agreed that it could be attributed to the anti-communist feelings in America at the time. During their trial the Rosenbergs had been blamed for a number of things, including the war in Korea. Many people outside America felt that they were victims of the excesses of McCarthy-ism. The Pope, the French President, the TUC, and the United States Ambassador in Paris all condemned the sentence.

Hostile public opinion led to the postponement of the original execution. Over the next two years there were numerous appeals, including three million letters asking for clemency being sent to the White House. However, it was all to no avail and on 19 June 1953 Julius and Ethel Rosenberg were sent to the electric chair. They maintained their innocence throughout.

Fellow spy

The most prominent British atomic spy of this period was Klaus Fuchs. Born near Frankfurt in 1911 he came to Britain in 1933 to escape Nazi persecution. He was a brilliant scientist and in 1943 was sent to America to help develop the atom bomb. In 1946 he returned to Britain to head the theoretical physics division at Harwell. All this time he was passing secrets to the Russians and in March 1950 he was arrested and sentenced to 14 years' imprisonment. He was released in June 1959 and moved to East Germany, where he was given citizenship and worked at a nuclear research centre. He retired in 1979.

Family ties

During the Rosenbergs' trial it was thought distasteful that David Greenglass should give evidence against his own sister. However, 30 years later, when Geoffrey Prime, the British electronics-information spy, was turned in by his wife she was applauded for being patriotic and loyal to her country.

Ruthven, William
(c.1541–84)

Conspirator

A Scottish nobleman who was involved in various plots against King James VI.

William Ruthven was the second son of Patrick, third lord of Ruthven. He was an opponent of Mary, Queen of Scots and in 1566 he took part in the plot to murder her secretary, David Rizzio. Following this he was denounced as a rebel and forfeited his lands.

In 1567 Mary was defeated at Carberry Hill by a group of rebel lords and Ruthven was responsible for guarding her at Loch Leven. However, after it was being sympathetic towards the Queen he was removed from this post. He redeemed himself in 1568 when he helped defeat Mary at Langside, following her escape from Loch Leven.

Double-dealing

Ruthven was an able soldier and acquitted himself well in several skirmishes with Mary's supporters: in 1570 he captured a garrison at Brechin; in 1572 he defeated his enemies at Jedburgh; and in 1573 he took part in the pacification of Perth. In addition to his military skills he had considerable diplomatic talents which he used to play off Mary's supporters' against those of the regent for James VI.

Ruthven always ensured he was on the winning side and in 1581 he was created Earl of Gowrie, being given the lands and barony of Gowrie. The following year he again had to take sides when the Earl of Arran and the Duke of Lennox quarrelled. He sided with Arran, only to discover that Lennox was planning to arrest them and charge them with treason. To avoid this he decided to kidnap James VI, without Arran's knowledge, which he did on 23 August 1582, in the Raid of Ruthven.

Forgiven

The King was taken to Castle Ruthven near Perth and, after turning against Arran and effecting his arrest, Ruthven guaranteed his own good favour with the King by helping him escape. In return he was pardoned on 23 December 1582 and appointed to the privy council.

In 1583 Ruthven's luck began to run out. Arran was allowed back into court and quickly ingratiated himself with James. He persuaded the King to banish Ruthven, citing his integral part in the Raid of Ruthven. In retaliation Ruthven joined with the lords of Angus and Mar in an attempt to capture the strategic stronghold of Stirling Castle.

Broken promise

Ruthven went to Dundee to finalize plans with his fellow conspirators but Arran had deduced what was happening and sent a force to capture his rival, which was done with relative ease. Ruthven was brought to Edinburgh on 18 April 1584. Under a promise of a pardon he made a full confession which, in keeping with his own methods, was then used against him at his trial. Predictably, he was found guilty and beheaded at Stirling on 2 May 1584.

Black magic
In addition to the charge of high treason Ruthven was also charged with witchcraft — a popular accusation at the time. However, he claimed this was malicious slander and the charge was dropped.

Sacco–Vanzetti case

(1921)

Nicolo Sacco and Bartolomeo Vanzetti

Two Italian immigrants who were tried for murder in America and executed six years after their trial.

Nicolo Sacco and Bartolomeo Vanzetti both emigrated to America at the beginning of the 20th century. Sacco was born in 1891 in the Adriatic village of Torremaggiore and worked in his father's olive fields, soon adopting his father's socialist beliefs. In 1908 he moved to America and settled with a friend of his father in Massachusetts, where he worked as a labourer and then as a shoemaker.

Vanzetti was born in 1888 in the Piedmontese village of Villafalleto and although he was an excellent scholar he made a living working in city bakeries. He arrived in America two months after Sacco and took a variety of jobs, eventually settling as a fish seller. He had strong socialist views and after leading a strike at a factory he was blacklisted from any factory work.

Nicolo Sacco and Bartolomeo Vanzetti

Anarchist activity

Sacco and Vanzetti met in 1916 and by this time they were both pacifists and anarchists — opposed to war and all kinds of organized government. When America joined World War I in 1917, they fled to Mexico for two years to avoid military service. They returned to Massachusetts in 1918 but it was a difficult time because anti-Communist feeling was running high following the Bolshevik revolution in Russia. Communists, anarchists and radicals were all looked upon with disdain and large numbers of them were deported.

On Christmas Eve 1919 there was an unsuccessful hold-up of a wage van in Bridgewater, 30 miles south of Boston. According to a witness several foreign men shot at the truck and then fled. The police discovered an Overland car that they thought had been used in the hold-up, in a local garage, and asked the garage owner to tell them if anyone came to pick it up.

Robbery and murder

Four months later, on 15 April 1920, another hold-up took place, this time in South Braintree. On this occasion the gang of four men successfully escaped with $16 000, but during the robbery they shot dead the paymaster and a guard. The police found the car that had been used in the attack and also tyre tracks that could have been those of the Overland. On 5 May four men came to pick up the Overland: Sacco, Vanzetti and two other Italians named Orciani and Boda. Before the police arrived the men became suspicious and fled.

Later that evening Sacco and Vanzetti were arrested on a street-car and found to be in possession of revolvers. Boda and Orciani were also arrested but released soon afterwards. The police suspected Sacco and Vanzetti of the Bridgewater hold-up and the Braintree murders. Since Sacco had an alibi for Bridgewater he was charged only with the Braintree murders. Vanzetti was charged with both offences.

Bridgewater conviction

Vanzetti was tried on 22 June 1920 for the attempted hold-up at Bridgewater. Five witnesses claimed to have seen him at the scene of the crime whereas 20 claimed he had been nowhere near Bridgewater on Christmas Eve 1919. Unfortunately he had been found in possession of cartridges similar to ones found in the abandoned car and this convinced the jury of his guilt. He was sentenced to 10 to 15 years' imprisonment.

It took almost a year for Sacco and Vanzetti to be brought to trial for the Braintree murders. By this time the newspapers had made the most of Vanzetti's conviction in the Bridgewater case. Their trial began on 31 May 1921 and much of the prosecution's case was based on circumstantial evidence. The issue of identification of the killers produced several conflicting statements, with 59 witnesses appearing for the prosecution and 99 for the defence. The forensic evidence concerning the murder weapon and the bullets used in the killings was particularly dubious.

Consciousness of guilt

One of the key issues of the trial was the prosecution's claim of the 'consciousness of guilt' of the accused. They based this on the fact that Sacco and Vanzetti had been carrying firearms and that they had lied in statements made after their arrest. The defence conceded this, but claimed that Sacco and Vanzetti were only conscious of their guilt in relation to their anarchistic and draft-dodging activities. Unfortunately for the accused the flimsy 'consciousness of guilt' evidence was given a lot more prominence than the physical evidence.

On 14 July 1921, after an unsatisfactory trial that lasted 30 days, Sacco and Vanzetti

were found guilty of first degree murder and sentenced to death. There was an immediate outcry both in America and abroad. Not only was it thought that the accused had not been found guilty beyond all reasonable doubt but it was felt that racial and political prejudices had also been a governing factor. Seven motions for a new trial were heard and dismissed, and several petitions for clemency were organized. These were signed by thousands of people, including H G Wells, Albert Einstein and John Galsworthy.

As a result of international and domestic pressure the governor of Massachusetts appointed an independent committee to review the case. Their report showed that although the trial judge, Judge Webster Thayer, had shown grave political bias, the verdict had been correct. Subsequently, Nicolo Sacco and Bartolomeo Vanzetti were electrocuted on 23 August 1927, more than six years after they had been convicted. Many people considered it to be barbaric to carry out the death sentence after such a long period of time. Grave doubts continued to be voiced about the case, until 1977 when Sacco and Vanzetti's names were cleared in a special proclamation signed by the governor of Massachusetts.

Anarchists

Both Sacco and Vanzetti were active anarchists and when he was arrested Sacco was discovered to be carrying a pamphlet advertising a speech to be given by Vanzetti: 'Fellow workers, you have fought all the wars. You have worked for all the capitalists. You have wandered all over the countries. Have you harvested the fruits of your labours? Does the past comfort you? Does the present smile on you? Does the future promise you anything? Have you found a piece of land where you can live like a human being? On this theme, the struggle for existence, Bartolomeo Vanzetti will speak'.

Trial of John Scopes

(1925)

John Thomas Scopes

Case of a Tennessee school teacher who was put on trial for teaching the theory of evolution.

In March 1925 a penal statute was passed in Tennessee that made it unlawful to teach 'any theory which denies the story of the Divine creation of man as taught in the Bible, and to teach instead that man is descended from a lower order of animals'. The statute was the work of religious Fundamentalists and it was immediately condemned by the American Civil Liberties Union (ACLU), who promised to defend any teacher who continued to teach Darwin's theory of evolution.

Darwinian disciple

At Rhea High School, Dayton, a biology teacher named John Scopes decided it would be against his principles to stop teaching evolution and, with his headteacher's support, he continued with his usual syllabus, which included Darwin's theory. He was duly arrested and sent for trial in Dayton in July 1925.

Scopes's trial promised to be a dramatic confrontation between the Fundamentalists and the ACLU and it attracted worldwide attention. The famous criminal lawyer Clarence Darrow (who had defended Leopold and Loeb (see p142)) offered to defend Scopes, and a renowned Fundamentalist and orator, William Jennings Bryan, gave his services to the prosecution.

Points of law

The trial began on 10 July and Darrow was immediately dealt a serious blow: the judge refused to allow his passionate argument for Darwin's theory, saying that the only relevant point was whether Scopes had broken the law or not. Darrow consoled himself with the knowledge that Bryan would be unable to broadcast his views.

The climax of the trial was Darrow's, cross-examination of Bryan, for he was at the peak of his powers and soon revealed Bryan to have a very shaky grasp of biological science. Darrow ridiculed him gently on his fundamentalist beliefs and at one point he asked, 'Where have you lived all your life?'. 'Not near you', was the indignant reply.

Fundamentalists discredited

Since Scopes had admitted breaking the law there was never any doubt about the verdict and on 21 July 1925 he was found guilty and fined $100. However, the trial was seen as an embarrassing and demoralizing defeat for the Fundamentalists, whose credibility had been destroyed by Darrow. To make matters worse for them Scopes appealed to the Tennessee Supreme Court and won on a technicality. The trial proved to be a devastating blow for Bryan and he died five days after its conclusion.

The 'monkey trial' as it was known had the effect of limiting Fundamentalist activity in other states; Mississippi and Arkansas were the only ones to introduce similar laws. Surprisingly, the law remained on the statute books in Tennessee until 1967.

Courtroom duel

Darrow was in a playful mood when he quizzed Bryan on the origins of man:
Darrow: 'Do you believe Eve was literally made out of Adam's rib?'
Bryan: 'I do'.
Darrow: 'Did you ever discover where Cain got his wife?'
Bryan: 'No, sir; I leave the agnostics to search for her'.

Sheppard, Jack
(1702–24)

Highwayman and house-breaker

One of the most famous criminals of the 18th century, who was renowned for his daring escapes from prison.

Jack Sheppard was born in Spitalfields, London, and his first employment was as an apprentice cane chair-maker and then as a carpenter. He frequented the Black Inn public house in Drury Lane and it was here that he was befriended by a prostitute named Edgeworth Bess and her friend Poll Maggott. It was Bess who suggested that he turn to crime and Sheppard was soon robbing the houses where he was working as a carpenter.

After teaming up with some local criminals, Sheppard had his first experience of prison when he tried to visit Bess in St Giles Roundhouse. At first the beadle refused to allow him entry, so Sheppard knocked the man out, took the keys and left with Bess. His audacity was greatly admired by the public, particularly the female population.

Expert in escape

Sheppard himself was imprisoned in April 1724 but escaped easily from St Giles Roundhouse by making a hole in the roof and leaving through the churchyard. He was arrested again in May 1724, for picking the pocket of a gentleman as he was crossing Leicester-Fields. He was imprisoned in New Prison with Edgeworth Bess but this did not unduly concern him — he cut through the bars on the windows with a file and then he and Bess lowered themselves into the courtyard by using knotted sheets.

During June and July 1724 Sheppard went on an orgy of burglary and highway robbery; as he himself admitted, 'I fell to robbing almost everyone that stood in my way'. At one point he was involved with the notorious Jonathan Wild but he got on the wrong side of this powerful figure of the London underworld.

Sheppard was betrayed by one of Wild's associates and he was arrested for the third time on 23 July 1724. He was tried at the Old Bailey on 14 August, sentenced to death and placed in the Condemned Hold at Newgate. This presented no problem to Sheppard though and he was soon at liberty again.

Luck runs out

For the next month Sheppard indulged in his criminal pastimes, until he was apprehended for holding up travellers on Finchley Common; he was taken back to Newgate and despite his being placed under a heavy guard, his jailers were dismayed the following morning when they discovered their prisoner had wriggled out of his chains and escaped up the chimney. It was a remarkable escape and he became a national hero.

Sheppard was captured for the final time about a week after his daring escape from Newgate. He was caught in a local alehouse, at the time so insensible from drink that he offered no resistance. Despite huge public support for him, Jack Sheppard was hanged at Tyburn on 16 November 1724.

Execution of a hero

Over 200 000 people were present at the hanging of Jack Sheppard, many of them sympathetic. Even to the last he hoped to escape the gallows: before he was hanged a small knife was found in his jacket, with which he had intended to cut himself free from the noose.

Simnel, Lambert
(c.1477– c.1534)

Imposter

A pretender to the English throne who was used to try and restore the Yorkist line in England.

In 1485 Henry VII became the first Tudor King of England, an event that enraged the Yorkist, who had just relinquished the throne following the termination of the wars of the Roses. One man who sought to rejuvenate the fortunes of the House of York was an unscrupulous Oxford priest named Richard Simon. He saw his opportunity when he was introduced to a young boy named Lambert Simnel whom Simon was convinced he could pass off as one of the 'princes in the Tower' believed to have been murdered by Richard III.

In 1487 Simon took Simnel to Oxford, where he gave him intensive coaching for the role he was going to fulfil. Initially Simon intended Simnel to impersonate Edward IV but changed his plan when he heard that Edward, Earl of Warwick, had supposedly escaped from the Tower.

Acceptance

Claiming that Simnel was now the Earl of Warwick, Simon took the young man to Ireland where there was still considerable support for the Yorkist cause. Most of the nobility and officials in Ireland accepted Simnel as the genuine Earl of Warwick; even Warwick's aunt, Margaret of Burgundy, announced that the impostor was her nephew and she persuaded her son-in-law Maximilian, king of the Romans, to send 1500 German mercenaries to help her nephew's cause.

When news of the events in Ireland reached Henry VII he tried to stem the wave of support for Simnel by parading the real Earl of Warwick through the streets of London. This had little effect though and Simnel's popularity continued to increase.

On 24 May 1487 Simnel was crowned at Dublin as Edward VI. To support this claim coins were struck and proclamations made. Following the coronation Simnel, who was almost totally under the influence of Simon, sailed to England with his supporters. They landed near Furness, in Lancashire, where they were joined by the German mercenaries and various prominent Yorkists.

Contemptuous defeat

By this time Henry VII was becoming thoroughly fed up with the impostor. He despatched a force to confront Simnel and his followers. They met at Stoke Field, Nottinghamshire, on 16 June 1487. The pretender and his men put up a surprisingly defiant fight but after a three-hour battle they succumbed. Simnel was taken prisoner, but Henry decided that he was so insignificant that he gave him a condescending free pardon. Simon, who was the driving force behind the conspiracy, and had hoped for an archbishopric, was not so fortunate and was imprisoned for life.

Following his pardon Simnel became a scullion in the royal kitchen and then a falconer enjoying this simple life more than the forced role of nobility. He died soon after 1534.

Perkin Warbeck

Another imposter during the same period was Perkin Warbeck, (c.1474–99), who tried to overthrow Henry VII. He was persuaded to impersonate Richard, Duke of York, and made a feeble invasion attempt in 1497. His forces were easily defeated and he was hanged after twice trying to escape from the Tower of London.

Slater case

(1909)

Oscar Slater

*Sir Arthur Conan Doyle led a
campaign for a man he believed
was wrongfully imprisoned
for murder.*

Marion Gilchrist was an 82-year-old spinster who lived in Glasgow. Her main pleasure in life was to look after her valuable collection of diamonds. On 21 December 1908 she sent her maidservant, Helen Lambie, to buy an evening newspaper. When Helen returned she found one of Miss Gilchrist's neighbours, Arthur Adams, at the outer door of the house, claiming to have heard a noise from inside. Before they entered they were passed by a tall, well-dressed gentleman. Inside the house they found the body of Miss Gilchrist, with her skull crushed. All that had been taken was one brooch.

Mistaken identity

Immediately after finding the body Helen ran to the home of Marion Gilchrist's niece, Mrs Margaret Birrell, and told her that she had recognized the man who had passed her at the doorway, but she was instructed that she must be mistaken, for she had mentioned the name of a respectable gentleman.

The police were anxious to make a quick arrest in the case and they were helped by a bicycle dealer who told them that he had been offered a pawn ticket by a man called Oscar Slater, for a brooch that was of the same value as the one missing from Miss Gilchrist. When the police went to Slater's house they found he and his mistress had left for America five days after the murder. When he was apprehended in New York

Slater claimed he knew nothing of the matter and returned to Britain voluntarily.

Unsatisfactory evidence

Slater was arrested for murder and brought to trial in Edinburgh in May 1909. The witnesses who claimed they recognized him gave very unsatisfactory evidence and Arthur Adams could only say that Slater 'closely resembled' the man he had seen. The prosecution made much of Slater's lack of morals, a fact that probably weighed heavily with the upstanding Edinburgh jury. Oscar Slater was found guilty by a majority verdict and sentenced to death. After three weeks in the condemned cell the sentence was commuted to life imprisonment.

Three years after Slater's conviction Sir Arthur Conan Doyle read of the case and, worried by the verdict, he began to investigate the affair with a tenacity with which his own Sherlock Holmes would have been proud. In a book entitled *The Case of Oscar Slater* he showed that Slater had pawned his brooch three weeks before the murder took place, demolished the convicting evidence of the eye-witnesses and pointed out that when Slater's entire wardrobe of clothes was searched there was not a single trace of blood or human matter to be found.

Conan Doyle's argument was a powerful one but it took another 15 years for the authorities to agree with him and release Oscar Slater. He received £6000 compensation for having had to spend 18 years of his life in prison.

Foregone conclusion
One of the eye-witnesses at the trial recognized Slater during an identification parade. However, she later admitted that this was only because she had been shown a photograph of him beforehand.

Smith case

(1857)

Madeleine Hamilton Smith

A case of arsenic poisoning that shocked the country due to the explicit love-letters written by the protagonists.

Madeleine Smith was born in Glasgow in 1836. Her father was a well respected architect and a pillar of Glaswegian society. She attended a finishing school near London and when she returned home at the age of 17 she was an accomplished young lady. Due to her situation she had little to occupy her time as she was required to wait patiently for marriage.

This lifestyle did not suit Madeleine, a flirtatious, passionate woman who had romantic fantasies. In 1855 she had the chance to indulge her desire for passion and romance when she began an illicit affair with a humble shipping clerk named Emile L'Angelier.

Social barriers

L'Angelier was of French extraction and had first come to Scotland in 1842, settling in Glasgow in 1852. Due to their respective social positions it would have been impossible for Madeleine and L'Angelier to meet under normal social conditions. However, when she was taking one of her unchaperoned walks the clerk approached her in the street. Attracted by his continental charm she encouraged his advances and the couple soon became lovers.

During the course of their affair Madeleine and L'Angelier wrote several highly intimate letters to each other, which not only discussed their proposed marriage plans but also related the fact that they had slept together.

Threat of exposure

By early 1857 Madeleine realized that the dangers of carrying on the affair with L'Angelier were too great. Her father had forbidden her to see her lover, and arranged for her to marry one of his friends, William Minnoch. When L'Angelier discovered this he was furious and threatened to disclose Madeleine's letters to her father — an action that would have compromised her position in society. She asked for all of her letters back, but in vain.

In March 1857 L'Angelier was taken ill with all the symptoms of arsenic poisoning. He died on 22 March and his body was found to contain 82 grains of arsenic, enough to kill over 50 men. Madeleine's letters were discovered and when it was revealed that she had bought arsenic a few days earlier she was and charged with murder.

The trial of Madeleine Smith, held in Edinburgh in June 1857, caused a sensation because of the explicit nature of the letters that passed between the accused and L'Angelier. The defence claimed that she intended to use the arsenic for a face-wash and also pointed to the fact that L'Angelier was a known arsenic-eater.

On 9 July 1857 the jury returned the uniquely Scottish verdict of Not Proven on Madeleine Smith. She left the country shortly afterwards and emigrated to America. She died in 1928, aged 93.

Love-letters

Following the first time they slept together Madeleine wrote to L'Angelier saying, 'Beloved, if we did wrong last night, it was in the excitement of our love. Yes beloved I did truly love you with my soul'. The judge at the trial was so horrified at this type of language that he refused to read some passages of her 'licentious' letters.

Smith, George Joseph

(1872–1915)

Convicted murderer

The 'Brides in the Bath' murderer who did not hesitate to kill for his own personal gain.

Smith was born in 1872 at Bethnal Green and by the time he was 24 he had served two prison sentences for larceny. He soon realized that there was a safer way of obtaining money and turned to members of the opposite sex to supply him with the wealth that he craved.

Despite the fact that he was bad-mannered and poorly educated Smith could be extremely charming; his secret seemed to lie in his eyes. His first bigamous wife, whom he married in 1899, said, 'When he looked at you — you had the feeling that you were being magnetized. They were little eyes that seemed to rob you of your will'.

In 1898 Smith, using the alias of George Love, married his only legal wife, Caroline Beatrice Thornhill. He quickly taught her everything he knew and she was soon working as a maid and stealing from her employers. In 1901 she was imprisoned for a year and on her release she left her husband and emigrated to Canada.

Courting for profit

In 1908 Smith married Florence Wilson and his treatment of her shows his calculating and callous nature. They were married after a three-week courtship and then Smith told her to withdraw her savings of £30 from the Post Office and give them to him. Once he had the money he took his wife to an exhibition at the White City where he made an excuse of going to get a newspaper and promptly walked out on her. Not stopping at this piece of chicanery, Smith then went back to their lodging house

Bessie Mundy *and **George Smith***

and sold all his wife's clothes and jewellery.

Later the same year Smith met Edith Pegler, and it seems he had some genuine affection for her, if only because he never tried to rob or murder her. They travelled around the south of England together until Smith decided he was in need of more money. In October 1909, calling himself George Rose, he married Sarah Freeman. Their marital bliss lasted seven days, by which time Smith had persuaded Freeman to give him her savings of £400 (equivalent to a working man's wage for four years) and deserted her at the National Gallery in the same way as he had Florence Wilson.

Smith returned briefly to Edith Pegler and bought a second-hand furniture shop in Southend. From here he made his next conquest and in August 1910 he married

Bessie Mundy at Weymouth. Having done his research carefully, he knew that his latest wife had over £2500 in gilt-edged securities. Initially, Smith was happy to deprive Mundy of the interest on her investment, which he did in September 1910 and then, true to form, he vanished.

From bigamy to murder

Smith spent the next two years with Pegler, who was apparently unaware of his bigamous activities. Then, while he was in Weston-super-Mare in March 1912, he met Bessie Mundy again. It was a coincidence that was to prove fatal for Mundy. She forgave her husband for his 18-month absence and they resumed their life together. They moved from town to town and the only work that Smith did was to enquire about how he might legally get his hands on his wife's fortune.

In July 1912 Smith was told by a lawyer in Herne Bay that if both he and his wife made wills and then she died, he would inherit everything. This was all that Smith needed to turn him into a murderer. Within a week the relevant wills had been drawn up and Smith had purchased a zinc bathtub.

The next part of Smith's plan was to prove that his wife was feeling unwell. He twice summoned a doctor to attend to her, claiming that she was having fits. Although the doctor was unconvinced he prescribed a sedative. Having done the groundwork, Smith then drowned his wife in the bath. An inquest returned a verdict of misadventure and Smith was free to collect Bessie Mundy's fortune.

Brief marriage

Having discovered how profitable murder could be, Smith set about looking for his next victim. In November 1913 he married Alice Burnham, a private nurse who worked in Southsea. He obtained £104 from her but by now greed was taking over and, in an attempt to make a greater profit from his victim, he insured her life for £500.

The couple went to Blackpool shortly after their marriage and Smith followed the course of action that had been so successful with Bessie Mundy. Burnham made her will, there was a visit to another doctor and then four days later the landlady in the Blackpool boarding house in which they were staying saw water coming through the ceiling of her living room. Predictably, Alice Burnham was found drowned in the bath. The landlady, Mrs Crossley, asked that Smith give his wife a good burial but he insisted on the cheapest available, saying, 'When they are dead they are done with'. When Smith left, Mrs Crossley made her feelings known by shouting, 'Crippen' after him (see p70).

Repetition leads to discovery

Smith's final victim was Margaret Lofty, whom he met and married in Bath in 1914. Being a man of little imagination, he disposed of her in exactly the same way as his first two victims, which proved to be his undoing: Mrs Crossley and Alice Burnham's father read of the crime in the newspapers and were so struck by the similarities with the previous deaths that they contacted the police. On 1 February 1915, just after he had collected the insurance money on Margaret Lofty, George Smith was arrested and charged with murder.

The trial of George Smith was the longest murder trial since that of William Palmer in 1856 and included 264 exhibits and 112 witnesses. On 1 July 1915 the jury took just 22 minutes to find George Joseph Smith guilty of murder. He was hanged at Maidstone prison on 13 August 1915.

Realistic demonstration
During Smith's trial there was a demonstration to show how he had murdered his victims — by lifting their legs up in the bath so their heads went underwater. This was so authentic that the nurse who had volunteered had to be revived by artificial respiration.

Snyder, Ruth May
(1896–1928)

Convicted murderess

A woman who tried to kill her husband on a number of occasions, and finally succeeded with the aid of her lover.

Ruth Snyder was a strong-minded Norwegian-American who lived in New York with her husband Albert Snyder, the art editor of a boating magazine. Her marriage was an unhappy one and in 1925 she began an affair with a corset salesman named Henry Judd Gray. Gray was a weak man and he was happy to let the dominant Ruth take control of his life. He called her 'Momsie' and she referred to him as 'Lover Boy'.

Murder in mind

After Ruth met Gray she made several attempts at killing her husband. She tried to gas him on a number of occasions and frequently left glasses of poisoned drinks around the house. Snyder was aware of what was happening but he was not unduly concerned; he recommended that his wife take a course of Christian Science in order to calm down.

By March 1927 Ruth tired of her futile attempts at murder and persuaded Gray to help her in disposing of her husband. Reluctantly he agreed—he rarely went against Ruth's wishes. The fact that Snyder was insured for $96 000 could have been the deciding factor.

Poor alibis

On 20 March 1927 Gray hid in the Snyder home with a sash-weight, a length of piano wire and a bottle of chloroform. When the Snyders returned home and Albert went to bed, Ruth and Gray clubbed him to death with the sash-weight. They then staged a fake break-in and Ruth was tied up and gagged.

The police were immediately suspicious of Ruth's story about a burglary. When some jewellery, that was supposed to have been stolen, was found under a bed she was arrested. Gray's name was found in her address book and when he was questioned he initially claimed he had been in a hotel in Syracuse at the time of the murder. But he soon broke down and admitted to the murder. Once Ruth heard of this she too confessed. They both claimed that the other had struck the fatal blow.

The 'Granite Woman'

Ruth Snyder and Gray were tried in April 1927, blaming each other for the crime. Gray claimed that Ruth had a peculiar power over him and he instinctively did what she told him. Ruth gave a much more powerful performance in court and she was dubbed the 'Granite Woman' by the press.

The jury took two hours to find Snyder and Gray guilty and they were both sentenced to death. While she was awaiting execution Ruth received 164 offers of marriage and also wrote her autobiography, which included a poem entitled 'My Baby'. Ruth Snyder and Henry Gray were electrocuted within four minutes of each other at Sing Sing prison on 12 January 1928.

Snapshot
A photographer gained a remarkable exclusive during the execution of Ruth Snyder. He had a miniature camera strapped to his ankle and managed to get a photograph of the moment of execution, as Ruth sat in the electric chair.

Sobhraj, Hotchand Bhawanni Gurmukh (Charles)

(1944–)

Smuggler, confidence trickster and convicted murderer

A habitual criminal who robbed and murdered travellers in Asia.

Born in Saigon, South Vietnam, Charles Sobhraj came from a wealthy family and enjoyed a privileged early life. However, his happiness came to an end when he was nine. His mother married a Frenchman and decided to send him to a Catholic boarding school in Paris. He hated the school, he hated France and he hated the fact that his living standards had dropped dramatically. He tried to return to his father in Saigon on several occasions but his efforts invariably ended in failure. The one time that he did reach Saigon he quarrelled with his father and was sent to stay with relatives in India. When this proved unsatisfactory he was forced to return to France.

Love of the easy life

Sobhraj married a Frenchwoman named Chantel, in 1969, and made a living by stealing cheque books and writing forged cheques. After some initial success he began taking a serious interest in fraud and theft. After writing 30 000 francs worth of fraudulent cheques Sobhraj and Chantel moved to India. Sobhraj took to crime with great enthusiasm and was soon making a considerable amount of money from diamond smuggling, currency deals and the sale of goods bought with stolen cheques. His natural charm and plausible manner were the perfect assets for his trade and also aided him in another of his sidelines — befriending tourists, then drugging them and stealing their passports and money.

Elusive character

In 1972 Sobhraj took part in an abortive jewellery raid in Delhi and was arrested. While he was on bail he and his wife escaped to Afghanistan, where they were soon jailed for stealing. Escape proved easy and the Sobhrajs moved on to Iran. Again a period in jail followed, after which Chantel decided that she had had enough and sued for divorce, leaving for America with another man shortly afterwards.

Sobhraj's next stop was Istanbul and he was joined by his younger brother Guy, who soon learnt the art of conning rich tourists. However when the two were recognized at the airport, Charles fled, leaving Guy to serve a prison sentence.

After meeting a Canadian girl named Marie-Andrée Leclerc, in 1975, Sobhraj invited her to live with him in Bangkok. By now he had become involved with drug-trafficking and sought to make large profits through the distribution of heroin. One of his tutors, André Breugnot, seemed to be dispensable; he was drugged at Sobhraj's flat and then drowned in the bath.

As Sobhraj's drug smuggling activities increased so did his propensity for murder. He frequently befriended travellers, took them back to his flat and then killed them. On 13 October a 23-year-old American went to his flat; her body was later found at Pattaya. This was followed by the deaths of a Turk, a French girl and a Dutch couple. All the victims were drugged, strangled, dowsed with petrol and then burned.

On the move

By the end of 1975 Sobhraj realized that he was beginning to arouse suspicion in Bangkok, so he moved his operation to Nepal; shortly afterwards the charred bodies of an

American and a Canadian were discovered near Kathmandu. The crime was traced to Sobhraj but after being questioned by the police he left Nepal for India.

By March 1976 the net was beginning to close around Sobhraj and a Dutch diplomat, Herman Knippenberg, had connected him with the deaths of the Dutch couple. But when the Thai Drugs Squad raided his flat they released him after payment of a substantial bribe. When Knippenberg searched the flat he discovered large quantities of drugs and personal documents belonging to over 20 people. Interpol were alerted and Sobhraj became the most wanted man in Asia. The authorities in several countries wanted to question him about numerous crimes, including a total of eight murders.

Overdose

Despite the knowledge that he was a wanted man Sobhraj continued to rob and con his way through Asia. He planned a large robbery in India but had to rethink his plans when one of his accomplices turned the tables and stole all of his money. To try and recoup some of his loses he drugged and robbed a French traveller, Luke Solomon. Unfortunately he miscalculated the dosage and Solomon died in hospital.

Sobhraj then turned his attention to a group of 60 French students staying in Delhi. He visited them at their hotel and gave them a number of pills that were intended to send them to sleep while he robbed their rooms. Again his calculations had gone awry and the students began to collapse in the lobby of the hotel. The police were alerted and on 5 July 1976 Charles Sobhraj was arrested.

Only culpable homicide

Despite his continuous criminal activity for over 10 years, Sobhraj was initially only charged with the murder of Luke Solomon. He was found guilty of culpable homicide and sentenced to seven years' hard labour, with a further two years' imprisonment for the drugging of the French students.

In 1982 Sobhraj was taken to Varanasi, in northern India, to face another murder charge. His trial was a sensational affair, with the defendant conducting his own headline-grabbing defence. It served little purpose though; both Sobhraj and Marie-Andrée Leclerc were found guilty and sentenced to life imprisonment. It is estimated that Sobhraj murdered a minimum of 10 people. Following his conviction for murder in India, Thailand and Nepal applied for his extradition. Sobhraj claimed that he would regain his freedom 'by legal means', but so far he has not lived up to his boast.

Comfortable existence

While in prison Sobhraj used his considerable charm and cunning to ensure that he had as comfortable a time as possible. He used hidden tape-recorders to blackmail the guards and in return he was allowed 'conjugal' visits from two women who wanted to marry him, and his cell was fitted with various luxuries. He also appealed to the High Court for the removal of leg irons and shackles. When he won his case he became a hero with his fellow prisoners but the prison officials always viewed him as a thorn in their side.

South Sea Bubble

(1720)

The South Sea Company

A fraudulent stock flotation that threw Britain into a financial crisis.

At the beginning of the 18th century speculators and investors were constantly seeking new markets for their capital. One of the main areas of expansion was South America. This followed several extremely successful expeditions by the adventurer Thomas Drover which netted him nearly £4 million. This interest in overseas trade coincided with a large rise in the National Debt — by 1711 the interest alone amounted to £3 million.

In September 1711 a group of men sought to exploit the potential of South America, take care of the National Debt, and make themselves a fortune in the process. A company named the South Sea Company was formed, with the idea of it taking over a large part of the National Debt in return for a complete monopoly of trade in the South Seas.

Crooked auditor

The guiding force behind the South Sea Company was John Blunt, an auditor who had already made a fortune from clothing the army and organizing the first state lottery. For the first few years of its existence the Company made moderate progress, but all the time Blunt was working on plans and manipulations that were to have repercussions for years to come.

Since the South Sea Company was committed to paying off the National Debt it was essential that its stock rose to an artificially high level. Blunt saw to this by first bribing various ministers to ensure that the necessary bills passed smoothly through Parliament, and then advertising the Company in such a way that when trading began, people were eager to buy as many shares as possible. The stock rose dramatically, reaching its peak at 1050 in June. Whenever there was a lull in the market Blunt invented fictitious pieces of news concerning the Company's good fortune, which the investors believed.

Bubble deflated

As the stock soared there were whispers that the Company's operations were falling well below expectations. Rumours began circulating and even Blunt was unable to stop them. It soon became clear that the South Sea Bubble had burst, and investors tried desperately to get rid of what was now worthless stock. The price plunged to 150 and fortunes were lost by thousands, including royalty and Parliament members.

The South Sea Bubble had a dramatic effect on the public's faith in stock investment and it took several years for their confidence to return. The Bank of England intervened to help steady the economy and several influential figures were prosecuted for their involvement in the fraud. One person who escaped punishment was John Blunt; he even managed to salvage £5000 from the fiasco.

> **Bizarre schemes**
> The South Sea Bubble gave rise to a number of wildly optimistic, and undoubtedly fraudulent, projects. These included companies for, 'supplying London with sea-coal', 'trading in hair', 'transmuting quicksilver into a malleable fine metal', and 'importing large numbers of jackasses from Spain'. The most incredulous scheme was 'an undertaking of great advantage, but nobody to know what it is'. The promoter made £2000 in a morning and vanished.

Stavisky, Alexandre Serge

(1888–1934)

Financial swindler

A Russian-born swindler whose activities caused the downfall of the French Government.

Apart from his birth in the Ukraine in 1888, little is known of Alexander Stavisky's early life. At some point he emigrated to France and obtained residential status. He settled in Paris and it soon became clear that he was capable of every possible trick. He was imprisoned twice for minor frauds; on his release he persuaded a rich widow to lend him money to open a nightclub, which attracted the rich and famous of Parisian society. Nevertheless Stavisky was also involved in company swindles, the drugs business and blackmail.

A face in the crowd

Outwardly Stavisky was an unremarkable man; the novelist Colette, who knew him by sight, commented, 'He excelled at having no face'. However, he had a peculiar talent not only for making money but also for developing friends in high places. How he did this has never been discovered but he was undoubtedly protected by the police and politicians. These connections frequently saved him when his actions warranted prosecution.

Bayenne bonds swindle

Stavisky's greatest swindle involved bonds issued by a pawnshop in the French town of Bayenne. In France, pawnbrokers are allowed to issue bonds to the value of the goods that they are holding. Stavisky took advantage of this by arranging to have an accomplice, Gustave Tissier, appointed as the director of a pawnshop in Bayenne.

Once he had done this he started depositing fake jewellery and issuing expensive bonds on the basis of these worthless assets. It is estimated that he made the equivalent of over £2 million in this way, and defrauded hundreds of investors.

In 1933 the fraud was discovered and Tissier was arrested. He made a full confession, implicating Stavisky and other members of his organization. This time Stavisky's friends could not, or would not, help him and he fled to the ski resort of Chamonix. The police tracked him down but before they could apprehend him he shot himself. It was rumoured that the police had murdered him to prevent him making embarrassing revelations, but there was no evidence to support this.

Riots in Paris

Following Stavisky's death there was uproar in France as people tried to unravel the cover-up concerning his affairs. There were riots in Paris by Fascist groups, and the left-wing prime minister was forced to resign. A right-wing Government headed by Henri Doumergue was installed and he restored order. An official inquiry followed but no one was prepared to say who was behind Stavisky. None of the money that he obtained was ever returned.

Suspicious death

One of the people involved in the Stavisky case was a judge named Monsieur Prince. He was known to possess documents that would have exposed Stavisky but he was told not to disclose them as they would compromise an unnamed Leftist politician. Shortly after this, Prince was found mutilated on a railway track near Dijon. Suicide was the official cause of death but many people believed it was part of a massive cover-up operation.

Stratton case

(1905)

Alfred and Albert Stratton

The first people in Britain to be convicted using the technique of fingerprinting.

Alfred Stratton, 22, and his brother Albert, 20, were two petty criminals who lived in Deptford, south-east London. They had several convictions for burglary and in March 1905 they heard that an elderly local tradesman, Thomas Farrow, kept a moderate sum of cash in his shop. On the morning of 27 March the brothers broke into the shop and started looking for the cash-box. Farrow was alerted by the noise but when he came downstairs he was beaten to death. The Strattons also attacked Mrs Farrow, before fleeing from the scene of the crime.

A vital clue

The body of Thomas Farrow was found the next morning and although his wife was still alive she died in hospital three days later. When the police arrived they found two crude masks made from stockings, and the empty cash-box. Crucially, the impression of a right thumb was on the metal plate. Everyone who had touched it (including the murdered couple) were fingerprinted but none of the prints matched the one on the cash-box.

The police reasoned that the murderers must be locals if they needed to disguise their appearance. They investigated all the petty criminals in the area and checked their alibis. They heard that the Stratton brothers had been out all night on 26 March and that when they returned Albert had burnt his coat. Albert's girlfriend also admitted that he had asked her for an old pair of stockings.

A new technique

The Stratton brothers were arrested and their fingerprints were taken. It was discovered that Alfred's thumb-print matched the one on the cash-box. This caused great excitement because it was the first case where the prosecution relied on the relatively new principle of fingerprinting.

The trial of Alfred and Albert Stratton took place in May 1905. Due to the revolutionary new fingerprint evidence there was enormous interest in this sordid and clumsy crime. The prosecution was led by Sir Richard Muir, one of the greatest counsels of the time. He explained to the jury the technicalities of fingerprinting and showed them 11 similarities between Alfred Stratton's fingerprint and the one found on the cash-box. To test the theory the jury had one of their own number fingerprinted to compare it with that of Stratton.

The defence tried to dismiss the principle of fingerprint evidence as unreliable and even the judge was not entirely convinced. The jury had no such qualms though and found the Stratton brothers guilty of murder. They were hanged together, blaming each other for the crime.

Fingerprinting

The theory of fingerprinting was first put forward by Sir Edward Henry in 1900 when he published an account of fingerprint classification. A year later he was appointed Acting Police Commissioner for the Metropolis of London. He has since given his name to the system used for fingerprint identification by police forces around the world, except South Africa. The Henry system is based on four groups of ridge patterns and has been used by the FBI to accumulate over 200 million records.

Sutcliffe, Peter William (The Yorkshire Ripper)

(1946–)

Convicted murderer

A sadistic mass murderer who preyed mainly on prostitutes and claimed he was driven to kill by voices in his head.

Peter Sutcliffe was born at Heaton Row near Bingley. He was a shy child and became easily embarrassed in the presence of girls. He attended Cottingham Manor School in Bingley, leaving at the age of 15. He worked in a variety of menial jobs before being employed as a gravedigger. It was work that fascinated him and he shocked his workmates by taking an unnatural interest in the corpses. He was sacked from his job in 1967 for bad timekeeping.

Also in 1967 Sutcliffe met Sonia Szurma, and the couple married seven years later. During their courtship they quarrelled frequently and on one occasion Sutcliffe turned to a prostitute. The girl conned him out of £5; he later claimed that this was the beginning of his hatred of prostitutes. Sutcliffe and Sonia were married in 1974 but they had numerous violent rows and Sutcliffe was dominated by his forthright wife.

Attacks begin

During the summer of 1975 two Yorkshire women were attacked with a hammer. Both survived, but on 30 October a prostitute named Wilma McCann was not so lucky. She was working in the Chapelton district of Leeds when she was attacked and savagely beaten with a ball-headed hammer and then stabbed repeatedly. Her murder attracted little attention but on 20 January 1976 Emily Jackson suffered a similar horrific fate. The West Yorkshire police, led by assistant chief constable George Oldfield, thought they were dealing with a psychopath.

There were no more killings for a year until 5 February and 23 April 1977, when two more prostitutes, Irene Richardson and Tina Aitkinson, were brutally battered and stabbed to death. The fifth victim of the man now dubbed the 'Yorkshire Ripper' was 16-year-old Jayne MacDonald. She was the first non-prostitute to be killed and it heightened the public awareness of the case. Jayne's father died two years after his daughter's death.

Flood of information

Despite one of the largest police operations ever mounted in the north of England the CID had virtually no clues as to the Ripper's identity. On 27 July a victim of the Ripper survived an attack and she told the police that her assailant had blond hair — which was later found to be incorrect.

On 1 October 1977 the Ripper moved his operation from Leeds to Manchester, where he murdered another prostitute, Jean Jordan. It was later discovered that she had been killed by 11 blows to the head and 24 stab wounds. There was one clue, however, a new £5 note that had probably been handed to Jordan by her killer. It was traced and during the course of their enquiries the police interviewed the entire staff of T and W H Clark, an engineering and haulage firm. One of the men interviewed was Peter Sutcliffe but he was cleared of any involvement in the case. The same pattern occurred another eight times in the next three years and each time Sutcliffe was released.

The Ripper's next victim was an 18-year-old prostitute in Huddersfield, named Helen Rytka. She was murdered in the

The 13 victims of the Yorkshire Ripper

usual brutal fashion on 31 January 1978. Two months later the body of Yvonne Pearson was also found. This was followed by the killing, in Manchester, of a 40-year-old prostitute named Vera Millward.

From this point the Ripper began killing women indiscriminately, not just prostitutes, as all the victims except Jayne MacDonald had been so far. On 4 April 1979 he murdered 19-year-old Josephine Whitaker, fracturing her skull from ear to ear.

Red herring

On 26 June 1979 the beleaguered police got what they thought was an important break. They were sent a taped message from a man claiming to be the Ripper. It was sent to George Oldfield and it taunted him for his inability to catch the killer: 'I see you are still having no luck catching me. I reckon your boys are letting you down, George. You can't be much good, can you?'. The accent was pinpointed to a district in Sunderland but it later transpired that the taped message had been a vindictive hoax. Oldfield was later taken off the case and

subsequently suffered a heart attack.

The Ripper struck again on 2 September 1979 when Barbara Leach, a student at Bradford University was his eleventh victim, stabbed repeatedly with a rusty screwdriver. There then followed two attacks in which the victims survived and it was not until August 1980 that the Ripper's next victim appeared, a civil servant named Margo Walls who, unusually, had been strangled with a piece of rope. On 17 November the Yorkshire Ripper claimed his final victim, 20-year-old Jacqueline Hill.

Fortuitous arrest

On 2 January 1981 Sergeant Robert Ring and PC Robert Hydes stopped a car in the centre of Sheffield for a routine check. A man and a woman were inside; unsatisfied with the answers they received, they decided to run a check on the registration. When it did not match the story the driver had told them, they took him to the police station. The officers were stunned a few hours later when Peter Sutcliffe identified himself and admitted to the Ripper murders.

Peter Sutcliffe's trial began on 5 May 1981 and he pleaded not guilty on the grounds of diminished responsibility, claiming that he had been on a mission from God and that voices in his head had driven him to murder. This theory was rejected by the jury and on 22 May Sutcliffe was found guilty on 13 counts of murder and seven of attempted murder. He was sentenced to life imprisonment on each count, with a recommendation from the judge that he should serve at least 30 years.

Warning note
A note that Sutcliffe kept in his truck read: 'In this truck is a man whose latent genius, if unleashed, would rock the nation, whose dynamic energy would overpower those around him. Better let him sleep'.

Police operation
During the course of the Yorkshire Ripper investigation 250 000 people were interviewed, 32 000 statements were taken and 5.2 million car registrations were checked. The total cost was £4 million.

Sutton, William Francis

(1901–80)

Bank robber

A master of disguise and impersonation who stole over $2 million from American banks.

Willie Sutton was born in Brooklyn and quickly moved into a life of petty crime, first shoplifting and then breaking into shops. During World War I he worked in a munitions factory and supplemented his wages by stealing from his employer. In 1920 he stole $20 000 and eloped with the daughter of a Brooklyn shipyard owner. He was soon discovered, imprisoned for a month and put on probation for a year.

When he came out of jail Sutton teamed up with Eddie 'Doc' Tate, an expert safe-breaker. For four years the two worked successfully together and it was during this time that Sutton learned the value of make-up. This did him little good when he committed his first solo robbery in 1925 — an informer went to the police and Sutton spent the next four years in Sing Sing.

Willie the Actor

When Sutton was released in 1929 he adopted a new persona, that of 'Willie the Actor'. He had become a master of disguise and he also realized that a uniform afforded a virtual open invitation into a bank or a jewellery store. Working with an accomplice named Jack Bassett, Willie the Actor carried out over a dozen bank raids during the next few months, netting over $2 million. They were all carefully planned and executed and Sutton appeared in a variety of poses: policeman, railwayman, messenger and window cleaner.

In 1932 Sutton and Bassett were arrested in connection with a number of robberies. Sutton proved difficult to convict because none of the eye-witnesses could recognize him in his own clothes. At last one man identified him and Willie the Actor was sentenced to 30 years' imprisonment in Sing Sing. However, the bank robber was free a year later, having escaped through supposedly 'escape-proof' doors. He committed two more raids before he was recaptured and this time he was placed in the East State Penitentiary.

New career

Sutton remained in jail for the next 13 years. He tried to escape four times, once nearly drowning in the prison sewer in the process. In 1945 he was moved to Holmesburg County Prison and two years later he made a successful escape attempt. He took a low-paid job in an old-folks' home on Staten Island. He worked happily there for five years, genuinely enjoying the job and taking a sincere interest in the home's inhabitants.

On 18 February 1952 Arnold Schuster, a clothing salesman, recognized Sutton and reported him to the police. He was convicted of a robbery that he almost certainly did not commit and gained a considerable amount of public sympathy. This evaporated shortly afterwards when Schuster was brutally murdered. No one was ever arrested for the killing but it did Sutton's cause little good and he was sentenced to 30 years' imprisonment.

Willie Sutton was released in 1969 due to ill health. He died in poverty in 1980.

Professional opinion
Shortly after his arrest for the final time, $7000 was found in Sutton's suit. When asked why he had not put it in a bank he replied, 'It's never safe in a bank'.

Teach, Edward

(?–1718)

Pirate

Known as Blackbeard, Teach is one of the most legendary pirates in history.

Edward Teach, or Tache, or Thatch, was a native of Bristol. At the turn of the 18th century he went to the West Indies to fight for the British during the War of the Spanish Succession (1701–13). He was employed to undertake privateering voyages against the Spanish and with his imposing physique and fearless manner he was a daunting opponent.

Enthusiastic pirate

In 1713 it seemed as though Teach's activities would be curtailed by the declaration of peace. However, he did not let this interfere with his vocation and instead he turned to piracy, plundering any Spanish or French vessels that came his way. His transformation from privateer to pirate was completed by 1716 and the following year he was in command of a sloop with his companion Benjamin Hornigold. Together they took several prizes including a French Guinea merchant ship which Teach re-fitted as a 40-gun warship and renamed *Queen Anne's Revenge*.

During 1717 Woodes Rogers was appointed Governor of the Bahamas and Hornigold took advantage of the king's mercy that was offered and gave himself up. Teach would have none of this and continued with his piratical ways. Whenever he went into battle he wore a silk sash and had six pistols around his waist. He also put lighted matches under his hat, to make himself look more menacing.

Carolina base

After tiring of the West Indies Teach and his crew sailed north and in 1718 they established their base in a small North Carolina inlet. They wreaked considerable havoc in the area and it was common for Blackbeard, as he was becoming known, to blockade harbours for 10 days, seizing all shipping that went in and out.

On 10 June 1718 when Teach was trying to go into Topsail Creek in North Carolina his ship was wrecked on a sand-bar. Another of his ships was also damaged and eventually Teach and his crew fled on their two remaining vessels. Shortly afterwards a dispute broke out amongst the crew and some decided to take to land. Teach was left with between 20 and 30 men, whom he took to Bath-town in North Carolina.

Obliging governor

Once Teach reached his destination he was relieved to find that he had allies in the form of Charles Eden, governor of North Carolina, and his secretary and Collector of Customs, Tobias Knight. The three entered into an agreement whereby Teach could continue his piratical acts as long as Eden and Knight received a share of the spoils. This was quickly put into practice when the pirate captured two French vessels. In their official capacity Eden and Knight condemned this action, but they were more than willing to accept the hogsheads of sugar which Teach offered them. They then obligingly disposed of the evidence by sinking the two ships.

When he was not plundering vessels off the Carolina coast Teach was engaged in a riotous life on shore. He forced the planters to supply him with all his needs and he spent his money in a cavalier fashion. To fill his coffers he charged heavy tolls for any ships that wanted safe passage in his inlet.

End of their tether

After a few months of living under the tyrannical rule of Blackbeard the residents of North Carolina were beginning to desire a more peaceful existence. They sought relief from Colonel Alexander Spotswood, the lieutenant governor of Virginia. After consultation with seamen experienced in dealing with pirates, Spotswood decided to send a small force under the command of lieutenant Robert Maynard to put a stop to Blackbeard's activities.

On 22 November 1718 Maynard made his way with two sloops up the Ocracoke Inlet to Teach's base. The pirate captain was well prepared and immediately opened fire. All the ships ran aground after only a few minutes and a vicious hand-to-hand battle ensued. During the course of the fighting 10 of Maynard's men were killed while the pirates lost eight of their number. Many others jumped overboard in an effort to escape.

Decapitation

At the height of the battle Maynard and Blackbeard became locked in a personal dual, which ended with the pirate being shot dead. Not content with this Maynard cut off his opponent's head and hung it over the end of the bowsprit.

When Maynard returned to Spotswood with Blackbeard's body Governor Eden was furious. Obviously annoyed that one of his best providers had been removed he threatened legal action against Spotswood but it did not materialize; instead 13 of the 15 captured pirates were hanged.

Missing treasure

A great many apocryphal stories have been told about Blackbeard. The most famous one concerns the large quantities of treasure that he accumulated and buried on an unidentified island. This has never been proved with any authenticity and no treasure has ever been found.

Reputation of fear

Blackbeard had no morals when it came to instilling fear into his enemies. On one occasion he sent some of his men to Charlestown to demand a medicine chest, with the threat that he was going to take hostages and kill them if the chest was not forthcoming. After they delivered the message his men ransacked the town to emphasize the point. By the time they were finished ample medical supplies had been provided and Blackbeard's name was feared throughout the area.

Teapot Dome scandal

(1923)

Albert Fall and others

A major American political scandal of the 1920s that involved the private leasing of vast oil reserves.

During the presidency of Woodrow Wilson (1913–21), the Democrats initiated a policy of federal conservation, which included the creation of huge naval petroleum reserves. In 1915 an emergency reserve was created at Teapot Dome in Wyoming.

With the election of the Republican president, Warren G Harding, in 1921, the policy of federal conservation began to be relaxed and people started voicing their opinions against it. One opponent was the new Secretary of the Interior, Albert Bacon Fall. His was one of several appointments by Harding that owed more to comradeship and past favours than to common sense.

Transfer of reserves

Albert Fall believed firmly in a free enterprise economy but unfortunately his enterprises were not always legal. One of his first tasks in office was to persuade the Secretary of the Navy, Edwin Denby, to transfer the oil reserves to the Department of the Interior. These included not only Teapot Dome but also vast reserves at Elk Hills and Buena Vista Hills in California.

Once Fall had control of the oil reserves he set about leasing them to two oil companies, which he did secretly and without offering the leases for competitive bidding. In April 1922 he leased the entire Teapot Dome reserve to the Mammouth Oil Company, owned by Harry Sinclair. A few months later he did the same with the Elk Hills and Buena Vista Hills reserves, this time offer-ing the leases to Edward Doheny's Pan-American Petroleum and Transport Company. The two oilmen, who now had the potential to create vast personal fortunes, rewarded Fall with gifts and 'loans' that exceeded \$300 000.

Senate committee

Despite Fall's attempts at secrecy the transfers aroused the curiosity of a trouble-shooting senator from Wisconsin, named Robert LaFollette, and a committee was set up to investigate the granting of the oil leases. It took them 18 months to prepare their case and by the time they were ready to present it, in October 1923, Fall had resigned and President Harding had died. It is uncertain how much he knew of Fall's activities, but the prospect of a major scandal had done little for his already fragile health.

The senate committee hearing into the Teapot Dome Scandal ran for the remain-der of the 1920s. In 1927 the leases for Teapot Dome, Elf Hills and Buena Vista Hills were invalidated and the two compa-nies who bought them were ordered to restore the reserves to their original levels. Sinclair and Doheny were cleared of con-spiracy charges but on 25 October 1929 Albert Fall was sentenced to one year in prison and fined \$100 000 for accepting bribes. He died in poverty and obscurity.

> **Few repercussions**
> The Teapot Dome Scandal had little long-term adverse effect on the Republican party; President Calvin Coolidge, who succeeded Harding, was able to show that his administration had investigated the affair thoroughly and fairly. One result of the scandal was a reassessment of the storage of America's natural resources.

Murder of Percy Thompson

(1922)

Edith Jessie Thompson and Frederick Bywaters

A love-triangle killing where the two murderers were convicted on the evidence of their love-letters.

Edith Graydon and Percy Thompson were married on 15 January 1915, when she was 22 and he was 26. He was a shipping clerk and she worked as a milliner's bookkeeper and manageress. They lived a rather monotonous life in Ilford, with their main entertainment being the theatre and an occasional meal with friends.

In June 1921 the Thompsons went on holiday to the Isle of Wight. They were accompanied by Edith's sister, Avis, and her boyfriend, Frederick Bywaters, a virile 19-year-old who was a steward on an ocean liner. During the holiday Edith and Bywaters spent a lot of time together and in August 1921 they became lovers, meeting almost daily before he went back to sea.

Incriminating love-letters

Between 9 September 1921 and 23 September 1922 Bywaters had five spells at sea, each lasting approximately two months. While he was away, Edith wrote to him frequently, bemoaning her dreary life in Ilford. On several occasions she made oblique suggestions about poisoning her husband and sent newspaper cuttings of poison cases in Britain. During these periods she constantly asked her husband for a separation but he obstinately refused.

When Bywaters returned home in September 1922 his affair with Edith intensified. On 3 October they met for lunch and in the evening she went to the theatre with her husband. They returned home at about midnight and as they were nearing Kensington Gardens they were attacked by a man in an overcoat and a hat. He knocked Edith to the ground and asked Thompson, 'Why don't you get a divorce or separation, you cad?' He then attacked Thompson, stabbing him in the neck. He died a few minutes later, choking on his own blood.

Incitement to murder

Bywaters and Thompson were both arrested on 4 October and charged with the murder of Percy Thompson. A week later 83 letters from Edith to Bywaters were found in a chest on his ship. These were to play a vital role in the trial which began at the Old Bailey on 6 December 1922. Forty-nine of them were used as exhibits to show that Edith had incited Bywaters to kill her husband. In one letter she wrote, 'Darlint, be jealous, so much that you will do something desperate'.

In his summing-up the judge was extremely hostile to the defendants and described Edith's letters as, 'the outpourings of a silly but at the same time a wicked affection'. The jury took two hours to decide that the accused were guilty.

Despite the fact that Bywaters claimed Edith knew nothing of his intention to kill Percy Thompson the couple were hanged on the same day, 9 January 1923; she, heavily sedated, at Holloway and he at Pentonville.

> **Needless witness**
> Edith Thompson's leading council, Sir Henry Curtis-Bennett, was convinced that she would have been acquitted if she had taken his advice and not testified: 'She spoiled her chances by her evidence and demeanour. She was a vain woman and an obstinate one. I could have saved her'.

Throckmorton, Francis

(1554–84)

Conspirator

A supporter of Mary, Queen of Scots, who tried to overthrow Elizabeth I and restore papal authority in Britain.

Francis Throckmorton's family came from Feckenham, Worcestershire; his father was a staunch and prominent Catholic who, in later life, was persecuted for his beliefs. Francis shared his father's opinions and was determined to try and further the Catholic cause, which was suffering under the regressive laws laid down by Elizabeth I.

Throckmorton attended Hart Hall, Oxford, in 1572 and four years later he was entered as a student of the Inner Temple. However, he disliked this sedentary lifestyle and in 1580 he went to the continent with his brother Thomas. He used the opportunity to visit leading Catholic exiles, discussing with them the various options that were available.

Plotting abroad

While in Madrid Throckmorton met Sir Francis Englefield, a leading Catholic dissident, and raised the idea of an invasion of England by a Spanish army. He then moved to Paris where he was entertained by two agents of Mary, Queen of Scots, Thomas Morgan and Charles Paget. Much of their debate centred around the feasibility of mobilizing Catholics in England to join forces with an army that Henry of Guise was raising against Elizabeth.

Throckmorton returned to London in 1583 and continued his conspiratorial activities. He rented a house at Paul's Wharf which was used as a nerve-centre by fellow conspirators. One of its main functions was to relay secret communications between the Queen of Scots and Bernardino de Mendoza, the Spanish ambassador at Elizabeth's court.

The Throckmorton Plot

Unfortunately, Throckmorton maintained very lax security and he was frequently seen visting Mendoza's house by Elizabeth's agents. The Queen was informed and in October 1583 she ordered his arrest. When the authorities went to his house they caught him red-handed, writing a coded letter to the Queen of Scots. Although Throckmorton managed to destroy a large number of incriminating documents, Elizabeth's principal secretary, Francis Walsingham, discovered lists of Catholics who were conspiring against the Queen, and plans for the landing of a foreign invasion force.

Although the evidence against him was reasonably conclusive Throckmorton had to be put on the rack three times within one week before he would confess that he and Mendoza had been plotting to aid Henry of Guise in his proposed invasion of England.

Throckmorton was tried for treason at Guildhall on 21 May 1584. He claimed in vain that his forced confession was not sufficient to convict him. His execution was postponed until he made another confession; then, on 10 July 1584, Francis Throckmorton was hanged at Tyburn. Shortly before the execution he revoked his second confession; he had only made it in the hope of gaining a pardon.

Agent abroad

Throckmorton's brother, Thomas, settled permanently in Paris in 1582, as one of the agents of Mary, Queen of Scots. In 1584 she tried to persuade the Pope to grant him a pension. He died on 19 October 1595, shortly before he was due to be married.

Troppmann, Jean-Baptiste

(1849–70)

Convicted murderer

A French mass murderer who killed an entire family in an attempt to get his hands on their money.

Jean-Baptiste Troppmann was born in Alsace into a poor family. He was spoilt by his mother, beaten by his father and constantly bullied at school. Although he developed considerable strength he looked insignificant and his morose character did little to endear him to people, particularly when they discovered that he was a compulsive liar.

In December 1868 Troppmann was sent by his father to Paris to install some weaving machinery. Once he had completed this he moved to Roubaix near the Belgium border. Here he met Jean Kinck, a diligent and successful businessman. Since he was also an Alsatian Troppmann immediately befriended him and tried to steal his money with various hair-brained and fraudulent schemes. Eventually Kinck fell for a story about precious metals in the mountains of the Upper Rhine and agreed to meet Troppmann in an abandoned chateau at Herrenfluch, Alsace. When Kinck arrived, on 26 August 1869, Troppmann poisoned him with home-made prussic acid and buried the body between Guebwiller and Bollwiller.

Money problems

After the murder Troppmann wrote to Kinck's wife and asked her to send 5500 francs for her husband, claiming he had broken his arm and so could not write himself. She sent the money but a suspicious postmaster refused to hand it over without identification. Exasperated, Troppmann wrote several times to Mme Kinck and it was eventually agreed that her eldest son, Gustave, should meet Troppmann in Paris and give him the money.

When Gustave arrived in Paris he did not have the money so Troppmann ordered him to send a telegram to his mother asking the rest of the family to join him. He then brutally killed the boy. When Mme Kinck and her five children, aged between two and 13, arrived in Paris they were met by Troppmann who said he would take them to Kinck. Instead he took them to Pantin on the outskirts of Paris and murdered them all with sadistic ferocity, using a spade to hack the bodies into pieces.

National sensation

The bodies of the Kinck family were found the following day, on 20 September 1869. The case caused a sensation and the whole of France became obsessed by the affair. It was even suggested that the Government had been behind the crimes in an attempt to divert attention from the serious international crisis.

After the murders Troppmann fled to Le Havre but despite trying to escape by diving into the harbour he was arrested and taken back to Paris, where the train was met by a massive crowd. He claimed initially that Kinck and Gustave had killed the other members of the family but when their bodies were found, Troppmann was found guilty of all eight murders and guillotined on 19 January 1870.

Goulish interest

After the discovery of the bodies of the Kinck family 100 000 curious Parisians visited Pantin to see the sight of the murders. Special trains were organized and street hawkers set up stalls selling food.

Turpin, Richard (Dick)

(1705–39)

Highwayman

England's most legendary high-wayman, who was also a vicious house-breaker and a horse-thief.

Dick Turpin was born in Essex and although he received a rudimentary education he grew up to be an unruly and ill-mannered young man. He was apprenticed to a butcher and by the time he was 21 he was running his own shop, which he stocked with sheep stolen from his neighbours' farms. When this was discovered Turpin gave up all pretences of leading a law-abiding life and joined the notorious Essex Gang.

The Essex Gang specialized in violent house-breaking, which consisted of ransacking the chosen houses and subjecting the occupants to terrible torture. Turpin quickly assumed the leadership of the gang and under his ruthless command they plundered a number of houses during 1735.

A reward of 50 guineas was offered for the Essex Gang and when this was increased to 100 guineas two of Turpin's lieutenants were informed upon, arrested and hanged. When Turpin heard of this he decided to turn to a career of highway robbery. While travelling to Cambridgeshire he encountered a well-dressed gentleman, whom he decided to rob. As he drew his pistol the gentleman laughed heartily, 'What, dog eat dog?'. The 'gentleman' was another highwayman, Tom King, and he and Turpin decided to form a partnership.

Accidental death

For safety, Turpin and King lived in a cave in Epping Forest, from which they made numerous raids on the highways. Since the reward for Turpin was still 100 guineas there were a number of attempts to track him down. One of these was undertaken by a Mr Thompson and on 4 May 1736 his servant, Thomas Morris, stumbled across the highwaymen's hideout. Sensing danger, Turpin invited the man towards his lair and then shot him. This increased the price on his head to 200 guineas.

For the next year Turpin and King terrorized the roads, earning a reputation for brutality and sometimes carrying out raids on several consecutive nights. In May 1737 King was apprehended on a charge of horse-stealing and in trying to save him Turpin accidentally shot his friend.

Apprehended

Turpin was so unsettled by this that he moved to Lincolnshire and lived under the assumed name of John Palmer . Although he took on the role of a country gentleman he was soon in trouble for sheep-stealing and moved again, this time to Welton in Yorkshire.

Turpin was finally brought before the authorities because one of his neighbours complained when he shot a gamecock. The mysterious Mr Palmer was investigated and when his true identity was discovered he was imprisoned in York Castle. He was tried at York Assizes, on 22 March 1738, for horse-stealing. He was found guilty and sentenced to death. Dick Turpin was hanged at York on 7 April 1739 and he went to his death bravely, even deciding to jump willingly from the ladder.

Turpin and Black Bess

Much of the legend surrounding Dick Turpin concerns his ride to York on the mare Black Bess. This was recounted in Harrison Ainsworth's *Rookwood* but in reality it was probably another highwayman, John Nevison, who made the ride and not Dick Turpin.

Vacher, Joseph

(1869–97)

Convicted murderer

A Frenchman who committed a series of murders that were compared to those of Jack the Ripper in London.

Joseph Vacher was born in the south-east region of France, near Belley. He was one of 15 children and he grew up a troubled child given to acts of unprovoked violence. In 1890 he was conscripted into the army and on one occasion he tried to cut his throat because his promotion to full corporal had not come through. When he started eyeing the throats of his comrades and talking about 'flowing blood' he was moved to the army infirmary.

Facial disfigurement

In 1893 Vacher became involved with Mlle Louise B of Baume-des-Dames, an ill-fated romance that ended with the volatile Vacher shooting his lover and then turning the gun on himself. One of the bullets lodged in his head, damaging an eye and causing facial paralysis. When consequently committed to Saint-Ylle asylum, his ravings amazed even his fellow inmates.

After a brief stay at Saint-Ylle Vacher was transferred to Saint-Robert asylum and on 1 April 1984 he was released, supposedly cured. Six weeks later a 21-year-old factory worker was found raped, disembowelled and stabbed near Vienne. Over the next three and a half years there were 13 similar murders — carried out mostly on women but sometimes on young men. People were quick to draw comparisons with Jack the Ripper and the only description the police had was of a black-bearded tramp with a scarred face and a damaged eye.

Ripper caught

On 4 August 1897 Vacher attacked a woman in the Bois des Pelleries. Thanks to the efforts of her husband she escaped and Vacher was overpowered. He received a three month prison sentence for offending against public decency. Once he was in custody the police realized that his description matched that of the man wanted for the Ripper murders. Vacher eventually confessed: 'Yes it is I who committed all the crimes with which I am charged — but I committed them all in moments of frenzy'.

Mad dog

Since no witnesses came forward Vacher was charged with only one murder, that of a shepherd boy named Victor Portalier, in 1895. He was tried at the Assizes of Ain in October 1897 and his defence was insanity. He claimed that he had been bitten by a rabid dog many years earlier and this had caused his madness. The jury did not believe him and he was found guilty. He was guillotined on 31 December 1897 and his head was later examined by experts to see if they could find any explanation for his barbaric behaviour.

Insanity plea

Before his trial Vacher was examined by a team of doctors, including the famous French criminologist Professor A Lacassagne. It was decided that he was sane enough to stand trial. Vacher himself had more unconventional methods of proving his insanity. When, during his trial, he went into vivid descriptions of his mental state and the murders to which it led him, the judge ordered that 'all decent women withdraw from the courtroom'.

Van Meegeren, Han
(1889–1947)

Art forger

A master forger who was only detected following an accusation of being a Nazi collaborator.

Van Meegeren was born in Deventer, Holland, and studied architecture at Delft University. However, he preferred painting to studying and failed his exams. He became a full-time painter and had an exhibition of his work in 1916. His work was well received at first but then it fell out of favour with the art critics and the public.

Following his early failure Van Meegeren yearned for recognition as a great artist and decided that forgery was his best option. In 1932 he undertook the necessary research and preparations and in 1937 he began work on *Christ at Emmaus* in the manner of the celebrated Dutch artist Jan Vermeer. When it was finished it was pronounced genuine by an expert and the painting was sold to the Boymans Museum in Rotterdam for £58 000.

Fooling the art world

Encouraged by this success Van Meegeren produced and sold other Vermeer forgeries, including *The Last Supper, Isaac Blessing Jacob, The Washing of Christ's Feet,* and *Christ and the Adulteress.* All the paintings were accepted by experts as being genuine and Van Meegeren sold them for a total of nearly £750 000. He explained this wealth by saying that he had won a lottery.

In 1945 the Allied Military Government Art Commission discovered a large number of paintings in a disused salt mine near Salzburg. Most of them had been looted by the Nazis during World War II and one of them was Van Meegeren's forgery of *Christ*

and the Adulteress. It had been bought by Field-Marshall Goering and when its origins were traced it was discovered that Van Meegeren had been involved with the sale. He was arrested and charged with being a Nazi collaborator.

Confession

For six weeks Van Meegeren refused to give the Dutch police any information about the origins of *Christ and the Adulteress.* But he was suffering from depression and eventually told his interrogators, 'I sold no great national treasure — I painted it myself!'. He went on to confess to his other forgeries.

Initially the police thought that Van Meegeren was mad so they ordered him to paint a forgery in the Vermeer style. He agreed and in two months he produced *Young Christ Teaching in the Temple.* He was accepted as a forger and the charges of collaboration were replaced by ones of fraud and forgery.

During his trial Van Meegeren became a hero to the Dutch public as the man who fooled the art world. He was very co-operative and when he was found guilty he was given the minimum sentence of one years' imprisonment. It is likely that Queen Juliana would have given him a free pardon but she never got the chance because Han Van Meegeren died of a heart attack on 29 December 1947.

The forger's art
To produce his paint Van Meegeren ground earth and stones together so that under a microscope the particles would appear irregular and not mechanically produced. He aged his canvases by baking them, and the forgeries could only be detected by X-ray.

Vicars, Henry Edward

(1888–1942)

Burglar

Known as 'Flannelfoot' he was responsible for over 1000 burglaries and break-ins.

Henry Vicars was born in Reading, the son of a butcher. He was a quiet and well-mannered youth who had a natural aptitude for burglary. In 1911 he was convicted of house-breaking for the first time and sentenced to nine months' imprisonment. On his release he joined the army and was discharged in 1918. At this point he decided that his future lay in a life of crime in the London suburbs.

Vicars was a meticulous thief who never used threatening behaviour and never caused unnecessary damage. He varied his operation between various London suburbs, always moving on when people in one area became suspicious. Friday nights were his busiest times, since houses were more likely to be empty and the weekly wage packet might be lying around. He gained entry to houses by forcing a window or picking a lock and he then performed the robbery in his socks. Because of this he became known as 'Flannelfoot'.

Attention to detail

Part of the reason for Vicars's success was the fact that he always worked alone and never associated with other criminals. He never left any fingerprints and was never attacked by guard dogs, a piece of good fortune that he later attributed to the fact that if he came across a hostile dog he usually threw it some food from the kitchen of the house he was robbing.

In 1932 Vicars left his wife, taking their daughter with him. Four years later the girl was found wandering the streets of London suffering from amnesia. She was reunited with her mother but was unable to tell her, or the police, the whereabouts of her father. If she could have remembered she may have told them that Flannelfoot was living in Royal Crescent, Holland Park, under the name of Henry Williams.

Police tail

The police soon traced Vicars using their own initiative; Superintendent Thompson from Scotland Yard, who had been tailing him for years, vowed that this time Flannelfoot would not escape. After several narrow escapes for the burglar, one night in October 1937 the police followed him. He went to Eastcote in Middlesex and shortly after he entered a house there the police interrupted him. He was caught red-handed with keys, pliers, gloves and several other house-breaking implements. He did not put up a struggle and the police were impressed by his smart clothes and his impeccable manners.

On 2 December Vicars pleaded guilty to numerous charges related to his burglaries. He was sentenced to five years' imprisonment and died soon after his release. There were several imitations of Flannelfoot's methods but none of them measured up to the real thing.

Flash crooks

Some thieves have been considerably more flamboyant than Flannelfoot: in Coventry a gang stripped £5000 worth of lead from a police station that was due to be sold; in Reading a crime prevention banner was stolen; in London during the 1980s a thief profited handsomely by using ice 'coins' in vending machines; and in Turin a gang broke into the house of a man who had made a fortune from manufacturing burglar alarms.

Vidocq, Eugene-François
(1775–1857)

Convict and private detective

A former criminal who founded the French Sûréte and created the forerunner of private detective agencies.

Eugene-François Vidocq was born in Arras, France and grew up to be an impetuous youth who was frequently in trouble with the law. At one stage he seemed to have a promising career in the army, fighting courageously at the battles of Valmy and Jemappes. However, he could not keep out of trouble and he served a number of prison sentences for petty offences. His time in prison was notable for two reasons: the French had difficulty finding a jail that was secure enough to hold him, and he studied the criminal classes and their methods intently. In 1809 he became a police spy, informing on his colleges in prison.

Crime chief

In 1811, during the reign of Napoleon, there was a dramatic rise in crime in France and the authorities were desperate to find someone who could reverse the trend. They settled on Vidocq, which, given his background, was a bold choice, reasoning that his knowledge of the underworld would prove useful. Added to this was his love of disguise, a reliable string of informers and a personality that would not baulk at any task.

Vidocq's appointment proved to be inspirational. He created his own squad of detectives, most of them from the criminal classes, which was to eventually grow into the Sûréte (now the Police Judiciaire) at the Prefecture of Police. With a total of 28 detectives in his squad Vidocq was responsible for a dramatic reduction in the crime rate. In his first year he and his men effected more than 750 arrests. There were rumours that he and his agents were responsible for some of the crimes for which they later arrested people but there was never any proof of this.

Private eye

In 1827 Vidocq resigned to set up a paper and cardboard mill, where he employed former convicts, but this was a failure and in 1832 he was recalled to the Sûréte by Louis-Philippe. He distinguished himself by putting down the rebellion of that year but he was dismissed only months later, for a theft that his enemies claimed he organized.

After his dismissal Vidocq created one of the first private detective agencies. He undertook private cases and also helped to protect people from swindlers. Some of the people at the Prefecture of Police resented this and tried to incriminate him, citing incidents from his criminal past. Vidocq went to great lengths to vindicate himself, and did so, although the costs were crippling.

Vidocq, who was friends with such people as Hugo, Balzac and Dumas, kept working up until his death in 1857 and became a self-appointed counter-espionage agent for Louis-Napoleon.

Author
Vidocq also had considerable literary talent. He wrote a reference book on the criminal classes, a book concerning the reclamation of criminals, and two novels. He was also an accomplished painter and at the age of 70 he exhibited some of his work in London. Several books were also written about him and he was the inspiration for Balzac's fictional criminal genius Vautrin in *La Comédie Humaine*.

Wainewright, Thomas Griffiths

(1794–1852)

Forger and probable poisoner

Comparable to the French criminal Lacenaire, Wainewright was an artistic man who turned to murder for gain.

Thomas Wainewright was born at Chiswick and, following the death of his parents when he was an infant, he was brought up by his grandfather at Turnham Green. His grandfather was the publisher of *The Monthly Review* and when Wainewright finished his education he had the chance to meet many of the literary and artistic talents in London.

When he was 18 Wainewright joined the army as a guardsman. However, this grated on his artistic temperament and he soon sold his commission, observing that an artist should only serve as a soldier if he is allowed to design his own uniform. Instead he became a dandy, exhibited paintings at the Royal Academy, and wrote innovative art criticism.

Forgery

In 1821 Wainewright married Frances Ward but he made no effort to try and curb his extravagant lifestyle. He loved to entertain on a grand scale and his expenditure greatly exceeded his income. To try and alleviate this he forged the signatures of his trustees on documents that would allow him to sell £2000 worth of stock. The Bank of England handed over the money without a murmur.

By 1828 Wainewright had spent this money and was heavily in debt again. He and his wife decided to move back to Turnham Green and live with his uncle George Edward Griffiths. Within a year Griffiths had a mysterious 'fit' and died.

Wainewright was consoled by the fact that the house and the property passed to him.

Unproductive poisoning

His relief was short-lived because almost immediately his mother-in-law, Mrs Abercromby, and her two daughters announced that they were coming to live with him and his wife. This put a great burden on the household budget and Wainewright decided that the best thing to do would be to rid himself of his bothersome guests. Mrs Abercromby died suddenly in August 1830 and one of her daughters, Helen, followed shortly afterwards. Wainewright had insured her life for a considerable sum and he arranged for his other sister-in-law to collect the money, but the insurance company refused to pay and Wainewright fled.

From Paris Wainewright brought an action against the insurance company but it took five years for the case to be concluded, with the final decision going against him. In June 1837 he returned to Britain, where he was recognized by a Bow Street Runner in connection with the stock forgeries. He was tried at the Old Bailey on 5 July 1837 and pleaded guilty to the forgeries. He was sentenced to transportation to Van Diemen's Land (Tasmania) for life. While he was awaiting his voyage he admitted that he had poisoned Helen Abercromby, offering as a reason the fact that her fat ankles had offended him. He made a considerable impact in Van Diemen's Land as a painter and died there in 1852.

> **Comparison**
> Wainewright has been compared with the Frenchman Lacenaire because of his literary ability and also because he was an 'intuitive criminal', who thought carefully about his crimes and their consequences. In addition, he shared Lacenaire's love of cats.

Wartime Ripper

(1942)

Gordon Frederick Cummins

A serviceman who murdered four women within a week during World War II.

Gordon Cummins was born in the Yorkshire village of New Earswick. Although he grew up to be handsome and charming he was also dishonest and unreliable. In 1936 he married a secretary and in 1941 he joined the RAF, training for the air crew. At the beginning of 1942 he was billeted in North London.

On 9 February 1942 the body of 42-year-old Evelyn Hamilton was found in central London. She had been strangled with a silk scarf and the only clue the police found was a set of fingerprints that indicated the murderer was left-handed. The following day a second body was discovered, this time in Soho. The victim was a 35-year-old prostitute named Evelyn Oately. Her throat had been cut and her lower body had been horrifically mutilated by someone who was obviously sexually disturbed.

Vital gas mask

On 13 February two more bodies were found, one of 42-year-old Margaret Lowe, and the other of 40-year-old Doris Jouannet. They were mutilated in a particularly sadistic manner and there was an abundance of fingerprints at the scene of each crime. Other than this the police had few clues.

The following day a married woman named Greta Heywood was persuaded to have a drink with a young serviceman. When they left the pub he tried to attack and strangle her, but a passer-by heard her screams and the assailant fled. In his haste

he left his gas mask, which bore the name Aircraftman Gordon Frederick Cummins. He still seemed intent on finding another victim because he then picked up a prostitute and tried to attack her. She was too quick for him though and again he made a hasty retreat. This time he left behind his RAF belt.

Ripper comparisons

Following the discovery of the gas mask the police easily traced Cummins and found that his fingerprints matched those found at the scenes of the four murdered women. He was arrested on 17 February 1942 and on 27 April his trial began at the Old Bailey. In keeping with the English law he was only tried for one murder, that of Evelyn Oatley, but the evidence was conclusive and the following day he was found guilty.

Gordon Cummins was hanged in Wandsworth prison on 25 June 1942. Because of the preoccupation with the war his case did not create as much interest as it might have done in peace-time. Nevertheless the police were convinced they had encountered a personality who shared the same lust for sadistic murder as Jack the Ripper and the press dubbed him the Wartime Ripper and the Black-out Ripper.

A handsome killer

It was never fully discovered why Gordon Cummins suddenly went on an orgy of killing. The man who guarded him before his trial saw little that was abnormal in his character: 'He chatted to me on everyday subjects as though he had not a care in the world. Observed at close quarters, he was not an obviously unpleasant man. He was deceptively gentle in manner — a man not unattractive to women'.

Watergate scandal

(1972)

Richard Nixon and others

An American political scandal that became a byword for high-level corruption.

Between 1969 and 1971, without prior court approval, the Republican President, Richard Nixon, authorized undercover surveillance of particular organizations and individuals whom he thought were a threat to national security. In 1972 various people, acting under instructions that had come indirectly from the President, broke into the Democratic National Committee (DNC) headquarters at the Watergate buildings in Washington DC. The Republicans hoped to discover important information about the Democrat's campaign for the forthcoming election. Several visits were made to the Watergate building, most of them to install electronic bugging equipment.

Watergate burglars

At 2.30am on 17 June 1972 five men were arrested while breaking into the Watergate building. They were all charged with burglary and wiretapping, as were, more significantly, E Howard Hunt, a former White House aide, and G Gordon Liddy, general counsel for the Committee for the Re-election of the President (CRP). Nixon was concerned about the arrests and he ordered documents that linked the White House to Watergate to be destroyed. Publicly he denied any knowledge of Watergate.

The seven Watergate burglars were tried before Judge John Sirica, the proceedings opening in January 1973. Five of them pleaded guilty while Liddy and James McCord, security co-ordinator for CRP, were tried before a jury and found guilty of burglary, conspiracy and illegal wiretapping. Before sentencing on 23 March 1973 Judge Sirica read out a letter from McCord that stated the White House was involved with a cover-up in relation to the Watergate break-in and that the seven defendants had been instructed to plead guilty. The implications were clear, and matters were made worse for the Nixon administration when another of the defendants, Stuart Magruder, changed his testimony and admitted that he had perjured himself at the request of the former Attorney General, John N. Mitchell, and John W. Dean III, counsel to the President.

Top level investigation

On 17 April 1973 President Nixon bowed to the growing clamour surrounding Watergate and ordered an investigation into the affair. Two weeks later three of his top aides, Dean, H R Haldeman, and John Ehrlichman, all resigned, as did the Attorney General Richard G Kleindienst. Despite this Nixon continued to insist that he had known nothing of Watergate or a subsequent cover-up.

Elliot L Richardson replaced Kleindienst as Attorney General and immediately selected Archibald Cox, a Harvard law professor, as special Watergate prosecutor. Meanwhile a senate committee, headed by Senator Ervin, was conducting its own investigation. John Dean testified that Nixon had been directly involved from the beginning. Then, on 16 July 1973, a former White House staff member, Alexander Butterfield, disclosed that secret conversations in the President's office had been recorded on tape.

Vital tapes

On 23 July both Cox and the Ervin Committee subpoenaed the secret tapes. However Nixon refused to hand them over, arguing

Judiciary Committee impeachment panel

that it was a matter of national security. Judge Sirica then stepped in and ordered Nixon to turn over the tapes. Again the President refused, even when the U.S. Court of Appeals upheld the order. Nixon knew that he would have to do something so he suggested a compromise — he offered to submit a written summary of the tapes, but only on the condition that no other presidential documents were dealt with. This was rejected by Cox and in frustration Nixon fired the special prosecutor in October 1973.

There was now intense interest surrounding the blossoming Watergate scandal and in December 1973 Nixon was forced by intense public pressure to release the tapes. This only ignited the affair further, since there were only seven tapes when there should have been nine. Even more damaging to the President was the fact that one of the tapes had a glaring 18-minute gap. Experts said that it could not have occurred by accident and Nixon was unable to explain the discrepancy.

On 1 March 1974 seven of Nixon's former aides were indicted for conspiring to hinder the Watergate investigation. Five of them were later imprisoned but by now attention had focused on the extent of Nixon's involvement. Judge Sirica gave the House Judiciary Committee evidence against Nixon and in April 1974 they impeached another 42 of the Nixon tapes. The President again refused to hand them over but he did agree to provide written transcripts. These did not specifically implicate Nixon but it was clear that he knew about Watergate and the resulting cover-up.

Impeachment

Sirica, and Cox's replacement as special prosecutor Leon Jaworski, refused to let go and they subpoenaed another 64 tapes and documents. Nixon claimed that he had absolute authority over whether they were released or not. In a historic judgment the Supreme Court disagreed with him and Nixon was forced to honour the subpoena.

This last batch of tapes were the most incriminating of all and between 27 and 30 July 1974 the House Judiciary Committee passed three articles of impeachment. On 5 August President Nixon played three tapes which left no doubt as to his role in the whole Watergate affair. His support in Congress disappeared and, facing certain impeachment, Richard Nixon resigned at noon 9 August 1974.

Sentences

Three of the leading Watergate conspirators, Haldeman, Ehrlichman and Mitchell, were sentenced to between two and a half and eight years in prison. Richard Nixon was spared from any further indignity when his successor, Gerald Ford, granted an unconditional pardon on 8 September 1974.

President's story

Several books were written about Watergate, the most popular being the bestselling *All the President's Men* by two investigative journalists on the *Washington Post*, Bob Woodward and Carl Bernstein. It was later made into a successful film starring Robert Redford and Dustin Hoffman.

Wild, Jonathan

(c.1682–1725)

Receiver of stolen goods and thief-taker

A master-criminal who was one of the founders of organized crime in Britain.

Jonathan Wild was born and baptized in the Staffordshire town of Wolverhampton. After a reasonable education he was apprenticed to a buckle-maker in Birmingham when he was 15. He remained there for seven years and then returned to Wolverhampton.

In 1704 Wild left Wolverhampton and went to London. He worked as a debt collector for a short time, but found the work dangerous and distasteful and soon returned home. His next visit to London was four years later. This time he himself fell into debt and spent four years incarcerated in Wood Street Compter.

Criminal research

While he was in the debtors' prison Wild endeavoured to find out as much about the criminal mind as possible. With its variety of offenders this was the perfect place to learn and when he was released, in 1712, he had numerous criminal connections.

One of the people that Wild had met while in the Compter was a prostitute named Mary Millner. When they were released they set up a brothel in Lewkenor's Lane, Covent Garden. Seeing little future in this Wild decided to buy a small public house in Cock Alley, Cripplegate, which was one of the centres of criminal activity in London and perfect for what Wild had in mind.

Fence

Due to his criminal connections Wild's pub became a central point for people wanting to sell stolen goods. Wild was happy to accommodate them and he soon built up a regular clientele of criminals. This also meant he had a great deal of power over the thieves — a power that he used to inform on them if it suited his needs, thus fulfilling the role of a thief-taker, or freelance policeman.

As Wild was building up his businesses as a receiver of stolen goods and as a thief-taker he was approached by Charles Hitchin. Hitchin was a corrupt City Marshall (a private police force in London) who ran protection rackets and informed ruthlessly on anyone who angered him. Wild and Hitchin worked together for two years, selling goods, informing on some criminals and blackmailing others. Eventually they quarrelled and Wild decided it would be more profitable to set up as a thief-taker on his own.

Gaining control

Wild's business was halted briefly when a statute was passed whereby receivers of stolen goods were regarded as accessories, which Wild overcame in an ingenious way. Instead of selling the stolen goods he contacted the people who had been robbed, either personally or by advertisement in newspapers, saying that he had located their goods and that for a fee he would arrange for their safe return. Thus the stolen items never passed directly through his hands. He encouraged his thieves to steal items such as accounts-books, diaries and letters, not only because they could realize high rewards from owners who were worried about being blackmailed, but also because the authorities would attach little monetary value to them if they were discovered.

Wild's business became so successful that he opened up an office in Little Old Bailey. By now his reputation was so great that people who had been robbed often came directly to him. He insisted on an initial fee and also a list of the missing goods. This way he could check and see whether the criminals were trying to trick him.

Crime boss

While to the general public Wild was something of a saviour, in reality he was one of the first ever instigators of organized crime. He divided London into various districts and assigned individual gangs to certain areas — always making sure that they kept to their own particular speciality. Since the police at the time had to keep to their own districts they had little chance of keeping watch on Wild's far-reaching activities.

In order to maintain his empire Wild was ruthless in turning over people he did not trust or who did not follow his instructions. He frequently informed on his own gangs, through a third party, and used his powers to track down criminals who came into opposition with him, the most notable one being Jack Sheppard. In his role of thief-taker Wild was responsible for sending at least 60 men to the gallows.

In 1719 an Act of Parliament known as Jonathan Wild's Act was passed, which made it a capital felony to take a reward under pretence of helping someone to recover stolen goods. This presented little obstacle to Wild, however, and he soon opened a branch office of his Lost Property Office. By now he was advertising himself as 'Thief-Taker General of Great Britain and Ireland', while at the same time he had warehouses full of stolen goods and a sloop that was used to smuggle stolen merchandise out of the country. To the authorities he was an instrument of justice and to the criminal world he was the undisputed boss.

Beginning of the end

By 1724 Wild had broken all the major gangs in London and was in complete control of the underworld. However, he had also made numerous enemies and in November 1724 'Blueskin' Blake, one of Jack Sheppard's accomplices, tried unsuccessfully to cut his throat in court, an incident that brought to the public's attention the fact that Wild was perhaps not the honest citizen that he professed to be; there was no great surprise when he was arrested on 15 February 1725 for accepting 10 guineas for procuring the return of some stolen lace.

Jonathan Wild was tried at the Old Bailey on 15 May 1725. He was acquitted of stealing the lace but found guilty of accepting a reward for its return. Despite naming 75 criminals whom he had helped convict, Wild was sentenced to death. He tried to commit suicide by taking laudanum but was deemed fit to be hanged at Tyburn on 24 May 1725. The man who had once been thought of as a public benefactor was pelted with mud and stones as he was taken to the gallows.

Above the law

When asked how he could return stolen goods without being in league with the robbers, Wild replied, 'When I receive information of a robbery, I make enquiry after the suspected parties, and leave word at proper places, that if the goods are left where I appoint, the reward shall be paid, and no questions asked. Surely no implication of guilt can fall on me, for I hold no interviews with the robbers, nor are the goods given into my possession'.

Fit of temper

Wild liked to consider himself a man of consequence; he dressed in lace clothing and on occasions even carried a sword. The first time he used it was when he quarrelled with his former lover Mary Milliner: he aimed a blow at her and cut off her ear. His sense of remorse led him to allow her a weekly stipend until her death.

Trial of Oscar Wilde

(1895)

Oscar Fingal O'Flaherty Wills Wilde

One of Britain's leading literary figures who was tried for committing acts of gross indecency.

Oscar Wilde was born in Dublin on 16 October 1854. His father was one of the leading surgeons in the British Isles and founded the first eye and ear hospital in Ireland. His mother was an impressive woman who took up the cause of Irish nationalism and wrote poetry and political articles under the pen-name Speranza.

From an early age Wilde showed a liking for the flamboyant and at the age of 13 he scolded his mother for sending him his brother's grey shirts instead of his own scarlet and lilac ones. He was a brilliant scholar; in 1871 he won a scholarship to Trinity College Dublin and in 1876 he went to Magdalen College Oxford. In 1878 he won the Newdigate Prize for his poem 'Ravenna'.

Leading light

After he graduated, Wilde chose to go to London and involve himself in high society. With his wit and powers of oratory he was an immediate hit and the Prince of Wales once remarked, 'I do not know Mr Wilde, and not to know Mr Wilde is not to be known'. Wilde published very little work during his first 10 years in London but he nevertheless became famous for his outrageous personality and his flamboyant dress-sense.

In 1884 Wilde married Constance Lloyd and although he soon tired of her sexually they remained very close throughout their lives. Wilde's first major literary success came in 1891 with the publication of *The*

Oscar Wilde and Lord Alfred Douglas

Picture of Dorian Gray. Although it was condemned for its constant hints of homosexuality it was adored by the public.

The following year Wilde had an even greater success, with his first play, *Lady Windermere's Fan.* It was a huge hit and not only increased Wilde's popularity but it also netted him over £7000, a fortune at the time. He followed this up with *A Woman of No Importance* in 1893 and his most popular play, *The Importance of Being Earnest* in 1895.

Double life

But while Wilde was enjoying his popularity as a celebrity and a leading dramatist he was also leading a double life. From an early age he had been fascinated by young men and in 1886 he became an active homosexual when he was seduced by a young admirer, Robert Ross, at Oxford. The two became lifelong friends but soon after their first meeting Wilde became increasingly more promiscuous with a variety of young male prostitutes. Wilde was undeterred by the Criminal Law Amendment Act of 1885, which laid down severe penalties for homosexuality.

In 1891 Wilde met Lord Alfred Douglas and within a year the two were lovers. It was a stormy relationship and may never have been made public if it had not been for Douglas's father, John Sholto Douglas, the Marquess of Queensberry, an eccentric character who had a fanatical hatred of homosexuals, Jews and Christians. In April 1894, when he saw his son and Wilde lunching together, he became infuriated and vowed to put an end to the relationship. He tried to address the audience on the opening night of *The Importance of Being Earnest* and denounce Wilde but he was thwarted by the police. Instead, he left a note at Wilde's club, the Albermarle, accusing him of 'posing as a sodomite'.

Ill-advised prosecution

When Wilde received Queensberry's note he was incensed and decided to sue for libel. Most of his friends advised him against it but Douglas urged him on since he wanted to see his father humiliated. On 1 March 1895 Queensberry was arrested and on 3 April the libel case against him opened at the Old Bailey. Wilde was the main prosecution witness and he delighted the court with his witty replies. But when he was cross-examined by the formidable Edward Carson he became less sure of himself and at one point, when asked if he had kissed a certain young gentleman he replied, 'Oh dear no, he was a peculiarly plain boy'.

At the end of the second day of the trial Wilde's council were becoming worried. They had discovered that the defence intended to call a number of male prostitutes to testify against Wilde and they knew that this would do irreparable damage to their case. On 5 April 1895 Wilde was persuaded to drop the libel charges, but that same afternoon he was arrested and charged

with committing acts of gross indecency with various male persons.

Scandal

Wilde was tried at the Old Bailey on 26 April 1895 and he faced 25 charges. He was tried with a man named Alfred Taylor, who had been responsible for supplying him with male prostitutes. Wilde's performance in court this time was very subdued but his defence council, Sir Edward Clarke, pleaded his case so forcefully that the jury were unable to reach a verdict and so a re-trial was ordered.

The re-trial commenced on 22 May. After three days Wilde was found guilty on all counts and sentenced to two years' imprisonment with hard labour. He began his sentence in Pentonville Prison and then moved to Wandsworth and finally Reading Prison. It was an existence he despised and he spent several weeks in the prison hospital.

Outcast

Wilde was released on 30 November 1897 and left Britain immediately for the continent. In 1898 he published his last published work, *The Ballad of Reading Gaol,* a bitter poem about his experiences in prison. He saw Alfred Douglas a few times on the continent but their meetings usually ended in bitter squabbles.

Oscar Wilde died in Paris on 30 November 1900, aged 46. He was a ruined and bitter man whose career had been destroyed when he was at the height of his powers. Since his death he has been re-established as the literary genius that he undoubtedly was.

From *The Ballad of Reading Gaol*
We sewed the sacks, we broke the stones,
We turned the dusty drill,
We banged the tins, we bawled the hymns,
And sweated on the mill:
But in the heart of every man
Terror was lying still.

Williams, Wayne Bertram

(1958–)

Convicted murderer

A serial killer who terrorized Atlanta in the early 1980s, murdering up to 28 people.

Wayne Williams was the only child of two school teachers and grew up in Atlanta as a lonely and spoilt child. He was highly intelligent and by the time he was a teenager he had built his own radio transmitter and was selling advertising time. After he left school he developed a great interest in police work, took up freelance photography and created his own advertising agency.

Between July 1979 and spring 1981 there was an epidemic of unsolved murders in Atlanta. All the victims were black, young, and, with one exception, there was no apparent sexual motive. As the number of murders grew, Atlanta became gripped by fear. Black activist groups were concerned that the killer might be a white racialist and complained that the police were not doing enough to try and catch the killer. A reward of $100 000 was offered for information leading to his arrest and celebrities including Frank Sinatra and Burt Reynolds offered their support in raising money to help fund the search for the killer.

Massive man-hunt

The investigation into the killings was one of the largest ever staged in America. Twenty-thousand people were interviewed, thousands of children were spoken to, 35 FBI officers were permanently stationed in Atlanta, and at its height the investigation was costing Atlanta a million dollars a month. Despite all these efforts the killings continued at a average of one every three and a half weeks.

By 22 May 1981 the number of murders attributed to the killer was 26. That evening the police were carrying out routine surveillance on the South Drive Bridge, over the Chattahoochee river, when they heard a splash in the water. All traffic going over the bridge was stopped and the drivers questioned. One of them was Wayne Williams, and although he was not detained he was placed under constant surveillance.

Forensic match

Two days later the body of 27-year-old Nathaniel Carter was found in the Chattahoochee River, and then another victim, 21-year-old Ray Payne was discovered near the same place. It was proved that fibres and dog-hairs found on the latest two victims matched those in Williams's station-wagon and bedroom. He was arrested and charged with the murders of Carter and Payne.

The trial of Wayne Williams ran from January to March 1982 and the prosecution case was a weak one. But crucially the judge ruled that the prosecution could also use evidence linking Williams to 10 other murders. It proved to be the turning point, but nevertheless the jury took 12 hours to find Williams guilty on both counts of murder. It was a dubious verdict and one that was undoubtedly influenced by the fact that following the arrest of Williams, the epidemic of murder in Atlanta stopped.

Wayne Williams was sentenced to two consecutive life terms and he remains in prison despite attempts to reopen the case.

> **Manichean**
> At his trial Williams was described as having a 'Manichean' personality, after the Manichees who were world-haters. Although he was talented he was also a pathological liar and felt himself to be a failure.

Young, Graham Frederick

(1947–   )

Poisoner and convicted murderer

A compulsive poisoner who was imprisoned for murder, released and then committed two more murders.

Graham Young was an intelligent but slightly sinister child. His idols were Adolf Hitler and the Victorian poisoner William Palmer (see p183). By the time he was 14 he was following in Palmer's footsteps and experimenting with the effects of various poisons on the human body.

Young's experimentation included giving antimony tartrate to friends and members of his family. In April 1962 his stepmother died of antimony poisoning, and several packets of antimony tartrate were found in Young's pockets. He said his family were expendable victims of his research, a claim which led to him being found guilty but insane. He was sent to Broadmoor for 15 years.

Young spent nine years in Broadmoor and on his release in 1971 it was stated that he had made an 'extremely full recovery'. Young found employment with John Hadlands, a firm in the village of Bovingdon, Hertfordshire. He worked as a general storeman and also made tea for his workmates.

The Bovingdon Bug

A few weeks after Young started work a mysterious illness began spreading through Hadlands. About 70 members of staff were affected and one of them, Bob Egle, died on 7 July 1971. Two months later the Bovingdon Bug struck again when Frederick Biggs died after a three weeks' illness.

As more people fell ill with the 'Bug' the management ordered a full medical enquiry. The chief investigator, Dr Arthur Anderson, was amazed at Young's knowledge of dangerous chemicals. At one point Young even asked, 'Do you think the symptoms are consistent with thallium poisoning?'

Young's expertise aroused the suspicions of the police and when his background was investigated his previous conviction for poisoning was discovered. His bedsit was searched and the police found a lethal quantity of thallium and a diary detailing his deadly activities at Hadlands. When Bob Egle's ashes were examined they were found to contain thallium.

At his trial in July 1972 Young seemed more concerned with showing his scientific expertise than protesting his innocence. The jury found him guilty of two murders, two attempted murders and two charges of administering poison. He was sentenced to life imprisonment and placed in a top security hospital.

Thallium

Thallium is a heavy metal, similar to lead and mercury. It is highly poisonous and ideal for murder: it is colourless, virtually tasteless and the symptoms of thallium poisoning can be confused with other illnesses such as influenza.

Zodiac murders

(1968–9)

Hooded astrologer

A series of unsolved murders in California where the killer frequently contacted newspapers and the police.

On 20 December 1968 the bodies of two teenagers, David Faraday and Betty Lou Jensen, were discovered at the roadside between Vallejo and Benica, near San Francisco. They had both been shot but there was no apparent motive for the killings as there had been no sexual assault and nothing had been taken. The police had no clues and the case was quickly forgotten and marked unsolved.

Six months later, on 5 July 1969, a man telephoned the Vallejo Police Department to report a double murder. The police found the bodies exactly where the caller had promised but one of the victims, Michael Mageau, was still alive and was able to describe the killer. Again, the police had few leads.

Zodiac signature

The first substantial clue to the killer's identity came in the form of letters to two San Francisco newspapers, describing details of the killings which could be known to the murderer alone. The letters were signed with the sign of the Zodiac, a cross surmounting a circle, and the author demanded that they were published or else he would go on a killing rampage.

On 27 September 1969 the Zodiac Killer telephoned the Napa Valley Police Department to inform them that he had struck again. This time the victims were two students from Pacific Union College and as in the previous case one of them, Bryan

Hartnell, survived. He told the police that his attacker had worn a hood with the sign of the Zodiac on it. The same sign was found in his car. The police also found the killer's fingerprints in a nearby phonebox but they did not match any on police records.

Contact on TV

The Zodiac Killer's fifth victim was a taxi-driver named Paul Stein, who was shot on 11 October 1969. The next day a San Francisco newspaper received a fragment of the dead man's bloodstained shirt and a letter in which the killer threatened to massacre a bus-load of schoolchildren. Stein was the last known victim of the Zodiac Killer but on 21 October a man claiming to be the murderer telephoned a prominent lawyer, Melvin Belli, on his early morning TV chat-show. He agreed to meet Belli but never turned up.

Although the killings stopped, the Zodiac Killer contacted the newspapers and the police on two more occasions, once in 1971 and again in 1974. He taunted the police for their inability to catch him and threatened to 'do something nasty' if he did not receive more publicity. He also claimed to have killed 37 people, which was undoubtedly an exaggeration, but it is possible he was responsible for up to a dozen unsolved murders.

Mass fingerprinting

The police knew that the Zodiac Killer probably lived in Napa or Vallejo. Once they had the unidentified fingerprints they could conceivably have fingerprinted the entire male populations of these towns to try and find a match. This had been done before when the entire town of Blackburn was fingerprinted during a murder investigation in 1948, an enormous task that proved effective and the killer was caught.

Index

Note: Entries in **bold type** refer to articles headed with the name shown.

Kennedy, Pres assassination of (1963) **126**, 127
Kennedy, Sergeant 124
Kennedy, William Henry 43
Kent, Constance 128
Kent, Francis Savile, murder of (1860) **128**
Kent, Samuel 128
Keyes, Robert 104
Kidd, William (c.1645–1701) **129**
Kilbride, John 167, 168
Killearn, Graham of 152
Kinck family 225
King, Tom 226
Kingston, Duke of 65
Kleindienst, Gen R G 233
Kleinschmidt, Lena 155
Knevett, Sir Thomas 104
Knight, Tobias 220
Knippenberg, Herman 213
Knox, Dr Robert 50, 51
Kominski 118
Kray Twins (1933–) **130**, 131
Krenwinkel, P 157, 158
Kreuger, I (1880–1932) **132**
Kurten, Peter (1883–1931) **133**, 134

L
LaBianca murders 158
Laborde–Line, Madame 139
Lacassagne, Professor A 227
Lacenaire, Pierre–François (1800–36) **135**
Lacost, Mademoiselle 139
Lady Chatterley's Lover trial (1960) **136**, 137
Lafarge, Marie Fortunée (1816–51) **138**
LaFollette, Robert 222
Laird, Maggie 50
Lambie, Helen 207
Lamphere, Ray 102
Landru, Henri Desiré (1869–1922) **139**, 140
Lane, Sir Allen 136
L'Angelier, Emile 208
Lauder, W (c.1680–1771) **141**
Lauria, Donna 24
Lawrence, Geoffrey 6
Le Neve, Ethel 70, 71
Leach, Barbara 218
Leclerc, M-A 212, 213
Leicester, Earl of 154
LeMay, Georges 41
Lennox, Duke of 201
Leopold, N (1904–71) **142**
Liddy, G Gordon 233

Lincoln Pres assassination of, (1865) **143**, 144
Lindbergh kidnapping (1932) **145**, 146
Lipton, Col Marcus 188
Loeb, Richard (1903–36) **142**
Lofty, Margaret 210
Lonigan, Constable 124
Lord Haw-Haw — see Joyce
Lorraine, Mary of 154
Louis–Napoleon 230
Louis–Philippe, King 230
Louise B, Mademoiselle 227
Lovat, dowager Lady 96
Love, George — see Smith
Lowe, Harriet 11
Lowe, Margaret 232
Lucan case (1974) **147**, 148
Luciano, C (1897–1962) **149**
Lupo, Salvatore 25
Lustig, V (1890–1947) 56, **150**

M
McCann, Wilma 217
McCord, James 233
MacDonald, Jayne 217, 218
MacDonnell, George 14
McDougal, Helen 50, 51
McGinnis, Joe 40
MacGregor, Robert (1671–1734) **151**, 152
McIntyre, Constable 124
McKay, Mrs Muriel 174
Mackenzie, Stuart 174
Maclean, Donald Duart (1913–83) 28, 49, **153**, 187, 188
Maclean, Evelyn Walsh 146
MacLennan, Hectorina 64
Macmillan, Harold 188
Macnaghten, Sir Melville 118
McNeil, Hector 49
Macpherson, James 182
McSwann, Donald 105
McSween gang 30
McVitie, Jack 'The Hat' 131
Madden, Sir Frederick 66
Mageau, Michael 241
Maggio, Joseph 11
Maggott, Poll 205
Magruder, Stuart 233
Mahon, Patrick Herbert 122
Maitland, W (c.1528–73) **154**
Makely, Charles 81
Malone, Edmond 116
Maloney, Kathleen 64
Mandelbaum, Fredricka (c.1825–90) **155**
Mandeville, Geoffrey de (?–1144) **156**

Manningham–Buller, Sir R 6
Mansfield, Edward 169
Manson family murders (1969) **157**, 158
Manuel, Peter Thomas Anthony (1927–58) **159**
Mar, Earl of 152
Mar, Lord 201
Marazano, Salvatore 149
March, Alice 68, 69
Marie–Antoinette, Queen 53
Markov, Georgi 29
Marshall, Doreen 109
Marshall Hall, Sir Edward 69, 90
Martin, Oswald 9
Martinetti, Mr and Mrs 70
Mary, Queen of Scots 12, 154, 201, 224
Masseria, Joe 149
Mathew, Sir Theobald 136
Matilda, Empress (Maud) 156
Maxwell, Pete 31
Maybrick, Florence E 160
Maybrick, James, murder of (1889) **160**
Maybrick, Michael 160
Maynard, Robert 221
Means, Gaston B 146
Mendoza, Bernadino de 224
Merrett J D (1908–54) **161**
Miles, PC Sidney (1952) **162**
Millner, Mary 235
Mills, Jack 100
Millward, Vera 218
Minnoch, William 208
Mitchell, Frank 131
Mitchell, John N 233, 234
Modyford, Sir T 169, 170
Molineux, Roland Burnham (1868–1917) **163**
Mona Lisa theft (1911) **164**
Monmouth, James, Duke of (1649–085) 93, **165**, 166
Montrose, 1st Duke 151, 152
Moors murders (1963–65) **167**, 168
Moran Gang 56
Moray, J S Earl of 154
Morgan, Sir Henry Johan (c.1635–88) **169**, 170
Morgan, Thomas 224
Morrell, Edith 6
Morris, Thomas 226
Morse, John 34, 35
Moskowitz, Stacy 25
Mosley, Sir Oswald 121
Mounteagle, Lord 104
Mowbray, William 67
Mudgett, Herman W 111